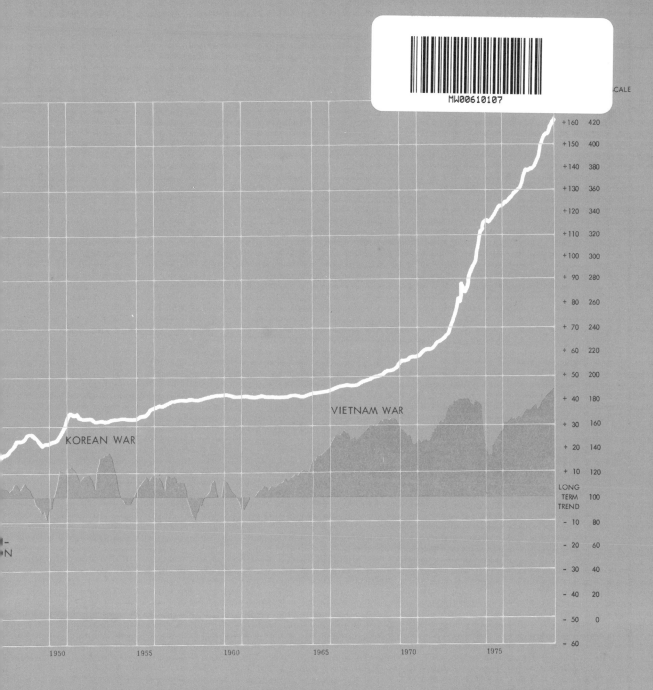

SCALE

+160 420
+150 400
+140 380
+130 360
+120 340
+110 320
+100 300
+ 90 280
+ 80 260
+ 70 240
+ 60 220
+ 50 200
+ 40 180
+ 30 160
+ 20 140
+ 10 120
LONG
TERM   100
TREND
- 10   80
- 20   60
- 30   40
- 40   20
- 50   0
- 60

VIETNAM WAR

KOREAN WAR

1950   1955   1960   1965   1970   1975

This chart from 1913 through 1978 shows fluctuations above and below the long-term
trend for wholesale commodity prices and industrial production. The solid line represents
the changes in wholesale commodity prices with 1926 having been selected as the base
year of 100. The solid portion of the chart indicates the index of industrial production with
percentage changes from the trend reduced to a per capita basis.

Source: The Cleveland Trust Company, Cleveland, Ohio.

An introduction to the American business enterprise

1980 FOURTH EDITION

Richard D. Irwin, Inc. Homewood, Illinois 60430

An introduction to the

American
business enterprise

JERRY B. POE
College of Business Administration
Arizona State University

ISBN 0-256-02280-1
Library of Congress Catalog Card No. 79–88790

Printed in the United States of America

3 4 5 6 7 8 9 0 K 7 6 5 4 3 2

Preface

Business is a vital part of our society. This Fourth Edition of *An Introduction to the American Business Enterprise* presents a balanced approach to the role of business. Changes occurring in business today are reflected in this edition, including the increasing influence of government on business, business's social responsibilities, equal opportunity for women and minorities, energy and pollution problems, and consumer interests. Because of the interest by students in owning their own enterprises, a new chapter has been added on small business.

Chapters open with statements and pictures taken from recent annual reports of publicly-owned corporations. These chapter openings reflect the dynamic nature of American business management today.

On the first text page of each chapter is an introductory statement of the general nature of the material covered, along with several major questions which can serve as learning objectives for your study. A system of major and minor subheadings provides a guide for outlining each chapter. An end-of-chapter summary reviews the major topics discussed.

The end-of-chapter Terms for Review list some of the key concepts and terminology. Because of the importance in an introductory course of learning the language of business, an extensive glossary of approximately 600 words and terms used in the book is included.

Throughout the book a series of career opportunity features give detailed information on careers for the 1980s. "Career Outlook" materials were taken from the *Occupational Outlook Handbook* published by the U.S. Department of Labor.

Questions at the end of each chapter draw on an understanding of specific concepts discussed in the text or require outside research or original thinking based on the background information presented in the chapter.

The Business Briefs at the end of each chapter provide a basis for understanding the dynamic nature of today's business world. Each business brief has been taken from public news reports of current interest. However, the basic issues in the business briefs reflect future problem areas as well as matters of topical interest.

The Cases contain discussion material which will help develop your capabilities for problem identification, evaluation of alternatives, and recommendations for action. The cases also present an opportunity for specific application of your understanding of the concepts discussed in the chapters. Questions at the end of each Business Brief and Case provide a starting point for your analysis. In analyzing a case the following approach is recommended:

1. Identify and state the issues or problems in the case. Indicate the most important or central problem facing management.

2. List the alternative solutions to the problems.
3. State your recommended course of action.
4. Indicate the reasons for your decision. Why is your recommendation better than other alternatives? What will be the probable consequences of accepting your recommendation?

My sincere thanks go to all the faculty members and students across the country who made constructive suggestions for this Fourth Edition. Clair W. Fisher of Des Moines Area Community College, Paul N. Loveday of University of Nevada, Las Vegas, and Gopal C. Pati of Indiana University–Northwest provided helpful reviews of the manuscript. Lohnie J. Boggs and Barry L. Van-Hook of Arizona State University made useful suggestions for the text and collaborated with James A. Carson of City College of San Francisco on the *Review Guide and Workbook* to accompany this book. Wilber C. Bothwell of Drury College made available his labor arbitration files for case materials and his writing on the motivations of workers in joining labor unions.

The following faculty members made positive recommendations regarding this edition: John S. Bowdidge, Southwest Missouri State University, Springfield; E. Wayne Chandler, Graceland College, Lamoni, Iowa; Helen Diamond, Citrus College, Azusa, California; Thomas P. Fullmer, Arizona State University, Tempe; Hal Holt, Glendale Community College, Glendale, Arizona; Albert Katz, Indiana University, South Bend, Indiana; Alfred M. Lubell, State University College at Oneonta, New York; Robert Paulson, Washtenaw Community College, Ann Arbor, Michigan; Phillip J. Peters, Fairfield University, Fairfield, Connecticut; Barbara R. Sunner, Iowa Central Community College, Fort Dodge; and Joe L. Terrell, Glendale Community College, Glendale, Arizona.

I also appreciate the cooperation of the many business people who provided case materials, examples, and pictures which illustrate the issues which managers face today.

Every attempt has been made to avoid errors; any of which remain are my oversight.

My thanks go to my family for their encouragement in this and past editions with special recognition to my wife, Carol, for her editorial assistance.

December 1979   Jerry B. Poe

Contents

SECTION TWO
Management of the business enterprise

agencies. The FTC and advertising. The Consumer Product Safety Commission. Other legislation. Private groups aiding consumers. Business aid to consumers.

business briefs

12   The marketing mix   261

The marketing mix. Product: *Product defined. Classification of consumer products. The importance of new products. Developing the product.* Promotion: *Personal selling. Advertising. Sales promotion. The total promotion mix.* Price: *Practical pricing considerations. Consumer demand. The importance of nonprice competition. Costs. Pricing strategies. Government controls.* Place: *Channels of distribution. Physical distribution. Storage.* Organization of the marketing department.

business briefs

13   Production   289

The location of production facilities: *The importance of factory location.* The production system: *Research and product design. Process design.* Production control and scheduling: *Orders and authorization of production. Production scheduling.* Purchasing industrial goods: *Steps in the purchasing process. Price and quality considerations. Selecting sources of supply.* The make-or-buy decision. Inventory control. The purchase of capital equipment. Other elements of the production system: *Motion and time analysis. Quality control. Maintenance.* Automation. The organization of the production department: *Manufacturing management. The factory foreman.*

business briefs

case

SECTION FIVE
Accounting and finance

14   Understanding accounting statements   313

The uses of accounting information: *Management uses of accounting. Outsiders' use of accounting information.* The basic accounting statements: *The balance sheet. The income statement. Statement of changes in financial position.* The financial analysis of accounting statements: *Measures of liquidity. Measures of profitability. Measures of solvency.*

SECTION SIX
Business in a changing world

The economic, political, and social environment of business

SECTION ONE

K mart reports . . .

In the United States today, we have what some analysts have described as the "big five" mass merchants. K mart is the second largest volume producer in the group and enjoys the most rapid sales increase. Other mass merchants include the large number of regional discount store chains and the discount subsidiaries of certain high-fashion department stores.

We at K mart consider ourselves mass merchants. But our strategy for gaining market share in this industry is somewhat different from the strategy of the other members of the "big five." Our most important competitive strategy is to use discount pricing. Our store buildings and fixtures are designed and built, our merchandise assortments are selected and our distribution systems are developed in order to offer a broad range of general merchandise at the lowest possible prices.

Customer acceptance of our stores and the turnover of merchandise that we achieve have permitted us to generate satisfactory gross profit dollars per square foot of selling area in spite of lower gross margin percentages on merchandise sold.

Perhaps our second most significant strategy is the development of free-standing stores throughout the country rather than concentrating our efforts in developing anchor stores in regional shopping centers. This decision has permitted the rapid development of stores and gives us the flexibility to build in rural areas or in high-density areas where sufficient land may not be available for regional centers. The development of free-standing stores was also strongly influenced by our conviction that convenience of location has become increasingly important in the minds of most consumers.

From annual report of K mart Corporation

1

The economic basis of business

The economic basis of business

The study of business provides insights into many of the challenges facing society. Over the years the provision of goods and services has been the main focus of business activity. However, the production and distribution of those goods and services have changed dramatically. The issues facing us in business today are more complex. New products and problems, unheard of only a few years ago, are becoming increasingly important.

Each of us is affected by business. Many of you are already working for business enterprises or are preparing for careers in business. Most Americans spend their adult lives producing goods and services as part of the business system. All of us are consumers of business products. We make vital decisions as to how our income will be spent. How well our economic system functions influences our individual standard of living.

After studying this chapter, you will be able to answer the following questions related to the economic environment of business:

What is the nature of economic activity?

How are societies organized to answer the three basic economic questions?

What are the major characteristics of the private enterprise system?

How do business enterprises create utility for consumers?

Why is the corporation such an important legal form of business organization?

THE NATURE OF ECONOMIC ACTIVITY

What is the most recent purchase you made? Was it breakfast this morning or gasoline if you drove to school or a Coke between classes? Have you ever bought a stereo set or a camera or a radio? Have you ever been faced with the decision of whether to spend or save money that you earned or were given? Although you may have been unaware of it, in all these actions you were involved in economic activity.

Economics defined

The word *economics* has its derivation in Latin and Greek. Originally economics referred to the management of a family household. The term was gradually extended to include not only the management of households but the management of businesses, communities, and governments. Therefore, *economics* may be defined as the study of how we manage the human and material resources available to society. Several aspects of the management of business enterprises are discussed in later chapters. However, the distinguishing feature of management is that it involves decision making. Business managers are required to make choices from among alternative courses of action.

The economic problem of scarcity

Economics may also be defined as the study of how scarce resources are allocated in a society of unlimited wants. Every society has an economic system which provides food, clothing, shelter, and other material goods and services for the basic and acquired needs of its people. Because these goods and services are available in limited quantities, with many people wanting them, they have value. Scarcity is a basic fact which underlies all economic activity. If there were a complete abundance of goods and services, then society would not have to be concerned with the issue of allocating scarce resources.

Limits are imposed upon us by nature and economic circumstances. There is only so much land we can till. Natural resources such as oil and minerals are definitely limited. At any particular time we have only so many factories equipped with machinery. There are only so many workers with the necessary knowledge and skills to produce goods and services which we consume. Our knowledge about how to produce more goods, although constantly expanding, is finite. In summary, we live in a world where material goods are limited.

Although the resources of our world are limited, our wants are not. Indeed, one of the important assumptions of economics is that total human wants can never be fully satisfied. No matter how much we have, we seem to want more. As people's incomes increase, so does their desire for more and better goods and services. How many times have you said, "If I could just have this particular product I would be completely satisfied." But when you obtained the good, perhaps an automobile, did it satisfy your material wants? It did not, if you are a typical person. When some material wants are satisfied, others take their place. This means that the economic system can never produce enough to satisfy everyone completely. Thus arises the need for a system of efficient allocation of the scarce goods of society among people who have unlimited wants.

The economic resources

Scarce economic resources consist of all the natural, synthetic, and human factors that go into the production of goods and services. These resources can be classified broadly as property resources and human resources.

Property resources consist of land and capital. *Land* refers to all natural resources which are used in the production process, including timber, oil and mineral deposits, and water, as well as land itself. *Capital* refers to all machinery, tools, equipment, and buildings required to produce goods and distribute them to consumers. The use of capital goods enables workers to produce more with the same amount of physical effort. Consider the productivity of a service station attendant hand-polishing automobiles all day compared with the productivity of another worker doing the same job with an electric buffing machine. The

career outlook

ECONOMISTS

Economists are concerned with how to utilize scarce resources such as land, raw materials, and human resources to provide goods and services for society. Economists analyze the relationship between the supply and demand of goods and services and study how goods and services are produced, distributed, and consumed. Most economists analyze and interpret a wide variety of economic data in the course of their work.

Economists who work for business firms provide management with information for decisions on the marketing and pricing of company products; analyze the effect of government policies on business or international trade; or look at the advisability of adding new lines of merchandise, opening new branch operations, or otherwise expanding a company's business. Business economists working for firms that carry on extensive operations abroad may be asked to prepare short- and long-term forecasts of foreign economies as well as forecasts of the U.S. economy.

Private industry and business will continue to provide the largest number of employment opportunities for economists because of the increasing complexity of the domestic and international economies and the increasing reliance on quantitative methods of analyzing business trends, forecasting sales, and planning purchases and production operations. Employers will seek those economists who are well trained in econometrics and statistics.

Persons who graduate with a bachelor's degree in economics through the mid-1980s are likely to face keen competition for jobs as economists. However, many of these degree holders will find employment in government, industry, and business as management or sales trainees or as research assistants. Candidates who hold master's degrees in economics should find good opportunities for administrative, research, and planning positions in private industry and government. Ph.D's should have favorable opportunities in government, industry, research organizations, and consulting firms.

addition of a piece of capital equipment greatly improves the worker's productivity.

Human resources consist of labor and entrepreneurial ability. *Labor* refers to all the physical and mental talents that indiviuals expend in producing goods and services with the exception of entrepreneurial talent, which is classified separately. Labor includes the manual labor of the trash hauler and the knowledge and skill of the brain surgeon. *Entrepreneur* was originally a French word which means enterpriser. The entrepreneur provides the managerial ability to bring together land, capital, and labor to produce goods and services. The entrepreneur assumes the risks associated with the organization and operation of a business enterprise and in return hopes to make a profit.

In traditional economic theory the compensation or return for labor is called *wages;* the return for the use of land is *rent;* and the return for capital resources

TABLE 1–1
Components of U.S. national income, 1968 and 1978

	Billions of dollars		Percent change
	1968	*1978*	
National income			
Compensation of employees	$520	$1,302	+150%
Rental income	19	23	21
Interest	27	106	293
Proprietors' income	63	113	79
Corporate profits	86	160	86
Total	$715	$1,704	138

Source: U.S. Department of Commerce, Bureau of Economic Analysis.

is *interest.* The return to the entrepreneur is the profit from business operations, although if the business enterprise is not well managed the profit may turn into a loss.

One measure of the returns to the various factors of production is national income as determined by the U.S. Department of Commerce. *National income* is defined as the total earnings of labor and property which result from the production of goods and services in our economy. National income is the sum of the compensation of employees, rental income, interest, proprietors' income, and corporate profits. The components of national income for 1968 and 1978 are compared in Table 1–1 along with the percentages of change over this ten-year period.

Technology

Another important part of our economic society is technology. *Technology* is the accumulated fund of knowledge which promotes efficient organization for the production of goods and services. Economic efficiency depends in large part on the technical state of knowledge of production and distribution processes. The state of technology in a particular business area is the practical application of science which has been accumulated from previous generations to the present.

TYPES OF ECONOMIC SYSTEMS

Whenever a society faces choices between alternative uses of scarce resources, an economic system must be organized. All economic systems must provide means of answering three basic questions:

1. What goods will be produced from the scarce resources that are available?
2. How will these products be produced?
3. How will these goods be distributed; that is, who will consume the goods?

How these questions are answered depends upon the nature of the economic system of the society being studied. There are two theoretical ways by which economic systems in industrialized countries may be organized—capitalism and socialism. Under *capitalism* the means of producing and distributing goods are privately owned and controlled. Under the economic system of *socialism* the means of production and distribution are owned and controlled by the government.

In practice the economic systems functioning in the world today have elements of both private and governmental ownership and control. However, there is quite a difference among the economic systems of major industrial nations ranging from the United States at one end of the spectrum to the Soviet Union at the other end. In between are the economies of countries such as Great Britain.

In describing the economic systems existing today, it is also important to consider the political environment within which economic activity takes place. Political systems may be organized on a democratic or totalitarian basis. Essential to the functioning of a *democracy* is the choice of governmental leaders by the people through free elections with freedom of speech, the press, and assembly. A *totalitarian* governmental system is one in which one party or group has absolute control. The people are not free to change their leadership through elections since candidates for office are chosen by the one party that is in power. Freedom of speech, the press, and assembly are restricted.

The following examples illustrate some of the basic differences in the organization of existing political-economic systems.

Great Britain

In Great Britain the political-economic system might be characterized as democratic socialism. Although there is still much private business ownership, basic industries, including gas, electric power, communications, transportation, steel, mining, and central banking, are owned and operated by the government. There is some degree of central planning. In the nationalized industries private profit is not a goal or a measure of the efficiency by which the economy's needs are met.

In a democratic-socialist country the people have free elections to choose political leaders who will legislate and govern their country. Strong opposition parties exist which compete for the votes and confidence of the people.

The Soviet Union

In the Union of Soviet Socialist Republics the political-economic system might be characterized as totalitarian socialism. The means of production and distribution are owned and controlled by the state. The concept of private profit is lacking in economic planning and motivation. There is a high degree of central planning for the economy. Generally the economic objectives are set by state planning agencies. These agencies emphasize the production of industrial and military goods rather than consumer goods.

In the Soviet Union there is no freedom to organize opposing political parties. Dissent from the established order is discouraged both in politics and in economics.

CAPITALISM AND THE PRIVATE ENTERPRISE SYSTEM

In the United States the political-economic system might be characterized as democratic capitalism. In general the means of production and distribution are owned and controlled privately. Private profit is an incentive to business to supply the goods and services desired by individual, industrial, and governmental customers.

In our political system individuals are free to organize or join political parties. Differences of view are often very much in the open.

The form that capitalism has taken in the United States is the *private enterprise system.* It is sometimes called the free enterprise system, the market economy, or the profit system. Our economic system has developed in a pragmatic fashion. Americans have been willing to experiment to solve economic problems. The result has been an economic system which, although predominantly capitalistic, has a definite role for government. Because of this willingness to use various means to achieve economic ends, we have a mixed economic system. The emphasis is on private ownership and the profit motive, but government is also involved in many aspects of the economy. There are five important characteristics of American capitalism:

1. Private property.
2. The profit motive.
3. The market system and competition.
4. The nature of the relationship between business and government.
5. Freedom of choice by consumers.

Private property

Private property is a basic element in a capitalistic society. Without it there could be no private ownership and use of capital. Private property means that individuals can own things of value and control their use. Especially important is the freedom of individuals to acquire, utilize, and dispose of the factors of production. An extension of this right is the legal contract, which specifies the conditions under which anything that is owned may be used by others.

Private property serves two important functions in capitalism. First, it places in the hands of individuals power over the use of productive resources. Economic activity cannnot occur unless someone makes decisions about which goods are to be produced and when and how they are to be produced. The more complex the method of production, the more crucial is the decision-making process. The owners of resources may delegate part of their powers to others, but for there to be capitalism the owners must have the final say as to how resources are used. Second, private property serves as an incentive for the accumulation of wealth. This incentive is necessary if the stock of capital in the economy is to grow. The right of property owners to benefit from the use of their property in the productive process encourages them to save and invest in capital goods.

"It seems like only yesterday we were debating whether the system worked."

Reprinted by permission The Wall Street Journal

In the United States the capital owned by individuals is used by them to make a profit through investing in the production process. In the Soviet Union individuals are permitted to own property for their own use but with few exceptions are not permitted to own property for the production or distribution of goods and services. One exception in the U.S.S.R. is the small truck farming plots where the individual family has about one-half acre of its own to cultivate, with the produce being sold in markets operated by the collective farm. These small private truck farms which occupy less than one percent of the Soviet Union's agricultural land reportedly produce 27 percent of the total value of Soviet farm output.

The profit motive

The profit motive is another important characteristic of capitalism. *Profit* is defined as the money difference between what it costs to produce and sell a product and the revenue from its sale. The term *profit motive* refers to the desire to engage in economic activity in order to earn profit.

In every economic system someone must decide how to combine the scarce resources of capital and labor to produce goods. In the American economy private enterprise management determines the most efficient balance between the factors of production, depending on their availability, quality, and price. The profit motive acts as the central controlling mechanism. Business managers are motivated by profits to expand the output of goods for which consumer demand is great and to cut back the production of less sought-after goods. Without the lure of profit the owners of business enterprises would not be willing to bear the risks inherent in the production process. To the extent that business owners activate the entire economic system and that their decisions are based on profit calculations, the profit motive is the key institution of the capitalistic economy.

In the U.S.S.R., except for the concept of planned profit used by government officials in setting industry goals, profit does not play an important role in the production process. Government planners can choose to subsidize industries in which the sales of goods do not cover the cost of labor and materials if it is to the state's advantage to do so. For example, in international trade it may be politically desirable to sell goods below cost. In a totalitarian planned economy the whole concept of "costs" is different from that in a free market economy. In the planned economy the government arbitrarily allocates the various kinds of costs to meet its objectives, rather than allowing the costs of labor and materials to be determined in the marketplace.

The market system and competition

In the private enterprise system the economy is organized as a system of markets in which buyers and sellers exchange money for goods and services. The market price which results from these exchanges reflects the behavior of the buyers and sellers. The market functions to match the supply and demand for each type of product. As a consumer you strongly influence what will be produced by exerting economic power in purchasing a product or passing it by for a competing product. Producers attempt to influence you by introducing new products, improving existing products, and using various types of promotional activities.

An essential characteristic of the marketplace in the American economy is that it is not formally regulated as to the type, quantity, and price of goods that are produced and sold. Our national policy is to encourage competition by business enterprises for the consumers' dollars. There are many ways to determine prices, but free and competitive market pricing is the one most consistent with the private enterprise system. It is this open market which is responsible for the creation and preservation of fair prices and economic efficiency. The degree to which the market system is permitted to function without excessive controls is a measure of the extent of democratic capitalism in the economy.

In socialistic economies there is an absence of competition and the free marketplace. In totalitarian socialism what will be produced and in what quantity are based on production quotas set by government planning bureaus. Prices are set to control the consumption of different types of products based on "costs" that have been set by government.

The relationship between business and government

Capitalism, particularly democratic capitalism, has always stressed the importance of individual freedom in economic affairs. In the 18th and 19th centuries the economic doctrine of laissez faire was associated with capitalism. Laissez faire is a French term meaning "let people do as they choose." This was the cry of businessmen in those days against the regulation by the state of their private economic activities. In its most extreme form laissez-faire capitalism limited the government's participation in economic activity merely to the provision of such vital public services as police and fire protection.

Today it is generally accepted that the role of government in our complex industrial society is different from what it was in the days of the laissez-faire capitalists. As a result of the depression of the 1930s, the American people expect our government to manage taxation, government spending, and the money supply so as to encourage the full employment of labor and other resources in the economy. A number of governmental agencies, such as the Federal Trade Commission, the Securities and Exchange Commission, and the Food and Drug Administration, show that we have recognized the need to be protected from harmful or deceptive business practices.

Government has assumed an increased role in economic affairs in the United States over the past 45 years. However, our economic system remains predominantly capitalistic. We still depend on individual consumers and business enterprises to make the vast proportion of economic decisions. About 80 percent of all the goods and services produced in the economy are purchased by individuals and private business enterprises, with the remainder being purchased by various levels of government.

Freedom of choice by consumers

One of the strengths of our form of democratic capitalism is that as consumers we have much freedom to choose what goods and services we will buy. We have many products to choose from. The freedom in the American economic system tends to encourage innovation and change, both for new products and for improved methods of producing and distributing them. Generally goods are distributed among consumers on the basis of their ability and willingness to pay the going market price. We cannot consume all the goods and services we want. Therefore, the existing stock of goods is allocated on the basis of the purchasing power and preferences of the many consumers.

In totalitarian economies one of the major criticisms by the people is the low quantity and poor quality of goods. Government planners have generally emphasized the production of industrial and military goods at the expense of consumer goods. Although in these countries people are relatively free to spend their limited incomes, the lack of consumer goods or their poor quality limits that freedom.

By American standards the marketing system of the Soviet Union is inefficient. Frequently people stand in one line to determine whether a product is available, then move to another line to pay for merchandise, and finally stand in a third line to receive their goods. In the Soviet Union more attention is beginning to be given to consumers, but the emphasis continues to be on the production of industrial goods.

CLASSIFICATION OF BUSINESS ENTERPRISES

From your point of view as a consumer, the end result of business activity is the goods you consume. *Goods* are anything useful in satisfying human wants. Goods may be tangible, such as automobiles and stereo sets; or they may be intangible, such as legal advice or schoolteaching. Intangible goods are usually called *services*. Goods also may be classified as consumer or producer goods. *Consumer goods* satisfy individual needs directly. They include nondurable items such as food and clothing and durable items such as automobiles, furniture, and appliances. *Producer goods* are the tools, machines, and equipment used to make consumer goods, and thus they satisfy individual needs indirectly.

Utilities possessed by goods

Utility is the power to satisfy human wants. For something to be a tangible good it must have four different types of utility:

1. *Form utility.* Goods must possess the proper physical characteristics. A motorist wants an automobile, not steel, rubber, glass, and paint.
2. *Place utility.* Goods must be where the consumer has access to them. The new automobile in Detroit is of no use to the prospective purchaser until it has been transported to the local dealer.
3. *Time utility.* Goods must be available when they are wanted. When you purchase a new car, you want delivery as soon as possible.
4. *Possession utility.* Goods must be owned or controlled by the people who consume them. Through credit arrangements you are able to possess an automobile even though you do not have enough money to pay for it immediately.

Types of business enterprises

A *business enterprise* is a privately owned and operated organization that brings together the factors of production to provide goods or services which are sold with the expectation of earning a profit. Business enterprises may be classified according to the four types of activities performed to provide goods with utility.

1. *Processing enterprises* transform the natural resources that come from the mines, forests, farms, and oceans into the raw materials used to manufacture goods.
2. *Manufacturing enterprises* fabricate consumer and producer goods out of raw materials.
3. *Marketing enterprises* distribute the finished goods to ultimate consumers.
4. *Facilitating enterprises* perform necessary auxiliary functions in such fields as finance, insurance, transportation, construction, and services.

Those business enterprises which engage in the same type of economic activity constitute an *industry*. For example, the manufacturers of passenger cars make up the automobile industry. However, this is a somewhat vague concept because many business enterprises produce more than one type of good or service. They really are a part of the much broader industry sector called manufacturing. Figure 1–1 indicates the broad industrial sectors which make up the economy and shows the percentage of national income which each sector supplied in 1978.

Figure 1–1 reveals the key role of manufacturing enterprises in our economy. This sector of business not only accounts for more than one fourth of national

FIGURE 1–1

Percentage of 1978 national income generated by different industries

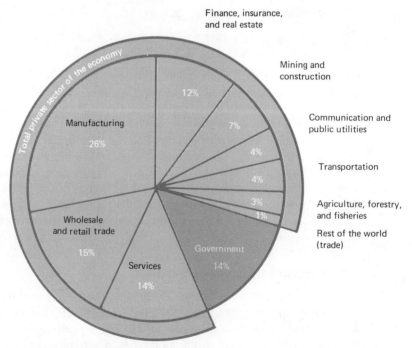

Source: U.S. Department of Commerce, *Survey of Current Business*, February 1979.

income but also greatly influences economic activity in such fields as transportation, trade, and finance.

LEGAL FORMS OF BUSINESS ORGANIZATION

The three most important legal forms of business organization in the United States are the proprietorship, the partnership, and the corporation. Table 1–2 shows a summary of the more than 14 million business enterprises in the United States according to their legal form of organization and the major type of economic activity they perform.

The proprietorship

The proprietorship is the simplest legal form of business organization. The proprietor is the sole owner of the business enterprise and is able to exercise complete control over its operation. The owner is personally liable for the debts and other legal obligations of the enterprise. The profits of the proprietorship are considered part of the owner's income. Therefore, there is no separate federal

TABLE 1–2
Number of enterprises operating in principal industries in the United States, period ending June 30, 1977

	Number of firms (000)		
Industry	Proprietor-ships	Active partner-ships	Active corpo-rations
Agriculture, forestry, and fisheries	3,470	121	62
Mining	60	18	15
Construction	963	60	198
Manufacturing	223	31	214
Transportation, communication, and public utilities	346	17	81
Trade	2,282	195	646
Wholesale	331	32	228
Retail	1,861	162	417
Finance, insurance, and real estate	827	447	414
Service	3,153	207	473
All industries	11,358	1,096	2,105

Note: Because of multiple-industry listings, totals are less than the sum of individual items.

Source: Department of the Treasury, Internal Revenue Service, *Preliminary Statistics of Income 1976, Business Income Tax Returns*, October 1978, and *Corporation Income Tax Returns*, June 1979.

income tax on the profits of the business. However, the owner has to report the enterprise's profits as personal income for tax purposes.

The proprietorship is by far the most common legal form of business in the United States, as Table 1–2 indicates. Proprietorships are most numerous in farming, services, and the retail trades. Generally they are small enterprises. Frequently proprietorships are not very profitable because of their size, problems of obtaining efficient management, and intensive competition. However, this form of legal organization continues to be popular because of the number of persons who want to have their own business and because of the ease in starting a proprietorship.

The partnership

A partnership is formed when two or more persons agree to start a business enterprise as co-owners. Each partner customarily contributes economic assets to the enterprise in the form of money, property, skill, or labor. Partners share in the profits or losses of the business according to an agreed-upon ratio. However, all general partners are liable for legal obligations, such as losses or court judgments against the partnership, to the full extent of their personal fortunes. This tends to limit the size of partnerships. Another limiting factor is that customarily when one partner dies a new partnership must be formed.

The control and management of a partnership are vested equally in the general partners, any one of whom has the power to make decisions. Therefore, a serious mistake by one partner can affect all the partners.

The profits of a partnership are considered to be part of the owners' incomes. Therefore, there is no separate federal income tax on the partnership's profits. However, the partners do have to report their portion of the enterprise's profits as part of their respective personal incomes for tax purposes.

The corporation

A corporation is a legal entity separate and distinct from the persons who are its owners. It comes into being when a charter is obtained from the state. The corporation has only those powers which are given by the state and expressed or implied in its charter. The owners exchange money or other assets for shares of stock in the corporation.

There is a legal distinction between the corporation and its stockholders. This permits the corporation to buy, own, and sell property; enter into contracts; sue and be sued; and carry out business activities as a legal entity separate from its owners. This separate entity concept also means that the income of the corporation is taxed by government. Any cash dividends which the corporation pays to its stockholders are taxed as personal income of the individual stockholders.

The stockholders of the corporation elect a board of directors to exercise control of the corporation. Usually each share of stock is entitled to one vote. Shareholders either vote in person at stockholders' meetings or by *proxy,* which is a written authorization for someone else to cast a stockholder's vote. The board of directors solicits proxies from stockholders which are then voted to support the incumbent board of directors. If a group of stockholders becomes dissatisfied with the board of directors they may solicit proxies in an attempt to gain control of the corporation. Such proxy fights are relatively rare and may be expensive to conduct when there are thousands of stockholders.

In the corporate form of legal organization there is a separation of roles. The stockholders are the owners. The president and other executives manage the corporation, and the board of directors exercises control. The board of directors is responsible for seeing that the corporation functions in the best long-run interests of the stockholders. Specific duties of the board include the election of the officers, including the chief executive officer or president. Other board responsibilities include the formulation of major policies, approval of important operating decisions, and the general exercise of control. Directors are usually elected annually by the stockholders.

Board members who are full-time employees active in the day-to-day management of the corporation are called *inside directors.* Such directors may include the corporation's president and various vice presidents. Directors who serve only on the board and are not full-time management employees of the corporation are called *outside directors.* Outside directors normally do not have as close an understanding of the detailed operation of the corporation as do insiders. However, outside directors should be able to take a more independent view of corporate activities since they do not have to work under the president.

There are considerably fewer corporations than proprietorships, as Table 1–2 indicates. However, Table 1–3 shows that the corporation has by far the greatest economic impact upon society in terms of business receipts (sales) and profits.

Advantages of corporations   The corporate form of legal organization has a number of advantages over the proprietorship and the partnership:

1. The liability of the owners of the corporation for the corporation's obligations is limited to the amount of their investment in the corporation. Therefore, stockholders' entire personal fortunes are not placed in possible jeopardy, as with the proprietorship and the partnership.

2. Depending upon the terms of its charter, the corporation may have perpetual life. Its existence does not depend upon any particular group of owners.

3. There is relative ease of transfer of ownership of the corporation. Stockholders can simply sell their shares of stock to someone else without directly affecting the functioning of the corporation or the other stockholders.

4. Because of the advantages of the corporate form, it is generally easier for corporations than for other legal forms of organization to attract the large amounts of capital necessary for many types of business operations.

5. Because the corporation can assemble large amounts of economic resources

TABLE 1-3
Business receipts and profits of U.S. enterprises in principal industries, period ending June 30, 1977 ($ billions)

Industry	Business receipts			Profit (less loss) before tax		
	Sole proprietorships	Active partnerships	Active corporations	Sole proprietorships	Active partnerships	Active corporations
Agriculture, forestry, and fisheries	$ 78	$ 13	$ 31	$ 5.7	$1.0	$ 0.6
Mining	4	5	83	0.2	*	30.0
Construction	38	13	149	5.6	1.1	2.7
Manufacturing	9	8	1,401	1.0	0.5	88.3
Transportation, communication, and public utilities	11	3	274	1.4	*	14.8
Trade	158	46	1,081	9.9	2.4	26.1
Wholesale	35	16	563	2.9	0.7	15.8
Retail	121	30	518	6.7	1.7	10.4
Finance, insurance, and real estate	15	38	182	5.3	*	18.1
Services	61	32	141	20.3	7.8	4.2
All industries	375	158	3,342	49.5	8.9	184.8

Note: Because of multiple industry listings, totals are less than the sum of individual items.
* Net loss exceeds net profit.
Source: Department of the Treasury, Internal Revenue Service, *Preliminary Statistics of Income 1976, Business Income Tax Returns*, October 1978, and *Corporation Income Tax Returns*, June 1979.

with relative ease, it frequently obtains managerial talent and specialized skills more easily than do other legal forms of organization.

The owners of a small corporation may not always be able to realize all the advantages listed above. For example, a bank may require the principal owners to personally endorse a loan which the bank makes to a small corporation. Such an endorsement negates the advantage of limited liability for those stockholders. If the corporation is unable to repay the loan, the bank has a legal claim against the personal assets of the endorsers. However, such an arrangement is not usual with the large corporation which has numerous stockholders.

Figure 1–2 is a summary comparison of factors relating to corporations, partnerships, and proprietorships.

SUMMARY

Economics is the management of the human and material resources of society. Economics can also be defined as the allocation of scarce resources in a society of unlimited wants.

Economic resources consist of all the natural, synthetic, and human factors that go into the production of goods and services. Property resources are land and capital. Human resources are labor and entrepreneurial ability.

The three basic economic questions which must be answered in every economic system are:

1. What goods will be produced?
2. How will these goods be produced?
3. Who will consume (or control) these goods?

Economic systems functioning today have elements of capitalism and socialism. The U.S. economic system is a modified form of capitalism called the private enterprise system. Private property, the profit motive, the market system, a particular relationship between business and government, and freedom of choice by consumers are important characteristics of the private enterprise system.

Goods, which may be either tangible or intangible, are useful in satisfying human wants. Intangible goods are called services. Goods may also be classified as consumer goods or producer goods.

In order for goods to have economic value they must have some type of utility. Utility is the power to satisfy human wants. Tangible goods have form, place, time, and possession utility.

Business enterprises may be classified by activity as enterprises for processing, manufacturing, marketing, or facilitating. Businesses may also be grouped by industry classification.

The three most commonly used legal forms of business organization are proprietorships, partnerships, and corporations. Corporations are the dominant legal form of organization in their impact on the economy.

FIGURE 1–2

Comparison of factors relating to corporations, partnerships, and proprietorships

Factors	Corporations	Partnerships	Proprietorships
Ease of formation	Most complicated. Must be chartered by state or federal government. May need city license.	Medium complexity. Partnership agreement needed. May require city or state license.	Least complicated. Individual starts business. May need city or state license.
Length of life	Life limited only by success of operations and charter.	Limited by life of each partner and partners' agreement.	Limited by life of proprietor or proprietor's sale of the business.
Transfer of ownership	Partial or complete ownership easily changed through sale of corporation's stock.	By mutual agreement of partners.	By sale or inheritance of assets of business.
Liability of owners	Limited to amount invested in corporation's stock.	At least one partner must have unlimited liability.	Unlimited liability for personal assets.
Ease of raising funds	Relatively easy to sell stock to many parties. Borrowing based on corporation's credit capacity.	Limited to partners' resources and ability to borrow.	Limited to owner's personal resources and ability to borrow.
Activities and flexibility	Limited by corporate charter which may be amended.	Limited to partnership agreement and partners' wishes.	Unlimited except by personal wishes of proprietor.
Taxation	Income taxes on corporate profits. Stockholders taxed individually on cash dividends.	Business income taxed as part of partners' personal incomes. Inheritance taxes.	Income taxed as proprietor's personal income. Inheritance tax liability at owner's death.
Information on operations and profits	Provided to stockholders. Large, widely owned corporations make much financial information public.	Provided to partners. Generally not known to public.	Known by proprietor. Generally not known by public.
Ownership, management, and control	Generally separated.	Exercised by partners. May have separate managers.	Generally exercised by proprietor.

THE SYSTEMS APPROACH TO BUSINESS

The systems approach to business has received attention in recent years because of the breadth and complexity of the issues facing management. These include changes brought about by exploding technological advances, vastly improved communications throughout the world, and questioning of the traditional priorities and values of society. The relationship between business and other institutions, along with the impact of economic, political, and social problems, has made it necessary for managers to reexamine their approach to the functioning of the enterprise.

The systems approach emphasizes the total functioning of the business enterprise in society. Business relationships are examined in relation to the total environment. The systems approach to business is useful because it emphasizes an understanding of the comprehensive nature of business activities and the structure and process through which these activities are carried out.

A *system* is defined as a set of elements which have a relationship to one another. The elements within a system are referred to as *subsystems*. Thus each system is composed of subsystems which in combination have a meaningful unity or wholeness. The elements within the system are interrelated and interdependent and constitute the internal environment of the system. If the economy as a whole is considered as a system, then individual enterprises would be viewed as subsystems. If, for purposes of study, a single business enterprise is considered as a system, then the various departments and functions performed are the subsystems which interact with one another.

Business functions as an open system which is continually influenced by factors in the external environment. As a result of information received, which is called *feedback*, business is constantly changing both to adapt to its environment and to influence the external systems with which it comes into contact.

When business is studied in the framework of the whole economic system, the total flow of economic activity by business and consumers is examined. This is referred to as *macroeconomic* analysis. The "macro" approach to business deals with the institution of business in its relationship with other systems in society.

Figure 1–3 shows the functioning of a simple model of the economic system which is influenced by a number of other systems in its external environment. This broad macroeconomic approach to business illustrates how business functions in the economic system and how it is influenced by other systems. Throughout this book several topics are discussed which relate the whole institution of business to its external environment. These topics are covered in such chapters as those dealing with government relationships, social responsibility, labor unions, consumers, and financial institutions.

Notice in Figure 1–3 how business enterprises use the inputs of labor, capital, land and management in order to produce the outputs of goods and services

FIGURE 1–3
The economic system in American society

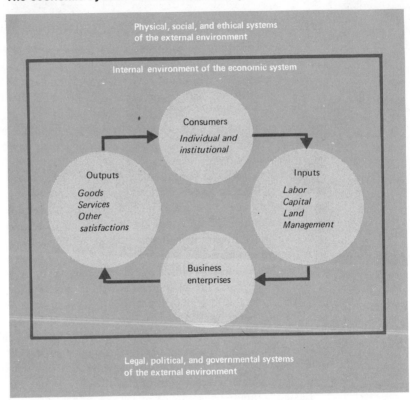

which are demanded by individual and institutional consumers. This activity takes place within the internal environment of the economic system.

The economic system is affected by other institutions in society and in turn influences them. The legal system is important to business because our economic system is based upon the concept of private property rights. Business operations depend upon contractual agreements which may be enforced through the courts of law. Business is involved in the political system because of the effect of political decisions on business operations and because of business influence on the governing process.

Since people are important in the functioning of the economic system, there is a system of social relationships which influences business. Business is influenced by cultural and religious institutions because of the interrelated nature of people's values and business activities.

Another way to study business is from the point of view of the functioning of the individual business enterprise. This approach is called *microeconomic* analysis. "Micro" analysis is concerned with the internal functioning of the subsystems of the enterprise and with the total management of the firm as it relates to its environment. Several chapters, including those on management, control, marketing, personnel, production, and finance, are devoted essentially to the study of the functioning of the individual business enterprise.

TERMS FOR REVIEW

economics
economic resources
national income
technology

capitalism
socialism
private enterprise system
profit motive

utility
proprietorship
partnership
corporation

QUESTIONS

1. Why is scarcity a fundamental part of the economic system?

2. *a.* What changes occurred in the components of national income from 1968 to 1978?

   b. Determine what recent changes have occurred in national income by checking the *Survey of Current Business, Economic Indicators,* or other government publications in the library.

3. *a.* What are the three basic economic questions which must be answered in every society?

   b. How are these questions answered in the United States today?

4. In what ways does the functioning of the U.S. economy differ from that of the Soviet Union? In what ways are the two economies similar?

5. *a.* Should some governmental body have the power to control prices and wages?

   b. What would be possible positive and negative consequences of such controls?

6. What kinds of economic utility are there? Give an example of each.

7. Under what circumstances would it be most advisable to organize a business enterprise as:
   a. a proprietorship?
   b. a partnership?
   c. a corporation?

8. Using Tables 1–2 and 1–3, analyze the relative importance of proprietorships, partnerships, and corporations in the various broad industrial categories. How do you account for these relationships?

9. In today's economy would you expect K mart's strategies described on the first page of the chapter to be successful? Why?

business briefs

CAMPUS RECRUITING

During the troubled times on college and university campuses in the 1960s and early 1970s, when the war was going on in Southeast Asia, many corporation recruiters were viewed with suspicion and disdain by students In the late 1970s unfavorable publicity re-garding product safety and pollution has given certain industries and corporations a negative image with some collegians.

In an attempt to build goodwill and hire more grad-uates, a number of corporations are making campus recruiting a comprehensive year-round activity. General Motors has developed a Key Institution Program instead of just an annual three-day visit in the spring. In its Key Institution Program GM has sent recruiting teams headed by top executives to more than 50 business and engineering schools. This program is also providing scholarships and financial aid, research support, summer jobs before graduation, and guest lecturers at the key campuses. The purpose of the program is to create closer ties with schools and to increase the number of students hired by GM in a competitive market for graduates. GM has increased its hiring goals for business students and engineers. In addition, GM is stepping up its attempts to recruit liberal arts graduates.

Other corporations which are broadening their campus recruiting programs include Dow, Ford, IBM, and Union Carbide.

1. *Why would GM and other corporations be interested in doing more than simply hold three-day recruiting sessions on college campuses?*
2. *What is the value for students of summer jobs with corporations before graduation?*
3. *What factors are important to you in a career job opportunity?*

RUBBERMAID'S RESPONSE

Rubbermaid Inc. is the leading manufacturer of plastic houseware products. The corporation's profits grew at an annual rate of 19 percent during the 1970s. This success in the marketplace and in profitability has attracted merger proposals from a number of larger corporations over the years.

The response of Rubbermaid's management to these merger proposals has been strongly negative. The desire of management is to keep the company as an independent enterprise. To help assure that Rubbermaid can resist the takeover attempts of larger corporations, at the 1978 annual shareholders' meeting the management received approval for the following plan:

> Removal of directors now requires the approval of two thirds of shareholders. Earlier a simple majority vote could remove a director from office.

> If a tender offer[1] receives 50 percent of Rubbermaid's shares, any stockholders not wishing to tender shares have the right to sell their stock to the company at the tender price or at any higher price that the stock may have traded for in the prior 18 months.

> If the acquiring corporation gets ownership of more than 25 percent of Rubbermaid's stock and starts a proxy fight with management, 85 percent of the shareholders must approve Rubbermaid's merger into another corporation. Also, Rubbermaid's shareholders would have the right to redeem their shares with the company for at least the tender price of the acquiring corporation.

Although this plan was approved, there was opposition by some shareholders.

1. *Why might the management of Rubbermaid desire to avoid having the enterprise merged into a larger corporation?*
2. *What advantages would these steps to prevent a merger have for shareholders?*
3. *What disadvantages might these antimerger steps have for shareholders?*
4. *What benefits could come for a smaller enterprise which merges with a larger corporation?*

---

[1] A tender offer is a public offer by another enterprise or investor group to purchase the stock of a corporation, normally at a price above the current market price. Tender offers are used to gain control of a corporation, either to change top management or to merge it with another enterprise.

Allied Chemical reports . . .

Oil production from Allied Chemical's North Sea fields rose rapidly during 1977, and income from operations of the energy products of our Union Texas Petroleum Division jumped to more than six times the 1976 level. Earnings of our oil and gas business are expected to be even higher in 1978.

These rising profits represent the first large-scale return on the heavy investments we have been making for the last several years in a worldwide search for new oil and gas reserves. In the British sector of the North Sea, Allied Chemical has a 20 percent interest in the Piper and Claymore fields, and we have committed about $330 million as our share of the capital costs of finding and developing those fields.

Piper, the larger of the two, started production in December 1976, and Claymore in November 1977. By early 1978 Piper was producing an average of 260,000 barrels a day and Claymore, 55,000. Facilities are being installed on the Piper platform to strip liquids from the gas brought up along with the oil. The gas will be piped ashore for sale to the British Gas Corporation. The new facilities, together with water injection wells, will permit Piper's production of oil to rise to an average of 300,000 barrels a day later this year. Claymore production should rise to an average of about 115,000 barrels a day by 1979.

Piper Field is estimated to contain recoverable liquid reserves of 642 million barrels, with the company's share, after royalty to the British government, being 112 million barrels. Claymore's recoverable liquid reserves are estimated at 409 million barrels, and the company's share after royalty is 72 million barrels.

Allied Chemical also began to realize profits in 1977 from its large gas discovery in Indonesia. Sales of gas from the Badak Field in East Kalimantan began in August 1977, following completion of a plant to liquefy the gas for delivery abroad. The liquefaction (LNG) plant is owned by Pertamina, the Indonesian state oil company, which has long-term contracts to supply the gas to Japanese industrial customers. The plant processes about 530 million cubic feet of Badak gas a day and Pertamina is considering expanding it. Allied Chemical has a 35 percent interest (reducible to 26¼ percent under certain circumstances) in the partnership that discovered and is developing the Badak Field.

From annual report of Allied Chemical Corporation

Photo opposite: Development of the Claymore Field in the North Sea is being carried out from this platform. Two wells can be drilled from the structure at one time.

2

The role of profits

The role of profits

Y ou need to understand the profit motive. It is one of the essential characteristics of the private enterprise system. The profit motive has been attacked in recent years as not being appropriate in today's modern and complex society. Even some business executives are apologetic about the profit motive. They turn discussions on profits to other aspects of business, such as the provision of goods and services, providing jobs, or supporting community betterment programs. Many attacks on the profit motive and apologies for profits may be traced to a lack of understanding of the role of profits in our economic system.

After studying this chapter, you will be able to answer the following questions regarding profit:

What is the profit motive?

How are profits defined?

How do risks relate to profits?

What are the functions of the profit motive?

How profitable are American corporations?

DEFINITION OF THE PROFIT MOTIVE

Both words in the phrase "profit motive" are important. *Profit* is what is left after all appropriate costs have been deducted from business revenues. A *motive* is a drive, impulse, or desire that moves one to action. Thus the *profit motive* refers to the financial difference between revenues and costs as an incentive to action. The profit motive is in operation when individuals, partnerships, or corporations undertake economic activity. An important aspect of the profit motive is that economic action is motivated by prospects of *future* profits. Business managers are influenced by past profits (or losses) only as these provide information about probable happenings in the future.

Although the profit motive may stimulate economic activity by business, there is no guarantee that profits will result. When a company's costs exceed its revenues, the company operates at a loss. Because of this risk of loss the private enterprise system is sometimes referred to as a *profit and loss system*. An enterprise may be able to operate at a loss for a time before being forced out of business. However, over the long run the private business enterprise must generate profits in order to survive.

CALCULATION OF BUSINESS PROFIT

Business profit is calculated by subtracting the appropriate portion of fixed and variable costs from the total receipts from the sale of a product. *Fixed costs* are those costs which continue whether or not the enterprise is producing goods. Fixed costs include such expenses as rent, property taxes, and the interest on borrowed money. *Variable costs* are directly influenced by the number of units produced. Variable costs include such expenses as materials used in the production of goods and the wages of production workers. In general the costs provide for returns to all factors of production except to the owners of the business enterprise. What is left after the deduction of all "outsiders" costs represents *business profit* and accrues to the owners of the business enterprise. The calculation of business profit is discussed in more detail in Chapter 14 on accounting. The business profit figure is on the bottom line of the accounting report called the income statement. The figure is labeled as net income or net profit if it is positive. If the total costs exceed income, the figure is negative and represents a business loss.

"If *you're* not making any money, the *packer* isn't making any money and the *rancher* isn't making any money, then the *cows* must have a bundle stashed away."

Reprinted by permission The Wall Street Journal

ECONOMIC PROFIT: AN ALTERNATIVE DEFINITION OF PROFIT

Definition of economic profit

Business managers and economists view profit somewhat differently. The distinction between business profits and economic profits depends upon the definition of the costs which are considered in the calculation of each. The concept of *economic profit* requires the subtraction of opportunity costs from business profits. *Opportunity cost* is an important economic concept and represents the cost assumed when persons or business enterprises forgo the alternative of making some other use of their economic assets. There are various ways in which economic assets may be employed. When persons elect to invest their money in a particular business enterprise they give up the opportunity of investing those funds in some other way, at least for the time being. The opportunity cost for those funds would be what they could earn if they were employed in some other manner and are subtracted from business profits to obtain an economic profit figure.

Opportunity cost can also be applied by individuals to the value of their labor as they consider how much their work efforts might be worth in another enterprise. In a proprietorship the opportunity cost of the owner's labor would be deducted from business profit to determine economic profit.

Example of the calculation of economic profit in a proprietorship

As an example of how the concept of economic profit might apply to an individual, consider a person who owns and works in a small retail store. The shop is organized as a proprietorship, and in 1979 a business profit of $15,000 was calculated for the year. In the proprietorship form of legal organization the owner's work efforts are not considered a business cost, so the owner does not receive a salary for working in the store. Any money the owner takes out of the enterprise is considered a withdrawal of part of the proprietor's investment in the store.

The owner has had an offer to work for a large discount store for an annual salary of $10,000 and is considering whether it would be better to continue as a business owner or to take the job at the discount store. The $25,000 presently invested in the retail store could be invested in some other way if the store were sold. Using the concept of economic profit to help make a decision, the store owner would make the following calculations:

Business profit for 1979		$15,000
(Total receipts from the sale of goods less appropriate portion of fixed and variable costs.)		
Less opportunity costs:		
Alternative salary cost	$10,000	
Imputed interest cost	1,250	
(Amount that could be earned from $25,000 derived from sale of store and invested at 5% in a bank savings account.)		
Total opportunity costs		11,250
Economic profit		$ 3,750

The proprietor, using this analysis, would see that in 1979 the economic profit was $3,750. What should then be considered are the advantages and disadvantages of owning one's own store compared with being an employee of the discount store. Some factors to be weighed are the independence of being one's own boss plus the additional $3,750 against the extra responsibility, longer hours, and greater uncertainties an owner faces.

Application and limitations of the concept of economic profit

The concept of economic profit may be valuable to a person in business in the selection of projects for the investment of economic resources. A careful appraisal should be made of the full range of possible investment alternatives before committing time or money to a particular project. Before a project is undertaken, the question "Is this the best opportunity available to me for the investment of money and effort?" can be a valuable check to see if profit prospects are consistent with the amount of risk the individual is willing to assume.

There are some significant problems involved in the determination of opportunity costs. Should the value of labor be calculated by its worth in another enterprise? A person might have an offer for employment in another business, but this would be the situation only in a limited number of cases. To change one's place of employment might mean severe personal adjustments which could be more costly than the money benefits to be gained. Generally it is difficult for people to determine what alternative value should be placed on their own work efforts.

Problems also arise when the concept of opportunity costs is applied to the money a proprietor has invested in a business enterprise. Should the alternative calculation be on an investment in the same risk class as the present business operation? Or should the calculation be made on a lower-risk investment such as government bonds or an insured savings account? The savings account may earn less than the present investment, but it would also have less business risk.

An awareness of the concept of economic profit with its consideration of opportunity costs, even though such costs are difficult to calculate, may provide useful insights in business decision making. However, the concept of business profit is used in this book since business profit provides the basis for our system of financial and investment analysis, taxation, and industry comparisons. Recall that business profit is calculated by subtracting the appropriate fixed and variable costs from the receipts for the sale of a product.

BUSINESS RISKS

The profit motive causes an owner of a business to assume the risks inherent in the production and distribution of goods and services in a private enterprise economy. Among the many risks involved in the operation of a business enterprise are the six illustrated in Figure 2–1.

Risk due to changes in overall economic activity

In our country there are fluctuations in the level of economic activity which are characteristic of industrialized economies. These fluctuations in business

FIGURE 2–1
Types of risks faced by business enterprises

activity affect both individuals and organizations in our economy. Business fluctuations are of concern to government because of their impact on orderly economic growth. Business managers are interested in business fluctuations because of their influence on operations and their impact on profitability.

Economists have identified three types of fluctuations in economic activity. These are the trend, seasonal changes, and business cycles.

The trend   The *trend* is the underlying long-run tendency which persists despite shorter term changes. In the United States the trend in overall economic activity has been upward at a rate of about 3 percent per year in real growth of goods and services. This upward trend is due to many factors, including the development of a new continent, natural resources, increases in population, increases in the stock of capital goods, improved productivity of labor, better management, and continuing technological development.

Seasonal changes   *Seasonal changes* are due to the changing seasons of the year, to holidays, or to the calendar. Certain agricultural products are available for processing only at particular times of the year. Both manufacturing and retailing enterprises are affected by sales demand stemming from the Christmas holiday period and the Easter season. Extra shopping days in a month due to variations in our calendar and the timing of paydays by business enterprises also contribute to seasonal changes in economic activity.

Business cycles   The trend and seasonal fluctuations are overshadowed in the short run by the recurring expansion and contraction of the level of business activity. These recurring variations are called *business cycles*. Starting from a low in cyclical business activity called a *trough* in the business cycle, the generation of demand for goods and services from a relatively low level causes business to expand production. Numerous factors may account for expansion of production, including increased government or consumer spending which increases demand for goods and services.

As production expands, earning power improves and the economy moves into a period of "recovery" or "expansion." Some industries show improved business conditions. This spreads to other industries, and the expansion continues until a *peak* in business activity is reached. The peak is followed by a decline in business activity called a "recession" or "contraction." The factors which contribute to the decline include reduced spending by business for capital equipment, excessive inventories built up during expansion which when cut back reduce production, and changing patterns of consumption. Recessions have also occurred in the adjustment of the economy following some of the wars in which the United States has fought. Should a recession become pronounced and prolonged, it is called a depression. Figure 2–2 illustrates the overall growth of the gross national product, the total goods and services produced in the economy. The trend line shows a 3.1 percent growth rate. Periods of recession in business activity are indicated in white on the chart.

Business cycles have been the subject of extensive study. A number of explanations have been advanced as to the cause of business cycles. These reasons include the cost and the amount of credit available; changes in consumption,

FIGURE 2–2
Gross national product in (1972) constant dollars and average growth rate

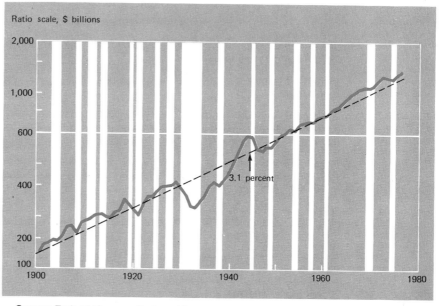

Source: Federal Reserve System, *Historical Chart Book,* 1978.

saving, and investment patterns; whether there are innovations which create opportunities for further investment, such as the invention of the automobile or the discovery of plastic; and the prevailing psychological climate—whether business or consumers tend to be generally optimistic or pessimistic about the future. Many economists believe business cycles are caused by a number of factors, with no single explanation being sufficient for this problem.

The National Bureau of Economic Research, a private nonprofit research organization, has identified economic indicators which normally tend to lead, lag, or coincide with the general level of economic activity. Examples of the leading series are:

Average hours worked per week by employees in manufacturing.

New building permits for private housing.

Changes in business inventories.

Prices of common stocks.

Orders for business plant and equipment.

Examples of economic indicators which tend to coincide with the business cycle are:

Employment in nonagricultural enterprises.

Index of industrial production.

Personal income less transfer payments.

Examples of economic indicators which tend to lag or follow the business cycle are:

Wage and salary cost per unit of output in manufacturing.

Average duration of unemployment in weeks.

Banks' prime rate of interest on short-term business loans.

The U.S. Bureau of the Census publishes the monthly *Business Conditions Digest,* which reports the state of these economic indicators.

Despite the complexity of business cycles and of forecasting them, business managers should attempt to anticipate fluctuations in the overall level of economic activity and make applications to their own industries and enterprises. Help is available from private sources such as trade associations and from federal government agencies which employ economists to measure the current state of the economy and attempt to forecast its direction of movement.

Risk due to changes in consumer demand

A business manager must also be concerned with the market demand for the enterprise's product. Even though the product is as good as or better than the competitor's product, there is no guarantee that a profit will be made. There may be a shift in consumer demand away from the entire industry. Look what the development of the automobile did to the sale of buggy whips!

Actions taken by competitors

The business manager must also be aware of what competitors are doing. Profits are threatened when new products are brought onto the market by competitors or when competitors take actions such as lowering the price of goods to customers.

Actions taken by government

Actions taken by government may substantially affect the profit of business enterprise. Such activities range from restriction by the Environmental Protection Agency on a manufacturer's dumping of waste products to an increase in the minimum wage passed by Congress.

Natural disasters

The impact on business profits of natural disasters, such as fire, hail, and wind damage, can be minimized by buying insurance, but it is not possible to eliminate all such risks. The business enterprise which has its plant located beside a river that periodically floods may find that the cost of flood insurance will be extremely expensive, if it is available. Also, it is difficult to measure the impact of a natural disaster on profits which would have been earned if the enterprise had operated normally without the disaster.

Poor management

The last of the risks faced by business, but not the least in importance, is the possibility of financial loss because of poor management. Big business is not immune to poor management, but the small business enterprise is especially vulnerable to this risk. A common problem of small businesses is that they are too small to obtain the management skills they need. The top jobs in small and medium-size business enterprises may require as much ability and greater versatility than similar positions in big business. The small business is faced with a lack of financial resources to hire competent management. Sometimes the business is family-owned, and the best jobs go to family members regardless of their qualifications. This tends to discourage good people from accepting employment in the small business. Too often small business managers are not willing to subject their decisions to outside advice, a common practice for the top management of a large-scale business enterprise.

The willingness of people to bear risks

With this long list of risks that could result in losses, you may wonder why people are willing to invest money in business enterprises. However, Americans show a surprising willingness to bear risk. The degree of risk investors are willing to assume depends on profit expectations. Normally, additional risks will be assumed only if there is a chance to earn profits high enough to justify the risks.

career outlook

ACTUARIES

Actuaries assemble and analyze statistics to calculate probabilities of death, sickness, injury, disability, unemployment, retirement, and property loss from accident, theft, fire, and other potential hazards. This information is used to determine the expected insured loss. Actuaries calculate premium rates and policy contract provisions for each type of insurance offered. Premiums are set so as to be profitable to the company yet be competitive with the rates charged by other insurance companies. Finally, actuaries must make sure that the price charged for the insurance will enable the company to pay all claims and expenses as they occur.

A good educational background for a beginning actuarial job in a large life or casualty company is a bachelor's degree with a major in mathematics or statistics; a degree in actuarial science is even better. Some companies hire applicants with a major in engineering, economics, or business administration, provided that these applicants demonstrate a thorough foundation in calculus, probability, and statistics (20–25 hours).

Of importance is the need to pass while in school one or more of the examinations offered by professional societies. Three societies sponsor programs leading to full professional status in their specialty. The Society of Actuaries gives nine actuarial examinations for the life and health insurance and pension field; the Casualty Actuarial Society gives ten examinations for the property and liability field; and the American Society of Pension Actuaries gives nine examinations covering the pension field.

Because the first parts of the examination series of each society cover similar materials, students need not commit themselves to a career specialty until they have taken about four examinations. Success in passing the first few examinations helps students evaluate their potential as actuaries.

The employment of actuaries is expected to rise faster than the average for all occupations through the mid-1980s. Job opportunities will be best for new college graduates who have passed at least two actuarial examinations while still in school and have a strong mathematical and statistical background.

Some industries have traditionally been more stable with less risk than those which are speculative in nature. An industry which has been relatively stable has been that of electric utilities. The well-defined growth of demand for electric power and the monopoly nature of electric utilities with government regulation of rates have generally assured profitable operations. However, even in the utilities industry the higher interest rates on borrowed money and the increased operating costs have demonstrated that no industry is without some risk. In 1974 Consolidated Edison, which supplies electric power to New York City, briefly eliminated cash dividends to common stockholders because of financial difficulties.

On the other hand, a much greater degree of risk is assumed by the "wildcat" oil drilling operator where there are wide ranges of profit potential. The possibilities for the oil driller range from a dry hole, with a complete loss of the money invested, to the gusher which will return substantial profits.

Why do some persons invest in utilities while others invest their last dollars in a drilling company which may bring either fortune or bitter disappointment? The difference is in the subjective values that these persons place upon risk bearing. The persons in the former group want security, and the slogan of the latter group is "nothing ventured, nothing gained." Neither group is right or wrong in its willingness to accept risk. The two types of persons merely express different preferences, and both types are needed to provide the wide variety of investments required in our complex private enterprise system. What is your attitude toward investment risk?

Business failures

When a business does not earn a profit for a period of time it is likely to go bankrupt. How long this will take depends on the financial strength of the enterprise, the amount of losses, the availability of credit, and the expectations for improved conditions.

The rate of business failures is shown in Figure 2–3. Failures declined from a high in 1939 of 70 for each 10,000 enterprises to a low in 1945 of 4. In 1978 the failure rate dropped to 24 from 43 in 1975 which was a recession year.

Characteristics of failing enterprises   Typically about two thirds of the business enterprises that fail owe less than $100,000 at the time of failure. This indicates that a high proportion of failures are in small enterprises. Many of

FIGURE 2–3
Business failure rates, 1939–1978

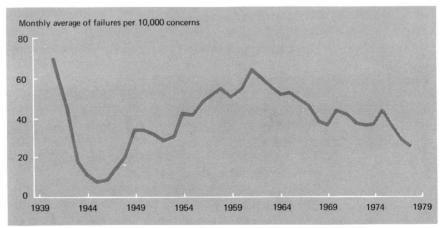

Source: U.S. Department of Commerce, *Business Statistics,* 1977 ed.; *Survey of Current Business,* March 1979; and Dun & Bradstreet, Inc.

these failures are in new companies. The majority of business failures occur in enterprises no more than five years old. Dun & Bradstreet, which specializes in the analysis and rating of business credit, reports that failure rates in 1976 were highest in retail stores selling sporting goods, men's and women's clothing, and furniture. Failure rates in manufacturing were relatively high in the furniture industry, transportation equipment, and textile manufacturing.[1]

Dun & Bradstreet indicates that in 90 percent of the business failures the cause could be classified under the general heading of poor management. The underlying causes of these failures are lack of experience in the industry, lack of managerial experience, and general incompetence. These resulted in an inability to compete, inadequate sales, heavy operating expenses, poor credit management, and improper inventory management. This evidence emphasizes the importance of effective management of the business enterprise, especially in its early years.

Use of economic resources   In the private enterprise system it is important that businesses have the freedom to make a profit, but it is also necessary that inefficient enterprises fail. The business enterprises that fail do so because they are not as efficient in meeting the needs of consumers as other enterprises are. The economic resources which were used by enterprises that failed flow to the successful enterprises to be employed so as to make a profit. The profit motive gives an incentive to produce goods and services at a competitive price and quality. Thus, the profit motive results in the efficient utilization of resources to provide those goods and services which you as a consumer desire to purchase.

FUNCTIONS OF THE PROFIT MOTIVE

The profit motive fulfills three important functions in the private enterprise system. These are the allocation of economic resources to the goods and services most desired by consumers, stimulation of the economy to greater levels of production and consumption, and the provision of a means for choosing among various investment opportunities.

The profit motive and the allocation of resources

In any society the supply of goods and services is limited in the short run. This means that all our material wants cannot be satisfied. At any given time there is just so much capacity for producing steel, assembling automobiles, processing food, or generating electric power.

How are resources allocated among various alternative uses in the economy? How do business managers determine whether to produce automobiles, or tractors, or motorcycles? In the private enterprise system in the United States the allocation of the economy's resources is accomplished in large measure by the expectation of profits on the part of those who control productive goods. A manufacturer produces ten-speed bicycles because of the belief that they can

[1] *The Business Failure Record, 1976* (New York: Dun & Bradstreet, Inc., 1977), p. 3.

be sold at a profit. If the manufacturer has correctly assessed our wants, there will be a demand for such bicycles. Basically, goods and services are provided by business in response to consumer demand, although at times consumer demand can be influenced by sales promotion programs.

The result of each producer marketing goods and services with the expectation of profit will theoretically be the allocation of resources to those goods which are most desired by our society. The statement that the profit motive results in the allocation of goods to fulfill the most desired needs is based on several assumptions: that producers are able to move freely into and out of markets, that competition exists among sellers, and that buyers have full knowledge of competing products. However, in the reality of our complex society these conditions are seldom, if ever, met. Because of large investment and the need for skilled workers and technological know-how, it is not possible to start or stop many business operations easily. A steel mill with its large investment in plant and equipment, skilled work force, and research laboratories is a good example of a business enterprise which cannot be established quickly even though the stimulant of profit prospects exists. Once a large investment has been made in a steel mill it is difficult to quit the steel business, sell its assets, and move the funds to some other type of business.

There are still some enterprises, such as the dry-cleaning business, which offer greater ease of entry and exit. As compared to the steel mill, dry cleaning requires far less capital, far fewer skilled workers, and a much narrower range of technological know-how. Furthermore, manufacturers of dry-cleaning equipment are generally willing to finance the necessary machinery, provide managerial assistance, and aid in determining a good shop location. If the business does not develop into a profitable operation, a market exists for the used equipment. Thus the entrepreneur may be able to withdraw from the dry-cleaning business with a minimum loss of capital. The larger and more complex the business enterprise, the greater the difficulty of entry and exit. Service enterprises and small retailing establishments provide the greatest ease of entry into and exit from the marketplace.

There are other limits to the statement that the profit motive results in the allocation of economic resources as desired by consumers. An enterprise may gain control of the production of some good. This control over the supply side of the market by one producer is called a *monopoly*. With monopoly control the producer may set prices higher than might be the case if there were many suppliers competing to sell that particular good. The higher profit which results from this control over supply is called *monopoly profit*. In order to protect the public, Congress has enacted laws to control the growth and actions of monopolists. These laws are discussed in Chapter 3.

In addition to the possibility of monopoly, there are other factors which influence the allocation of resources in our economy. These include government controls, especially in time of national emergency; geographic limits on both producers and consumers; and traditional preferences toward goods, such as consumer allegiance to brand names.

Despite these limiting factors, when profits occur this is a good sign that our society wants a particular industry to expand. When an industry or a firm does not make a profit and suffers losses, this is often a signal that consumers are not anxious to have more resources devoted to a particular purpose. The absence of profits for a year or so is not necessarily proof that the resources should be changed to some other type of operation, since profits or losses are dependent on many factors. However, when losses occur, management should investigate to determine whether future capital should be allocated to fields where the expectation of profits is greater.

The profit motive and the increased production of goods and services

Because of the expectation of profits, the entrepreneur is stimulated to invest resources in a business enterprise. This sets off a chain reaction throughout the economy whereby demands for other goods and services are stimulated by utilizing the human and material resources of our economy more fully. As the goods or services produced by business are purchased by consumers, consumption needs are being met. The production of these goods provides employment for more workers and a higher level of personal income. As the result of increased income, individuals are able to consume more goods and services. This in turn stimulates the demand for additional production. Buildings are purchased or rented, and the rents can be spent by landlords. Machinery is purchased from other manufacturers who employ workers and capital resources. All this activity stemming from the enterprise's investment based on expected profits tends to stimulate the economy.

Profits may result if the entrepreneur provides a new product or a significant improvement or greater variety of an old product. When this happens, profit is a reward for venturing out and providing a new good or improving an existing product. The entrepreneur's ventures do not succeed in every case. However, the profit motive encourages men and women to make other innovations to meet our basic and ever-changing acquired needs.

The profit motive and the choice of investment alternatives

The profit motive provides a criterion for management in determining which investment projects to select from a variety of alternatives. The rate of profit expected on a project in relation to its risk may be the key factor in deciding which machine to purchase, whether to build a new factory, or how to market a new product. Usually not enough funds are available for all investment possibilities. Therefore, some screening device must be adopted to establish project priorities. The rate of expected profit on each project is an excellent criterion for investment suitability.

The simplest way of measuring profitability is to calculate the percentage of profit in relation to the asset value of the investment. Thus if profits on a piece of machinery were anticipated at a level of $3,000 annually and the machine cost $15,000, including installation, the expected return on this investment would be 20 percent.

THE PROFITABILITY OF AMERICAN CORPORATIONS

Critics of the American private enterprise system sometimes say that the profits earned by corporations are too high. Let us examine some of the data which are available to determine the magnitude of corporate profits.

Table 2–1 shows the ratio profits to sales for all manufacturing corporations in the United States and for selected industries for 1975 and 1978. Corporate

TABLE 2–1
Manufacturing corporations' profits as a percentage of sales, 1975 and 1978, after federal income taxes

	1975	1978
All manufacturing corporations	4.6	5.4
Drugs	12.2	12.5
Tobacco manufactures	9.2	9.5
Instruments	7.6	9.2
Petroleum and coal products	7.6	7.2
Chemicals	6.9	6.9
Electrical equipment	3.2	5.7
Motor vehicles and equipment ...	2.2	4.9
Aircraft and parts	2.9	4.9
Iron and steel	5.0	3.3
Food and kindred products	3.2	3.2
Textile products	1.2	3.1

Source: Federal Trade Commission and Securities and Exchange Commission.

profits in 1978 were $119 billion after taxes, which was a historic high. The year 1975 was a year of recession with a drop in profits to $71 billion.

Table 2–1 indicates that the profit percentage on sales for all manufacturing corporations was 4.6 percent after taxes in 1975 and 5.4 percent after taxes in 1978. The highest return on sales was in the drugs, tobacco, and instruments industries. Several industries earned less than 4 percent on sales after taxes.

Another way of measuring profits is to determine the ratio of profits to the owners' equity. This is the measure of profitability on the invested capital of corporation stockholders. Table 2–2 shows the ratio of profits to owners' equity for all manufacturing corporations in the United States and for selected industries in 1975 and 1978.

In periods of recession, business profits are reduced, as Tables 2–1 and 2–2 indicate. Pressures from competing business enterprises, labor unions, and government tax policies also tend to reduce unusually high profits. Historically,

TABLE 2–2
Manufacturing corporations' profits as a percentage of owners' equity, 1975 and 1978, after federal income taxes

	1975	1978
All manufacturing corporations	11.6	15.0
Drugs	17.8	18.8
Tobacco manufactures	15.9	18.3
Instruments	13.5	17.8
Aircraft and parts	11.0	17.1
Motor vehicles and equipment	6.2	17.0
Electrical equipment	9.0	16.8
Chemicals	13.2	14.6
Food and kindred products	14.4	13.8
Petroleum and coal products	12.5	13.3
Textile products	4.2	11.6
Iron and steel	10.9	9.0

Source: Federal Trade Commission and Securities and Exchange Commission.

business profits have been unstable although trending upward. This is illustrated by Figure 2–4, which shows corporate profits before taxes, taxes, dividends (profits paid to stockholders), and undistributed profits (profits retained by the business enterprise) from 1947 through 1978.

Any statement about the level of profits being good or bad represents a value judgment on the part of the person making the statement. Would you be willing to go into business, assume the risks of investing your own money, and then have a return on your investment of no more than that shown? It may be that the critics of the profit (and loss) system are focusing on individual cases of excesses or abuses and not on the overall level of profits.

What about profit maximization?

Business enterprises seldom attempt to maximize profits at the expense of everything else. An enterprise which makes a product of shoddy quality to be sold at a premium quality price may succeed until consumers become aware of the inconsistency. However, this enterprise's share of the market is likely to decline when the product's shortcomings are discovered. This will result in lower sales and perhaps substantial losses to the manufacturer. The best-managed enterprises take a long-run view of profit potential.

It is questionable whether a realistic objective of today's business enterprise is to *maximize* profits, especially over a short period of time. Also, there is the further question of whether the business manager is able to determine at just what point profits are being maximized. Although economists can describe

FIGURE 2–4
Corporate profits, taxes, and dividends, 1947–1978

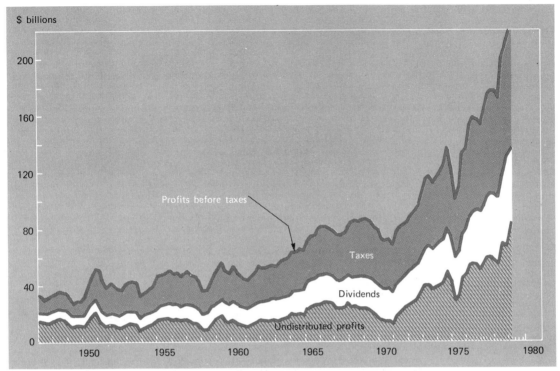

Source: Federal Reserve System, *Historical Chart Book* and U.S. Department of Commerce, *Survey of Current Business,* May 1979.

the theoretical conditions when profits will be maximized, it is very difficult for management to determine this in an actual business situation.

Even though business managers may not be able to determine the point at which their operations return maximum profits, this does not reduce the importance of the profit motive to business. Executives of corporations proclaim the importance of business's social responsibility to the community and provide financial support by business for charitable, educational, and welfare projects. However, such support comes from business enterprises which are operating profitably and furnish a rate of return on the owner's investment that is satisfactory considering the degree of risk involved. A satisfactory level of profits may be defined as profits which are high enough to attract sufficient capital investment to provide the level of goods and services desired by the consuming public.

Profit is an essential element of the private enterprise system where capital is privately owned and controlled. Just as individuals do not always act only as economic beings, so business enterprises which are managed by humans do not always operate strictly on a dollar profit basis. However, the expectation of profit represents the carrot of incentive that stimulates individuals and enterprises to invest money to produce goods and services which we consumers want.

SUMMARY

One of the essential characteristics of the private enterprise system is the profit motive which moves individuals and business enterprises to undertake economic activity because of the prospects of receipts which are greater than the expenses necessary to generate the receipts.

Business profits are calculated by subtracting appropriate fixed and variable costs from the total sales receipts of an enterprise. The difference between the revenues and the attendant costs is the profit.

Economic profit is the concept of profit which deducts opportunity costs from business profit to take account of alternative uses of the material or human resources used in a business.

Although business managers seek a profit from enterprise operations, there are a variety of risks which may result in losses. Business risks include changes in the overall level of economic activity, changes in consumer demand, actions taken by competitors, actions taken by government, natural disasters, and poor management.

A business enterprise can be expected to fail if it does not earn a profit over a long period of time. When an enterprise fails, the capital resources which were used by it flow to enterprises which appear to have better prospects for profitable utilization.

Thus, the profit motive serves to allocate economic resources to those goods and services which are most desired by consumers. It stimulates the economy to greater levels of production and consumption, and it provides an important criterion for choosing among various investment opportunities.

Two ways of calculating profits are to determine the ratio of profits after taxes to sales and the ratio of profits after taxes to owners' equity.

Most enterprises do not attempt to maximize profits in the short run because it is difficult to determine the operational point at which profit is being maximized and because businesses may have other goals in addition to the pursuit of profit. Most owners and managers seek a satisfactory level of profits, which may be defined as profits high enough to attract capital investment in sufficient quantity to provide the level of goods and services desired by the consuming public.

TERMS FOR REVIEW

profit	*trend*	*ratio of profits to sales*
profit motive	*seasonal changes*	*ratio of profits to owners'*
business profit	*business cycle*	*equity*
opportunity cost	*economic indicators*	
economic profit	*monopoly profit*	

QUESTIONS

1. What is business profit? How is it determined?

2. How does the concept of economic profit differ from business profit?

3. Explain how different industries are subject to the various types of business risks.

4. By checking publications such as *Business Conditions Digest, Survey of Current Business,* or the *Federal Reserve Bulletin,* determine the status of economic indicators outlined in this chapter and the present state of the business cycle.

5. *a.* Why do business enterprises fail?

   b. Do you agree with the statement "It is necessary that inefficient enterprises fail"? Give the reasons for your answer.

6. How may the profit motive serve the public interest?

7. *a.* What explanations might there be for the wide variation in profit percentages among different manufacturing industries (see Tables 2–1 and 2–2)?

   b. Explain the variation in profit percentages in the same industry from one year to another.

8. Would you expect the profits from Allied Chemical's operations described on the first page of the chapter to justify the risks when the investments were first made? Why?

---

business briefs

WILDCAT OIL EXPLORATION

In the summer of 1978 several oil companies engaged in exploratory drilling in the Baltimore Canyon area offshore from New Jersey. Thirty-nine companies had spent more than $1 billion to purchase leases from the federal government to drill for oil in the area. The initial results provided the oil companies with a mixed bag for their billion-dollar-plus investment in oil leases and drilling expenses.

Shell Oil announced that its first attempt at wildcat drilling[1] off New Jersey had resulted in a dry hole. This hole cost Shell and its drilling partners about $6.4 million. The dry hole went to a depth of 14,000 feet, which was deeper than had originally been planned, before being abandoned. Although executives were disappointed, a company representative said that more wells would have to be drilled to determine the potential of the Baltimore Canyon area.

The drilling rig for the dry hole was moved about 50 miles south to another lease area. In the new area Shell and its partners planned to drill a 16,000-foot test well.

Earlier in 1978 Continental Oil struck out with a 12,000-foot dry hole in the first wildcat operation in the Atlantic Ocean. This attempt was also off New Jersey and was just a few miles from Shell's efforts.

Farther out in the area Exxon was drilling for oil, but a broken drill pipe at over 13,000 feet delayed operations. The broken pipe could not be recovered. Maintenance problems and bad weather forced further delays in this drilling.

Texaco hit the first successful gas well in the area and began drilling another well nearby to determine whether enough gas was available to make it commercially worthwhile to pipe it to the mainland. The first reports from Texaco were cautious. However, the company's optimism about the Baltimore Canyon was indicated by its payment of $36 million for leases in the area before its drilling operations began.

1. *Why would oil companies pay millions of dollars for offshore drilling rights in unproven oil fields?*

2. *If you were an executive of an oil company, would you be willing to invest additional millions of dollars for further wildcat drilling after hitting dry holes?*

3. *In view of America's need for more oil reserves,*

---

[1] Wildcat drilling refers to seeking oil or natural gas in areas where reserves have not been proven to exist.

should further government incentives be provided for wildcat drilling operations?

FLYING IS THE ONLY WAY TO FLY

In 1978 the Civil Aeronautics Board (CAB), which regulates routes and rates for the nation's domestic airlines, took steps to encourage more fare reductions and greater route competition.

The response of the airlines was tremendous.

"Fly Me!" "Top Banana!" "Super-Saver Fares!" "Super Fares!"

These and similar headlines screamed out at prospective flying customers across the country in page ads in newspapers. Radio and television commercials pounded forth the message, "You can fly for less money now than ever before."

TWA promoted great savings to great cities and proclaimed a savings of at least 40 percent on certain coach flights. American Airlines pushed its own discount flights. United Airlines, the nation's largest air carrier, reconfigured 145 planes to provide almost 2,000 additional seats to meet the increased demand without additional aircraft.

These promotions were designed to attract more persons to fly on the huge 747 and DC-10 planes. The number of seats reserved for discount fares was limited, and passengers had to make reservations and pay for tickets in advance. Some fares required booking at least 30 days in advance. Discount service was not available on some holidays and during certain other periods. Even with these restrictions there was a surge in air passengers, and many airlines reported increased profits.

1. *How can an airline increase its profits by lowering ticket prices?*
2. *What potential problems does discount ticketing raise for airlines?*
3. *How can an airline justify charging one price for a discount ticket and regular coach prices to other travelers on the same plane?*

---

case

JACK ANDERSON

Jack Anderson graduated ten years ago from a large school of business administration located near his hometown in the Southwest. While in college, Jack had studied management under Professor Montgomery, who had taken a personal interest in him and had followed his career since graduation. When he was visiting in his hometown, Jack would drive over to the university to chat with Professor Montgomery about his work and economic conditions in general. The following conversation took place during Jack's most recent visit.

"Dr. Montgomery, I'm facing a crossroads in my life," said Jack Anderson. "As you know, after I graduated I joined a large New York department store in their merchandising training program. While the starting salary wasn't as good as some of the other job offers I had, the opportunities developed very nicely for me. I was made an assistant buyer and then promoted to the job of buyer of women's coats. Two years ago I joined a New York firm which provides smaller merchants across the county with assistance and buying power in the major clothing markets. I like this job. It has broadened my experience, and I have made many contacts in the industry.

"Last year I had an offer to take a buying job with a major chain store organization which would have meant a move to Chicago. After my wife and I talked it over, we decided against the change. It would have narrowed my contacts in the industry, and the money wasn't that much more than I was already making.

"Now we're faced with another major decision. Two weeks ago I was contacted by the owner of a clothing store in Orlando, Florida. He wants to sell out and retire because of a heart condition which his doctor has just diagnosed. He contacted me because I had helped him on sales promotions which gave us the chance to become acquainted over the past two years.

"The business apparently is considered to be one

of the better clothing stores in the community. While the store does most of its business in men's clothing, there is a women's clothing department which has been remodeled and has shown a good increase in sales recently. This department specializes in women's sportswear.

"My wife and I would have to invest all of our savings in the down payment for this store. The present owners would be willing to finance the rest of the purchase price by a loan which would have to be paid over the next ten years. There is a bank in the community which has been providing short-term loans to finance the purchase of merchandise for the principal selling seasons. I suppose they would continue these credit arrangements if I were to purchase the business.

"We've enjoyed living in New York City these past years. I guess it would take some adjustment to a smaller city, although both of us grew up in small towns in the Southwest. My wife is concerned about schools now, since our boy will be six years old his next birthday.

"I doubt that I would be able to draw as large a salary out of the business as I'm presently making in New York. But if the area looks like a good prospect for retail sales growth, I should be able to do very well after a year or two.

"I don't feel that I absolutely have to make a move at this time. I'm doing well where I am. Also, I think there will be other opportunities in the future if I want to get out of the rat race in New York. However, the idea of owning my own business is one I've toyed around with for some time. This is an attractive situation, and the price would probably work out to be a fair one.

"I suppose the reason I came by today, Dr. Montgomery, is that I want you to react to these ramblings of mine. What do you think of this situation?"

1. *Assume that this conversation occurred in the context of the present economic conditions. How would you respond to Jack Anderson's conversation if you were in the professor's position?*
2. *What factors should Anderson take into account in arriving at a decision?*
3. *How could Jack Anderson obtain answers to the questions which would be raised in Question 2?*
4. *If you were in Jack Anderson's position, what would you do next? Why?*

Sperry reports . . .

The 100 largest defense contractors in the United States received orders exceeding $34 billion from the Department of Defense during the 12 months ended September 30, 1977. Sperry, which ranks 14th, received more than $650 million.

Sperry's reputation in the aerospace and defense business has been built by successfully supplying major long-term projects with important guidance and control systems and by continuing to update the technology for those systems. Many have at their hearts a digital computer.

Our efforts are concentrated where there is a strong demand for highly specialized equipment and expertise. Sperry has been successful in anticipating that demand with the right technology. For example, both the U.S. Coast Guard and the U.S. Navy are emphasizing smaller ships today. Sperry is a major supplier of newly designed navigation, command and control, and stabilization systems for these small ships.

That kind of market anticipation is the key to our planning and strategy. We know the technology in our markets—in many cases we developed it—but we also have the foresight and flexibility to adapt the technology to new uses.

A large investment in research and development is being made now that will affect Sperry's position in aerospace and defense in the years ahead. The work is being done at our divisions and at the corporate research center in Massachusetts.

From annual report of Sperry Rand Corporation

Sperry digital air data computers are used aboard U.S. Air Force F-16 fighters.

3

Business and government

Business and government

Government has always had an influence on business. A basic responsibility of government is to provide society with a system of equity, order, and protection. This is necessary if our economic system is to function efficiently. The Constitution gives the federal government power to regulate interstate and foreign commerce and to provide a monetary system.

In our complex economic society the impact of government on business has become increasingly important. Laws passed by Congress and the regulatory actions of many government agencies affect business. The courts settle disputes involving business and provide for the enforcement of legal contracts. Business and consumers pay billions of dollars in taxes to government. Government purchases significant amounts of goods and services from business enterprises.

After studying this chapter, you will be able to answer the following questions regarding business and government:

What taxes does business pay to support government?

What services are provided by government?

How is business regulated by government?

In what ways does government subsidize business?

What enterprises are government-owned and -operated?

TAXATION OF BUSINESS

The activities of government are paid for with tax collections, receipts from users of government services or goods, or borrowed money. When government borrows money, interest is paid for the use of these funds. Ultimately the borrowing must be repaid through the collection of taxes or by additional borrowing.

In addition to raising revenue, taxes may be used for the regulation of business. An example of this is the taxation of narcotics under the Federal Narcotics Act, which restricts dealings in narcotics to scientific and medical purposes. The taxes on these narcotics are relatively low, and little revenue is produced. However, the regulations require record keeping which emphasizes the criminal nature of unauthorized traffic in drugs. Therefore, the primary purpose of the tax on narcotics is not to raise revenue but to regulate the flow of drugs.

The principal revenue-producing taxes levied by the federal government include individual and corporation income taxes, social insurance taxes, and excise taxes on specified manufacturers' and retailers' sales transactions. The main tax sources of state and local governments include sales taxes, income taxes, property taxes, and various types of fees. Figure 3–1 illustrates the relative

FIGURE 3–1

Sources of federal and state and local government revenue dollars, 1979–1980

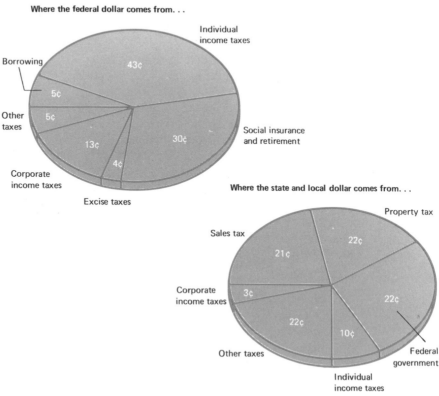

Where the federal dollar comes from. . .

Where the state and local dollar comes from. . .

Source: *The Budget of the U.S. Government, Fiscal Year 1980,* and Bureau of the Census.

importance of various types of tax revenues to federal, state, and local governments.

Types of taxes

Income taxes   Income taxes are levied on both personal and corporate income by the federal government and by many state and local governments. Corporate income is taxed after the deduction of business expenses. The income of proprietorships and partnerships is taxed after the deduction of business expenses as part of the personal incomes of the owners of these enterprises.

The income tax is viewed by many authorities on taxation as a desirable type of tax. It is relatively easy to collect, falls upon those who have the ability to pay, and produces substantial revenue. Critics claim that high income tax rates reduce profits, which lessens the incentive of individuals and business enterprises to take risks by investing funds. However, to some extent business may be able to pass on the effect of income taxes to its customers through higher prices.

In 1979, corporate profits were taxed by the federal government at a rate of 17 percent on the first $25,000 of taxable income; 20 percent on income between $25,000 and $50,000; 30 percent on income between $50,000 and $75,000; 40 percent on income between $75,000 and $100,000; and 46 percent on income over $100,000. In addition, many states have corporate income taxes, though the rates of these taxes are considerably lower than those of the federal income tax.

Sales taxes   Sales taxes are levied on the sale of goods to consumers and sometimes on consumer services. Sales taxes provide the largest single source of tax revenue for state governments. *General* sales taxes apply to all, or nearly all, retail sales. *Selective* sales taxes apply to some specific product such as cigarettes, liquor, or gasoline.

Property taxes   Property taxes are levied on the assessed value of real estate and on tangible and intangible property. For the business enterprise this means that taxes are levied on the assessed value of its land and buildings, equipment, and inventories. Property taxes are determined by annual rates based on the appraised value of property. Property taxes are vital sources of revenue for local governments, making up 80 percent of local tax collections. They are insignificant sources of revenue for state governments and are not used by the federal government.

Other taxes   A tax paid by business but passed on to the consumer is the excise tax. This is either a *manufacturers excise tax* or a *retailers excise tax,* depending upon which type of enterprise collects the tax. Manufacturers federal excise taxes are levied on such items as tires, liquor, tobacco, motor fuel, firearms, fishing equipment, and sugar. These taxes take the form of added costs which you as a consumer pay—usually without knowing that they have been collected by the manufacturer of the goods. Retailers excise taxes have been levied in the past on jewelry, silverware, and other luxury items. Most federal excise taxes on retailers have been repealed, although these taxes are still collected on motor fuels, liquor, and tobacco products. Federal excise taxes are collected on such services as air transportation and telephone service.

Employment taxes are paid by employers and employees who come under the Federal Insurance Contributions Act (FICA). These taxes provide for old-age, survivors', and disability insurance benefits and for government health insurance. Self-employed individuals are also subject to this tax. In 1979, employers and employees were each taxed 6.13 percent on the first $22,900 of each employee's annual wages. These taxes pay the Social Security benefits which are received by millions of retired, disabled, and dependent Americans.

Business also pays *unemployment insurance taxes* and *workers' compensation taxes* under a national system administered by the states. The states use unemployment insurance taxes to finance payments for a stipulated number of weeks to workers who are out of work and searching for employment. Workers' compensation insurance covers employee payments for job-related injuries. Some states have state coverage, and some states permit employers to purchase private insurance protection against accidents. The costs depend on the employer's accident record and the type of work in which the employees are engaged.

Customs duties are taxes collected on goods imported into the United States from other countries. These serve both as a revenue measure and as a means of protecting American producers from competing lower-priced imports.

A variety of other taxes are levied upon business at different levels of government, including licenses, incorporating fees, and utilities taxes. The importance of these taxes to business depends on the nature of the enterprise's operations and the location of the enterprise.

PROVISION OF PUBLIC SERVICES

In return for the taxes paid by business and individuals, government provides a wide variety of services, ranging from national defense to police and fire protection and social services.

Federal government services

The variety of federal programs is illustrated by the federal government's budget expenditures for 1979. Figure 3–2 shows the major categories of these expenditures.

Spending for income security is the largest category of federal government spending. This includes payments to individuals for Social Security retirement, disability, and dependents' benefits. National defense and veterans' benefits ac-

FIGURE 3–2
Federal government spending programs, 1979

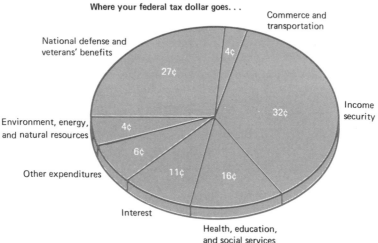

Source: *The Budget of the United States Government, Fiscal Year 1980.*

count for the second largest category of federal spending. About 11 percent of federal spending goes for interest on the national debt, which is money borrowed to finance past governmental programs.

State and local government services

Many of the functions of government which directly affect the business enterprise and individual citizens are performed by state and local governments. Figure 3–3 shows the spending of state and local governments based on the nature of the service provided.

FIGURE 3–3
State and local government spending by function

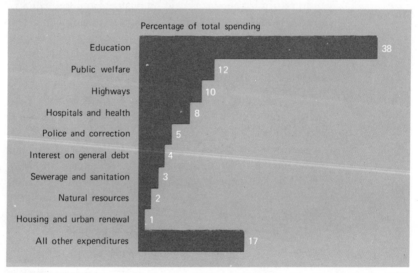

Source: U.S. Bureau of the Census, *Statistical Abstract of the United States: 1978.*

Government's impact on the economy

The relationship between tax receipts and governmental expenditures has an effect on the overall economy. When government collects more taxes than it spends, a budget surplus occurs. The general effect of a budget surplus is to reduce the level of economic activity.

Government spending that exceeds government tax receipts, called *deficit spending,* has an expansionary effect on the economy. When the economy is operating at less than the full employment of people and productive capacity, the general effect of deficit spending is to stimulate economic activity and increase the flow of goods and services. When the economy is already operating at or near capacity, the result of deficit spending is further stimulation of the economy which contributes to inflationary price increases.

Definition of inflation   *Inflation* is an economic condition in which prices are rising for goods and services and the factors of production. The long-run trend of consumer prices has been upward, as shown in Figure 3–4.

Inflation and its impact on different segments of society are difficult to measure. Two widely used indices of price changes are the consumer price index and the producer price index. The *consumer price index,* shown in Figure 3–4, includes prices for food, durable and nondurable goods, services, and housing. The *producer price index* includes prices for finished goods, consumer and capital equipment, and materials used in the production of food and nonfood products.

Not all price increases stem from inflation. Higher quality or changed characteristics of products may result in higher prices. Higher wages accompanied by a proportionate increase in productivity are not inflationary.

Effects of inflation   Inflation generally reduces consumers' buying power and results in a redistribution of income among the various groups in society. Inflation favors borrowers over lenders since debts are repaid in the future with dollars which have lower purchasing power. Persons on fixed incomes suffer from inflation if they do not receive additional income to maintain their

FIGURE 3–4
Consumer prices: All items and food

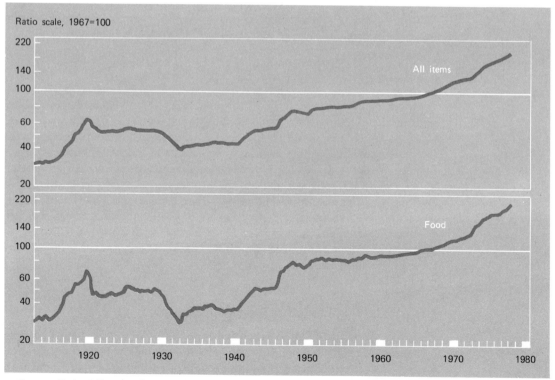

Source: Federal Reserve System, *Historical Chart Book,* 1978.

standard of living. Business profits tend to rise in inflationary periods if managers are able to maintain profit margins by passing on increased costs through higher prices. If workers get wage increases equal to or greater than the inflation rate, they are able to maintain or improve their economic position.

Causes of inflation   The causes of inflation are complex. Economists have identified two types of inflation. *Demand-pull inflation* occurs when an excess in purchasing power pushes prices up. This type of inflation results from an excessive demand for available goods and services. The demand may be from consumers, business enterprises, or government.

If the money supply is increased through government deficit spending or by the Federal Reserve System when the economy is operating at or near capacity, inflation results. This is the classic condition for inflation, when more dollars chase the same amount of goods. The result is higher prices. The roles of the U.S. Treasury and the Federal Reserve System in managing the federal government debt and influencing the money supply are discussed in Chapter 15.

Cost-push inflation results when groups in the economy are able to exert economic power to raise the prices of products or the factors of production. Examples of this include the ability of large corporations to raise prices and the power of labor unions to get wage increases above the increase in labor's productivity. Today prices and wages tend to increase before the economy operates at capacity and before full employment is reached. Cost-push inflation is difficult to control in a complex economy where freedom of economic decision making is a goal.

REGULATION OF BUSINESS

Government influences business through legislation, judicial review, and actions by the executive branch and administrative agencies. The laws passed by Congress which affect business are wide-ranging and complex. In addition, all the states and municipalities have laws regulating the conduct of business. Much significant national legislation is discussed in other chapters. Legislation relating to environmental pollution and energy is discussed in Chapter 4, along with laws on equal employment opportunity. The Occupational Safety and Health Act is discussed in Chapter 9. In Chapter 10 the labor-management laws are covered. Government protection of the consumer is discussed in Chapter 11. This chapter's discussion covers the impact of government's influence on business through the antitrust laws.

The background of antitrust legislation

During the period following the Civil War, America was industrialized. The corporation became the dominant form of business organization. The corporation fostered the growth of business and increased concentration in many industries. The economic fluctuations following the Civil War caused business to seek relief from cutthroat competition. This was done by combining operations, dividing markets, controlling industry practices through trusts, and by other actions which were characteristic of monopolies. A *monopoly* results when one producer or distributor has enough control over the supply of a product to determine prices independently. By the 1880s, major industries such as petroleum, cottonseed oil, linseed oil, whiskey, sugar, and lead were essentially monopolies in the United States.

These monopolies functioned through a form of organization called a *trust*. A trust was created when the owners of the controlling shares of stock in competing corporations transferred the control of their shares to a group of trustees. In exchange for their controlling shares, the former corporate shareholders received trust certificates and were entitled to a share in the profits of the combined corporations. The trustees voted the stock certificates in all the participating corporations, thereby electing corporate directors and controlling corporation policies. The result was that several corporations were run as a single business. The laws dealing with these trusts came to be known as *antitrust laws*. This phrase is applied broadly to any legislation which deals with restrictions on trade and business organization.

The trusts which developed in the latter part of the 19th century adversely affected many different groups in the community. Farmers, laborers, producers of raw materials, and small businesses were all forced to conform to the policies laid down by these industry giants. The powerful economic actions of the trusts resulted in a political reaction from those groups which felt oppressed. As a result, in 1889 a number of states passed antitrust laws and the way was opened for national legislation which was enacted in 1890.

Antitrust laws

The important antitrust legislation passed by the U.S. Congress started with the Sherman Act and includes the Clayton Act, the Federal Trade Commission Act, the Robinson-Patman Act, and the Antimerger Act of 1950.

The Sherman Act (1890)   The Sherman Act, passed in 1890, declared trusts, monopolies and other practices which would restrain trade to be illegal. United States attorneys under the attorney general could institute civil and criminal proceedings against those who allegedly violated the law. The criminal penalties included fines and prison sentences. Persons or enterprises injured by illegal restraint of trade or monopolies were entitled to sue for triple damages.

Administration of the Sherman Act, 1890–1912   The Sherman Act was the only significant antitrust legislation for nearly a quarter century. Its enforcement varied from one presidential administration to another.

Several large corporations were prosecuted during Theodore Roosevelt's administration. However, Roosevelt felt that not all trusts were bad and that those which had developed as a result of natural business growth should not be bothered as long as they operated within the law. Regulation, not destruction, became Theodore Roosevelt's answer to the trust problem. He stated, "We do not wish to destroy corporations, but we do wish to make them subserve the public good."

In 1912 Woodrow Wilson was elected president. Wilson felt that the answer was to restore competition and, unlike Roosevelt, contended that excessive size of corporations was in itself bad. He wanted a strengthening of the antitrust laws, tariff reduction, and a reform of the national banking system.

The Clayton and Federal Trade Commission acts (1914) In 1913 Congress passed laws establishing the Federal Reserve System, reducing tariffs, and instituting the federal income tax. In 1914 the problem of monopoly received detailed congressional attention. Extensive hearings preceded the passage of the Clayton Act, which outlawed price discrimination, exclusive and tying contracts, intercorporate stockholdings, and interlocking directorates.

The principal provisions of the Clayton Act included:

> Section 2, which forbade sellers to discriminate in price between different purchases of commodities unless there were differences in the grade, quality, or quantity of the commodity sold, where the lower prices made only due allowance for differences in the cost of selling or transportation and where they were offered in good faith to meet competition.
>
> Section 3, which prohibited sellers from selling or leasing commodities on the condition that the purchaser or lessee could not deal in the commodities of a competitor.
>
> Section 7, which prohibited any corporation engaged in commerce from acquiring the shares of a competing corporation or from purchasing the stocks of two or more corporations that were competitors.
>
> Section 8, which prohibited interlocking boards of directors between business corporations where one of them had capital accounts of more than $1 million and where the elimination of competition between them would constitute a violation of any of the provisions of the antitrust laws.

The provisions of Sections 2, 3, and 7 were not absolute prohibitions and applied only where the effect of violating them would be to substantially lessen competition or would tend to create a monopoly.

In the Federal Trade Commission Act unfair methods of competition in commerce were declared unlawful. The Federal Trade Commission (FTC) was set up to police the antitrust laws. The general provisions of the Sherman Act were made more explicit by the Clayton Act. The FTC dealt with both the prevention and the punishment of practices which reduced competition.

The Robinson-Patman Act (1936) With the growth of large chain stores, smaller business enterprises began to demand increased protective legislation. They charged chain stores and other mass merchandisers with obtaining price concessions which were greater than the saving in costs allowed under the Clayton Act. In 1936 the Robinson-Patman Act revised the Clayton Act to give increased protection to smaller retailers, including grocers and druggists, from large competitors. The Robinson-Patman Act outlawed:

1. Discounts on volume purchases which could not be justified by the lower cost of selling and delivering large quantities.

2. Payments of a broker's commission (in effect a reduction in price) when an independent broker was not employed.
3. Allowances for advertising and promotion on purchases made by volume buyers which were not available on proportionally equal terms to smaller competing buyers.
4. Discounts which varied for the same quality of merchandise in the same quantities to different purchasers.
5. Sales of goods at unreasonably low prices where the practice was for the purpose of destroying competition or eliminating a competitor.

The Miller-Tydings Act (1937)   Owners of small businesses had also been active in securing protective legislation at the state level. By 1937 most of the states had passed fair trade legislation. This permitted manufacturers or distributors of branded merchandise to establish the minimum retail price for which the product would be sold to the consumer. However, these state laws on fair trade practices were applicable only in intrastate commerce. In interstate commerce, where manufacturers and retailers or wholesalers were in different states, the resale price maintenance contracts violated the antitrust laws. Because the majority of branded goods moved across state borders, the effectiveness of the state fair trade laws was limited. The Miller-Tydings Act was passed by Congress in 1937 as an amendment to the Sherman Act. It exempted resale price maintenance contracts from antitrust laws if they were permitted by state laws.

The McGuire Act (1952)   Congress passed the McGuire Act in 1952. It permitted the states to include nonsigner clauses in their resale price maintenance laws. The nonsigner clause bound all retailers in a state by resale price agreements as long as one retailer in the state signed such an agreement.

The Consumer Goods Pricing Act (1975)   Fair trade pricing was not popular with consumers. Several states repealed their resale price maintenance laws. In December 1975 Congress passed the Consumer Goods Pricing Act. This act repealed the exemption from federal antitrust laws for the fair trade laws that were still in effect in 21 states, thus nullifying the Miller-Tydings and McGuire acts. This killed fair trade pricing, which had been practiced in some states for almost 40 years.

The Antimerger Act (1950)   The Clayton Act was strengthened by the Antimerger Act of 1950. This legislation provided that not only was the purchase of the stock of a competing corporation a violation of the antitrust laws but that it was now illegal to acquire the assets of a competing firm. Thus all types of mergers were prohibited if the Federal Trade Commission could demonstrate that the result might be a substantial lessening of competition. This included horizontal, vertical, and conglomerate mergers.

A *horizontal merger* occurs when two or more companies which manufacture or distribute the same product join together. For example, in 1974 the Standard Oil Company of Indiana proposed a merger with Occidental Petroleum which would have been a horizontal merger. A *vertical merger* occurs when enterprises involved in successive stages of the production or distribution of a product

FIGURE 3–5
A review of federal antitrust laws

Year enacted	Legislation	Goal
1890	The Sherman Act	To eliminate the monopoly power of big business by making restraint of trade and monopolization federal offenses with prosecution by the U.S. Justice Department.
1914	The Clayton Act	To make more explicit the antimonopoly provisions of the Sherman Act by outlawing: Price discrimination. Exclusive and tying contracts. Intercorporate stockholdings. Interlocking boards of directors.
1914	The Federal Trade Commission Act	To prevent and punish monopolistic business practices and to establish the Federal Trade Commission to police the antitrust laws along with the Justice Department.
1936	The Robinson-Patman Act	To protect small retailers by outlawing: Volume purchase discounts without cost justification. Payment of broker's commission if no broker is used. Advertising and promotion allowances only to large purchasers. Discriminatory discounts to different purchasers. Sales of goods at unreasonably low prices to reduce competition.
1937	The Miller-Tydings Act	To aid small business by permitting the establishment of minimum retail prices (fair trade prices) if allowed by state law.
1952	The McGuire Act	To strengthen state fair trade laws by legalizing state nonsigner clauses in which all retailers in a state were bound by one retailer's signing of a resale price agreement with a manufacturer.
1975	The Consumer Goods Pricing Act	To repeal the Miller-Tydings and McGuire acts, thereby nullifying the exemption of state fair trade laws from federal antitrust laws.
1950	The Antimerger Act	To outlaw all types of mergers where the result might be substantial lessening of competition whether by merger of the stock or assets of competing enterprises.

are joined. For example, in the automobile industry the acquisition of a glass manufacturer or a steel producer by an automobile maker would be a vertical merger. A *conglomerate merger* exists when enterprises producing or distributing unrelated product lines are joined. An example is Litton Industries, which has acquired companies with product lines ranging from books to electric typewriters and missile guidance systems.

GENERAL IMPACT OF THE COURTS ON BUSINESS

Our judicial system has an impact on the conduct of business, just as do the laws passed by legislative bodies. The courts function to adjudicate disputes between business enterprises or between business and its customers. The courts provide a mechanism for the interpretation and enforcement of contracts. The legal system constitutes a framework for the orderly transfer of property among parties. Court rulings along with laws provide a set of ground rules for the basic conduct of business. The courts also interpret questions regarding legislation and actions taken by other government agencies. The Supreme Court acts as the interpreter of the U.S. Constitution in economic matters as well as in social and political areas.

The interpretations of the courts are not completely rigid. Constitutional interpretations reflect in part the needs of the economy in a given era. With changes in the nature and structure of the economy there have been changed legal interpretations. The interpretations and laws which were relevant for the rural economy of the last century often hinder the solution of the complex problems of today's urban, manufacturing economy. Within the past 45 years interpretations of how business activities are affected by the public interest and interstate commerce have changed drastically from the views prevailing at the turn of the century. The rights for women and minorities provided by the Civil Rights Act of 1964 would probably have been viewed differently by the courts in an earlier era of American social and economic development.

INFLUENCE ON BUSINESS OF THE EXECUTIVE BRANCH AND ADMINISTRATIVE AGENCIES

Along with the various legislative bodies of government and the courts system, the executive branch of government and administrative agencies have an influence on the conduct of business.

Influence of the president on business

The president of the United States exercises influence on business in a number of ways. The president may recommend legislation to Congress to deal with economic problems. Although Congress is not obliged to follow these recommendations, presidential influence with the legislative branch of government is substantial.

The president appoints top officials of government agencies which directly influence and in some instances control the conduct of business. These appointments range from the president's cabinet to the commissioners of various administrative agencies. The president has direct control over cabinet officers. However, the president has only indirect control over the administrative agencies. Once commissioners in these agencies are appointed, they are customarily independent of the president's direct control during their term of office.

The president is able to influence public opinion toward business and other groups in society through speeches broadcast over nationwide television and radio and through press conferences. The influence of the president may be used to bring industry and union leaders together to press for a solution to labor disputes which threaten the nation's economy.

The president may appeal personally to business leaders to influence business decisions. Such personal appeals can be effective because business owners are reluctant to refuse a request from such a high public official. They are also aware of the considerable powers that the president has. These powers include administrative leeway under laws passed by Congress in matters affecting business. The government's important purchasing agencies in the Department of Defense and the General Services Administration have a profound influence in their negotiations for goods and services. The Office of the President has standby powers in import and export controls, the stockpiling of strategic materials, and credit controls. The threat of investigations from governmental agencies concerning alleged antitrust activities, tax return irregularities, or other violations of the law is another power of government over business. These investigations, whether or not the executive is ultimately found guilty, are difficult for business because of the time and expense required in answering the government's charges.

An example of how the president can influence business was President Kennedy's public denunciation in 1962 of some major steel producers which attempted to raise prices. In view of the economic situation, the president said that the higher steel prices would be inflationary and therefore contrary to the public interest. At the same time, the Department of Defense indicated that it would buy steel products only from those producers which did not raise prices and the Justice Department talked of initiating antitrust studies of the steel industry. Following these actions the increases in steel prices were revoked by the industry.

The Council of Economic Advisers

The president is assisted in economic matters by a Council of Economic Advisers. It consists of three members who are appointed by the president and approved by the Senate. These three council members are professional economists who analyze and interpret economic developments and recommend national economic policy to the president.

The council was created by Congress with the passage of the *Employment Act of 1946*. The Employment Act states that it is the responsibility of the federal government to assist the private sector of the American economy to promote maximum employment, production, and purchasing power. The Employment Act also requires that early in each regular session the president give an economic report to Congress. This report covers the state of employment, production, and purchasing power in the United States. The president also reviews federal government programs and may recommend laws to improve the economy. The Employment Act also established the Joint Committee on the Economic Report, composed of members of Congress, to guide legislative thinking on economic matters.

The *Humphrey-Hawkins Full Employment Act of 1978* sets goals for economic conditions without prescribing specific steps for their achievement. These include:

1. A central goal of reducing the unemployment rate to 4 percent by 1983.
2. A national goal of reducing the inflation rate to 3 percent annually by 1983 and to zero percent by 1988.
3. Reduction of the federal government's share of the economy to the lowest possible level "consistent with national needs and priorities."

The administrative agencies

The federal administrative agencies established by Congress are important in determining government's relationship to business. Administrative agencies act to regulate various sectors of the economy. By law they are given certain policy-formulating powers, such as the Federal Reserve System's power over the nation's money supply and the general level of interest rates. Some agencies exercise judicial functions. For example, the National Labor Relations Board determines whether actions by business and labor unions are unfair labor practices.

The investigative function of these federal agencies is important. Without the ability to do fact-finding, the effectiveness and purpose for which these agencies were created would be severely hampered. Therefore, sufficient staffs and budgets are required if administrative agencies are to be effective. Indeed, one of the prime means of control which Congress has over most federal administrative agencies is through budgetary appropriations, which are made on an annual basis.

The federal administrative agencies are increasingly important in the complex pattern of business-government, labor-government, and individual-government relationships. Examples of federal administrative agencies which are discussed in other chapters include the National Labor Relations Board; the Securities and Exchange Commission, which deals with financial markets and the protection of investors; the Board of Governors of the Federal Reserve System; and the Small Business Administration. Other federal agencies include the Federal Deposit Insurance Corporation; the Internal Revenue Service; the Export-Import Bank, which aids in financing trade between the United States and other nations; the Civil Aeronautics Board; the Federal Power Commission; and the Interstate Commerce Commission, which regulates carriers engaged in interstate commerce. This list is by no means exhaustive of the more than 85 federal agencies

"Don't jump, Wilkins! We've found somebody who *cares* . . ."

that regulate business. However, it illustrates the scope and importance of these agencies.

Effects of government regulation

The philosophy behind government influence over business has been to protect the public interest and to benefit the economy as a whole. However, over the past 20 years the many new laws passed by Congress have significantly increased the number of regulations with which business must comply. The cost of this regulation has had an impact on business and on the prices paid by consumers for goods and services. For example, in 1978 the Joint Economic Committee of Congress reported that federal safety and environmental regulations added $666 to the price of a new car. The same committee's study indicated that the price of a new home increased between $1,500 and $2,500 because of federal, state, and local regulations. Government and private studies have shown that the cost of government regulation to the economy was about $100 billion for fiscal 1979. This is reported to be 57 percent more than the cost of regulation in 1976.

Business and public officials agree that there is a need for some regulation. However, there are differences on how much and what kind of government regulation serve the economy best.

GOVERNMENT AS A CONSUMER

Even though the private sector of the economy consumes the vast majority of the goods and services produced in America, government is also an important consumer. The magnitude of government's importance as a purchaser of goods and services over the years is illustrated in Table 3–1. This shows government expenditures for goods and services in relation to the gross national product, the total value of the goods and services produced in the nation.

Table 3–1 is shown in constant 1972 dollars, which means that the dollar amounts for each year are stated in terms of the 1972 price level. This adjustment for price changes makes the dollar amounts from one year to another comparable in terms of real goods and services.

TABLE 3–1

Government purchases of goods and services in relation to gross national product in constant dollars (billions of 1972 dollars)

| Year | GNP | Government purchases of goods and services | | | |
		Total	Federal	State and local	Percent of GNP
1940	$ 343	$ 65	$ 27	$ 38	19%
1945	560	265	234	31	47
1950	534	98	47	51	18
1955	655	151	87	64	23
1960	737	173	91	82	23
1965	926	210	101	109	23
1970	1,075	250	111	139	23
1975	1,202	263	97	166	22
1978	1,385	275	100	175	20

Source: *Economic Report of the President, 1979.*

Government purchases of goods and services amounted to 20 percent of GNP in 1978. This does not include $226 billion in current dollars of government transfer payments to individuals. The recipients of transfer payments decide how these funds will be spent. *Transfer payments* consist of income paid to persons from whom no services are currently received. Transfer payments include payments under Social Security, state unemployment insurance, veterans' benefits, and direct relief.

As was indicated earlier, a large portion of federal spending is for national defense. In areas such as armaments and the aerospace industry the federal government is virtually the sole purchaser of goods produced by private business enterprises. Such large corporations as McDonnell-Douglas, General Dynamics, and North American Aviation are greatly dependent on government contracts. Corporations such as General Electric, RCA, and General Motors supply significant amounts of goods to governmental agencies. Medium-size and small business enterprises share in government spending directly and as subcontractors to prime contractors. The Apollo program, involved in putting American astronauts on the moon, used some 20,000 different business enterprises employing an estimated 300,000 workers in nearly every state in the nation.

The fact that government purchases account directly for 20 percent of GNP expenditures shows the importance of government as a consumer. This huge amount spent by a single class of consumers is very influential in the overall functioning of the economy.

SUBSIDIES TO BUSINESS

Government has acted to promote business through subsidies that began with protective tariffs against imported goods in the early 1800s. Business has received substantial direct subsidies over the years, along with government assistance to other groups in the economy.

The growth of this country was fostered by government assistance in the development of transportation systems. This assistance included early government programs to encourage the building of roads and canals and the development of rivers and harbors. In the 19th century the government provided subsidies to railroads to encourage the development of the rail system. These subsidies included large land grants and guaranteed loans.

Subsidies have gone to the ocean shipping industry for the difference between the higher cost of constructing ships in American shipyards and the cost of constructing them in foreign shipyards. Certain preferences for government-financed cargoes in U.S. flagships, mail payments, and tariff benefits have aided the ocean shipping industry.

The U.S. airline industry has benefited by subsidization which began with mail subsidies in the 1920s and has continued to the present. Airlines also receive government help in the form of aids to navigation and aeronautical research and development expenditures.

The trucking industry, along with the general public, has received the benefit of the highway system which has been built with state and federal funds provided by gasoline excise taxes.

Another form of subsidy to business has been the lower postal rates given to mail other than first-class mail. Newspapers and magazine publishers have benefited from these lower rates, as have businesses which send their merchandise or advertising through the mails. In general the cost of carrying other than first-class mail has not been fully covered by the postal charges on second-, third-, and fourth-class mail.

Several general government aids and subsidies to business exist, including the monopoly protection given to invention and written creativity under the patent and copyright laws. The federal government is also important in the financing of research and development by industry. As discussed in Chapter 5, the Small Business Administration actively assists small business enterprises.

Reductions in federal income taxes are available to business through investment tax credits and accelerated depreciation allowances on new factories and equipment. The tax laws have also provided special depletion allowances to benefit the oil and mining industries. These allowances have had the effect of reducing the income taxes paid by companies in these industries.

Over the years the federal government has stockpiled strategic materials, including mineral products, which has provided price supports for these products.

A number of subsidy and assistance programs have been available to agriculture in the United States. These include commodity price support programs, programs to remove surplus production from the marketplace, programs to restrict the production of farm goods, and programs to assist in conservation, farm credit, technical assistance, and research.

GOVERNMENT OWNERSHIP OF BUSINESS

The general practice of government in the United States has been to purchase goods and services from private industry. However, in a number of instances government owns and operates businesses. This is true at the federal, state, and local levels.

Federal business operations

The ownership of business operations by the federal government ranges from the production and sale of electric power to retail enterprises located on military reservations. In service areas such as finance and insurance the government has active agencies which directly serve private business and individual consumers.

The federal government is deeply involved in the production and sale of electric power. The Tennessee Valley Authority, which came into being in the 1930s, is one of the largest government hydroelectric power operations in the world. In addition to producing and distributing electricity, TVA controls floods

career outlook

FEDERAL CIVILIAN GOVERNMENT WORKERS

The federal government is the nation's largest employer. It employs about 2¾ million civilian workers. Training in business administration can be useful for many different government jobs.

Entrants into administrative and managerial positions are usually not required to have knowledge of a specialized field. They must show potential for future development by graduation from a four-year college or by responsible job experience. Entrants usually begin at a trainee level and learn the duties of the job after they are hired. Typical jobs in this group are budget analyst, claims examiner, purchasing specialist, administrative assistant, and personnel specialist.

More than nine out of ten jobs in the federal government are under a merit system. The Civil Service Act, administered by the U.S. Civil Service Commission, covers 61 percent of all federal jobs. This act was passed by Congress to ensure that federal employees are hired on the basis of individual merit and fitness. The act provides for competitive examinations and for the selection of new employees from among those who make the highest scores. The Civil Service Commission, through its network of about 100 Federal Job Information centers, examines and rates applicants and supplies federal departments and agencies with the names of persons who are eligible for the jobs to be filled.

Applicants are told whether they have achieved eligible or ineligible ratings. The names of eligible applicants are entered on a list in the order of their test scores. When a federal agency requests the names of eligible applicants for a job vacancy, the civil service sends the agency the names at the top of the appropriate list. The agency can select any one of the top three. The names of persons not selected are restored to the list so that these persons can be considered for other job openings.

Although total federal government employment is expected to rise somewhat, federal employment is expected to grow more slowly than the average for all industries through the mid-1980s.

and shipping, creates recreational areas, and encourages industrial expansion. Other important hydroelectric power facilities owned and operated by the federal government include the Hoover Dam and projects on the Colorado, Columbia, St. Lawrence, and Missouri rivers. Some of these projects are carried out in cooperation with private utility companies and local governments.

The Department of Defense operates a variety of business activities on military bases which directly or indirectly compete with private business. These include restaurants and bakeries, laundries, motion-picture houses, and military post exchanges and commissaries. The military manufactures some products which help make it independent of civilian sources of supply. Where feasible, however, the Department of Defense has generally chosen to purchase goods and services from private commercial producers.

The financial and insurance agencies of the federal government include the Social Security System, the Federal Deposit Insurance Corporation, and the Federal Savings and Loan Insurance Corporation. The Federal Home Loan banks and other agencies act to encourage the construction of residential housing. The Rural Electrification Administration and other agencies assist in improving the economic condition of the farmer.

There are other important government-sponsored business operations. The U.S. Government Printing Office is the largest publishing house in the world. In 1971 the National Railroad Passenger Corporation (Amtrak) began the operation of railway passenger service in the United States. Also in 1971 the U.S. Postal Service, organized as an independent government agency, took over the mail service formerly provided by the Post Office Department.

State and local government business operations

Business operations are not limited to the federal government. State and local governments also own a variety of businesses, sometimes in competition with private business.

Municipalities frequently operate their own electric, water, and gas utility distribution systems. City ownership and operation of airports, harbors, and local transportation facilities are common.

A number of states operate liquor stores for the purpose of control and for the substantial revenue that this brings. In some areas where state liquor stores exist, private businesses may be licensed to sell beer and wine or to sell liquor by the drink, with package sales of hard liquor limited to a state-owned monopoly.

SUMMARY

Government has an impact on business through taxation, the provision of public services, regulation, subsidization, and its role as a consumer of goods and services produced by business.

Income taxes are the greatest source of revenue for the federal government. Sales taxes and property taxes provide significant tax revenues for state and local governments.

Important antitrust laws which affect business include the Sherman Act, the Clayton Act, the Federal Trade Commission Act, the Robinson-Patman Act, and the Antimerger Act of 1950. The Justice Department and the courts have been influential in determining how the antitrust laws are administered and interpreted.

The president of the United States exercises influence over business by public statements and personal prestige, by legislation recommended to Congress, and by appointments made to the cabinet and the administrative agencies.

The Employment Act of 1946 placed responsibility on the federal government to assist the private sector of the economy to promote maximum employment, production, and purchasing power. The act created the Council of Economic Advisers to assist the president in economic matters.

The various administrative agencies of government are becoming increasingly important in government's relations with business, labor organizations, and the public.

Government is an important purchaser of goods and services from private business enterprises. Governmental units have generally chosen to purchase goods from private business rather than to establish government production facilities. In some instances, such as in electric power production and military retailing operations, the government produces and distributes goods or services in competition with private business.

Government has acted to promote business through subsidies to transportation, agriculture, publishing, mining and petroleum, and other industries.

TERMS FOR REVIEW

income tax
sales tax
property tax
excise tax
FICA taxes

deficit spending
inflation
monopoly
trust
antitrust laws

merger
Council of Economic
  Advisers
Employment Act of 1946
gross national product

QUESTIONS

1. What types of taxes are most important at the federal and state and local levels of government?

2. *a.* What types of taxes are paid by business enterprises?
   b. Which taxes does a business enterprise have to pay whether or not it makes a profit?

3. Give at least five examples of business enterprises which would receive direct benefits from government spending even though for most enterprises these spending programs would provide only general benefits as part of society.

4. *a.* Why is business regulated?
   b. Why were the Sherman, Clayton, and Federal Trade Commission acts passed?

5. *a.* What is the difference between horizontal, vertical, and conglomerate mergers?

   b. In what ways might these different types of mergers be contrary to the public interest?
   c. How might these different types of mergers serve the public interest?

6. How do the courts have an impact on business?

7. How can the president of the United States influence business?

8. *a.* What advantages might there be for a business enterprise if a substantial portion of its sales were made to a unit of government?
   b. What problems might be created for such a business enterprise?

9. What risks are accepted by Sperry Rand's management in being a major Department of Defense contractor as described on the first page of this chapter?

business briefs

FEDERALLY ASSISTED TORTILLAS

The Community Services Administration, a federal agency, made a grant of $1.5 million to a Phoenix, Arizona, Chicano group to provide employment for a section of Phoenix that was heavily populated with minority persons.

In the summer of 1978 the Chicano group, known as Chicanos por la Causa, used a portion of the $700,000 that had been earmarked for a tortilla factory to purchase a controlling interest in an established Mexican food enterprise. About $250,000 was spent to build a new tortilla factory. Not only tortillas but spices and other Mexican foods would be marketed by the government-financed enterprise. In addition to the government grant, the Chicano group obtained a line of credit for $300,000 from a large Arizona bank.

A sales campaign was planned to promote the merchandising of tortillas and other Mexican food products in the Phoenix area. An outside advertising firm was hired to help market the production of the expanded enterprise. Market surveys were conducted which indicated that the demand for Mexican food products was increasing faster than the demand for other food commodities. The expected increases in Arizona amounted to 15 percent annually. On a national basis the demand for Mexican food was expected to increase more than 25 percent a year. The firm had reportedly received inquiries concerning the sale of tortillas in Japan.

Chicanos por la Causa used $800,000 of the federal grant to establish a real estate firm and to set up a marketing and research organization to conduct surveys among minorities. The firms will train and hire minority persons as employees.

1. *What specific benefits could come from this grant by the Community Services Administration?*
2. *Should federal funds be used to assist minority business enterprise in this way? Why or why not?*
3. *What problems, if any, could come from this type of government support for minority enterprise?*

STEEL INDUSTRY REGULATION

According to the federal Council on Wage and Price Stability, in the late 1970s there were at least 5,600 separate federal regulations with which the steel industry had to comply.

This list of rules was contained in a 235-page catalog released by the council. A government official said that the long list of regulations, "portrays how a major industry, such as iron and steel, can hardly make even routine decisions without taking into account the directives of some federal agency."

An estimated 4,000 of the 5,600 regulations were issued by the Labor Department's Occupational Safety and Health Administration. The council report pointed out that the regulations were growing rapidly in number, were extending into the daily routine of plant operations, and increasingly told the industry what it must do rather than what could not be done.

The issuance of the list of regulations was reportedly the first step by the council in a study of the inflationary effect of federal regulation on the steel industry.

1. *What positive effects may result from government regulation of the steel industry?*
2. *What problems have been created for the steel industry by the 5,600 regulations reported by the council?*
3. *What possible effects can these regulations have on the various public groups which have an interest in the steel industry?*

FEDERAL CHARTERS FOR ALL CORPORATIONS?

Traditionally business corporations have been chartered by the states. Competition has existed among the states to be chosen as the state of incorporation for major business enterprises. Delaware has been a popular state for incorporation. Generally Delaware's law permits the most flexibility in corporation charters. About one third of the nation's largest corporations are chartered in Delaware. Incorporation fees provide an estimated 15 percent of that state's annual budget.

Critics of corporation chartering by the states include followers of Ralph Nader and some members of Congress. These critics claim that stockholders' rights are not adequately protected by state incorporation laws. Stockholder voting procedures tend to keep current managements in office. Also, the management flexibility permitted by some state charters fails to emphasize management's responsibility to such groups as consumers, employees, and the general public.

Persons opposed to federal charters for business corporations indicate that the 1934 Securities and Exchange Act already protects stockholders against management fraud and negligence. These persons argue that more information is being made public about corporations' operations and activities without federal chartering. Opponents of federal charters believe that requiring federal charters could lead to political control of corporations. In Great Britain a number of key industries have been nationalized. In West Germany laws provide for employee and public representatives on corporation boards and there is partial state ownership of corporations.

The United States already has federal chartering for banks and savings and loan associations. However, there is also a system of state charters for these financial institutions. Therefore, a bank or a savings and loan association may operate under either a federal or a state charter.

1. *What is the purpose of the corporate form of business organization?*
2. *How should corporations be governed in the 1980s?*
3. *What advantages and disadvantages would there be for the public in a federal chartering system for business corporations?*

Reynolds reports . . .

Recycling of aluminum cans, foil and other scrap into new aluminum is making a major contribution not only to the conservation of energy in the aluminum industry, but to the source of metal supply as well.

In 1977 Reynolds recycled more than 67,000 tons of household aluminum, including cans and foil, paying recyclers $22.9 million through its consumer program. This was equal to about 7 percent of Reynolds domestic primary aluminum capacity. Included were about 2.9 billion cans, equivalent to more than 55 percent of the cans the company manufactured last year. And because aluminum can be recycled at a 95 percent energy savings, about 1 billion kilowatt-hours of electricity were conserved by recycling at these levels.

The company now operates 73 permanent recycling centers, including three new centers opened this year in Texas, Louisiana and California. More than 150 mobile recycling units help bring the recycling program to people at more than 800 locations across the country.

There is more to the recycling story. Reynolds is actively pursuing research to extract aluminum from solid wastes such as municipal refuse and junked automobiles. The company is working closely with communities around the nation to ensure that aluminum recovery is included in resource recovery programs. The company currently has long-term contracts to purchase scrap aluminum recovered from five municipal waste processing operations. Others are being negotiated. As millions of pounds of discarded aluminum—from consumer products, junked cars, old appliances and other refuse—arrive at recycling smelters, a new era in the recyclability of this fundamental metal is beginning.

From annual report of Reynolds Metal Company

4

The social responsibility
of business

The social responsibility of business

The vast social changes in the United States and around the world emphasize the total environment within which business functions. The great human and material resources available to business provide business enterprises with an opportunity to contribute to the solution of the social problems we face. This chapter discusses the responsibilities of business to society and what is being done to meet these challenges.

It is appropriate for you to consider the role of business in our society. In the years to come you and other students will be the decision makers not only in business but in the many other groups which make up society.

After studying this chapter, you will be able to answer the following questions:

What does society expect business ethics to be?

Does business have a responsibility to support philanthropic projects?

How can public relations aid in improving the relationships between business and other groups in society?

What can business do to improve the economic condition of women and minorities?

What can business do to reduce environmental pollution and help our energy situation?

What response can business make to the continued urbanization of America?

BUSINESS AND SOCIETY

Business enterprises have an important role in providing consumer goods and services which can be sold at a profit. The private enterprise system has provided the vast majority of the American people with a higher standard of living over the years. Table 4–1 shows that even with our high rate of inflation there was an increase of 11 percent in median family income over a recent ten-year period.[1] The dollar amounts are shown in constant 1977 dollars, which means that they have been adjusted for the higher prices caused by inflation and are stated in 1977 buying power.

There are other vital factors besides profits to be considered in the successful long-run conduct of business. Business has a responsibility to produce and distribute goods and services at a price consistent with their quality and purpose.

---

[1] The term *median income* means that half of the families had incomes higher than the stated figure and that half had lower incomes. Thus the *median* represents the midway point in a series of data which divides the number of units in half.

TABLE 4–1
Median family income in the United States
(in constant 1977 dollars)

1977	$16,009
1967	14,398
Increase	$ 1,611

Source: U.S. Bureau of the Census, *Current Population Reports*, series P-60, no. 116, July 1978.

These goods should be fairly advertised and merchandised. Consumer protection, of interest to both business and government, is discussed in Chapter 11. Employees should have fair wages and satisfactory working conditions. Enterprises and managers should contribute a portion of their resources to improving the community. Business needs to assist efforts to solve the social problems of our time. American business does not function in an economic vacuum. To fulfill its role in a responsible manner, business must relate positively to the society of which it is a part.

ETHICS IN BUSINESS

We expect persons in business to conduct their activities in an ethical manner. *Ethics* is a code of conduct and values that is accepted by society as being right and proper. In general, business managers support a concept of business ethics that is based on honesty, fairness, and adherence to the law. However, there is always the possibility of a divergence between what is considered to be ethical and what is actually practiced. From time to time incidents of expense account padding, bid rigging, and price-fixing come to light that contradict the consensus of what are ethical business practices.

In the mid-1970s there were numerous revelations of illegal payments by American corporations in this country and abroad for bribes, questionable commissions, political contributions, and protection. After a crackdown by the Securities and Exchange Commission, more than 400 enterprises reported a total of $1 billion in questionable payments. Following these public disclosures managements generally tightened their internal controls to prevent such payments.

There are several influences which shape the ethics practiced by persons in business. These include:

1. The individual's personal code.
2. The behavior of colleagues.
3. The attitudes and actions of superiors in the enterprise.
4. Financial circumstances.
5. The enterprise's policy on specific ethical questions.
6. The ethical practices of the enterprise's industry.

From this list it is apparent that no single factor determines the manager's actions when a hard decision arises. However, a case could be made that the individual's personal code and the views expressed by the boss are especially important. This places great responsibilities on the superior in a business situation to set the proper ethical climate. As discussed in Chapter 8, the top management in an organization has the responsibility for setting the basic tone of the enterprise.

In every industry there are generally accepted ways of doing business. Industry practices also influence the ethics of a given enterprise. When industry practices leave something to be desired, the responsibility for improvement lies with top managements. An industry which continues to ignore the basic codes of conduct considered to be right by society can expect the public to demand changes. In past years these changes have come through government legislation and increased regulation of business. Enlightened self-regulation is one of the best ways to avoid more government control of business conduct.

CONTRIBUTIONS TO EDUCATIONAL, HEALTH, AND CHARITABLE INSTITUTIONS

A wide range of views may be found regarding business philanthropy. At one extreme are those who maintain that the corporation should not practice philanthropic giving, leaving the support of nonprofit institutions to individual shareholders and employees. The proponents of this negative attitude toward corporate giving hold that the sole function of business is to provide goods and services which can be sold at a profit. Persons with this viewpoint say that corporate giving is an indirect tax which results in shareholders receiving lower dividends, employees receiving lower wages, and customers paying more for goods and services.

At the other extreme are those who favor devoting a much greater share of corporate wealth to socially desirable projects. Advocates of substantially higher contributions by business enterprises point to increasing profits which they say demonstrate the ability of business to support such gifts. These advocates suggest that private business ought to meet recognized social needs which otherwise would not be met, or would be handled less effectively by government.

Most business managements follow a practice between these extremes. Corporate contributions amounted to $2.0 billion in 1978, according to the American Association of Fund-Raising Counsel. In corporate giving decisions managers consider a variety of factors. They do not wish to antagonize shareholders or employees by excessive gifts. They also consider the extent that contributions can be deducted from federal income taxes. A corporation may deduct charitable contributions which do not exceed 5 percent of the corporation's taxable income. For the nation as a whole, total corporate giving in past years has amounted to about 1 percent of corporate income before taxes.

Although corporate giving may be thought of in strictly financial terms, the time and effort devoted by managers and other employees to philanthropic projects should not be overlooked. Civic projects and organizations benefit from the work of many persons who are engaged in business. With the approval of top management, much of this work is done during business hours. In a very real sense this represents corporate giving to a wide range of socially approved projects.

PUBLIC RELATIONS IN BUSINESS

Public relations at its best relates the business enterprise to the different groups constituting the public. Identifiable groups with which the enterprise needs to communicate include shareholders, customers, employees, suppliers, and governmental agencies. There are four ways in which public relations can aid in improving the relationship of the business to others in the society.

First, the public relations department or outside counsel can assist management in clearly defining the company's broad economic and social objectives. Second, the public relations department can help translate these goals into imaginative programs which can be achieved. Third, this department can provide advice as to how the image of the socially responsible business enterprise may be effectively communicated to the groups which have an interest in the firm's activities.

Fourth, the public relations department should be sensitive to misunderstandings between the enterprise and its public. After a diagnosis of these problems, recommendations for correction can be made to management. In some cases the difficulties may be due to an inaccurate and unjustified public image that stems from ignorance or misinformation. However, the problems can sometimes be traced to unsound policies or actions by the enterprise. When this is the case, the public relations function is to assist in improving the enterprise's policies and actions.

This broad definition of the public relations function makes public relations much more than gaining publicity for the enterprise through the press or presenting a picture of the enterprise which is not wholly accurate. In the long run the public relations program of the business enterprise should clarify the needs of society and suggest ways for the enterprise to help meet those needs.

BUSINESS AND THE POLITICAL PROCESS

As the result of changes in political campaign financing laws in the mid-1970s, corporations are permitted to create separate, segregated political funds to receive collections from managers and other parties. Corporations may solicit funds for these political action committees (PACs) from employees and shareholders. PACs may contribute up to $5,000 to individual candidates for a specific election. Trade associations and individual corporations have established PACs. In the 1978 elections about 700 corporate PACs were active, including committees sponsored by General Electric, International Paper, and Standard Oil of Indiana. For many years labor unions have been permitted to have PACs, with

career outlook

PUBLIC RELATIONS WORKERS

Public relations workers apply their talent for communication in many different areas. They may handle press, community, or consumer relations; sales promotion; political campaigning; interest-group representation; fund raising; or employee recruitment.

Public relations workers put together information that keeps the public aware of their employer's activities and accomplishments and keeps management aware of public attitudes. Public relations is more than telling the employer's story, however. Understanding the attitudes and concerns of customers, employees, and various other publics—and communicating this information to management—is an important part of the job.

Public relations workers also arrange and conduct programs in which company representatives will have direct contact with the public. Such work includes setting up speaking engagements for company officials and writing speeches for them.

Public relations workers must have considerable ability to gather information, write, speak, and deal effectively with people. A college education combined with public relations experience is an excellent preparation for public relations work. Courses in journalism, business administration, psychology, sociology, political science, advertising, English, and public speaking help in preparing for a public relations career.

Extracurricular activities such as writing for a school publication or a television or radio station provide valuable experience. Many schools help students gain part-time or summer internships in public relations which provide training that can help in competing for entry positions.

The employment of public relations workers is expected to increase faster than the average for all occupations through the mid-1980s. Competition for beginning jobs is keen, for public relations work has an aura of glamour and excitement that attracts large numbers of jobseekers. The prospects for a career in public relations are best for highly qualified applicants—talented people with sound academic preparation and some media experience.

the AFL–CIO's COPE (Committee on Political Education) being one of the most active.

In addition to supporting political candidates financially, many business managers are active in political parties and in communicating with elected officials. There are numerous examples of business executives who have turned to full-time politics. Senator Charles Percy of Illinois was president of Bell & Howell before running for political office. Senator Barry Goldwater of Arizona was active in department store management before being elected to Congress.

Business's views are heard when political issues affecting the economy are being debated. Business groups such as the U.S. Chamber of Commerce and the National Association of Manufacturers express the collective views of their members. Trade associations, business study groups, and individual corporate executes are active in political matters which influence local and national economic conditions.

BUSINESS AND SOCIAL PROBLEMS

As one of the significant groups in society, business can have an important role in taking actions to help deal constructively with the socioeconomic problems we face. It is difficult to forecast the future. However, an examination of our present society reveals certain socioeconomic problems that require long-run solutions. Socially responsible business enterprises are needed to help solve problems arising from discrimination in employment and income, minority business ownership, environmental pollution, the energy shortage, and increasing urbanization.

EQUAL EMPLOYMENT OPPORTUNITY

A socioeconomic problem that is receiving major attention from business is the discrimination in employment and income that women and members of minority groups have traditionally faced.

Women in business

A dramatic change in the American economy in recent years has been the increase in the proportion of women in the labor force. Of the 15 million persons who entered the work force from 1970 to 1977, 57 percent were women. By 1978 there were 41 million women workers who made up 41 percent of the civilian labor force.

Women's earnings Women earn 60 percent of men's wages when median earnings for year-round full-time workers are compared. In 1976 the median earnings for women were $8,200 and for men $13,700. This difference in earnings may be explained by a variety of factors. These include length of work experience, amount of training or education, and number of hours worked weekly.

The occupational status of women One of the significant causes of the difference between the earnings of women and men has been the concentration of women in certain lower-paying occupations. As can be seen from Figure 4–1, the occupational distribution of women differs greatly from that of men. Almost 70 percent of employed women work in three occupational groups. In clerical occupations women are mainly stenographers, typists, secretaries, and bookkeepers. In the service category women predominate in occupations such as waitresses, practical nurses, dental assistants, and beauticians. In the professional-technical category more women than men are employed as elementary and secondary teachers, registered nurses, social workers, librarians, dietitians, physical therapists, and dental hygienists.

Society has traditionally assigned certain roles to men. Higher-paid occupa-

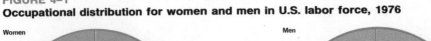

FIGURE 4–1
Occupational distribution for women and men in U.S. labor force, 1976

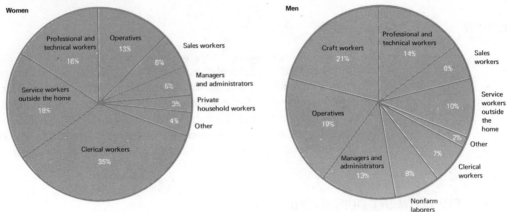

Source: U.S. Bureau of the Census, *Current Population Reports,* series P-60, no. 114, July 1978.

tions such as physician, dentist, airlines pilot, architect, and certified public accountant are male-dominated. However, more women are beginning to enter these male-intensive occupations.

Women have also made inroads into the traditionally male-intensive category of the self-employed. In the mid-1970s, 26 percent of self-employed persons were women, compared with only 17 percent in 1940.

The changing job interests of women   Because women typically are spending more than 20 years of their adult lives working outside the home, they are becoming more career-minded while attending school and in choosing an occupation. Women now view paid employment not just as an interlude between completion of their formal education and marriage, but as a long-range commitment. Therefore, the choice of an occupation and the satisfactions of a particular job have become more important to them. These changes in women's attitudes toward careers have important implications for employers in their hiring, training, and promotion of women.

Minority employment

The largest minority group in American society are the blacks, who make up 11.5 percent of the population. The second largest minority group are the Spanish-speaking Americans, who account for about 5 percent of the population. Asian Americans comprise about 1 percent of the population. Less than one half of 1 percent are American Indians.

The occupational status of minorities   Like women, members of minority groups are generally concentrated in occupations and industries with the lowest earning potential. However, in recent years there has been improvement in the occupational status of blacks and other minorities.

There have been significant increases in the proportion of male minority workers who hold white-collar jobs, especially as professional and technical workers. More members of minority groups are being employed in skilled craft positions. Also, significantly more black males are being hired and trained for managerial positions.

The change for women minority workers has been even more dramatic. The proportion of minority women employed as white-collar workers has almost doubled. Minority women have made sizable gains in the professional and technical category and the clerical category. There has been a large decline in the number of minority women who are employed as service workers because of the drop in the number of private household workers.

Minority earnings   In spite of the shift in minority employment into more highly paid occupations, the wage level of blacks is still considerably below that of whites. Figure 4–2 compares median income levels for year-round full-time black and white workers by sex. These data show that there has been improvement in nonwhite income relative to white income since 1967, especially

FIGURE 4–2

Comparison of earnings for full-time workers by race and sex, 1967 and 1976

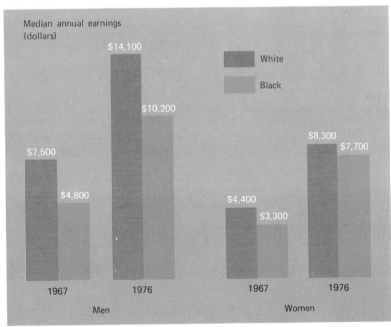

Source: U.S. Bureau of the Census, *Current Population Reports*, series P-60, no. 97, January 1975, and series P-60, no. 144, July 1978.

for black females. However, the wages of blacks are still below those of whites. Also, over the 1967–76 period the absolute difference in dollar wages increased for white males compared to black males.

Government equal opportunity actions

Government action to improve the employment status of women and minorities has come through legislation, court decisions, and executive orders.

The Civil Rights Act of 1964   At the federal government level the Civil Rights Act of 1964 is the most important antidiscrimination legislation of this century. The act has a number of titles, including those outlawing discrimination in voting, public accommodations and schools, federal assistance programs, and employment. Title VII, which was amended by the Equal Employment Opportunity Act of 1972, deals with employment.

Title VII bans discrimination in employment by business, educational institutions, government, labor unions, employment services, and apprenticeship programs. Private employers with 15 or more employees are covered. Under Title VII the hiring, promotion, and discharge of persons is to be based on ability and qualifications, without regard to race, color, religion, sex, or national origin.

The Equal Employment Opportunity Commission (EEOC) was set up to receive and investigate charges of job discrimination. When the EEOC finds reasonable cause for the charges, it attempts through voluntary agreements to eliminate the discriminatory practices. If this approach fails, the 1972 amendments give EEOC power to go directly to court to enforce the law. This has resulted in a significant increase in EEOC legal actions against employers that practice job discrimination.

The Equal Pay Act of 1963   This law, which was amended in 1972, requires employers to pay men and women in an enterprise equally for work of the same skill and responsibility. In a ten-year period the Department of Labor found that more than 150,000 employees, nearly all women, were underpaid by more than $75 million under the Equal Pay Act. Small wage differentials often added up to large amounts. This is illustrated by the $200,000 paid to 197 women nursing aides in Kentucky who were receiving 30 cents an hour less than male orderlies for the same work.

The Age Discrimination in Employment Act of 1967 prohibits employers of 25 or more persons from discriminating in the employment of persons between the ages of 40 and 65 because of age.

State and local legislation   Fair employment practice (FEP) legislation outlawing various kinds of discrimination has been passed in a majority of the states and in many cities. FEP laws generally establish a commission which can investigate complaints of discrimination, conduct public hearings, and attempt to resolve complaints through conciliation.

Many states have laws which were passed in earlier years to protect women from work that was dangerous or imposed heavy physical demands. With improved safety conditions and extensive use of machinery to replace physical labor, these laws have excluded women as a group from many well-paying jobs that some women might have the capacity, ability, and desire to perform. EEOC guidelines and court decisions have held that the equal employment requirements of Title VII replace these state protective laws. Now the employer must consider women as individuals in determining their capacity to do particular jobs.

Court decisions

Women and minorities have turned increasingly to the courts to overcome discrimination by employers and unions. When discrimination is determined to exist, the courts have ordered employers to establish affirmative action plans. An affirmative action plan begins with an analysis by the enterprise of its present work force to identify jobs and departments where few women or members of minority groups are employed. Then specific hiring and promotion goals are set up to compensate for the effects of past discrimination. The goal of affirmative action is the measurable, yearly improvement in hiring, training, and promoting minorities and women throughout the business enterprise.

The federal courts have held that a small number of women or minorities in any job classification in relation to their number in the population or the work force constitutes strong evidence of discrimination. When such statistics are found, the burden of proof is on the employer to show that the situation is not the result of discrimination.

In a well-publicized case the American Telephone & Telegraph Company agreed to a court order in 1973 calling for an estimated $15 million in backpay for women and minorities. AT&T agreed to increase its hiring and promotion goals for women and minorities. In 1975 AT&T and some of its operating companies agreed to another court order providing for the payment of an additional $2.5 million in compensation and penalties because of failure to comply fully with the 1973 order. The new order awarded backpay of $125 to $1,500 each to an undetermined number of employees whose promotions may have been delayed. Although AT&T agreed to step up its minority hiring goals, several unions with which the Bell System had contracts challenged the court agreement on the ground that it violated seniority provisions of existing labor contracts.

Executive orders

Another means of enforcing equal access to job opportunities is an executive order issued by the president of the United States. A number of executive orders have been issued since 1941 to prevent discriminatory employment practices. The Office of Federal Contract Compliance (OFCC) was set up in the U.S. Department of Labor to administer these orders.

One of the most important is Executive Order 11246 (as amended by Executive Order 11375), which covers all employers who have federal government con-

"Can't those Equal Opportunity people leave well enough alone??"

Reprinted by permission The Wall Street Journal

tracts. About one third of the labor force is employed by business enterprises having government contracts. This order forbids discrimination based on race, creed, color, sex, or national origin. Also, it requires employers to have affirmative action plans and to state in all job advertisements that they are equal employment opportunity employers. Subcontractors and labor unions are included in the order's provisions.

Business actions in equal employment

Management can develop its own nondiscriminatory employment system. This involves a commitment throughout the enterprise to provide opportunity for equal employment. The present work force should be analyzed to determine where minorities and women are underutilized. Specific hiring and promotion goals for minorities and women need to be set, with target dates for attaining these goals. All employees should be committed to the enterprise's affirmative action program if the program is to be successful.

Some job descriptions may need to be revised if they specify higher qualifications than are necessary to perform the job. For example, requiring a high school education as a condition of employment or promotion tends to disqualify minorities at a higher rate than others. For some blue-collar jobs there is no evidence that a high school education is necessary for satisfactory performance.

Care can be taken to ensure that help-wanted ads do not indicate any race, sex, or age preference. If a job opening has traditionally been typed as "male" or "female," the help-wanted ad can emphasize interest in recruiting both sexes.

Discrimination is most likely to occur in the process of selecting the employee for the job. Care needs to be taken that any tests used are valid predictors of success for the job in question. Instead of traditional tests, a work-sample technique may be used. For example, an applicant for a production job could be asked to assemble nuts and bolts or electrical components in a certain sequence. This would test the applicant's manual dexterity, ability to follow directions, and tolerance for repetitive routines.

The person who conducts the job interview should be free of stereotyped images about minorities' or women's abilities for particular jobs. One commonly held stereotype is that women are more prone to absenteeism or job turnover than men. However, studies show that there is little difference in the absentee rates of men and women. Job turnover is more related to the type of job and the level of pay than to sex. The applicant's previous work record is usually the most valid evidence of employee stability.

Management and unions can adopt company-wide promotion plans and publicize job promotion opportunities to all workers. Apprenticeships, on-the-job training, and management development programs should also be open to all employees.

An example of what business is doing to provide job training and opportunities for the hard-core unemployed is the National Alliance of Businessmen. This organization was formed after the Detroit riots of 1967 to expand employment opportunities, especially for persons who had been considered unemployable because of a lack of job skills. Many large corporations and thousands of smaller business enterprises are participating in this program.

MINORITY BUSINESS OWNERSHIP

Most students of American society feel that better opportunities for job training, employment, and promotion are vital to improve the economic status of minorities. However, the following statement, made by the late Whitney M. Young, Jr., when he was executive director of the National Urban League, points up the importance of minority business ownership as well as job opportunities:

Important as jobs in the larger society are—and creation of such jobs must be the main thrust of economic efforts toward equality—there is a pride and dignity in ownership that must be satisfied within the black community, as it is within the white.

Although blacks, Spanish-speaking Americans, Asians, and Indians make up about 18 percent of the U.S. population, only about 4 percent of the nation's business enterprises are owned by members of these minority groups. Minority-owned enterprises are usually small, and they account for less than 1 percent of the economy's business receipts and assets.

Aids to minority-owned business

There are numerous ways in which majority businesses can aid in the further development of minority enterprises. A number of the more than 85 federal government programs aid minority business ownership require participation from private enterprise.

One of the federal agencies which assists minority-owned enterprises is the Office of Minority Business Enterprise (OMBE) in the Department of Commerce. One of OMBE's roles is to coordinate federal assistance programs to encourage minority citizens to take advantage of these opportunities. The Small Business Administration (SBA) discussed in Chapter 5 provides management and financial assistance to small enterprises. The General Services Administration has committed millions of dollars to purchase goods from minority suppliers.

Private financial help has come through Minority Enterprise Small Business Investment companies (MESBICs), which are private investment companies licensed by the SBA. MESBICs specialize in providing long-term capital funds and management assistance to minority business enterprises.

Less than one half of 1 percent of the banks in the United States are minority-owned. Since most are small, their capacity to provide loans to other minority enterprises is limited. Large enterprises can place deposits in minority-owned banks. This not only strengthens the minority bank but also provides more funds to be loaned in the minority community.

Another way business can help is by purchasing goods and services from minority suppliers engaged in manufacturing, processing, packaging, and other services. Lists are available to aid purchasing agents in locating these new suppliers.

Sometimes the managements of a majority and a minority business enterprise will work together by contracts or in partnership on a joint project. The minority business manager often has specialized skills and knowledge in dealing with the $30 billion minority market. By working together, the majority enterprise can gain entry into a specialized market while the minority firm can obtain the management skills and capital resources it needs in order to operate profitably.

Franchising can be a valuable technique in developing minority enterprises. The well-known name of a successful franchise will tend to attract customers who recognize that they will be getting a quality product or service. Also, the national franchisor provides much assistance in the form of management training, marketing techniques, and accounting and financial systems. All of these factors help reduce the risks of failure for the minority enterprise.

ENVIRONMENTAL POLLUTION

Many persons believe that environmental pollution has reached a critical point in the United States. Pollution of our air and water, solid waste pollution, and noise pollution are recognized problems which affect business as well as the rest of society.

Federal legislation on pollution

Pollution occurs without respect to state or municipal boundaries. Therefore, federal legislation has been necessary to improve environmental quality. A flood of federal environmental legislation has been passed, beginning in the 1960s. A summary of the broad laws affecting business follows.

National environmental policy   The *National Environmental Policy Act of 1969* is a major statement of our environmental policy in the same way that the Employment Act of 1946 is a statement of our economic policy. The 1969 act states that the continuing policy of Congress is "to use all practicable means . . . to create and maintain conditions under which man and nature can exist in productive harmony and fulfill the social, economic, and other requirements of present and future generations of Americans."

Federal agencies must consider the environmental impact of their programs and cooperate with the Council on Environmental Quality (CEQ) established by the act. The CEQ, which has three members, is responsible for studies, policy recommendations, and preparation of the annual Environmental Quality Report.

The Environmental Protection Agency (EPA) was established to carry out the policies of the CEQ. The EPA's activities cover programs for air and water pollution control, pesticide usage, radiation control, and ecological research.

Air pollution legislation   The *Clean Air Act of 1963* authorized federal grants to state and local air pollution control agencies to establish or improve programs. The federal government was empowered to take action in interstate air pollution cases.

In 1965 and 1966 amendments to the Clean Air Act authorized the secretary of health, education and welfare to establish emission standards for new automobiles.

The *Air Quality Act of 1967* called on the Department of Health, Education, and Welfare (HEW) to define geographic air-quality control regions and to develop air-quality standards. Air-quality monitoring programs were undertaken in cooperation with the states. When health is endangered by air pollution practices, the government can go to court to halt the practices.

The *Clean Air Amendments of 1970* set auto emission standards through the mid-1970s. The law also established emission controls on new stationary sources of pollution and provided new antipollution regulation for auto and aircraft fuels and aircraft engines.

The *Clean Air Amendments of 1977* set standards for auto emissions into 1983 for hydrocarbons, carbon monoxide, and nitrogen oxides. The amendments relaxed emission controls for 1978 auto models. The EPA was authorized to delay 1981 carbon monoxide and nitrogen oxide auto emission limits for up to two years if the required technology was not available. This law provides for continued air-quality improvement and economic growth in areas that have not attained the air-quality standards. Also, deterioration in air quality is to be avoided where air is cleaner than the national standards.

Water pollution legislation   The *Water Quality Act of 1965* and the *Clean Water Restoration Act of 1966* established water-quality standards and plans for their implementation. The federal government is working with state governments for improved treatment of municipal and industrial sewage.

The *Water Quality Improvement Act of 1970* provided that operators or owners of a vessel or a facility can be held liable for the cleanup costs of an oil spill unless it can be proved not to be their fault. This act also covers nuclear power plants, mine acid drainage, and ships and pleasure craft. *Water Pollution Control Act Amendments of 1972* set the national goal of eliminating all pollution discharge into U.S. waters by 1985, with an interim goal of making waters safe for fish, wildlife, and people by 1983.

The *Clean Water Act of 1977* modifies the 1972 amendments while retaining the national goal of eliminating the discharge of pollutants into our water. The act strengthens the EPA's authority to control toxic pollutants.

Solid waste legislation   The *Resource Recovery Act of 1970* emphasized the recycling and recovery of materials and energy from solid waste. Earlier federal programs had mostly dealt with the disposal of wastes.

The *Resource Conservation and Recovery Act of 1976* gave the EPA authority to regulate hazardous wastes and to ensure their safe disposal. *The Toxic Substances Control Act of 1976* gave the federal government authority to control or stop the production or use of chemical substances that might be an unreasonable risk for health or the environment.

Actions by business

American business because of its technology and economic resources has the capacity to contribute significantly to the reduction of environmental pollution. Business is conducting research on pollution control at its source. Once pollutants have been released into the environment, it is difficult, if not impossible, to correct the situation.

Auto industry technology   Automobile manufacturers are working with petroleum producers to develop better methods for reducing auto exhaust emissions. Beginning in the late 1960s automobiles were equipped to emit fewer pollutants than did earlier models. Improvements have been made progressively through the 1980 models, with further reductions in harmful emissions scheduled. Some persons have suggested abandonment of the internal-combustion engine in favor of electric or battery-powered cars. However, the present state of technology does not make this a likely alternative in the immediate future. Research continues for an internal-combustion engine which will reduce pollution and improve gas mileage.

Actions of other industries   Many industries are involved in the battle against pollution. Spending has been increased to reduce the contaminants in production processes and products. The Department of Commerce reports that the nonferrous metals industry spent 19 percent of its total plant and equipment funds in 1976 for pollution control. In the iron and steel industry 15 percent went for pollution control equipment. The paper industry spent 15 percent; petroleum and chemicals, 11 percent each. Since 1973 the investment in pollution control facilities by American industry has averaged over 5 percent of total plant and equipment spending.

In 1977 Du Pont had total capital funds of $626 million committed to pollution control facilities in the United States. The chemical company's operating costs for pollution control are estimated at $220 million per year.

Allied Chemical spent $74 million in 1977 on new environmental facilities, which was 16 percent of the corporation's total capital spending. Allied expected to spend $200 million or more in 1978–80 for environmental capital improvements. Allied's annual operating expenses for environmental facilities range up to 40 percent of the capital cost, depending on the nature of the equipment.

It is costly for industry to meet government antipollution standards. However, compliance provides an opportunity for the modernization of plants to improve production efficiency as well as to achieve pollution control. In some instances older factories and processing plants are closed down because of the cost of meeting new standards. The financial impact of investment in control equipment is reduced in most enterprises by writing off the cost of this equipment as a tax-deductible expense over a period of years. Nevertheless, investments in antipollution equipment generally add to the costs of doing business.

Problems for business

There are a number of problems for business in dealing with pollution abatement. These include setting and enforcing standards, the limitations of present technology, and the problems of recycling waste products.

Problems in setting and enforcing standards   Some enterprises are reluctant to install expensive pollution control systems because government standards are not completely developed or are in conflict from one level of government to another. Clear regulations are needed.

There has been a lack of uniformly applied pollution control standards both within industries and in various areas of the country. This places enterprises which have spent millions of dollars on pollution control at a cost disadvantage in competing with firms in the same industry which have not taken this socially responsible action. Enterprises which have spent money on pollution control must either increase prices or absorb these costs with lower profits.

This indicates the need for uniform federal standards, applied equitably. Then enterprises can act in a socially responsible manner and still maintain their competitive position in the marketplace. Without uniformity across the country, the temptation exists for business to relocate where regulations are more lenient or where they are not enforced by state or local governments.

Problems in developing antipollution systems There is no easy or simple method to correct much of our present environmental pollution. In some instances a control mechanism will have wide applicability in easing the harmful effects of pollution. For example, in auto emissions control a technical development can be utilized widely. However, pollution abatement in most industrial situations requires each solution to be somewhat unique to correct specific problems. Variables such as topography, climate, size of industrial equipment, and population density make it necessary for solutions to be custom tailored. This makes pollution control expensive in money, time, and technical resources. Furthermore, although control equipment is being improved, it is still inadequate in some situations. Scientific knowledge of pollution reduction is generally more advanced than the engineering technology to prevent pollution or to deal with pollutants already in the environment.

Problems with synthetics and recycling Although technology can aid in abating pollution, sometimes it furthers it. Research by both government and business tends to contribute to the introduction of new materials. Many of these release contaminants into the environment which have unknown effects. Modern technology has spawned the development of thousands of synthetic substances and products. Some of these synthetics are resistant to the natural process of decay which recycles waste products into a form compatible with the environment. We have produced aluminum beverage cans that do not rust, radioactive wastes that continue to be toxic for centuries, and inorganic plastic products that will not decompose.

Who will pay for pollution control?

The cost to society of the environmental pollution caused in the manufacture and ultimate disposal of goods has usually not been considered in the pricing of products. Manufacturers and processors have generally considered bodies of water and open air to be free for the disposing of pollutants. Thus, polluters that do not have to pay for the costs of their pollution are able to sell their goods cheaper than if they were forced to bear the extra costs of manufacturing without polluting the environment. On the other hand, a plant downriver from a major polluter may face extra costs before it can use needed water. This tends to raise unfairly the costs of the second manufacturer's goods.

For example, a pulp and paper mill which is free to dump its wastes into a river may have its costs understated. Downriver a chemical plant which incurs extra costs in purifying the polluted water tends to have its costs overstated. The net result of this example would be that users of chemicals unknowingly subsidize users of pulp and paper products.

Methods of encouraging pollution reduction   There are different ways to stimulate business to include the full costs of manufacturing products and disposing of wastes without damage to the environment. These methods range from public pressure by irate citizens to tough enforcement of antipollution laws which may even halt production until the production process is cleaned up.

One way to discourage pollution by industrial enterprises would be to make the penalty cost of pollution more than the cost of cleaning up production processes or installing better waste disposal systems. One plan to do this proposes a system of "effluent charges" which would require industry to pay by the pound for the pollutants it discharges. If it were less expensive for industry to avoid pollution than to pay the effluent charges, industry would be stimulated to install antipollution systems. However, enforcement would be difficult.

To encourage the development and use of containers that would be either biologically degradable or economically recycled, a container tax could be imposed, based on the difficulty of recycling.

A system of incentives could be worked out through which special tax credits would be given to encourage pollution reduction. This would tend to make the public as a whole bear the cost of pollution abatement rather than the manufacturers or consumers of a particular product.

In the late 1970s the EPA adopted an "emission-offset" policy. Before a proposed new factory could be built in an area that had air pollution problems, the owners would have to agree to clean up more existing air pollution than the new factory would produce. This policy has permitted Volkswagen to establish an auto plant in Pennsylvania and oil refiners to set up new operations in Texas. Standard Oil of Ohio agreed to improve the air quality in the Long Beach, California, area by paying almost $80 million for pollution control equipment for a utility power plant there. In exchange, SOHIO was permitted to proceed with plans for a port terminal to receive Alaskan oil for distribution across the country. SOHIO finally decided to drop the project because of excessive delays and increased costs.

The ultimate cost of pollution   Although business profits will be reduced in some instances, over the long run the cost of improving the environment will be borne in large measure by consumers and individual taxpayers.

Consumers will pay for reductions in industrial pollution through higher prices for goods and services. For example, because unleaded gasoline is more expensive, American drivers pay several hundred million dollars more each year for gasoline to reduce air pollution. To reduce the thermal pollution of Lake Michigan, consumers may have to pay up to 25 percent more in monthly electric bills.

Taxpayers pay the cost of government programs at all levels of government.

Many believe that even though the cost of these improvements is high, the price tag for the individual consumer is low compared with the benefits both now and in the future.

THE ENERGY PROBLEM

Another problem for business is the shortage and the increased cost of energy. For several decades Americans were encouraged to consume more energy. Electricity, gasoline, and natural gas prices were kept low by government policy. By 1973, with only 6 percent of the world's population the United States consumed about one third of the world's total energy output. Then, in 1974, the United States experienced what has been called an "energy crisis." A number of domestic and international factors contributed to our energy problems.

After World War II the search for new oil reserves focused on foreign lands. Most of the oil in easy geographic and geologic access to the continental United States had already been discovered. Significant oil discoveries were made by the international oil companies in the Middle East, Venezuela, Africa, and the North Sea. Refinery capacity also shifted to other parts of the world.

Increased attention to environmental pollution in the United States caused delays in developing new energy sources. Construction of the Alaskan pipeline to bring newly discovered oil from the North Slope was delayed several years while the environmental impact of the project was determined. Environmental considerations over strip mining limited the development of our huge coal reserves. The slowdown in building nuclear power generators has been caused in part by disputes over possible environmental pollution. Before these problems could be resolved, massive changes on the international scene created the energy crisis.

Beginning in the early 1970s, the cartel of the Organization of Petroleum Exporting Countries (OPEC), led by Saudi Arabia started raising oil prices. The price increased from less than $1 for a 42-gallon barrel to almost $3.50 a barrel in October 1973 at the start of the Arab-Israeli war. Then the energy crisis hit with a fury as the Arabs embargoed all oil shipments to the United States because of our support of Israel. OPEC also continued to raise oil prices. After the embargo was lifted in 1974, Americans were paying more than $10 a barrel for Arab oil. It was apparent for America that the era of cheap energy had ended. By 1979 OPEC had raised oil prices to over $20 a barrel.

Better technology needed

There has been a past acceptance of inefficiency which has wasted much of our energy. The following examples show the need for improved technology to utilize energy more efficiently.

Car engines fail to use most of the energy potential in gasoline. The rest is thrown off in heat and exhaust. In 1975 the *Energy Policy Conservation Act* set fuel economy information requirements and fuel economy standards for future automobiles. Under the *National Energy Act of 1978,* starting with the 1980 models, low-mileage cars will be taxed on the basis of fuel consumption. Taxes and mileage standards will rise through 1986. Manufacturers will have to achieve new-car fuel economy averaging 27.5 miles a gallon by 1985, compared with 19 miles a gallon for 1979 models. More efficient engines and smaller, lighter cars will be required in order to meet these standards.

Other consumer products need to have improved design to emphasize efficiency and reliability as well as appearance. For example, better-insulated refrigerators require less electricity.

Modern steam power generating plants are only about 40 percent efficient in energy utilization. Most of the energy loss occurs when heat energy is transformed into mechanical energy to turn steam turbines. The Soviet Union is reportedly using previously wasted power plant energy to heat homes and buildings in the vicinity of the generating plants. The overall efficiency of these plants is said to approach 70 to 80 percent.

Alternatives for energy conservation

The present structure of utility rates tends to encourage excessive use of electricity since lower rates are usually charged when larger amounts of power are consumed. Eliminating the lower rates for larger amounts of electricity might reduce consumption. Also, demand for power by individual and industrial consumers tends to peak at certain times of the day. Electric utilities have expanded their facilities to meet the need for electricity at times of maximum use. This results in substantial excess capacity at most other times.

One way to reduce the need for higher peak capacities is to charge premium rates for electricity during peak times. Also, rates could be set lower for electricity used in off-hours. Electric utilities and public service commissions have conducted a number of experiments with rates based on *when* electricity is used instead of simply on the amount consumed. The first results show that time-of-day rates are acceptable to customers.

Experiments are also under way with radio-controlled switches on customer-owned electric water heaters. During peak-need times the electric utility will automatically cut off these water heaters, thus reducing peak needs.

About 10 percent of our energy is used to heat and cool indoor space. Therefore, substantial conservation could result from designing buildings that would be heated, cooled, and lighted more efficiently. The practices of using great expanses of glass, which is a notoriously poor insulator; of installing minimum insulation; and of lighting halls in office buildings with candlepower sufficient for desk work all assume that cheap and ample energy is a basic fact of life.

Each of the five major energy-consuming industries—steel, aluminum, paper, oil refining, and chemicals—can reduce its use of energy and install more energy-efficient production processes. As long as energy was cheap, there was little incentive to economize. In the past, when a manufacturer's costs for energy were only 5 percent of total expenses, plant managers frequently gave conservation programs a low priority. Now companies such as Union Carbide, Dow, Du Pont, Alcoa, and Greyhound have extensive programs under way to conserve energy, and these programs are paying off in cost savings.

What government can do

Business can be encouraged to be more energy efficient by governmental policies. Tax and regulatory policies can be adopted to encourage investment in energy-efficient facilities. Attainable standards can be set for business and consumers in transportation, construction, and public utilities.

The *National Energy Act of 1978* was passed after much debate and compromise. Its major provisions include the following:

1. There is a gradual move toward the deregulation of newly discovered natural gas in 1985, with gas price increases until then. Intrastate natural gas becomes subject to federal price controls for the first time. It is hoped that this will result in more exploration and increase our gas reserves.

2. As indicated earlier, gas-guzzling cars are subject to a special tax, beginning in 1980. Also, business enterprises and homeowners are granted tax credits for the installation of energy-saving devices such as solar water heaters and insulation.

3. New electric power plants and factories are required to burn coal instead of oil or natural gas, since coal is abundant in this country.

4. Energy conservation is encouraged by requiring utilities to offer information and to arrange financing for residential users of energy-saving insulation. New efficiency standards were established for major appliances by the Department of Energy.

5. State regulatory agencies are encouraged to consider different rate structures to force more energy conservation. The Department of Energy can participate in these deliberations.

Realizing both energy and environmental goals

Environmental and energy problems are closely linked. The head of the Environmental Protection Agency has stated, "Our energy ills and our environmental ills stem, essentially, from the same source: from patterns of growth and development that waste our energy resources just as shamefully as they lay waste our natural environment."[2]

Environmentalists and energy conservationists agree that better land-use planning and more mass transit can achieve mutual benefits. Both approaches can reduce the need for automobiles.

Recycling, long an environmental objective, is also a useful means of saving energy. For example, far less energy is required to produce aluminum from scrap than from bauxite. According to the industry, the recycling of aluminum cans saves 95 percent of the energy needed to produce aluminum from ore.

---

[2] *The Wall Street Journal,* January 3, 1974, p. 1.

Progress is being made in recycling. In the United States about 25 percent of the aluminum, 25 percent of the steel, and 40 percent of the copper consists of reprocessed scrap.

We must recognize that the price of energy will continue to rise. The added costs of energy resources, like the costs of cleaning up our environment, will ultimately have to be borne by the consuming public.

The goals of a cleaner environment and more efficient use of energy reinforce each other. Many of the actions already proposed or taken can help slow the growth rate of energy consumption. Over the long run the adjustment of the American economy to higher energy prices is part of the larger issue of world economic development and population growth.

INCREASING POPULATION AND ITS CONCENTRATION

Another of our socioeconomic problems is the increasing population and its concentration in metropolitan areas. Figure 4–3 shows the Standard Metropolitan Statistical Areas (SMSAs) designated by the U.S. Bureau of the Census as urban areas having at least one city with a population of 50,000 or more.[3] The 272 SMSAs contain about 73 percent of the country's population. Major problems facing many of these areas include increased costs of government; high property taxes; traffic congestion; robberies, assaults, and other crimes; a need for improved housing and recreation areas; and racial tensions.

Some businesspersons have developed a fight-or-flight response to these urban problems. Some managements are relocating home offices and other facilities outside central city metropolitan areas. One example which made national headlines occurred in late 1978 when American Airlines announced that its corporate headquarters would be moved from New York City to the Dallas–Fort Worth area to reduce expenses and to be closer to its center of operations. Such moves tend to aggravate the problems of central cities by decreasing the property tax base and reducing the jobs available to inhabitants of the inner city.

Other business managements have chosen to stay in the cities and become more involved in community action. For example, in St. Louis business leaders helped in developing and carrying out programs to clean up the Mississippi River waterfront. In Los Angeles and Chicago, business people joined in supporting improved law enforcement. In numerous cities men and women in business have helped in improving slum housing, providing municipal recreational areas and downtown parking, and supporting public education needs.

THE ROLE OF PRIVATE ECONOMIC POWER

The issue of business's relation to our society may be summed up in the question "What is the proper role of private economic power in the last two

___

[3] A county with a city of less than 50,000 may be an SMSA if the addition of nearby densely settled areas would bring the city up to the 50,000 level and if the SMSA has at least a 75,000 population.

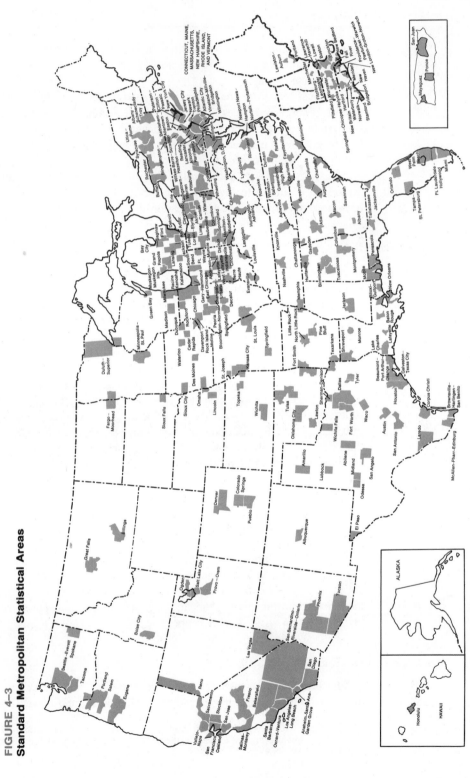

FIGURE 4–3
Standard Metropolitan Statistical Areas

Source: U.S. Bureau of the Census.

decades of the 20th century?" This basic question includes many other social issues in addition to those discussed in this chapter. American business can also work with government to solve the problems of inflation and unemployment. Business can assist other nations in their economic development. The role of private economic power in the United States will have to be resolved in all these issues.

In summary, when we consider the proper role of private economic power, it should be emphasized that economic power is not an end in itself. Indeed, even the goods and services produced by business for industrial and individual consumers are not the ultimate objectives of our economic society. The end purpose of our economy is to provide a fuller measure of freedom for our citizens. The wealth of the American economy should be used so as to further individual dignity and meaningful living.

Because of the concentration of private economic power at the command of business managers they bear a great burden of responsibility for good steward-ship of that power. The words of the late Robert G. Menzies, former prime minister of Australia, spoken to America as a nation, also apply for today's business leaders: "Great power can breed great selfishness unless it is wedded to great responsibility."[4]

SUMMARY

Society expects business to fulfill its role in a responsible manner. Persons engaged in business should be ethical in the conduct of their activities.

Business enterprises contribute to a wide range of philanthropic projects both in money and in employees' time.

The public relations department can help the business enterprise relate its purposes and programs to the various groups in society.

Business may be active in the political process through political action commit-tees and the activities of individual businesspersons.

Business's responsibility to society goes beyond providing goods and services. Business cannot solve all our social problems. However, socially responsible business actions can help solve such problems as employment discrimination against women and minorities, minority business development, environmental pollution, the greater cost of energy and energy conservation, and increasing population and urbanization.

Changes are occurring in our economic society. We need to be concerned with the question "What is the proper role of private economic power in the last part of the 20th century?"

The provision of goods and services by business is important. However, our economy should function so as to provide a fuller measure of freedom for all citizens. American private enterprise can help promote this objective.

---

[4] From an address delivered at Drury College, October 15, 1966.

TERMS FOR REVIEW

ethics
philanthropy
public relations
occupational distribution
median income
Civil Rights Act of 1964
Equal Employment
   Opportunity Commission

Equal Pay Act of 1963
affirmative action plan
MESBIC
National Environmental
   Quality Act of 1969
Environmental Protection
   Agency
OPEC

National Energy Act of 1978
Standard Metropolitan
   Statistical Area

QUESTIONS

1. What factors influence the ethics practiced by a business manager in a particular situation?

2. *a.* Develop an argument to support the following statement: "As a stockholder in American corporations, I resent their gifts to charitable, educational, and community projects. I would rather have corporate boards of directors declare higher cash dividends for stockholders and let individual stockholders give to the philanthropic projects of their choice."

   b. Develop an argument to refute the above statement.

3. What is the function of a positive public relations program for an enterprise and its publics?

4. How has discrimination affected the economic status of women in the United States?

5. *a.* How has the economic status of blacks improved in the past ten years?

   b. In what ways has the economic position of blacks either declined or improved only slightly in recent years?

6. Comment on the merits and the problems involved in giving women and blacks preferential treatment in hiring, training, and promotion to improve their economic status.

7. Outline the solutions to combating environmental pollution. What would be the effects of your solutions?

8. What problems are there for business in reducing environmental pollution?

9. What *negative* results might occur for individuals and communities as the result of governmental actions to reduce environmental pollution?

10. From sources referred to in the *Reader's Guide to Periodical Literature* and the *Business Periodicals Index,* prepare a brief giving reasons for and against the continued development of nuclear power after the difficulties at the Three Mile Island nuclear plant at Harrisburg, Pennsylvania, in March and April 1979. What conclusions do you draw from your study?

11. After a study of current publications, prepare a 300-word summary of the social issues that you think will be most important to business in the next three to five years.

12. Discuss the benefits from the recycling efforts of Reynolds Metals as described on the first page of this chapter. Who gains from such programs?

business briefs

SHIP THE STUFF OVERSEAS?

Ralph Nader claims that American corporations sell products overseas which have been banned for safety reasons in the United States. The well-known consumer advocate has expressed concern that U.S. laws permit the export of products that do not meet safety or health standards for Americans.

Governmental agencies such as the Environmental Protection Agency, the Consumer Product Safety Commission, and the Food and Drug Administration have legal responsibility for setting standards for products sold in the United States. A number of pesticides have been banned for sale here because of their potentially harmful effects on the environment, agricultural workers, or consumers. Some of these pesticides which have been proven effective against harmful insects are still manufactured and sold in foreign markets.

Some new drugs for combating human and animal illnesses are not permitted for sale in the United States because of delays in approval from the Food and Drug Administration. A number of these drugs have been used in foreign countries after testing by drug manufacturers.

Other consumer products banned in this country are manufactured here for export. In some cases American-controlled corporations manufacture and sell such products in foreign countries where local laws permit these activities.

In 1978, imports of merchandise into the United States totaled $34 billion more than we exported to other nations.

1. *Should American products banned for safety reasons in the United States still be sold abroad? Justify your answer.*
2. *Should new drugs which have been tested in overseas use be permitted in the United States without further testing?*
3. *Should domestic regulatory agencies such as the EPA and the FDA be permitted to set standards for the rest of the world?*

ATTACK THE LITTER

The cost of picking up rubbish and litter in our country has been estimated at $1 billion annually. Oregon, Michigan, Vermont, and South Dakota have passed mandatory deposit laws for bottles and cans to reduce this litter.

In 1971 Oregon's legislature passed a tough law banning no-deposit, no-return bottles and pop-top cans. Before the law was passed, empty beverage containers had accounted for up to 75 percent of roadside litter. Since the law was passed, the volume of bottles and cans in roadside litter has been reduced up to 90 percent.

In order to give bottlers and retailers time to prepare for compliance, Michigan's law went into effect in late 1978, two years after having been approved by voters. The Michigan law requires a ten-cent refund deposit on nonrefillable containers and a five-cent refund on refillable bottles. It also outlaws cans with pop-tops.

Some container and beverage industry executives have expressed concern about these laws. Returnable bottles are generally more expensive than one-way containers. It costs money to pick up returnable empties and to prepare them for refilling or reprocessing by bottlers.

Alcoa and Reynolds, large aluminum producers, have accepted these laws as an opportunity for a major recycling program for aluminum cans.

1. *What are the likely results of antilitter laws?*
2. a. *What costs will be avoided by such legislation?*
   b. *What costs will be incurred as the result of these laws?*
3. *What alternative solutions are there to America's litter problem?*

A NEW VENTURE

Control Data, a large computer manufacturer, has put some of its money where its corporate mouth is. The enterprise has long held that taking care of society's problems is good for business. Now Control Data has formed City Venture Corporation, which will plan and manage programs designed to improve conditions in economically depressed inner-city areas and to benefit business enterprises that locate there.

The emphasis will be on creating new jobs. Inner-city residents need increased training in basic and vocational skills in order to be attractive to business. City Venture will emphasize adult remedial courses in basic skills such as math and language as well as vocational programs. Computers can deliver the training in such a way that persons can progress at their own speed. City Venture will also seek to help inner-city residents solve personal problems and area needs instead of simply throwing money at city problems in programs which are too depersonalized.

Control Data officials point out that they have acquired much expertise in the special requirements for employing the poor from their previous experience in profitably building and operating plants in poverty areas in St. Paul, Minneapolis, and Washington, D.C.

Control Data is the major stockholder of the new enterprise. Other stockholders include the Minneapolis Star and Tribune Company and a Chicago architectural firm. Other Minnesota-based corporations are considering buying stock in City Venture. About $3 million is being committed initially to the new enterprise.

City Venture will cooperate with governmental agencies. The eventual goal of the new enterprise is to become a national center for information on urban revitalization. Control Data computer systems will be used to store and exchange information and solutions regarding urban problems, so that successful ideas can be shared across the country.

1. *Why would Control Data organize and invest money in an enterprise such as City Venture?*
2. *Why have a separate enterprise for such activities?*
3. *What problems face the managers of City Venture Corporation?*
4. *In what ways can taking care of society's problems be good for business?*

cases

PERSONAL DECISIONS IN BUSINESS

I

"See you in the morning, Norma."

"Good night, Mrs. Keating."

Norma Spalding looked up from her typewriter and watched as her boss stopped at the supplies cabinet before leaving the office. It was a common practice for executives of the company to take note pads, pens, and other items for use at home. Although these were, in part, used for company work, they were often used for other purposes in the home. Norma had never before given much thought to this practice. It seemed to be accepted by employees and executives of the company. Now, however, as she turned back to her work, she wondered whether it was "right" to take company supplies for one's personal use.

II

"It's silly to go out and buy this stuff," Bruce said, as he reached into a carton marked "rejects." "Here, take one of these." Tom reached out and caught the can of car polish which Bruce had tossed to him.

Tom Farber was finishing the second week of his summer warehouse job. He had been assigned to work with Bruce Bartels, lift truck operator and senior worker on the warehouse crew. Bruce was a good-natured, easygoing, middle-aged worker who knew his job well. Tom had already learned a good deal from Bruce, not only about the warehouse, but about people. In his relationships with his peers and superiors Bruce demonstrated an understanding of human nature which had quickly won Tom's confidence and admiration.

Turning the can of car polish in his hands, Tom found the reason it had been "rejected": a small dent in the side of the can. Although such rejects were not given to employees, it was not uncommon for warehouse personnel to "help themselves" when they had a need for some item. "After all," they reasoned, "these rejects are to be destroyed, so it's no loss to the company."

III

Laura Peters looked over her travel expense form. She had just returned from her first sales trip with the Sun-Ripe Food Company. During her training period Laura had been associated with several of the other salesworkers of her district. From her conversations with these workers Laura understood that it was common practice for the salesworkers to report travel expenses equal to the amount allowed by the company, whether they spent that amount or not. For example, a salesworker who spent only $25 of the allotted $50 per day would report the full $50 and keep the difference. The salesworkers justified this practice in the following manner: "If the company is willing to have me spend $10 on a steak dinner, but I would just as soon have a hamburger, why shouldn't I keep what I save?"

IV

Helen Schelling studied her shipping records carefully. There seemed to be no question about it—one of the tank cars which had been shipped that morning was contaminated.

Helen was the shipping coordinator for the Ace Chemical Corporation. Most of the company's products were shipped in railroad tank cars to a wide variety of industrial customers. Since a variety of products were shipped, a tank car had to be flushed out if the chemical it shipped was different from the chemical it had carried previously. Helen's subordinates had told her that no cars has been flushed that morning because they had all previously contained the same chemical that was being shipped then. Helen's records, however, clearly showed that this had not been the case. One car had carried a different chemical and therefore should have been flushed.

Helen considered the possible consequences of letting this shipment continue. She knew that the contaminating chemical would not react with the shipment. Furthermore, there seemed to be little chance that the customer would encounter difficulties in processing the chemical. This, however, would depend upon the use to which the chemical was put. For some uses it was possible that the "batch" in which the chemical was used would be ruined. The customer in question was a small plant which ordered only about five cars each year from Ace. Schelling knew that she would risk losing this customer if it should encounter problems with the shipment. However, she felt confident that the chances of such problems arising were quite slim.

On the other hand, the cost of correcting the error would undoubtedly be very high. The shipment would have to be called back and another sent in its place. The contents of the shipment would have to be reprocessed or disposed of. Helen estimated that the cost of such an effort would be between five and ten thousand dollars. In addition, the customer had placed a "rush" on this order and would not appreciate a delay.

1. What factors will probably influence the individual actions taken in each of these situations?
2. What could an enterprise do to help employees attain a higher standard of ethics in dealing with these situations?
3. Under what circumstances, if any, should an ethical position be compromised?

SOUTHWEST RENDERING COMPANY, INC.

The Southwest Rendering Company has a plant located just outside the city limits of a Midwestern community of 125,000. The plant has been in its present location for almost 40 years.

The rendering process consists of dehydrating and separating grease and protein elements in animal matter. Rendering companies convert waste products of the meat-packing and poultry-processing industries, dead animals, and restaurant greases into products which are used in both industrial and consumer markets. Tallow and grease extracted in the rendering process are used in many products, including soap, animal feeds, lubricants, cosmetics, and plastics. Protein products, including meat, bone meal, and dried blood, are important nutritive additives in all types of livestock feeds and pet foods.

The raw materials from which grease and protein elements are extracted consist of waste fat, bones, and meat scraps from meat-packing plants, poultry-processing plants, restaurants, and food stores. These materials are picked up by the renderer's trucks on a regular route basis—generally daily. In addition the rendering company picks up dead livestock on farms and cooperates with public officials in removing large animals which may be littering highways.

These waste products are dumped into two large hoppers (each of which has a capacity of 30,000 pounds), crushed, and ground to ⅛-inch particles. The particles are continuously fed from the grinder to cooker tanks. Here the raw materials are cooked for at least 30 minutes under steam pressure at approximately 240° F.

During the cooking process the greases are drained off into settling tanks. The protein materials are pressed through a system of expellers which reduces it to a mashlike substance that is then dried and transferred to bins for storage and blending into animal and poultry feed.

The Southwest Rendering Company had been relatively isolated from the city, since it was located to the north of the city limits, with little other economic or residential development in the immediate vicinity. When a new high school was located nearby and a residential area was developed subsequently, the management of the plant began to get complaints about odors coming from the plant.

The management of Southwest Rendering began to adopt various odor control devices similar to those used throughout the industry. A deep well was used to provide cold water for jet condensers. A hot well was added, along with an afterburner, to take care of gases which could not have their odors reduced without heat. Despite these attempts to reduce odors, complaints from the neighbors continued. Management then adopted an in-plant spray system using chemicals to mask the odors created in the rendering process. Although this reduced the number of complaints, citizen criticism of the rendering plant continued.

Following studies by outside engineers, management decided to incorporate a stack dilution process with a new type continuous dry rendering system. An equipment manufacturing company was requested to design equipment utilizing the latest known technology to make the plant as odor-free as possible. This new equipment was installed at a cost of $20,000.

However, the plant was located in a valley 90 feet below the surrounding terrain. The gases from the rendering plant were of relatively low temperature. The plume of gases coming from the 150-foot stack did not have sufficient buoyancy to carry it high enough to dilute the odors adequately before they reached ground level.

The company continued to receive complaints about odors. Deciding that the stack was not sufficient, it added a chemical air-scrubbing system which treated the gases before they were blown up the stack into the open air.

By now, the company's total investment in air pollution control equipment had reached $68,000, with an annual operating cost of $32,000, or $5 additional cost per ton of produced material. Company records indicated that 18 percent of the original equipment cost was for air pollution control equipment and that 15 percent of plant operating costs were for the control of odors.

Because of continued complaints, the county prosecuting attorney contacted the state health department, requesting an investigation into the possibility that the plant was a health menace. A report made by a health officer of the state division of health indicated that the overall sanitation in and around the plant appeared to be satisfactory. There was no offensive odor at the time of the inspection. In view of his inability to uncover any diagnosed illness as the result of the odors, the health officer could not certify that the plant was a public health hazard.

Upon receiving this report, the county prosecutor visited the licensing and inspecting authority in the state veterinarian's office. The prosecutor quoted the state veterinarian as saying that the plant was one of the most modern rendering plants in the United States; that the firm was not a public nuisance; and that there would be a public nuisance if the plant were closed, because there was no other firm in the area to dispose of dead animal carcasses. The prosecutor concluded that he had no legal basis for court action unless new evidence was uncovered.

The Southwest Rendering Company was collecting over 30 million pounds of decay-prone waste annually for processing. Over $160,000 was paid to grocery stores, restaurants, meat-packers, and poultry-processing plants for these raw materials. Some 5,500 tons of high-energy protein and animal feed were being produced by the company and sold to area feed companies to mix into feeds for livestock, poultry, and pets. The company's annual sales were approximately $2,000,000, and over 40 employees were paid over $250,000 in wages.

In a letter sent with a report to the state air conservation commission, the president of Southwest Rendering Company said:

[Ours] is a perfect case history of what can happen to a firm when it moves ahead too rapidly in the almost nonexistent methods of controlling air pollution. We moved entirely too fast in acquiring suggested, but unproved, equipment, the expense of which placed us in a position of having costs in excess of our competition, resulting in a net operating loss. . . . [now] there is no question that we have a unique economic disadvantage in our industry. We cannot add the cost of air pollution control to the selling price of our finished product [because of competition]. We must compete on an open market governed by the economic law of efficiency, or by lowering our raw product costs. In any event, we must be prepared to control our odors within the limits of what it is economically possible to do.

1. *What factors have increased the problem of pollution for the Southwest Rendering Company?*
2. *How responsive was the management of Southwest Rendering in dealing with this problem?*
3. *Discuss the dilemma faced by the management of the Southwest Rendering Company in operating its business in the public interest.*

Management of the
business enterprise

SECTION
TWO

General Semiconductor reports . . .

In our 1977 annual report I stated, "We have entered the year 1978 with optimism for the continued growth of General Semiconductor." It is with a great deal of satisfaction that we are able to report our reasons for optimism were well founded.

Sales reached $8,552,000, up 31 percent from 1977's $6,544,000. Net earnings increased by 36 percent to $968,000, up $256,000 from 1977's $712,000. Earnings per share were $0.80, up from 1977's $0.61, a 31 percent increase.

We finished the addition to our facilities on schedule in early 1978, and we are presently occupying substantial portions of it. Based on present product mixes and forecasted average prices, we still feel that our facilities will support $15–20 million in sales.

During February of 1978, we held a training session in Tempe, Arizona, for 21 of our export representatives. The purpose of the session was to train and stimulate them with the goal of increasing our percentage of export sales by 25 percent, to approximately 20 percent of our total sales. By year-end, 24 percent of our 1978 shipments were exported.

We in management continue to battle the problems faced by many in this day of inflation. Continuing to produce products profitably in the face of rising costs, especially labor and labor-related costs, becomes an increasingly greater challenge. Typically in the semiconductor industry, selling prices continually decrease every year, despite cost increases. Therefore, to maintain an increase in sales per employee, productivity becomes a very key factor. During 1978 each average employee produced $25,079 in sales, a $661 increase over 1977's $24,418.

We enter 1979 with what appears to be a great deal of economic confusion. Forecasters are forecasting various downturns for the economy and readjusting the time frame for the occurrence. In looking at our major customers and their industries, which are forecasting increases of up to 20 percent for 1979, we feel that as a company we may not experience, during fiscal 1979, the effects of the forecasted downturns.

Dalton L. Knauss
Chairman and President

From the annual report of General Semiconductor

5

Small business

Small business

During your business career many of you will think about going into business for yourself. There is a great appeal to the thought of being one's own boss. The desire of Americans to be economically independent is strong. This leads to the organization of new businesses or to the purchase of established enterprises. The personal satisfaction of starting and building a business enterprise can be one of the real rewards of entrepreneurship. Also, the prospect of monetary rewards from a successful enterprise is attractive to many persons. Even with all their problems, small businesses and individual entrepreneurship are important to the economic fabric of the United States.

After studying this chapter, you will be able to answer the following questions related to the small, independent business enterprise:

How is small business defined?

What are the advantages of small business ownership?

What problems may be encountered in the small enterprise?

Which questions should be answered before you enter business for yourself?

How does one get started in a small business?

What assistance is available for small business enterprises?

DEFINITIONS OF A SMALL BUSINESS

The U.S. Small Business Administration (SBA) defines a small business as an enterprise which is not dominant in its field and is independently owned and operated. In order to receive assistance from the SBA a small business is limited in either the amount of its annual sales or the number of its employees. For example, depending on the industry, the following maximum standards apply for SBA loan assistance:

Retail enterprises—annual sales not exceeding $2 million to $8 million.

Service enterprises—annual receipts not exceeding $2 million to $7.5 million.

Wholesale enterprises—annual sales not exceeding $9.5 million to $22 million.

Construction enterprises—annual receipts not exceeding $9.5 million.

Manufacturing enterprises—employment not exceeding 250 to 1,500.[1]

Several years ago the Committee for Economic Development (CED) defined a small business as having at least two of the following characteristics:

---

[1] *The Small Business Administration: What It Does* (Washington, D.C.: Government Printing Office, 1977), p. 2.

1. The management of the enterprise is independent. Generally the owners are also the managers.
2. Ownership capital is provided by an individual or a small group.
3. The area of operations is mainly local. Owners and employees live in a single community. However, the markets served need not be local.
4. The size of the enterprise must be relatively small when compared with that of the largest companies in its industry.

Both definitions of the small business enterprise emphasize independence, owner management, local operation, and relative smallness.

THE IMPORTANCE OF SMALL BUSINESS IN THE UNITED STATES

Small business plays an important role in the United States. There are between 9.5 million and 13 million small business enterprises in our economy, the number depending on what definitions and statistical sampling techniques are used.[2]

About 6 million small business proprietorships and partnerships have annual business receipts of less than $25,000. Yet small businesses are an important source of employment. The SBA 1977 annual report indicates that 36 million persons were employed in small business–related industries in 1977. This was 40 percent of total civilian employment. Small business accounts for more than 40 percent of the gross national product.

Other indications of the economic importance of proprietorships, partnerships, and corporations, the vast majority of which are small enterprises, may be reviewed in Chapter 1 in Tables 1–2 and 1–3.

ADVANTAGES OF SMALL BUSINESS OWNERSHIP

A small business enterprise can have a number of advantages over a giant corporation. These advantages include innovation, flexibility, and personalized attention. In addition, for the owner of a small business there are personal advantages such as financial rewards and independence.

Innovation

Small enterprises are frequently innovators for important new products in both consumer and industrial markets. The independent entrepreneur may have ideas for new or better products, processes, or services which would not be encouraged in the large corporation. A single new product that could spell success for a small enterprise might be so insignificant to a large corporation's sales that it would not be developed. Corporations such as Polaroid, Eastman Kodak, and Hewlett-Packard are examples of enterprises which started small but provided creative innovations that won the approval of consumers.

---

[2] *The Study of Small Business,* part 2: *What Is a Small Business?* (Washington, D.C.: Office of Advocacy, U.S. Small Business Administration, 1977), p. 17.

career outlook

INSURANCE AGENTS AND BROKERS

Insurance agents and brokers sell policies that protect individuals and businesses against future losses and financial pressures. They may also help plan financial protection to meet the special needs of a customer's family; advise about insurance protection for an automobile, a home, a business, or other property; or help a policyholder obtain settlement of an insurance claim.

An insurance agent may be either an insurance company employee or an independent businessperson who is authorized to represent one or more insurance companies. Brokers are not under exclusive contract with any single company. Instead, they place policies directly with the company that best meets a client's needs. Otherwise agents and brokers do much the same kind of work.

Agents and brokers should be enthusiastic, self-confident, and able to communicate effectively. Because agents usually work without supervision, they need initiative to locate new prospects. For this reason, many employers hire as agents people who have been successful in other jobs.

Although many employers prefer to hire college graduates for insurance-selling jobs, most will hire high school graduates with potential or proven sales ability. College training may help the agent grasp the fundamentals and procedures of insurance selling more quickly. Courses in accounting, economics, finance, business law, and insurance subjects are helpful.

All agents and most brokers must obtain a license in the state where they plan to sell insurance. In most states, licenses are issued only to applicants who pass written examinations covering insurance fundamentals and the state insurance laws.

The employment of insurance agents and brokers is expected to grow about as fast as the average for all occupations through the mid-1980s as the volume of insurance sales continues to expand. However, the employment of agents and brokers will not keep pace with the rising level of insurance sales, because more policies will be sold to groups and by mail. In addition, each agent should be able to handle more business as computers take over some of the time-consuming clerical tasks.

Flexibility

Large corporations may lack the flexibility of small business because of complex organizational structures, established bureaucracies, and high overhead costs. Decision making in the small business frequently depends on only one or two persons. The management and the work force in the small enterprise may be more adaptable to change than those of the large corporation. Even if a union exists in the small business, the work rules may be less rigid than in large corporations. Many small enterprises do not have a large investment tied up in plant and equipment. This may allow them to react more quickly to changing market conditions or to modify a product for a customer more easily than could a big business.

Personalized attention

Small businesses tend to have close communication with their customers, suppliers, and employees. The small business may succeed because the owner-manager knows the firm's customers and their special needs. Its sales can be based on quality and service rather than quantity and price, as is frequently the case in large business operations.

Both management and blue-collar employees in the small business can be treated as individuals. Managers can be given freedom in decision making and provided with a variety of responsibilities. Blue-collar workers, often of necessity, can be given a number of jobs and encouraged to innovate, thereby reducing boredom in the workplace. Lines of communication are direct between owners and employees.

Financial rewards

The small business entrepreneur is still a prime example of the American dream when it comes to taking risks for the sake of financial reward while bearing the risks of loss. Even though many new enterprises fail, as was discussed in Chapter 2, the lure of profits causes Americans to enter business for themselves. Once an enterprise is established and begins to generate profits, the owner is on the way to financial independence. The owner's employment and salary are not subject to the decisions and evaluation of other managers, as would be the case if the small business owner worked for a larger corporation.

Independence

Owners of small business enterprises have a degree of freedom which is not customary for managers in most big corporations. This freedom makes for a larger measure of self-motivation. Often this freedom of small business owners means the right to work harder and longer hours than they would if they were employees of big business. However, the psychological and financial satisfactions that come from enterprise ownership are powerful rewards for the risks of going into business for oneself.

For those persons who prize independence, entrepreneurship is attractive. Once an enterprise is established, the owner may devote less time to its routine operations. Then more time may be spent in leisure activities, community projects, or further creative business pursuits. However, the independence of the small business owner is restricted because of responsibilities to customers, employees, and the general public. As was discussed in Chapter 3, all levels of government limit business enterprises in many ways. Therefore, the independence of all business owners is limited in today's society.

PROBLEMS OF SMALL BUSINESS OWNERSHIP

Although the advantages and the rewards of a small business may be substantial, many problems confront the owners of small enterprises. These problems may be summarized as inadequate management, insufficient financing, and inability to cope with growth.

Management problems

Good management is very important for the small business. Frequently the person who starts a new enterprise already has good technical skills, high sales ability, or detailed product knowledge. The best mechanic in a large car dealership may go out and start an independent auto repair shop. An excellent salesperson may have a lifelong desire to own a clothing specialty shop. An inventive engineer may leave a promising career with a large corporation to begin a new manufacturing enterprise. However, these capabilities alone are not enough to assure success in a new enterprise.

More is required for the owner of a successful auto repair shop than being able to tune up an engine. The work efforts of other persons employed in the enterprise must be coordinated. Financing must be secured and adequate business records maintained. Taxes must be paid on schedule. Required reports must be filed with various governmental agencies. Raw materials and parts must be purchased. Appropriate advertising and promotion programs must be carried out. Customers' needs must be met. If credit is granted it must be supervised. In summary, our outstanding mechanic may not have time to tune engines because of other pressures relating to the overall management of the enterprise. As was indicated in Chapter 2, poor management is the dominant reason for business failure.

The owner of the small enterprise typically lacks expertise in management. Yet because of financial limitations the small business owner is often forced to become a generalist in management. This means that the owner must perform virtually all of the management functions discussed in Chapter 6 and possess the human relations skills discussed in Chapter 8.

Assistance in such areas as accounting, taxes, legal problems, and advertising is available from specialized enterprises. However, these services are costly and they do not provide the overall enterprise management that is necessary for success.

A basic problem of the small enterprise with one good manager is that the enterprise's success may hinge on the health and the continued effectiveness of this one person. This risk may be reduced by consciously developing the managerial talents of other employees and by providing the enterprise with key-person insurance against the untimely death of the executive.

Financial problems

As was discussed in Chapter 2, the risks of failure are high in new businesses. Therefore, it is often difficult to secure adequate financing for a new enterprise. Large, established corporations have access to a variety of sources of funds, some of which are unavailable to small businesses. Frequently persons starting

"I didn't ask you where you got the money so why should you ask me what I'm going to do with it?"

Reprinted by permission The Wall Street Journal

new enterprises lack large sums of money themselves. This means that many small enterprises are started without adequate investment by the owners and must operate on a financial shoestring.

Money is needed by the new small business to finance current operations and to provide funds for production or marketing facilities, such as buildings and equipment. Funds for current operations, called *working capital,* include money devoted to merchandise inventories, accounts due from customers, and supplies as well as cash to pay wages and other expenses.

The new enterprise also needs funds to finance long-term assets, which are referred to as *capital.* Capital assets include equipment, buildings, land, and other assets which will last more than one year. Tying up a small enterprise's limited funds in buildings and land may be avoided by renting facilities. However, generally at least some investment must be made in equipment, machinery, or fixtures to carry out business operations. Sometimes equipment may be leased. This avoids the immediate payment of large sums of money, with lease payments being made like rental payments.

Because of the risks inherent in small business and the general lack of owners' investment, loan funds for both working capital and long-term assets are hard to obtain on reasonable terms. Bankers generally do not make loans on unproven business prospects to persons without managerial and financial experience. In those cases where banks will lend to small business enterprises, the banker is interested in answers to the following questions:

1. What is the specific purpose of the loan?
2. To which particular uses will the funds be put?
3. When can the loan be repaid with interest?
4. What security (collateral) can the borrower provide?

The small business owner-manager should be prepared to provide this information before seeking bank credit.

Commercial finance companies and factors, discussed in Chapter 15, are other potential sources of loan funds for small enterprises. The Small Business Administration and small business investment companies, discussed later in this chapter, are also sources of funds for small business.

An additional complication for small business owners is that typically they lack the financial training and experience to deal with the financial, accounting, and control problems which arise. Fortunately assistance is available from bankers, professional accountants, financial consultants, lawyers, and government-sponsored programs. However, these outside sources are no substitute for the owners' personal knowledge of financial management. Numerous courses designed for small business operators are available at colleges and universities. These college classes are sometimes held in cooperation with the Small Business Administration, chambers of commerce, or other organizations.

Problems of growth

In addition to the problems associated with starting a small business enterprise, there are problems associated with the growth and success of such an enterprise.

Growth in sales and the level of operations eventually brings about the need to increase the number of employees. Besides making more personal interactions necessary for the owner-manager, this increase puts a greater emphasis on organizational structure. In a manufacturing firm more supervisors will be needed to coordinate the work of additional production employees. In a marketing enterprise additional salespersons and an improved inventory control system will probably be needed for successful growth. This means that the owner-manager will have to do more managing and less of the production, sales, or engineering work.

The growth of the enterprise will also require decisions as to what new investments should be made in such items as inventories, equipment, plant, and research. Careful planning is important to avoid spending scarce money for things which are not really needed. The natural optimism arising out of success has to be controlled to avoid unplanned expansions. Emphasis should be on *profitable* growth instead of expansion for its own sake.

The finances of a small business are tested with growth. A substantial increase in sales means that more funds will be needed for inventories and accounts receivable from customers. Even if the enterprise is operating profitably, the increase in profits will usually not provide enough funds to finance the higher level of assets. This again raises the problem of acquiring additional funds by increasing the owner's investment, borrowing from suppliers through trade credit, or obtaining loans from banks or other lenders.

Increasing equity (owners' investment) by selling stock to outsiders or by taking in partners may provide an additional source of funds at this point in the enterprise's development. However, frequently the owner-manager is reluctant to bring in outside partners or stockholders because of a desire to maintain complete ownership and control of the business. Also, new outside owners in the small business may expect to have some role in its management. At the very least they will want the clear prospect of a substantial profit on their investment because of the risk involved.

QUESTIONS BEFORE GOING INTO BUSINESS

Before deciding to become involved in a small business, there are a number of questions you should answer:

1. What is the general state of the economy?
    a. What is the present state of the business cycle? Is this the time to start a new business enterprise?
    b. Is consumer income or industrial demand strong, given the general economic conditions?
    c. What are the employment conditions in the community where the product or service will be sold?
2. What is the future of the industry of the prospective enterprise?
    a. Is demand for the product or service increasing or on the decline? Are the profit prospects good?
    b. If the industry is subject to rapid technological change, can a small business survive and prosper?
    c. What governmental regulations are involved? What are the prospects for additional regulation which may affect profits or industry survival?
3. Where should the enterprise be located?
    a. Are the demographic characteristics of the population in the area right for this enterprise? (Don't start a children's clothing store in a retirement community unless you expect lots of purchases by doting grandparents.)
    b. Are enough potential customers available?
    c. Is there an adequate labor supply?
    d. Is there enough parking, or are transportation facilities available?
    e. Is the tax situation right?
    f. How much competition is there in the area? What chances will the new enterprise have of competing successfully with large enterprises which may be present?
4. Am I right for this type of business?
    a. Do I really want to assume the responsibilities and risks of business ownership?

b. Is this particular type of enterprise consistent with my personal values? (Don't start a liquor store if you have a strong aversion to the consumption of alcoholic beverages.)

c. Do I like to make decisions, even those which may involve some unpleasantness? (Can you dismiss an employee and not develop an ulcer?)

d. Am I willing to work hard to make this business a success?

This lengthy list of questions should be supplemented with many other specifics relating to every step of the organization and management of a new enterprise.

Assistance and answers to some of the questions may be obtained by studying data from agencies such as the U.S. Bureau of the Census, the U.S. Department of Commerce, the Small Business Administration, state industrial development commissions, local chambers of commerce, and industry trade associations. Much of the specific analysis of a particular area and type of enterprise will have to be developed individually. However, the time and effort taken for a detailed analysis *before* funds are invested in a small business can help reduce the risks of failure and improve your chances for profitable operations.

Ownership interests in a small business, even if the enterprise is incorporated, are often difficult to sell to someone else. This makes the investment relatively illiquid. Therefore, careful consideration is needed before you tie up your money in a small business.

STARTING IN A SMALL BUSINESS

The person who wishes to become involved in small business ownership may either buy an established business concern or start a new enterprise.

Buying an established business enterprise

There are several possible advantages if you buy an established business enterprise. The plant and equipment are in place and operating. Customers are already acquainted with the business, and the location has been proven satisfactory. Employees are familiar with the operations of the enterprise. A credit relationship has already been established with suppliers and commercial banks. If the seller is eager to dispose of the enterprise, perhaps in order to retire, the price may be a bargain. Last, but not least, the enterprise should have an established record of profits.

Before you rush off to find an established small business to buy, consider a few of the possible problems associated with such a move. The equipment may be in poor operating condition or technologically outdated. The neighborhood may be changing, and the location may no longer be a prime one. The inventories may include obsolete stock. Employee relations may be poor. Credit relations with suppliers and banks may be strained because of slow payment. The asking price for the enterprise may be too high, and the enterprise may be unprofitable.

Your own analysis can reveal which of these two sets of conditions best fits a particular situation. In addition to making your own investigation, it is well to hire a certified public accountant (CPA) to audit the financial records of the enterprise. Check the enterprise's inventory carefully. Talk with suppliers to see whether trade credit will be granted to you. Contact the firm's banker to determine whether borrowing agreements will be continued if you purchase the enterprise. Especially if a retail or service enterprise is under consideration, see that the present owner signs an agreement not to go into a similar line of business within certain geographic and time limits. Otherwise the former owner may start another enterprise nearby in competition with yours.

Starting a new business

An advantage of starting a new business enterprise is that you will be able to determine the nature and the location of operations without being limited by prior conditions. You can take advantage of new opportunities without being burdened with old methods. You can utilize the latest technology. You can select and train employees to your specifications. You can begin your operations without having the financial and space burden of obsolete inventory. You can set objectives, plan, and develop a system for monitoring results with more freedom if you start your enterprise from the ground up.

Starting a new business has some disadvantages. The lack of a proven record may make suppliers, bankers, and potentially large customers reluctant to make much of a commitment early in the enterprise's life. All the problems of determining the nature and the location of the enterprise must be faced by the new firm. Despite the care with which planning is done, a new business usually requires a larger amount of funds in its start-up period than was originally anticipated. Delays may occur in constructing and equipping the business. Unexpected problems in designing facilities and beginning operations may delay the production or sale of goods or services. The inexperience of owners and new employees frequently contributes to the above difficulties. All of these possibilities make the new enterprise a risky undertaking.

LEGAL FORMS OF BUSINESS ORGANIZATION

The proprietorship, the partnership, and the corporation are the three most widely used legal forms of business organization. These have been defined in Chapter 1, where Figure 1–2 compares a variety of factors relating to each form of organization. Some additional considerations are included here, especially regarding the formation of a new business enterprise.

The proprietorship

The proprietorship is certainly the easiest way to start a new enterprise. All that is required of the proprietor is to secure a license to do business from the city, county, or state government, depending on the laws in the particular location. Some types of enterprises are subject to special regulations and restrictions. These include firms dealing with alcoholic beverages, food service, gambling, transportation, health care, and child care.

The proprietorship is also the simplest type of enterprise to discontinue. All that the proprietor has to do is close the doors and indicate the "final return" on any required government reports, such as FICA and withholding tax reports.

However, the disadvantages of the proprietorship outlined in Figure 1–2 may mean that it is not the most desirable form of legal organization for the new business. These potential disadvantages include difficulties in raising additional ownership funds, unlimited liability for the owner, taxes, and life for the enterprise limited to the owner's lifetime. Just because the proprietorship is the simplest legal form does not mean that it is the best legal form for the new enterprise.

The partnership

The problems associated with the partnership form of organization that were discussed in Chapter 1 apply to the newly established business enterprise. The dangers of unlimited liability for other partners' actions and of disagreements among the partners raise serious questions about the desirability of this form of organization. Also, any change in the general partners dissolves the partnership so that a new partnership must be formed to continue operations. This could occur with the death or withdrawal of a general partner or with the admission of new partners.

The comments above refer to *general partnerships,* in which all partners have unlimited liability. However, in the form of organization called the *limited partnership* the liability of some partners is limited to the amount of their ownership investment in the enterprise. Still, even the limited partnership must have at least one general partner with unlimited liability. If limited partners are to be protected from unlimited liability they must refrain from being active in the management of the enterprise. In addition, the limited partnership must give public notice as to who the limited partners are, usually through registration at the county courthouse. Such registrations generally conform to the Uniform Limited Partnership Act, which applies in most states.

The corporation

The advantages of the corporation discussed in Chapter 1 make it an appropriate form of organization for the new enterprise as well as the large, established business. The concept of the corporation as separate from its owners provides the new owner with limited liability. It also provides a means for raising additional ownership funds through the sale of more stock, should this be necessary. The corporate form of organization provides for the continuous life of the enterprise apart from its original founder.

Although it is more expensive to form a corporation than a proprietorship, the process is relatively simple. The business corporation is formed by making application to an appropriate state office such as the state corporation commission or the secretary of state. The application includes a copy of the proposed enterprise's articles of incorporation. This document states the name of the corporation, the nature of its business activities, and the types and amount of stock to be authorized for sale.

Once the state laws regarding incorporation have been met, a charter is issued for the new corporation. The cost of forming the corporation includes the required filing fees, a tax on the number of shares of the corporation's capital stock, and fees paid in any states where the corporation conducts its business activities other than the state of incorporation. The amount of these expenses varies among the states.

The corporation does not have to be chartered by the state in which it conducts its business activities. However, incorporation in its home state may be the most practical and inexpensive course for the new enterprise.

Subchapter S corporations

Under certain conditions an enterprise may be incorporated and still be taxed like a partnership. Such an enterprise is called a *Subchapter S corporation.*

Subchapter S corporations were permitted by legislation passed in 1958 to encourage small enterprises to obtain the benefits of limited liability through incorporation. However, the Subchapter S corporation avoids the double taxation which occurs when corporate income is taxed and then taxed again when stockholders receive it in the form of cash dividends.

The income of Subchapter S corporations is not taxed at the corporate level. Like the income of the partnership form of organization, it is taxed only once as the personal income of its stockholders. Unless the individual stockholders already have very large personal incomes, this arrangement will yield substantial tax savings. For example, assume that an enterprise is organized as a Subchapter S corporation and has 15 equal stockholders. On $150,000 taxable income each of the stockholders in a Subchapter S corporation would pay personal income taxes on $10,000, whereas an ordinary corporation would pay an income tax on $150,000.

Subchapter S corporations may be organized subject to a number of limitations and provided that there are no more than 15 stockholders.

Legal assistance

Regardless of the form of legal organization that you are considering for your new enterprise, you would be well advised to seek the best legal advice available.

You may form a proprietorship or a partnership without the aid of a lawyer. In some states the services of a lawyer are not required in order to apply for

REAL ESTATE AGENTS AND BROKERS

Real estate agents and brokers represent property owners in selling or renting their properties.

Real estate brokers are independent business people who not only sell real estate but also rent and manage properties, make appraisals, and develop new building projects. In closing sales, brokers usually arrange for loans to finance the purchases, for title searches, and for meetings between the buyers and the sellers at which the details of the transaction are agreed upon and the new owners take possession. Brokers also manage their own offices, advertise properties, and handle other business matters.

A growing number of brokers, currently about one in five, have entered into franchise agreements with national or regional real estate organizations. Under this type of arrangement, which resembles that of many fast-food operations, the broker pays a fee in exchange for the privilege of using the widely known name of the parent organization. Although franchised brokers often receive help in training salespeople and in running their offices, they bear the ultimate responsibility for the success or failure of their own firms.

Real estate agents are generally independent sales workers who contract their services with a licensed broker. Agents show and sell real estate, handle rental properties, and obtain listings (owner agreements to place properties for sale with the agent's firm).

Every state requires that real estate agents and brokers be licensed. They must pass a written examination—more comprehensive for brokers than for agents—which includes questions on basic real estate transactions and on laws affecting the sale of property.

As real estate transactions have become more complex, many of the large firms have turned to college graduates to fill sales positions. However, personality traits are fully as important as academic background. Brokers look for applicants who possess such characteristics as a pleasant personality, honesty, and a neat appearance.

The employment of real estate agents and brokers is expected to rise faster than the average for all occupations in order to satisfy a growing demand for housing and other properties.

a corporate charter. Moreover, the services of a good attorney will be an additional expense for the new enterprise. However, the money and time required for competent legal services before and during the organization of a new enterprise is well spent. Numerous problems can be avoided by using an attorney who specializes in new business ventures. Specific suggestions for the names of such specialists may be obtained from your banker, successful small business owners, or the American Bar Association's directory.

FRANCHISING

The franchise approach to starting a new enterprise is widely used today by small business owners. The *franchise* is an agreement by a manufacturer or an operating company (the franchisor) to give an individual or an enterprise (the franchisee) rights to the sale of a product and the use of trademarks, methods, or name identification. In return the franchisee agrees to promote the franchisor's products.

This type of enterprise has grown rapidly in recent years. Well-known franchises include McDonald's drive-ins, Kentucky Fried Chicken, Coca-Cola bottlers, H & R Block income tax service, Holiday Inns, Western Auto Stores, and automobile dealerships. The U.S. Department of Commerce estimates that franchise operations have accounted for 30 percent of total retail sales. Most of these sales were made by auto and truck dealers and gasoline stations. However, fast-food and convenience food enterprises account for billions of dollars in sales.

Benefits to franchisees

The franchise provides the small business entrepreneur with the opportunity of ownership and independence. At the same time it enables the franchisee to sell a good or service which is already established positively in the consumer's mind. Before the franchisee starts operations, the franchisor typically provides location analysis, loan assistance, and management training.

Once the franchise is operating, the small business owner is assisted with standardized operating methods, centralized purchasing, advertising layouts, and continued management assistance. In a mobile economy in which millions of Americans move every year, the nationally known franchise symbols provide a means of easy identification and ready acceptance by potential new customers.

Problems for franchisees

Although many franchisees are successful and obtain significant help from their franchisors, problems may arise with this type of enterprise. The cost of the goods and services provided by the franchisor may be relatively expensive. Items sold by the franchisor to its franchisees may not always meet local tastes or conditions. The franchisor does not always live up to the expectations of the franchisee. This may be due to misunderstanding on the part of the small business owner. In some instances the franchisor simply does not deliver what was initially promised. Whatever the case, such situations emphasize how important it is for the small business entrepreneur to investigate the franchise opportunity thoroughly and to get good legal advice before entering into a franchise agreement.

The name and the trademark of the franchise may be valuable nationally, and this identification may be valuable in a local market. However, the quality of the service and products provided by the individual franchisee will be critically important in maintaining repeat business. This is especially true in such fields as fast foods and automotive services, where substantial competition exists from local enterprises and other franchises. Even with the support of a national franchisor, the individual small business owner still faces the basic need to provide good management if the business is to be a success.

GOVERNMENTAL ASSISTANCE TO SMALL BUSINESS

A number of governmental agencies and programs are available to assist small business enterprises in a variety of ways. The principal federal agency charged with this responsibility is the U.S. Small Business Administration. Other governmental agencies involved with small business include the Department of Commerce, the Department of Agriculture, the General Services Administration, state development companies, and local development companies. The SBA is discussed here because of its importance in fostering small business.

FUNCTIONS OF THE SBA

The Small Business Administration was created by Congress in 1953 to provide assistance to prospective, new, and established small business enterprises. The SBA's services range from financial assistance and help in securing government contracts to management training and counseling. The SBA maintains a network of over 100 field offices across the country.

Financial assistance

The SBA provides a wide range of loan programs. Their purpose is to help small enterprises that are unable to obtain credit from conventional lenders at reasonable terms.

SBA financial assistance may take the form of SBA participation in a loan to a small business that is made by a bank or some other type of conventional lender. In other cases the SBA guarantees up to 90 percent of a loan which a bank or another lender agrees to make.

If a loan for a worthwhile small business project is not available through participation or guarantees, the SBA may make a direct government loan to the enterprise for the entire amount of the funds needed. However, such direct loan funds are limited, and the demand for these loans usually exceeds the SBA's available funds. Most SBA loans are made on a participation basis with commercial banks.

Loan funds may be used to expand or construct facilities or to convert them to other purposes. Loans are also made for the purchase of machinery, equipment, or working capital items, such as inventory and supplies.

The SBA is also authorized to make a number of other types of loans. These include loans for physically handicapped small business owners, economic injury loans in situations where federal laws have hurt small enterprises, and loans implementing a variety of disaster loan programs.

Procurement assistance

The SBA has federal procurement specialists throughout the country to help small business managers obtain business from various government agencies. This assistance includes counsel on how to prepare bids, obtain government contracts, and get on bidders' lists. In recent years about one third of federal government purchases have been made from small business.

The SBA Minority Vendors' Program helps small enterprises owned by socially or economically disadvantaged persons to make contact with governmental agencies or large corporations. These small business vendors are listed in an SBA computer bank and are available for referral to potential customers to whom they might furnish products.

Management assistance

As was indicated earlier, good management is very important to the success of a small business. The SBA has a Management and Technical Assistance Program to improve the management skills of owners and managers engaged in small business. This program includes free counseling by retired and active business executives and by university students and faculty; courses, conferences, workshops, and clinics; and a variety of publications.

Counseling

The SBA has management assistance specialists who provide counsel on specific problems to individuals and enterprises. Free advice is also available from volunteers from the Service Corps of Retired Executives (SCORE) and the Active Corps of Executives (ACE). Various national professional associations also have volunteers to help owners and prospective owners of small business who have problems.

A number of college and university schools of business administration work through the Small Business Institute (SBI) to provide senior and graduate students for on-site management counseling. The students work under the direction of a faculty member and an SBA management assistance officer.

Courses and workshops

The SBA actively cooperates with schools and business groups to offer courses in management for small business people. Conferences and workshops covering such topics as sources of financing, types of business opportunities, site selection, and business forecasting are held across the country.

Publications

An extensive program provides hundreds of management, technical, and marketing publications to prospective or established business owners. Most of the management publications may be obtained free from the SBA. Other publications are available for a small charge from the superintendent of documents at the U.S. Government Printing Office in Washington, D.C. Lists of all SBA publications are available from local SBA offices.

Assistance to minority-owned small businesses

In addition to the Minority Vendors' Program discussed earlier in this chapter, the SBA has a comprehensive Minority Small Business Program. This program brings together all SBA services to help minority persons take advantage of business opportunities. These special staff persons also cooperate with local business development organizations in assisting minority persons to go into business.

SMALL BUSINESS INVESTMENT COMPANIES

The Small Business Investment Act of 1958 authorized the creation of small business investment companies (SBICs). An SBIC is a privately owned investment company. Its purpose is to provide equity and long-term debt capital to new enterprises operating on the frontiers of new technologies and markets. Enterprises financed by SBICs typically need venture capital and are riskier than those to which commercial banks would usually make loans.

The SBA cooperates with SBICs by loaning funds to the investment companies. These funds are combined with the SBICs' equity capital to provide a larger pool of financing to assist new, innovative enterprises. Since the SBIC program began, about 50,000 small enterprises have received financial assistance of about $3 billion.

The companion organizations to the SBICs are the Minority Enterprise Small Business Investment companies (MESBICs). These organizations, discussed in Chapter 4, provide financial and management assistance to enterprises owned by minority persons who may be hampered by economic or social disadvantages.

SIMILARITIES BETWEEN SMALL AND LARGE ENTERPRISES

Many of the opportunities and problems associated with the small business are the same as those of the large corporation. The factors that pertain especially to small business have been discussed in this chapter. However, such topics as personnel, marketing, production, and finance are important for all persons interested in business. These topics are covered later in this book. The functions of management and control have to be performed in all enterprises, regardless of size. These functions are discussed in the next two chapters.

SUMMARY

A small business is an enterprise which is not dominant in its field and is independently owned and operated. Small businesses have an important impact on U.S. employment and productivity.

The advantages of small enterprises include innovation, flexibility, and personalized service as well as financial rewards and independence for their owners.

The problems which confront small business owners include poor management, insufficient financing, and difficulties in dealing with growth.

There are numerous economic and personal questions to be answered before one begins a small business. A person may enter small business by buying an established enterprise or by starting a completely new operation. Each approach has advantages and disadvantages which should be investigated.

Proprietorships, partnerships, and corporations may all be used as a legal form of business organization. Under some circumstances the Subchapter S corporation may provide the advantage of limited liability and also avoid the double taxation of corporate income and stockholder dividends. Good legal advice is desirable before starting a small business.

Franchises have been widely used to provide local small business owners with the advantages of national production, promotion, and distribution.

A variety of governmental agencies and programs are available to assist small business. The principal federal agency responsible for this is the Small Business Administration.

Small business investment companies are privately owned investment firms which provide equity and long-term debt capital to new enterprises.

TERMS FOR REVIEW

small business
working capital
general partnership
limited partnership

Subchapter S corporation
franchise
Small Business
    Administration

small business investment
    company

QUESTIONS

1. What criteria are used to define a small business?

2. How can a small business enterprise compete successfully with a large corporation? Give a specific example.

3. What problems are faced by the person who is about to become involved in a small business? How can these problems be minimized?

4. a. Would you like to own a small enterprise? Explain your answer.

   b. If you were to become a business owner, what type of industry would you like to be in? Why?

5. Why is the corporate form of legal organization frequently preferred over the proprietorship and the partnership forms?

6. Discuss the advantages and disadvantages of owning a franchised business enterprise.

7. Outline the various forms of assistance provided by the Small Business Administration.

8. Why might a small business be able to secure financing from an SBIC when a bank loan would be difficult, if not impossible, to obtain?

9. What successes and what problems are reflected in the annual report of General Semiconductor Industries as outlined on the first page of this chapter?

business brief

UNFAIR COMPETITION

Following newspaper publicity about a federal grant of $1.5 million to Chicanos por la Causa in Phoenix (see "Federally Assisted Tortillas" business brief on p. 71), an outcry arose from owners of Mexican food businesses throughout the area. Most of the Mexican foods and spices enterprises in Phoenix are small "mom and pop" operations.

An owner of a Mexican spices enterprise in south Phoenix complained, "It just gripes me that the government takes our tax money and gives him [the firm receiving the grant] an advantage." This enterprise employs seven persons and has been in business more than 25 years. "It was a long, hard struggle," the owner stated. He said that for about 25 years he worked six to seven days a week for up to 14 hours daily. Until two years ago this Spanish-speaking owner had not taken a vacation.

Owners of other Mexican wholesale food enterprises complained about the government grant to Chicanos por la Causa. One owner was fearful that consumers might think they could help disadvantaged workers only if they bought from the government-supported enterprise. "However," this owner pointed out, "almost every *tortillaría* [tortilla shop] hires these kinds of people."

These comments were made by managers of Mexican American businesses: "I don't know how they got the money when we can't even borrow any. They must be sharp people to get it." "It's going to hurt everybody. We had to work a lot to get where we are the past five years. It took friends and relatives."

1. *What is the basis for the concerns expressed by minority business owners regarding the government grant to Chicanos por la Causa?*
2. *Should federal grants be made to minority business enterprises which may compete with established enterprises?*
3. *If such grants are made, what investigation should precede the awarding of the grants?*
4. *What action, if any, can Mexican food producers in the Phoenix area take to protect their enterprises?*

case

THE DRIVEWELL CORPORATION

The Drivewell Corporation has been in business for one year. It is engaged in the design and manufacture of devices and component parts for manufacturers in the trucking industry. The founder of Drivewell, Jim Schollenbach, had been a successful engineer in the industry for a number of years. He had had considerable experience in the invention of new products and had supervised the establishment of a new manufacturing plant for a former employer. Schollenbach organized his company after he became dissatisfied with the management of the firm where he had worked. He had dreamed of going into business so he could be his own boss. He felt his products were simpler and more efficient than competing products, and could be sold profitably for the same or slightly lower prices.

During the early months of the Drivewell Corporation most of Schollenbach's time was spent in handling the many details necessary to starting a new enterprise. Finances had been a limiting factor, although he had been able to negotiate borrowing arrangements with a local bank to go along with limited equity funds. A draftsman, a sales manager, and a few machinists were hired, along with a part-time clerical employee who kept the company's books with the assistance of a local certified public accounting firm.

Manufacturing operations were carried out in a small plant which was rented on a monthly basis. Emphasis was placed on developing pilot models to be used as samples that prospective customers could try out. These pilot models met with a good response in the industry. Within a few months some small orders were being produced and shipped.

However, Schollenbach was disappointed that things were not moving as rapidly as he had hoped. He discussed his problems with Herb Johnston, a friend who had been helpful in organizing the enterprise.

"Even though we knew it would take time to get operations started," began Schollenbach, "I never dreamed that details would take so much of my time. Also, we have encountered numerous delays in obtaining parts. For example, one of our main products requires a type of rubber bushing which is not standard in the industry at present. As is the customary practice, we paid for a special mold which we put in the hands of a large rubber manufacturer when we placed our initial order. It turned out that there was a strike in the rubber industry. Then, when production started again, our order must have been pushed down the line. The bushings arrived seven weeks later than the date I had been promised. We were delayed in getting out pilot models and in filling an initial order for a customer because of the failure to get the batch of bushings."

"How about other materials?" asked Johnston. "Do you have this problem with other suppliers?"

"Partially," answered Schollenbach. "Since we are a small purchaser we can't command much respect from the big companies in getting special treatment for our orders. We have been able to buy steel from a local distributor. Much of our steel fabrication for the pilot models is done in our shop. Later we will place special tooling in the hands of a steel manufacturer, which will reduce our fabricating costs. However, the tooling will cost several thousand dollars and we aren't ready for that now, either in production volume or in finances.

"Another problem we have had is getting delivery on the proper springs. One of the spring manufacturers we have been dealing with shipped us an order of the wrong spring. We were able to adapt our models to this spring because of the necessity of getting our orders out. But this has been time consuming and more costly than we anticipated.

"The most encouraging part of our business so far has been the excellent reception our pilot models have received in the industry. Enough pilot models are now in use that we expect to receive some substantial orders in the near future. Morale is high among our employees because we all believe in our products, but it will be good to get some profitable contracts under our belts."

1. *What are the major problems that Jim Schollenbach faces in expanding the Drivewell Corporation's operations?*
2. *What, if anything, can Schollenbach do to deal with these problems?*
3. *From the point of view of a purchasing agent for a large manufacturer, at present what would be the advantages of ordering component parts from the Drivewell Corporation? What would be the disadvantages in placing an order with Drivewell?*

Burroughs reports . . .

Burroughs' overall strength as a company is built on the individual excellence of Burroughs people. Throughout the world, in all areas of operation, the talents, spirit, and dedication of our employees represent the key element in our success.

Employing outstanding people at every level of the organization is a two-dimensional resource: it enables us to provide the highest quality products and services to our customers, and it gives us an international reservoir of talent and experience for the management of our company.

In building our fundamental strengths, no area has been more important than the development of a highly professional, self-renewing management organization. This program begins with the selection of highly trained men and women from leading schools of engineering, science, business administration, and the professions—a practice we began over 40 years ago. It continues with ongoing training, both on the job and in the classroom, with emphasis on individual development as well as career development. Typically, Burroughs people are assigned their first management responsibilities relatively early, and their responsibilities are increased as they mature and grow in experience.

This dynamic process has continually provided the company with a team of skilled, experienced leaders.

From annual report of Burroughs Corporation

Photo opposite: To maintain the high caliber of people it requires, Burroughs recruits outstanding students from leading colleges and universities around the world.

6

Management

Management

Business management has been called the oldest of the arts and the youngest of the professions. From the time people began to specialize their labors, problems of coordination have arisen which have required managerial attention. Earlier studies of management have come from schools of public administration, where techniques for the administration of governmental bodies were developed. Today the practice of management has benefited from the findings of the behavioral sciences of psychology, anthropology, and sociology. The systems concept, adapted from the natural sciences, and the use of electronic computers also aid management. Many of the generalizations regarding management are applicable to any institution or group which has common objectives. However, our discussion will center on the business enterprise as the focal point of managerial activities.

After studying this chapter, you will be able to answer the following questions regarding management:

What is the nature of management?

How does the systems approach relate to management of the business enterprise?

Why is planning necessary for successful operations?

What factors are considered in developing the organizational structure of the business system?

How do authority-responsibility relationships apply to management?

What is the relationship between line and staff functions in the business system?

THE NATURE OF MANAGEMENT

Management may be defined as achieving results by coordinating the activities of other people. There are many dimensions to managerial activity. A supervisor in a factory acts as a manager when scheduling production runs and making work assignments for employees. The vice president for marketing acts as a manager when conferring with district sales supervisors to work out a new marketing program. In turn the district sales supervisors act as managers when they organize and direct their salespeople to sell the enterprise's products. In all these examples the function of the manager is to provide an environment in which others perform the actual work involved in the production and distribution of the enterprise's products.

An individual who is designated as a member of management may on occasion also do some specific work in producing or selling the enterprise's product. Sometimes even the president will act as a salesperson in entertaining important customers or in working out an important contract. However, when a person has the label of "manager," this means that the individual's main responsibility lies in indirect achievement rather than in the actual production of goods or services.

Management has also been called the art of decision making. Some of the outstanding managers in this country have been able under difficult conditions to make decisions which have been proven to be sound by the events that followed. The types of managerial decisions vary from those made by the board of directors and the president of an enterprise as to whether to produce a new product to a supervisor's responsibility for assigning workers to particular jobs.

A SYSTEMS APPROACH TO MANAGEMENT OF THE BUSINESS ENTERPRISE

In the appendix to Chapter 1 the systems approach to business was introduced. The systems concept can be applied to the management functions of an individual

FIGURE 6–1
General model of the system of a business enterprise

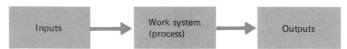

business enterprise. Although the external environment is important, in this chapter the internal system of the individual enterprise is emphasized. This is done to focus attention on the internal functions of management. The basic system of the enterprise is illustrated in Figure 6–1.

Figure 6–1 shows how the inputs flow into the work system where they are processed and become outputs. The inputs consist of material and human resources. The outputs are goods and services and other means for satisfying human needs.

As a business enterprise increases in size and complexity, further division of labor is required for efficient functioning of the work system. Specialized workers and capital equipment are used to make the work system more productive. To achieve an orderly flow of work in an increasingly specialized organization, coordination and direction by managment are necessary. The work system may be thought of as being composed of technical, organizational, and human subsystems. The addition of these subsystems to the model of the business enterprise is illustrated in Figure 6–2.

The *technical subsystem* consists of the equipment, layout, and technology required to produce and distribute a particular product. The nature of the technical subsystem depends on the requirements of the product and varies widely from one industry to another. For example, a research laboratory of a chemical manufacturer requires a technical subsystem which is quite different from that of a magazine publisher. The requirements for a technical subsystem relate

FIGURE 6–2
Model of a business enterprise depicting the technical-organizational-human subsystems

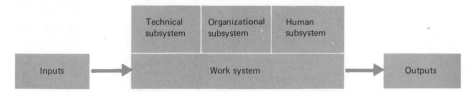

closely to the human and material inputs that are needed to make the subsystem function effectively. Chapter 13 on production deals extensively with the functioning of the technical subsystem of the business enterprise.

The *human subsystem* exists in all enterprises and consists of the values, motivations, and interactions of the persons in the enterprise. This subsystem involves management in the practice of human relations. Because of the importance of developing a good human relations climate in the business enterprise, Chapter 8 is devoted to a discussion of this subject.

The *organizational subsystem* is the means by which the technical and human subsystems are organized, directed, coordinated, and controlled by management. This involves planning, departmentalization, staffing, and authority relationships. The organizational subsystem can be considered as the formal means by which the technical and human subsystems are related to each other.

There are numerous interactions among the technical, organizational, and human subsystems. Changes occurring in the technical subsystem can affect the human subsystem and may necessitate changes in the organizational subsystem. For example, the installation of automated equipment may reduce the need for some production employees or require workers with different skills than those now on the job. Such a technical change will have an impact on the morale of the work force and thus create a problem requiring the attention of management. As an example of a different type of change, the development of a new product will cause changes in the human and organizational subsystems. New production facilities and the marketing program for the new product expand the requirements for personnel and an organization to direct their activities.

In any business system the various subsystems are constantly adjusting to changes caused by internal and external forces. The job of management is to deal with these change agents so that the enterprise will function efficiently to produce outputs desired by society.

TRADITIONAL FUNCTIONS OF MANAGEMENT

The activities of management can be incorporated into the model of the business enterprise in the organizational subsystem. The traditional functions of management are planning, organizing, direction, and control. These functions are systematized in Figure 6–3.

FIGURE 6–3
The functions of management

The relative importance of each of these management activities at a particular time depends on the stage of the enterprise's development, its growth rate, its competition, and other factors in the environment. Planning and organizing are discussed in this chapter. Direction is discussed in Chapter 8 along with human relations, and control is discussed in Chapter 7.

PLANNING—REQUISITE FOR SUCCESSFUL OPERATIONS

Planning is a primary function of management. In the new enterprise planning precedes the other functions of management. In the established enterprise planning is a continuing part of the total management process. Without adequate planning the manager frequently deals only with immediate problems and fails to consider future needs. The management that does not plan will function on a random, day-to-day basis. The executives in such an enterprise never seem to have time to anticipate the problems which may arise tomorrow. They do not create conditions within the enterprise to reduce future emergencies. Thus, *planning* may be called the process of rational decision making done sufficiently in advance to promote the more effective operation of the enterprise. This involves determining objectives, policies, procedures, and the organizational structure which will provide a framework to achieve the enterprise's broad goals.

Objectives

The first step in the planning process is formulating objectives. *Objectives* include the broad goals toward which the group activity of the business enterprise is directed. The following statement is the published objective of the Ideal Cement Company of Denver, Colorado:

> To manufacture and sell cement of the types and qualities, in such quantities, at such times and places, and to do such things in connection therewith, as will result in increasing the returns to the Company to the greatest extent with due regard for the rights and proper interest of customers, stockholders, employees, and all others affected by the activities of the Company.

This statement is an overall enterprise objective. To be effective it should be supplemented with more specific objectives throughout the subsystems of the organization. Meaningful subgoals are needed for each division and department of the enterprise. A subgoal of one of the manufacturing departments might be to produce the necessary quantity of cement at the lowest possible cost. The traffic division might have a subgoal of maintaining shipping dates.

The formulation of enterprise objectives is a necessary first step in the planning process, since objectives establish the basis for operations.

Management by objectives One approach for appraising the performance of an enterprise's managers is to measure their progress toward a specified set of goals or objectives. This concept of *management by objectives* emphasizes evaluation based on measurable results rather than on subjective, personal judgments of higher management. Planned objectives are agreed upon by both the manager and his or her boss. Then the manager is evaluated on how well these objectives are fulfilled. A number of business enterprises, including General Electric, have emphasized management by objectives.

Policies

A *policy* is a framework for decision making that is consistent with the objectives of the enterprise. Good policy statements are important as guidelines for supervisors in dealing with issues which arise. Without policies each situation might have to be rethought completely by management before action could be taken. Areas in which business enterprises typically have policies include new product development (does the company lead in research and new product development, or does it follow other enterprises?), production (does the enterprise produce only for specific orders, or does it emphasize long production runs with a buildup of inventory?), and finance (are funds for expansion provided by the owners or by borrowing?).

Policies may be broadly stated so as to give considerable discretion to executives, or they may be quite specific as to what actions are to be taken. The amount of discretion allowed by a policy statement is usually greater the higher in management one goes. At the top management level, consisting of the board of directors and the chief executive officer, policy statements provide for considerable freedom of thought and action. At the first-line supervisor's level, policies are usually more specific and less flexible. For example, a fairly specific statement regarding enterprise policy on absenteeism is most helpful to a supervisor who oversees many persons where production schedules are important. At the top management level, work schedules are less rigid and responsibilities much broader. Therefore, a less specific policy about hours of work and presence in the factory or office is appropriate. Figure 6–4 illustrates the concept of freedom of policy interpretation discussed above.

Despite less latitude for policy interpretation by first-line managers, some flexibility of policy interpretation is important here too. It is almost impossible to write a statement which will be applicable in every set of circumstances.

FIGURE 6–4

Therefore, a certain amount of policy flexibility is usually desirable at the level of the first-line supervisor to provide for varying circumstances.

Although flexibility in policy administration is desirable, it does come into conflict with the concept of consistency of policy application. Policy flexibility tends to lead to variations in application by individual supervisors. Wide inconsistencies in a policy's application can result in lower levels of employee morale. Even though a particular policy does not meet with the complete approval of employees, it is generally accepted if it is consistently applied. Management should be aware of the conflict between flexibility and consistency of policy application and should seek to achieve a balance between these two important elements of policy administration.

As a part of policy administration, executives should understand that there is often a difference between the formal stated policy on an issue and the actual application of that policy in the enterprise. Where circumstances have made the formal policy obsolete and resulted in informal policy changes, management should be prompt to update written policies. Problems have arisen for managements which have openly tolerated vast differences between stated policies and actual policy administration in the areas of employee safety, operational efficiency, and customer relations.

For policies to be most effective they should be well understood throughout the business system. Policies should be clearly stated and written so that employees will understand the basic framework within which decisions will be made. The old joke, "There's no good reason, it's company policy," has no place in today's business enterprise.

Procedures

Procedures are the third element of the planning process. A *procedure* is a series of steps carried out in a particular sequence to implement a given policy. Procedures provide little or no discretion on the part of the individual. They may be used to carry out certain policies where a chronological sequence of events is important. For example, procedures may relate to matters such as how information about the enterprise's profits shall be released to the public or what steps must be taken to ensure the safe operation of machinery.

TO ERR IS HUMAN
TO FORGIVE IS
NOT COMPANY POLICY

Reprinted by permission
The Wall Street Journal

In implementing company policies and in establishing guidelines for employee conduct, management should make clear whether a particular statement is a rule or a guide. *Rules* are statements which must be obeyed. *Guides* represent recommendations for action. A rule is usually stated in a negative manner, such as "No Smoking in This Area" or "No Admittance without Safety Glasses." Even if a rule is stated in a more positive manner, such as "Safety Glasses Must Be Worn Here," the negative connotation is still present. Rules should be applied only when necessary to govern employee conduct.

Good planning is essential

The planning process culminates in the development of programs which are a mixture of policies and procedures to achieve the enterprise's objectives. These programs include the necessary financial budgets to support them.

Planning is a continuous process to meet changing conditions and new needs of the business system. Planning reduces unproductive work. It provides a necessary basis for controlling operations by setting a standard against which results may be measured.

No enterprise should spend more money on planning than the value of the anticipated benefits. The measurement of the dollar benefits of planning is difficult. The amount of money that could be spent on evaluating alternative courses of action and forecasting probable results could be unlimited. Each management must determine how much it wishes to spend to get the information necessary for good planning. Time and the available executive talent are also limiting factors in the planning process. However, good planning reduces the chances that executives will be forced to make snap decisions on critical issues without adequate information. Careful planning provides a sound basis for the other management functions of organizing, directing, and controlling.

ORGANIZING THE BUSINESS ENTERPRISE

Organizing the business enterprise is the second important management function. The various activities must be systematically arranged and assigned for efficient use of time and energy. The factors to consider in developing the organizational structure of any business system include departmentalization, staffing, authority-responsibility relationships, span of control, and line and staff relationships.

Departmentalization

The many different activities of the business enterprise must be assigned so that the employees will clearly understand who is responsible for which activity. Can you imagine a large store that sells many different kinds of merchandise and does not have any departments? Suppose that each morning all employees were assigned to their workplaces for that day on a random basis without any relationship to what they had done the day before. The result of this unorganized situation would be chaos!

Departmentalization provides the basis for organizing the work to be done in the business enterprise. When the business enterprise is thought of as a system, departments can be viewed as subsystems. Viewing the departments as subsystems emphasizes the interrelatedness of departments in achieving both their own objectives and those of the enterprise. Such an approach stimulates individuals in the various departments to expand their view beyond a single narrow activity.

The usual ways of organizing an enterprise into departments are by function, by product time, or by geography. Other methods of departmentalization include those based on the type of customer served or on individual projects.

Functional departmentalization   When an enterprise is departmentalized on a functional basis, activities of a similar nature are grouped together. Thus, the activities of production and marketing are placed in separate departments and function as different subsystems. Other functional departments customarily include personnel, finance, and accounting. Figure 6–5 illustrates the typical manufacturing enterprise's top management structure departmentalized by function. The five major departments illustrated in Figure 6–5 perform such an important role of many business enterprises that separate chapters are devoted to an analysis of each of these functions.

Product line departmentalization   A business enterprise may be organized according to the various types of products it manufactures and sells. This is product line departmentalization, and under this method each product is handled almost as a separate system. Product line departmentalization is used in the

FIGURE 6–5
Simplified organization chart of a typical manufacturing corporation on a functional basis

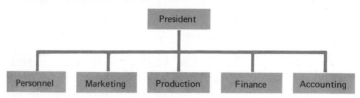

automobile industry. The major automobile manufacturers have separate divisions for the production and distribution of each line. This concentrates management attention on the problems peculiar to each segment of the market.

Departmentalization by geography   *Geographic departmentalization* is logical when activities are carried on over a wide territorial range. Geography provides a good means for departmentalization when different markets and conditions exist across the country.

Other means of departmentalization   Sometimes an enterprise may find it profitable to departmentalize on the basis of the *type of customer served.* This is done many times by enterprises producing both civilian and governmental products. Enterprises which sell products to the Department of Defense often have a separate division for defense contracts. This helps such enterprises to maintain close control over standards and to keep up to date on the complex requirements for dealing with the federal government. These same enterprises may use separate departments to produce and sell products for civilian use. Sometimes commercial banks organize departments on a type-of-customer-served basis, such as departments for loans to retail stores, to consumers, or to farmers.

In engineering and construction industries the *single-project type of departmentalization* is useful where large one-time projects are undertaken which will extend over a period of months or years. Highway construction contracts serve as a logical basis for single-project departments. Once the project has been completed, the personnel and equipment are reassigned to other activities.

Staffing and management succession

Once the organizational structure has been planned, the next step is providing managerial personnel to fill the decision-making positions. *Staffing* is the provision of qualified managerial personnel for the enterprise. A key element in a good staffing program is to develop an adequate plan for management succession. No matter how competent particular executives are, these persons will not always be with the enterprise. Therefore, management should have a program to provide qualified managerial personnel as replacements.

Sources of executive talent   There are two ways of obtaining executives. The first is to promote employees from lower management levels or from nonmanagerial levels. The second is to bring in executive personnel from the outside.

Generally executive morale is higher if promotion comes from within the company ranks. However, if inside promotion is practiced, this means that executive training programs should be in operation to assure that personnel will be prepared when vacancies occur. Also, there is a danger that inbreeding may tend to stifle new ideas.

Hiring executives from outside the enterprise can also have merit. Besides bringing new ideas into an organization, an executive hired from the outside is generally ready to assume the responsibility for a given position immediately. The lead time required for training may be cut down by hiring experienced executives from other business enterprises. This practice is especially useful in companies where no management training programs have been undertaken.

Management training   When management is faced with a shortage of trained personnel, this may reflect a weakness in the management training program. There are four ways in which personnel can acquire managerial training to qualify them for promotion. These are job rotation, special assignments, formal training programs, and staff assignments.

Job rotation involves the transfer of employees through a series of different positions to acquaint them with the different elements of the enterprise's operations. This is especially helpful for the young person who is new to the enterprise, and it provides a basis for a more permanent assignment.

More experienced personnel may be given *special assignments* in which they can show their ability to organize and carry out a program. Special assignments provide a measure of one's ability to deal with new situations.

Formal training programs can be conducted within the enterprise. These programs include lectures, special training, and discussions. Or the executive may go to a college or a university for professional management training. Such a program tends to broaden the scope of the executive's knowledge outside a special field such as marketing or accounting.

Placing an individual in a *staff position,* such as an assistant to a member of top management, can provide a real insight into the operation of the enterprise. The assistant's role, when used as a training device, should include work at various levels in the organization. As a staff official, the individual acts to provide assistance or information but does not have to bear the final responsibility for decision making. Such assignments give young managers a better understanding of the complexities of the decisions made by top executives and improve their grasp of the total managerial job.

Authority-responsibility relationships

In organizing the business enterprise, management must determine the nature of the authority-responsibility relationships. *Authority* is the delegated power to make decisions. Sometimes authority is defined as the right to direct the actions of others. However, in a free society an employer is neither able to command enthusiastic cooperation from employees nor able to make employees obey commands they do not understand. Therefore, good communications, respect for the individual worker, and reasonable work standards are critical in the exercise of authority in the modern industrial enterprise.

Responsibility   Those with decision-making power are held accountable for their decisions. Responsibility is closely tied to accountability. Supervisors at all levels of business know that they are responsible for the results obtained from the employees and the materials put under their direction. However, one of the most frequent complaints of supervisory personnel is that they do not have authority in decision making which is equal to their responsibility. With every responsibility should go sufficient authority to make the decisions necessary to achieve the desired results.

Delegation of authority   Another aspect of authority-responsibility relationships is the importance of proper delegation of authority to subordinates. A particular responsibility, as such, cannot be delegated by a superior to a subordinate. However, a superior can delegate authority to make decisions to a subordinate and then create a new responsibility relationship from the subordinate to the superior. This does not relieve the superior of responsibility to higher management, but it does make possible the disposition of work assignments.

Consider the example of the office manager who is responsible for the work of many clerks and other office employees. The office manager is not relieved of these responsibilities when the office workers are divided into four sections, with a supervisor appointed for each section. The office manager is still responsible for the smooth functioning of the office. However, new responsibility relationships have been created from the section supervisors to the office manager.

In this example, the office manager should make clear to the section supervisors what their responsibilities are and what authority is delegated to them to meet these responsibilities. Without a clear understanding among supervisors and employees as to authority and responsibility, morale will deteriorate. Employees will be unable to have their questions answered by supervisors. Employees may bypass section supervisors and go to the office manager with their problems. This not only creates misunderstanding but negates the purpose of the section supervisor: that of performing many administrative details in the office to enable the office manager to concentrate on broader matters of more long-run importance.

Degree of decentralization of decision making   In recent years many large enterprises such as General Electric Company have become very interested in applying the concept of decentralization of decision making to their organizations. The concept of complete centralization of decision making is not appropriate to the large business operation. The relevant question is not whether there is to be decentralization but to what extent decision making shall be decentralized. Even in medium-size and small business enterprises, where problems of geographic distances and multiplant operations are not present, decentralization of decision making is appropriate.

In view of the interest in decentralization, the answers to each of the following five questions will give some guidelines for the appropriate extent of decentralization in a particular business enterprise.

1. What is the significance of the decision? In those instances where the decision is relatively minor it ought to be made by operating personnel on the spot. The cost of having the problem passed up through the organization may exceed the value of the decision itself. When the decision is critical to the overall success of the enterprise it should probably be made by more senior executives.

2. Who in the organization has the information necessary to make an informed decision? Most decisions should be made at the level in the organization where the needed information is readily available. With more complex decisions the need to draw information from several areas of the enterprise means that clear channels of communication will be required.

3. At what level in the organization do personnel have the capacity to make the decision? Authority should normally be delegated as far down in the organization as employees have the experience and knowledge necessary to render a sound decision. There are times when personnel at the operating level of management are better equipped to make a decision than higher management because of their close association with the problem.

4. How rapidly must the decision be made? Some authority must be placed at the point of impact of the decision making. There is no sense in requiring permission from the plant manager before taking a fire extinguisher and putting out a trash fire in a wastebasket! On the other hand, a major decision relating to expansion of plant capacity can wait until sufficient evidence is gathered.

5. How will employee morale be affected by the degree of decentralization in the enterprise? Generally decentralization improves initiative and creates good morale among employees. People like to feel that they can influence events where they are employed.

Span of control

A concept closely related to the issue of decentralization of authority is that of executive span of control. *Span of control* refers to the number of subordinates a manager can effectively supervise. There are three main factors that tend to limit the number of persons whom any single manager can supervise. These are the executive's available time and energy, the executive's mental capabilities and personal abilities for dealing with individuals, and the nature of the supervisory problems that will be encountered on the job.

The more face-to-face contacts that are necessary each day in the conduct of a department's affairs, the more time consuming and demanding is the supervisor's role. Generally, the more complex the supervisory situation and the greater the variety of activities that a person directs, the more limited will be the number of individuals who can be supervised. Consequently the span of control is narrower. Some authorities indicate that at higher levels in the enterprise fewer persons can be effectively supervised. This leads to a narrower span of control than exists at lower levels in the organization, where problems are not of such great magnitude. However, in those enterprises in which considerable decentralization of authority exists, a wider span of control at the top management level can be very effective. In such cases the shorter lines of communication from the bottom to the top of the organization and the fewer levels of management personnel can improve the morale and the effectiveness of subordinates. Figure 6–6 illustrates the difference in organizational structure between a wide and a narrow span of control.

Notice in Figure 6–6 that the number of production workers in each company is the same. However, the two organizational structures are quite different. There are 18 production workers in each supervisory work unit in Company A and only 8 in Company B. In Company A there are only two levels of management between production workers and the president. In Company B four levels separate workers from the president. Although it is rather unrealistic to assume that workers will have much direct contact with the president, communication is more direct when fewer levels of supervision exist. The danger that

FIGURE 6–6
Comparison of organizational structures with wide and narrow spans of control

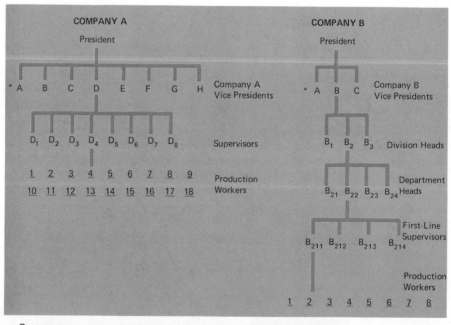

Summary:

Company A	Company B
1 President	1 President
8 Vice presidents	3 Vice presidents
64 Supervisors	9 Division heads
1,152 Production workers	36 Department heads
1,225 Total employees	144 First-line supervisors
	1,152 Production workers
	1,345 Total employees

* Each level below the departmental level has a similar structure of supervisors and production workers as shown for Department D in Company A and Department B in Company B.

communication will be impaired is greater where the span of control is narrow and there are many levels of supervision. In Company A more authority and responsibility are placed with individual supervisors than in Company B, where authority is likely to be more divided among the various levels of supervisors.

There are 120 more supervisory personnel in Company B than there are in Company A. It can be asked whether these additional salaries are necessary. Top management should always attempt to determine whether additional levels of supervision with more executives can be economically justified. Although in view of their greater responsibilities some supervisory personnel in Company A may be more highly paid than those in Company B, the total executive wage bill will probably be higher in Company B.

Despite the issues which have been raised concerning the organizational structure of Company B, it would be wrong to assume that a wide span of control is always best. The optimum span of control or supervision for each level in the enterprise should be determined by the variety and importance of the activities being supervised, the stability of enterprise operations, the abilities of the executive, the abilities of subordinates, and the importance of executive salaries as an expense item in the enterprise.

Whether the span of control is wide or narrow, it is important that employees know the chain of command. The *chain of command* concept involves having all employees understand to whom they are directly responsible. All persons should understand the nature of authority and how it is to be exercised.

Line and staff relationships

Problems arise in the organization of the business enterprise because of misunderstanding of line and staff functions. The *line function* consists of those activities that directly result in the achievement of the goals of the enterprise. Thus, line activities in a manufacturing enterprise would be those relating to producing and selling the product. The *staff function* includes all other activities which assist the line in fulfilling the enterprise's objectives. Activities such as finance, personnel administration, and accounting are normally considered to be staff functions. This means that line and staff functions may be defined in terms of the kinds of activities accomplished. Those which are part of the mainstream of enterprise goals are line functions, and those which support line activities are staff functions. Both types are illustrated by Figure 6–7.

Line and staff functions may also be defined with regard to authority relationships. The concept of chain of command implies a direct line of authority running throughout the enterprise's system. In this sense, the line executive is one who has direct authority over another employee. Line authority consists of the power to make decisions and follow through to see that a mission is accomplished. The role of the staff executive is that of advice and consultation, not of final decision making. In terms of authority relationships the staff function is not decision making or direction but provision of assistance to improve decisions made by persons with line authority.

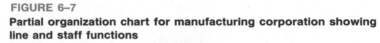

FIGURE 6–7

Partial organization chart for manufacturing corporation showing line and staff functions

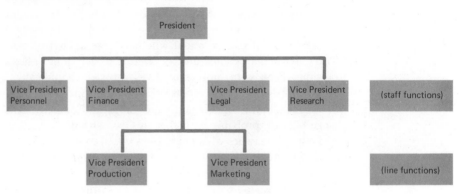

Thus, the concept of line and staff may be defined either according to the kind of activity accomplished or in terms of authority relationships. A particular executive may be considered to perform both line and staff functions. For example, the personnel manager is head of the personnel department and exercises a line function with respect to that department. However, personnel administration is generally considered to be a staff function since it provides advice and assistance to other departments.

Dimensions of the staff function   Although any staff function represents an activity that is necessary to support the line, there are different dimensions to the staff function. Staff personnel include technical advisers, personal assistants, housekeeping staff, and specialized staff.

Technical advisers are personnel such as legal counselors, public relations experts, and engineers who provide information of a highly specialized nature. Much advice given by technical staff members is almost a directive. The line manager may ignore the advice, but is unlikely to be in a position to make a different decision which will be sounder technically.

Personal assistants provide busy executives with information or handle details that the manager may not have time for. This type of staff person is often titled as "Assistant to . . ." The exact nature of the responsibilities involved will be determined by the top executive.

Housekeeping staff means just what the name implies. This includes the large number of personnel who perform custodial and maintenance duties, record keeping, health services such as giving physical examinations and providing first aid, and routine personnel functions such as interviewing prospective employees and providing testing services.

Specialized staff includes a variety of staff personnel whose common denominator is understanding in a particular field of knowledge that can be of vital assistance to the line executive. The accounting function in the business enterprise is generally considered a specialized staff role, as are elements of finance, purchasing, and engineering.

What constitutes a staff function in one business enterprise may be a line function in another. Purchasing for many manufacturers is considered a staff function, but in a large retailing enterprise the buying or purchasing function is a vital line responsibility that is coupled with successful selling or marketing. Whatever represents the main thrust of an enterprise's economic function may properly be called the line, and those elements that support and assist may be called the staff.

SUMMARY

Management consists of achieving results by coordinating the activities of other people.

The systems approach to management of a business enterprise focuses on the coordination of inputs of material and human resources into the work system, where they are processed and become outputs of goods, services, and other means for satisfying human needs. The work system is composed of technical, organizational, and human subsystems.

The traditional functions of management are planning, organizing, direction, and control.

Planning is the process of rational decision making done in advance to promote the enterprise's more efficient functioning. Planning includes the formulation of objectives, policies, and procedures.

Organizing enterprise activities is an important function of management. The organization process includes departmentalization, staffing and providing for management succession, and establishing authority-responsibility relationships. Persons in the enterprise need to understand the span of control and the nature of line and staff relationships.

Authority is the delegated power to make decisions. When decision-making power is delegated, an authority-responsibility relationship is created. Decentralization of decision making is an important trend in management today.

The line function consists of those activities which directly result in the achievement of the enterprise's goals. The staff function includes all other activities which assist the line in fulfilling enterprise objectives.

TERMS FOR REVIEW

management	*procedure*	*span of control*
work system	*departmentalization*	*chain of command*
planning	*staffing*	*line function*
objectives	*authority*	*staff function*
policy	*responsibility*	

QUESTIONS

1. How is the management of organizations such as government and educational institutions similar to the management of business enterprises? How does the management of business enterprises differ from the management of other institutions?

2. Discuss the relationships between the technical, organizational, and human subsystems in a business enterprise. Give a specific example of how changes in one subsystem affect the other two subsystems.

3. An owner of a small business recently commented, "I can't afford to take the time to plan because of all the immediate problems I have to solve." What comments would you make to this businessperson about the importance of planning and its benefits?

4. Why is consistency of policy adminstration important in managing the enterprise? Does consistency mean that there should never be variations in policy administration? Explain your answer.

5. Determine the nature of departmentalization in a business with which you are familiar, or obtain a copy of a corporation's annual report from a stock brokerage firm or by writing to the secretary of the corporation. Draw up an organization chart of the enterprise showing its present form of organization. What other methods of organization could the enterprise have utilized? What possible advantages could be gained from a different form of organization?

6. a. When vacancies occur in key management positions in the business enterprise, what are the advantages of filling these positions with persons presently employed by the enterprise?

   b. What are the advantages of filling key management vacancies with persons from outside the firm?

7. What problems can arise if supervisors do not understand their responsibilities and the authority delegated to them?

8. What are the strengths and weaknesses of:
   a. A narrow span of control?
   b. A wide span of control?

9. Would you like to work for a company with an approach as reflected in the annual report of Burroughs on the first page of this chapter? Why?

business briefs

"WHEN YOU CARE ENOUGH"

When Hallmark is mentioned, most persons think of greeting cards. Today Hallmark's product line extends considerably beyond greeting cards, and in the future its product line will be even wider.

Hallmark is the leader in the greeting card industry, and its card sales have been growing at a 2 to 4 percent rate annually. However, Hallmark is now selling such items as books, candles, costume jewelry, pewter figurines, and crystal animals. Noncard sales amount to more than $300 million per year and make up almost half of the enterprise's sales.

In 1976 Hallmark acquired Trifari, a costume jewelry manufacturer. Trifari has designed an extensive line of jewelry for exclusive sale through Hallmark card shops.

The backbone of Hallmark's distribution system is the 6,000 independent dealers who own card shops. They account for half of the company's sales. The remainder of Hallmark's sales come from 30,000 card accounts in department stores and other retail outlets, plus a handful of company-owned card shops.

Not all the products Hallmark has introduced have been successful. Board games were withdrawn because their sales were too seasonal and because discount stores proved to be the most popular outlet for board games. Large, expensive coffee-table books were also withdrawn as slow-moving items. In contrast, tiny hardback books with greeting card themes have been big sellers. Some of the items that Hallmark is now experimenting with are puzzles, calendars, photographs, and a large array of bath products for gift giving.

1. *Why would Hallmark want to diversify its product line when it is the leader in the greeting card field?*
2. *What are the risks of such diversification?*
3. *What elements already exist that will tend to aid expansion of the Hallmark product line?*
4. *What criteria would you suggest for Hallmark's new products?*

BEHAVIOR MODELING

A wide variety of enterprises, including the Ford Motor Company, Lukens Steel, Exxon, AT&T, and General Electric, are using a form of management training called behavior modeling with considerable success.

A behavior modeling program begins with a short discussion with both inexperienced and experienced supervisory trainees of some principles of behavior based on good human relations. These principles may include helping the employee to feel at ease, asking the employee for ideas on how a job can be made more interesting, and emphasizing the importance of maintaining and enhancing the employee's self-image.

After these basic points are discussed with the management trainees, a videotape or a training movie is viewed which lasts about 15 minutes and shows a manager in a discussion with an employee. The manager is applying the basic principles being taught. By watching another supervisor deal with a potentially difficult situation, the management trainees are provided with a model rather than simply being lectured to or assigned a textbook.

After the videotape or training movie, the trainees act out a role-playing situation dealing with a specific issue or employee problem, such as excessive absenteeism, tardiness, or performance improvement. Trainees take turns playing supervisor and employee. Then, guided by an experienced management trainer, they critique each other's performance in applying principles of good management.

Management consulting firms across the country have developed packaged videotaped modules, cassettes, and slides dealing with various behavior modeling situations. Many enterprises, especially larger firms, prefer to develop their own programs, using managers who are known to trainees in the modeling demonstrations.

The emphasis in behavior modeling sessions is on problem solving and not on disciplining a particular employee with whom a problem has been encountered. Follow-up sessions are sometimes held to reinforce trainees' learning after they have had time to put their training into practice.

1. *What might be some advantages of the behavior modeling approach of supervisory training over conventional classroom learning?*
2. *What might be possible problems of behavior modeling?*
3. *List some of the advantages of packaged programs and of custom programs.*
4. *What might be some positive effects of working with employees to solve problems rather than concentrating on disciplinary action?*
5. *How may the effectiveness of behavior modeling programs for managers be measured?*

case

UNITED INSURANCE COMPANY

Sharon Findlay, office manager of the Aton district office of United Insurance Company, was faced with the question of what to do about the absenteeism of one of the most efficient typists in the office.

Sharon prided herself on having been consistent in applying personnel policies since she had been promoted to office manager eight months ago. Under her supervision were five analysts, four typists, three filing clerks, and a mailroom clerk. Typing and clerical work were sent into the office from other departments of the Aton district. The analysts worked on specific policy problems which were reported by the agents and referred by the district sales manager for detailed study.

The written personnel policies issued by the company's home office were quite explicit regarding absenteeism. Employees were expected to be at work on time. Absenteeism was viewed as a serious matter except for genuine cases of personal hardship. District managers, who were in charge of all operations, were directed to draw up specific procedures to be followed in dealing with absenteeism in their districts. The Aton district's written personnel policies stated that the procedure to be followed for unexcused absenteeism was:

First unexcused absence—oral warning by the supervisor.

Second unexcused absence—written warning by the supervisor.

Third unexcused absence—two days' suspension without pay.

Fourth unexcused absence—discharge of the employee.

Whether the absence was excused was left up to the supervisor. However, the district manager indicated that absences due to personal illness, family illness, or death of a relative would be considered excused, provided that the supervisor was notified at the time. Other reasons for being absent would have to be evaluated by the immediate supervisor. United Insurance Company had a company-wide policy allowing up to seven working days annually for such "excused" absences.

Shortly after she was named office manager, Sharon Findlay fired one of the filing clerks for excessive absenteeism. The young woman had failed to come to work for reasons which Sharon had not considered "excused." She had been warned according to the established procedure. After the fourth absence Sharon Findlay dismissed her after briefly outlining the case to the district manager.

Now a similar situation had arisen with one of the best typists in the office. Jayne Jones had been absent three times in the past four months without what Sharon Findlay considered to be a satisfactory explanation. Following the third absence Sharon sent Jayne home for two days without pay. At the time, Jayne indicated that she had been having problems with her parents and really needed her job to enable her to pay some debts and then to move into an apartment she had been looking for. Jayne had been hired about six months ago and had proved to be an excellent worker except for the recent absences.

On Monday morning, two weeks after her third absence, Jayne called in sick. Late that afternoon an agent for the company returned to the office and remarked to Sharon Findlay as he passed her desk, "Say, I saw Jayne Jones this afternoon at the Crestview shopping center. I thought she worked in this office."

The agent's remark disturbed Sharon Findlay. She knew that Jayne had a number of friends in the office force and that the typing section functioned more smoothly when Jayne was there. Sharon was aware that some managers were more liberal than she in the interpretation of unexcused absences. On the other hand, she wanted to avoid future morale problems in the office which could occur if she "let Jayne get away with something." Sharon knew that her future promotion depended on how well she managed the office and on whether the work was done efficiently. She wondered what she should do about Jayne.

1. *What should Sharon Findlay do at this point? Discuss both the immediate and long-range actions to be taken.*
2. *Discuss the merits and limitations of consistency in policy administration.*

Merck reports . . .

Management has long been of the opinion that the primary responsibility for the integrity and objectivity of the company's financial statements rest with management and the Board of Directors. The financial statements report on management's stewardship of company assets, and are prepared in conformity with generally accepted accounting principles. To this end, management maintains a strong system of internal controls and procedures which provides assurances that financial information is reliable and assets are safeguarded. Fundamental to the control system is the careful selection, training, and development of professional operating and financial managers; an organizational alignment that provides appropriate division of responsibility; and a communications program aimed at assuring that company policies and procedures are understood throughout the organization. A staff of internal auditors is used worldwide to evaluate the adequacy and application of these controls, compliance with company policies and procedures, and the accountability and safeguarding of company assets.

The company's financial statements are examined by the independent public accountants. The auditors' report expresses an independent, informed judgment as to the fairness of management's reported operating results and financial condition. To arrive at this judgment, the auditors review the company's accounting and internal controls and perform other tests and auditing procedures as they deem necessary.

The Board of Directors pursues its responsibility for the company's financial statements through its Audit Committee, which was established in 1956 and consists solely of outside directors. The Audit Committee periodically meets with the independent public accountants, management, and internal auditors to assure that all are carrying out their respective responsibilities. The independent public accountants have full access to the Audit Committee, and meet with it, without management present, to discuss the scope and results of their audit work, including the adequacy of internal controls and the quality of financial reporting.

From the Annual Report of Merck & Co., Inc.

Photo opposite: New antibiotic facilities in Virginia. Supervisor monitors automatic filling operations for Merck's new antibiotic, *Mefoxin,* assisted by two other employees.

7

Control

Control

Control is sometimes referred to as the last step in the management process of planning, organizing, directing, and controlling. However, a good control system will be built into the management process from its beginning.

The control system provides a means of informing management whether other systems are functioning according to plan. Controls also provide a basis for correcting problems which have already occurred.

After studying this chapter, you will be able to answer the following questions regarding control:

How does the process of control relate to management?

What are the elements of a control system?

What are the requirements for effective control systems?

Why is the budgeting process a key management device?

How may the break-even chart be used in controlling profits?

THE PROCESS OF CONTROL

Without a good system of control the technical, organizational, and human subsystems of the business enterprise may be ineffective. The control system measures the progress of the enterprise toward its objectives. Control systems relate to the planning which is done throughout the enterprise. Also, feedback from the control process points out the need for adjustments in plans.

Control enables management to coordinate different activities by measuring actual output against expected performance. Control systems usually focus on a limited number of measurements. This means that management should concentrate on control systems for enterprise activities which are both controllable and important. Standards in the established enterprise should relate to past performance as well as absolute standards set by management.

If the enterprise is to achieve its goals, many persons must work together for the common good. There is a need for cooperation and a certain amount of conformity on the part of employees. Control systems help maintain individual behavior within limits which make possible the efficient operation of the enterprise. However, the control system should also allow for creative changes if the business enterprise is to function at its best.

THE ELEMENTS OF A CONTROL SYSTEM

Whether it is control of production, product quality, personnel performance, or cash, there are three essential elements in a control system. There are the

FIGURE 7–1
Elements of a control system

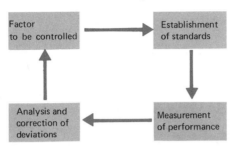

establishment of standards, the measurement of performance, and the analysis and correction of deviations from planned standards. Figure 7–1 illustrates these basic elements.

Establishing standards

Standards provide the guidelines for control systems. There are different types of standards, including monetary standards, physical standards, and intangible standards.

Monetary standards generally relate to the cost of operation, such as materials or labor cost per unit produced. Sometimes monetary standards are stated in terms of revenues, such as the average sales per person. Monetary standards are widely used in business as a means for control when quantitative measurement is possible.

Physical standards, like monetary standards, are frequently quantitative, but they may also be qualitative. Physical standards are quantitative when they are used to measure such things as number of units produced hourly or amount of energy used per unit of production. The qualitative aspect of physical standards includes factors such as the consistency in a color or the tensile strength of metals or fabrics.

Intangible standards cannot be stated precisely in either monetary or physical terms and therefore tend to be difficult to determine. How do you judge the effectiveness of the enterprise's public relations program? Or establish loyalty standards for the president's secretary, who has access to confidential data? Intangible standards are difficult to define but this does not diminish their importance.

In setting standards, the broad objectives of the business must always be kept in mind. Management may become overly impressed with specific quantitative standards which can be easily measured. At the same time management may miss the significance of broader issues which will have a greater impact on profits. For example, a sales manager may keep logs on long-distance telephone calls in an attempt to eliminate unnecessary telephone expense. However, a telephone expense account may be overcontrolled. Greater use of the telephone might increase sales and profits. Similar examples can be found in other areas of control.

Measuring performance

If a standard has been set properly, the measurement of performance should be relatively simple. With routine production work the question may be direct. Do the results meet the standard? On the other hand, measuring performance against a standard is not so easy in a shop where all work is custom orders and each order requires a different combination of patterns and materials. In such a job-lot shop the careful analyst may be able to set meaningful standards. However, more allowance for variations may be necessary than in the routine production line.

A more difficult area is the evaluation of managers. A production manager can be evaluated by the performance of the production department, or a sales manager by the number of units sold. However, there may be conditions beyond the control of these managers which will affect the results in their departments. Evaluation of the performance of a staff executive such as a personnel manager is even more difficult. As a staff executive, the personnel manager may give excellent advice, but line managers may choose to ignore it.

Analysis and correction of deviations

A good control process includes an analysis of deviations from standards and suggests the corrections needed to bring performance back within acceptable limits. The analysis of deviations illustrates how controls should be built into the total management of the enterprise and not be added on after plans are made, resources assembled, and action initiated. Management should establish expectations for results throughout a project's development cycle and should devise means for making corrections before the project encounters serious problems.

Most control systems tend to emphasize the negative factors of performance. Management becomes concerned when productivity in a department fails to reach expectations or when the sales of a product do not meet quotas. In these cases the control system seeks an explanation for the unexpected deviations. Production or sales personnel are prodded to meet goals. Too often management fails to give praise when something is done correctly or when an objective is exceeded by good performance. Mobilizing employees to do their best is likely to be most effective when communication is not limited to criticism of an individual or a department for below-standard performance.

REQUIREMENTS FOR EFFECTIVE CONTROL

The controls needed in an enterprise will vary, depending on its size, the nature of the work performed, and the degree of accuracy and detail required.

However, certain characteristics apply to any good control system. Controls should be diagnostic, therapeutic, accurate, timely, understandable, and economical.

Controls should be diagnostic

Controls should apply to significant processes or problems. Controls ought to point out mistakes and deviations for management attention. Controls should be sensitive enough to report deviations in time so that action may be taken to remedy the situation before too much harm is done.

Controls should be therapeutic

The effective control system not only calls attention to deviations but also suggests a means of curing the difficulty. Today's automated processes have built-in corrections for variations from standards. Even in less automated systems the controls should suggest a solution to the problem. Sometimes the reasons for deviations will be difficult to determine. A skilled analyst may be required to solve the problem.

Controls should be accurate and timely

Controls should be both accurate and timely in reporting deviations. This may create conflicts. In striving for a high degree of accuracy, more time may be required to seek additional data to increase the certainty of one's conclusions.

An example of conflict between accuracy and timeliness can be seen in a typical problem of the market research director. To determine the success of a new product the market research director might require a carefully selected sample of sales reports and reactions from customers. After receiving this information and processing it to remove sampling errors, the marketing executive would be prepared to report how closely the demand for the new product conforms to expectations. However, consider the time and expense required for such a lengthy analysis. Often management cannot wait this long before setting production schedules and starting sales promotion programs. More rapid analysis, based on less elaborate data, may be necessary for immediate control. Later more detailed analysis can be used in a report on total campaign effectiveness.

When time and accuracy come into conflict in controlling operations, then management must decide which is more critical. The answer will depend on the importance of the decision, the time pressure under which management is operating, and how helpful the additional information is likely to be in making a better decision.

Controls should be understandable

The most sophisticated control systems are likely to be worthless if they are not understood by those who need the information they provide. Technical

career outlook

STATISTICIANS

Statistics are numbers that help describe the characteristics of the world and its inhabitants. Statisticians devise, carry out, and interpret the numerical results of surveys and experiments.

Often statisticians are able to obtain accurate information about a group of people or things by surveying a small portion, called a sample, rather than the whole group. Statisticians determine the type and size of the sample group, decide where to get the data, and develop the survey questionnaire or the reporting form. They also prepare instructions for workers who will tabulate the returns.

Statisticians who design experiments prepare mathematical models to test a particular theory. Those in analytic work interpret collected data and summarize their findings in tables, charts, and written reports.

About two out of three statisticians are in private industry, primarily in manufacturing, public utilities, finance, and insurance companies.

A bachelor's degree with a major in statistics or mathematics is the minimum educational requirement for many beginning jobs in statistics. For other beginning statistical jobs, however, a bachelor's degree with a major in an applied field such as economics or natural science and a minor in statistics is preferable.

Required subjects for statistics majors include mathematics through differential and integral calculus, statistical methods, and probability theory. Courses in computer uses and techniques, if not required, are highly recommended. For quality control positions, training in engineering or a physical or biological science and training in the application of statistical methods to manufacturing processes are desirable.

The employment opportunities for persons who combine training in statistics with knowledge of a field or application are expected to be favorable through the mid-1980s. Private industry will require increasing numbers of statisticians for quality control in manufacturing. Business firms will rely more heavily than in the past on statisticians to forecast sales, analyze business conditions, modernize accounting procedures, and help solve management problems.

and staff personnel have a special responsibility to explain control systems to line personnel who will be judged by those controls. Line management must be made aware of how controls may improve operations and profitability. Then the line manager should see that subordinates understand the controls appropriate to their areas.

Frequently, the most significant difficulties in initiating new control systems are not technical problems but involve human relations and communications. A new report form, thrust into the hands of a supervisor without an adequate explanation, may not be filled out properly. You should not be surprised if the form, for which the supervisor sees no clear purpose, ends up at the bottom of a pile of paperwork.

Controls should be economical

The cost of controls should be justified in terms of the profit objectives of the business system. Controls should not be so elaborate that they become an end in themselves. The amount spent on controls should depend on the importance of the process being controlled, the loss which might be incurred without controls, and the size of the enterprise's operations. The elaborate control systems with sophisticated computers used by McDonnell-Douglas Corporation and the National Aeronautics and Space Agency to track space explorations are obviously ridiculous for the small clothing shop. However, economy is a relative concept. Effective controls for a small enterprise are just as necessary for profitable management as are the extensive control systems used in a giant industrial firm. Under any circumstances, the cost of controls should not exceed the savings to be gained from them.

THE BUDGET—A KEY MANAGEMENT DEVICE

The budget is a key device for management in the planning, coordination, and control of operations. Budgets outline in quantitative terms the planned operations of the enterprise for a specified period of time. The budgeting process begins with the goals of top management for the enterprise. Data are gathered from marketing and production and translated into budgets which will become a financial plan of expected expenditures, receipts, and profits. Thus, budgeting translates the goals of the enterprise into quantitative terms and also sets a basis for control. The budget provides a guideline for informing departments of their part in the overall plans of the enterprise.

Though budgeting practice varies among business enterprises, three types of budgets are widely used in business. These are operations budgets, cash budgets, and capital budgets.

The operations budget

The *operations budget,* sometimes called the revenue and expense budget, consists of a forecast of expected sales along with an estimate of the costs necessary to achieve the sales goal. Usually this budget will be made up in detail for the year ahead, though sometimes estimates for two or three years are also made. However, the most important part of the operations budget is the estimate of revenues and expenses for the coming year.

The revenues portion of the operations budget comes from a forecast of sales. Since the sale of goods or services is the main source of operating revenues for business enterprises, the sales forecast is a key variable in operations budgeting. The information for developing the sales forecast comes from both external and internal sources.

External sources of sales estimates are economic data developed by public and private agencies. The federal government is the most important source of national economic data. The U.S. Department of Commerce issues the monthly *Survey of Current Business,* which contains information useful for all business enterprises. Both the *Federal Reserve Bulletin,* published monthly by the Board of Governors in Washington, D.C., and *Economic Indicators,* issued by the staff of the Joint Congressional Committee on the Economic Report, contain timely economic data. The U.S. Bureau of the Census provides useful information to business on a national or regional basis.

Private sources of business news include the daily *Wall Street Journal,* the weekly *Business Week,* and a number of magazines such as *Fortune* and *Dun's Review.* These publications provide information on general business trends and an analysis of economic developments. A wide variety of trade publications are also available for particular industries. Trade journals not only interpret the broad economic view but through the cooperation of member firms collect and present data for their own industries.

General economic data obtained externally must be analyzed by the particular enterprise and integrated with other material. Sampling techniques are available whereby the enterprise can conduct its own surveys to obtain information about consumer attitudes or reactions to its products. This market research is valuable when the sample is properly prepared and the survey is well done.

The enterprise must also use internal data in preparing the sales forecast. These data come from reports of sales personnel, marketing managers, and top executives, and from an analysis of past sales.

After the sales forecast has been made, a sales budget is drawn up. This

"Explain it? Flowers, cocktails, dinner, champagne . . . come now, Mr. Strickland—don't be naive."

Reprinted by permission The Wall Street Journal

sales budget translates plans into quantitative terms not only for anticipated revenues but also for the expenditures necessary to generate those revenues. This means that anticipated costs for product development, advertising, and sales promotion are part of the operations budget.

To check on results, the sales budget is broken down by products and months. Without this detailed breakdown a comparison of actual results with expectations would be relatively useless for good direction and control. All salespersons should have their own budgets so that they can check their own performance as well as be subject to management's evaluation.

Budget review and flexibility   A means of review and revision is necessary if the operations budget is to be useful as a control device. The prompt reporting of actual sales results and comparison with the budget provide the basis of control. There is no point in setting up a budget and blindly pursuing it without regard to later developments. Marketing executives should be able to make immediate adjustments to new opportunities or difficulties.

This does not mean that the basic operations budget is changed every time the actual results vary from the projected sales or every time circumstances change. The basic budget should serve as a frame of reference, with an explanation being made for variations which are bound to occur. This should not prevent revisions during the year, as circumstances dictate, to make the budget more meaningful for coordination of the activities of the enterprise.

Sometimes two operations budgets representing the extremes of business optimism and pessimism will be drawn up for a year. One will be based on the assumption of excellent economic conditions, with the highest level of sales projected. This will be compared with a budget projecting the lowest level of operations and assuming less positive economic circumstances and less effective results from management programs. Then the most likely forecast, which normally comes somewhere between the extremes, will be outlined. This most probable expectation is adopted as the budget for the coming period, with spending programs and expected sales being based on it. However, contingency budgets are prepared to be put into effect if results improve beyond expectations or if they do not measure up to budgeted figures.

Simplified example of an operations budget

Figure 7–2 is an operations budget for a small retail enterprise showing operating results for 1979 and the operations budget for 1980. The management is projecting an increase in sales of 20 percent based on its analysis that 1979 was not a good year for retail sales in the area because of a high level of unemployment. Also, the owner plans to increase advertising spending by 50 percent in 1980, which should stimulate sales. This budget was prepared during the latter part of 1979 and finalized as the 1980 budget period began.

The operations budget is a means of systematic planning for the future and a basis for control. Actual results can be compared with budgeted plans to determine whether operations are conforming to expectations. In practice the

FIGURE 7–2
Tot-Teen Shop operations budget—1980

	Actual 1979	Budget 1980
Sales	$70,000	$84,000
Cost of merchandise sold	42,000	50,000
Gross profit on sales	$28,000	$34,000
Operating expenses		
Selling expenses		
Sales salaries	$10,200	$10,400
Advertising	2,400	3,600
Miscellaneous selling expenses	400	500
Total selling expenses	$13,000	$14,500
General expenses		
General salaries	$ 4,800	$ 5,200
Rent	2,400	2,400
Utilities	900	1,000
Miscellaneous taxes	700	900
Insurance	300	300
Miscellaneous general expenses	1,200	1,600
Total general expenses	$10,300	$11,400
Total operating expenses	23,300	25,900
Profit from operations	$ 4,700	$ 8,100
Income taxes	1,200	2,100
Net profit	$ 3,500	$ 6,000

owner of the Tot-Teen Shop would prepare more detailed budgets for each department or for major items in the budget. This would aid remedial action if results were below expectations. Also, the annual budget would usually be broken into quarterly or monthly budgets to improve its timeliness and usefulness.

Cash budgets

The cash budget is an estimate of the business enterprise's cash receipts and cash payments over a specified period of time. This budget is used to forecast requirements for cash during future periods. It is a helpful means of justifying a request for a short-term loan from a bank to finance a seasonal increase in business operations.

The cash budget usually extends over the year ahead, with cash receipts and disbursements being estimated on a monthly basis. When closer control is justified, the inflows and outflows of cash will be estimated on a semimonthly, weekly, or daily basis. The cash budget can be adapted to any time period which will help management do a better job of estimating cash needs, planning for short-term loans, or investing surplus cash. The complexity of the cash budget will depend on the needs of the enterprise and on the nature of cash inflows and outflows and the degree of their predictability.

The cash budget can be useful as a planning tool since it requires management to review the entire operation. Besides being used for planning normal cash receipts and disbursements for operations, the cash budget can be used to plan future capital spending for equipment or building improvements.

Capital budgets

The capital budget consists of investment plans for assets which will last longer than a year. Such capital budgeting items include machinery, buildings, land, and improvements to facilities. Like the operations budget, the capital budget is usually prepared for the year immediately ahead. However, capital budgets are also prepared for a longer period in the future to program large-scale investments and to coordinate finance, production, and marketing activities associated with major long-term programs.

The capital budget is a list of proposed investment projects, and it normally includes a justification for each item on the list. One important criterion for justification of a capital investment proposal is the rate of return which the project is expected to yield. However, not all projects requiring capital investment can be evaluated on the basis of their profit returns since not all generate profits or savings. Capital expenditures such as money spent on an employees' cafeteria or on paving the parking lot cannot be measured by the percentage of return on the investment. Instead, this type of expenditure is usually justified by improved morale, convenience, appearance, or safety.

Approval of the capital budget is normally done by the board of directors after budget committees have analyzed the capital budgets of the various departments of the business enterprise. Once a major capital expenditure has been approved in principle, the managers who have responsibility for the project present detailed plans for final authorization of actual cash spending commitments.

The level of management which actually authorizes specific capital expenditures depends on the amount of money involved and on the policies adopted in each enterprise. An example of the type of authority required for capital expenditures might be something like this:

Departmental superintendents may authorize capital spending up to $500.

The factory manager may approve capital investments of $500 to $2,500.

The finance committee of the board of directors may approve projects of $2,500 to $20,000.

Full board of directors' approval is required on all capital investment projects of over $20,000.

Once approval has been granted for a capital investment project, control should be a continuing part of the procedure. Reports should be prepared to show how nearly actual expenditures are in line with planned spending. This check continues through the construction and installation phases. After the project begins operation, the anticipated rate of return on the investment or the expected savings are compared with the amounts projected when the proposal was approved. Postcompletion audits of capital budgeting projects are essential to check on profit progress and to improve future budget planning.

COST ACCOUNTING FOR CONTROL

The accounting system in the business enterprise provides a means for control. Cost accounting generates data which can be used to establish centers of managerial responsibility for judging performance. Responsibility centers can be established for a division, a department, or at the supervisor's level wherever costs can be controlled. Cost accounting provides a basis for analyzing the controllable costs in a responsibility center.

When a responsibility center's activities generate measurable revenues, it is possible to designate a profit center where not only costs but also profits are analyzed. It is not feasible to designate all responsibility centers as profit centers since not all subsystems have operations which directly produce revenues. A manufacturing department can usually be divided into profit centers. However, the engineering department which provides staff services is not judged on its profit contributions but on how well it assists other departments.

Another important aspect of cost accounting is assigning the proper costs to each unit of production. This helps determine product costs, pricing decisions, and profit planning. Cost accounting may also be used to provide information on the expected costs of taking various courses of action in the future. Cost accounting is a valuable planning and decision-making tool as well as being useful for control purposes.

The accounting statements discussed in Chapter 14 provide information which is the basis for other financial controls.

BREAK-EVEN ANALYSIS

The technique of break-even analysis can be a useful management planning and control device for understanding the relationship between costs and revenues at different levels of operations. The break-even chart, sometimes called the profitgraph, assumes a particular pattern of variable and fixed costs and provides management with an estimate of profits or losses that would occur at various levels of sales. In constructing a break-even chart, first the cost functions are analyzed and then the sales revenue function is added.

Recall from Chapter 2 that *variable costs* are directly influenced by the number of units produced. Variable costs include such expenses as the materials used in the production of goods and the wages of production workers. *Fixed costs* are those costs which continue whether or not the enterprise is producing goods. Fixed costs include such expenses as rent, property taxes, and the interest on borrowed money.

FIGURE 7–3
Estimated cost structure

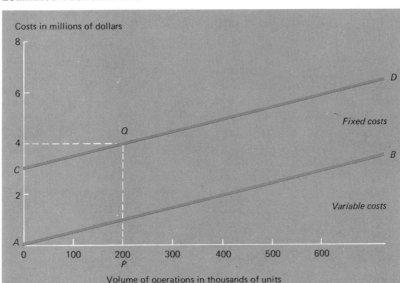

Variable costs are calculated at $5 per unit.
Fixed costs are at a level of $3 million for the range of operations from 0 to 600,000 units annually.

Figure 7–3 illustrates fixed and variable costs. At any volume of operations the sum of fixed and variable costs equals total costs at that level of units. Variable costs in this example are estimated at $5 per unit. Therefore, the variable costs line, *AB*, increases at a rate of $5 for each additional unit produced to reflect the added costs of materials and labor for the extra units. Thus at the zero level of production there are no variable costs, while at the level of 200,000 units of production the total variable costs equal $1 million.

Fixed costs of $3 million remain constant regardless of the level of output for this particular business enterprise. Fixed costs are shown on Figure 7–3 as the vertical distance between the *AB* and *CD* lines on the chart. At a level of zero units of production the fixed costs of $3 million are shown by the distance between points A and C.

Total costs of operations for the enterprise are represented by the *CD* line, which includes both the total variable costs and fixed costs at any particular volume level. Total costs can be verified for any level of production by multiplying the units produced by the $5 variable costs per unit and adding the $3 million fixed costs. For example, if the 200,000 units of production are multiplied by the $5 per unit variable cost, this equals $1 million. The $1 million variable cost figure added to the $3 million fixed cost figure means that the total cost of producing 200,000 units is $4 million, the distance from *P* to *Q*.

In the second stage, Figure 7–4 is the complete break-even chart. It has the same cost structure as Figure 7–3. However, now a sales revenue line,

FIGURE 7–4
Break-even chart

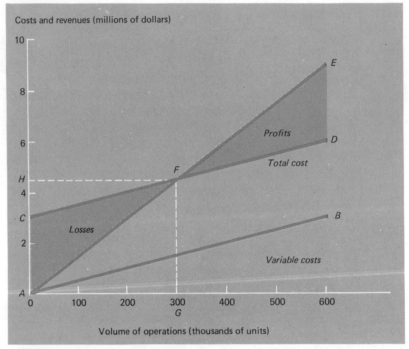

Costs and revenues (millions of dollars)

Volume of operations (thousands of units)

Variable costs are calculated at $5 per unit. Fixed costs are calculated at $3 million total. Sales revenue is calculated at $15 per unit.

designated as *AE,* has been added to complete the revenue and cost relationship. Sales revenue increases at a rate of $15 per unit, the assumed price for which each unit of the enterprise's product could be sold. The rate of sales revenue increase is constant, which implies that each unit is sold at the same price, regardless of the number of units sold.

Notice that the total revenue line, *AE,* crosses the total costs line, *CD,* at point *F.* Point *F,* called the break-even point, is where revenues equal costs. In this example this is at a level of sales of 300,000 units, marked by point *G,* and at a cost of $4,500,000, marked by point *H.* At the break-even point the enterprise is neither earning a profit nor incurring a loss. At sales levels higher than *G* the enterprise generates a profit from operations. Below the break-even point, sales revenue is insufficient to cover total costs and the enterprise suffers a loss.

The break-even chart is useful in demonstrating the factors which affect profits and the ways in which profits may be controlled. The break-even chart shows that profits will vary for each level of operations. The level of profits increases as sales increase past the break-even point. There are four ways in which the profit of a business can be increased, each of which can be analyzed through break-even analysis:

Variable costs per unit can be decreased.

Fixed costs can be decreased.

The selling price per unit can be increased.

More units can be sold.

In order to see the limitations in the use of break-even analysis you should keep in mind the assumptions on which the chart is based. It is assumed that variable costs increase at a constant rate; that is, materials costs and direct labor costs are the same for each additional unit of production. Fixed costs are the same throughout the given range of operations, assuming no changes in the level of capital invested or changes in overhead which would alter the fixed costs. It is assumed that there will be no changes in the market which may affect selling prices.

SUMMARY

Control is an important part of the management process. Control provides a means for measuring the progress which an enterprise is making toward its objectives. The three elements of control are the establishment of standards, the measurement of performance, and the analysis and correction of deviations from expectations.

Control systems will vary with the nature of the enterprise. However, any good control system should be diagnostic, therapeutic, accurate, timely, understandable, and economical.

The budget is a key control device. Budgets outline in quantitative terms the planned operations of the business system for a specified period of time. A variety of budgets are used, including operations budgets, cash budgets, and capital budgets.

Cost accounting generates data which can be used to establish centers of managerial responsibility for judging performance. Cost accounting can be used to assign costs for each unit of production for the determination of product costs, pricing decisions, or profit planning.

Break-even analysis is a useful planning and control device for understanding the relationship between costs and revenues at different levels of operations.

TERMS FOR REVIEW

control

standards

budget

operations budget (revenue
   and expense budget)

sales budget

cash budget

capital budget

cost accounting

break-even chart

QUESTIONS

1. What is the purpose of control in the business enterprise?

2. What recommendations would you make to the owner of a new manufacturing enterprise for the development of a control system? What different types of controls would be needed?

3. Explain the requirements of an effective control system.

4. What is a budget? Why are budgets important?

5. Outline a step-by-step procedure for developing an operations budget for a manufacturer supplying replacement auto parts to wholesale supply distributors on the West Coast. How would you develop the sales forecast for such an enterprise?

6. What is the relationship of the capital budget to the operations budget and the cash budget?

7. In what ways is cost accounting useful to management?

8. Describe the elements of Merck's control system outlined on the first page of this chapter. Why should the corporation's directors be concerned with these controls?

business brief

ZERO-BASE BUDGETING

An approach to budgeting which has attracted increasing attention is zero-base budgeting.

Zero-base budgeting requires a justification of every dimension of an operation which is being done and which is proposed to be done. Instead of simply showing proposed budget increases for the coming period (as is usually the case for the operations budget), managers must justify the total functioning of their departments and the funds necessary to continue operations. Alternatives must be presented showing any increases or decreases in department activities. Such an approach requires a complete analysis and justification of operations or new investments from the ground up. This tends to prevent managers from simply asking for a fixed dollar amount to increase their budgets or a percentage increase, perhaps to carry out activities not really essential to the business enterprise.

The zero-base budgeting approach began in the 1960s with Texas Instruments, the large electronics firm based in Dallas. The first application of the concept came in developing a system for evaluating research and development projects. This consisted of describing the project, the consequences of not proceeding with the project, alternative courses of action, and the estimated costs and benefits. This analysis made up a decision package which provided information on whether to proceed with a specific project.

In addition to Texas Instruments, a variety of other large corporations have used the concept of zero-base budgeting. These include Allied Van Lines, Westinghouse Electric, and Xerox.

1. *What advantages does zero-base budgeting have over the conventional operations and capital budgets?*

2. *What problems have to be overcome when starting zero-base budgeting in an enterprise?*

cases

JIM RADER, PROPRIETOR

After several years as foreman and chief estimator for the McGill Cabinet Shop, Jim Rader quit to begin his own woodworking shop. Two of the best craftsmen at McGill quit to join Jim's operation. Some custom orders were received, and an initial order was obtained from a local lumberyard for preassembled door frames and windows which would keep the men occupied for a period of time.

Despite this good start for his new enterprise, Jim Rader was concerned as he recalled the nature of the control system used by his former employer. Jim felt that if his business were to prosper he would need controls on the costs and quality of his products. However, he was dissatisfied with the control system which he had seen in the McGill Shop.

Jim called his friend Larry Thomas, a certified public accountant and a partner in a local accounting firm. He asked for an appointment to discuss the new business and the controls he would need.

"Larry," began Jim, "I want to approach you for some help with my new business. We have been successful initially in generating business, and I am pleased with the quality of our work force. However, at McGill I never did get a clear understanding of their control system. If what they had represents good controls, I don't want any part of it. I would like you to analyze my business and indicate what controls I need."

"We are prepared to do a control analysis for you," responded the consultant. "Most of my time is spent in providing management consulting services to our clients rather than more traditional accounting work.

"Why don't you tell me about the controls you didn't like at your former situation and what your present operations are like. After that I can proceed with a preliminary written report for you. Then we can talk it over before any elaborate system is designed. Among other things, you will need to control such items as the cost of consultants!"

"To begin with," Jim said, "it seemed like McGill's management was penny-wise and pound-foolish. One thing that really bugged me was telephone usage in the shop. Part of my job consisted of contacting customers as a technical adviser. It would have been easier to call out-of-town customers than to write letters.

But Bill McGill, the company president, put his foot down on the use of long-distance telephone calls and said that such calls would be held to a minimum. Also, every time I made a long-distance call I had to fill out a chit for the bookkeeper so when the phone bill came in it could be checked to see that none of us were making personal calls which were billed to the company.

"Another thing I didn't like was the way the bookkeeper kept pestering the foremen for their time sheets and materials-in-process reports. You would have thought that everything revolved around the bookkeeper's office in that shop. I guess Mr. McGill thought so too, since he was always complaining to the office force about not having reports completed on time.

"We never knew how we stood with the company, although the Christmas bonuses paid out by the McGills were sure nice. However, very little was ever said on how things were going in the shop unless McGill came down to complain about something going wrong.

"I wonder," continued Jim Rader, "why I stuck it out as long as I did at McGill's. The old-timers said that Mr. McGill had been like that ever since his son was killed in Vietnam in 1967. Also, the firm does have a good reputation for quality work. I learned a lot there, and the money was good. When I quit, Mr. McGill seemed surprised. He said he had me picked to be promoted to general manager of the shop when Sam Jones retired in a few years! That was news to me, and by then I had already made up my mind to start my own business.

"There was one good thing done in McGill's shop. That was the care which all the foremen were forced to use in keeping the jobs separate. Most of their business is custom work. Every stick of wood that went into a job was accounted for. They knew which jobs they came out on and which lost money. Not many jobs lost money!

"My business is a small one at present. We have two men working in the shop. I also employ a student part time. Most of the office work is done by my wife who comes in when she can. I do all the selling and order all the raw materials. I think we have the beginning of something which could work out very nicely, but I don't want to foul it up by too many controls or not enough."

1. *Appraise the control system in the McGill Cabinet Shop as described by Jim Rader. Discuss positive and negative elements of the system as it is understood by Rader.*
2. *What steps could the management of the McGill Cabinet Shop have taken to improve the effectiveness of its control system?*
3. *Outline a preliminary report from the accountant's office suggesting the basic nature of the controls needed by Jim Rader at this time. Does Jim Rader need to be concerned with a control system for such a small business? Why or why not?*

A PROBLEM IN PROFIT ANALYSIS

The ABC Manufacturing Corporation had one main product line, for which management believed rather accurate costs had been calculated. Between production levels of 30,000 and 150,000 units it was estimated that the variable costs were $10 per unit. At these levels of production the fixed costs were about $700,000. The current sales price of the product was $30 per unit in the quantities purchased by most customers.

Required:

1. *Construct a break-even chart showing cost and revenue functions over the range of production indicated.*
   a. *What is the break-even sales volume in units and dollars?*
   b. *What is the amount of profit or loss at 30,000 units of production and sales? At 100,000 units? At 150,000 units?*
2. *In what ways could this analysis be helpful to the management of ABC Manufacturing Corporation?*
3. *What limitations are there to this analysis?*

Human elements
of administration

SECTION
THREE

Borg-Warner reports . . .

Middle managers keep getting messages from the top about how to succeed. These usually don't stress being a manager of people; they stress being a profit maker. Unless the messages from the top change, the managers won't.

Somebody has to take the initiative: a strong leader in control of one segment of the business, who wants to change the way it manages human resources. Often this happens in a crisis, when a company must find some new chemistry to survive. But well before that, enlightened managers will say: "We're just holding our own, and that's not good enough. We're going to shoot for a new level of productive effectiveness, by getting our people involved."

Of course without a strong backup of job security, productivity improvement can be seen as a threat. Workers know if you increase efficiency faster than sales, you'll need fewer people. So workers and unions resist it.

How do you build trust, so people involve themselves without fear? There are two ways to reward contribution: the individual approach, which is antisocial. It's like a piecework incentive, where you reward the ratebuster who makes the others look bad. If group performance improves, you penalize them by raising the standard. It's not fair.

The other way is by team building. We're learning more and more that work fulfills a need for social contact. As the family is weakened and divorce rates go up, we find a third of the labor force living as "singles." People want more teamwork and interaction. Really, the sociology of life must be more integrated with the sociology of work.

Society changes faster than the workplace. Look where we've gone in this decade on abortion, open marriage, the 18-year-old vote, women's rights. Then look at the workplace; you find a fortress mentality. Organizations have made only surface adaptations to changing social behavior, allowing such things as long hair and jeans on the job. But a participative organization is what people want.

A new Yankelovich study shows 62 percent of young workers say they have a right to participate in job decisions, and half of *all* workers agree, regardless of age. Another study deals with authority. In 1969, 70 percent said they'd accept orders from a boss, whether or not they agreed with the order. By 1975, 70 percent said they would not follow orders they disagreed with.

The risks in dealing with people stop most managers from experimenting. It's easier to work on tangible aspects of productivity: investment, product mix, technology.

You've got to make a value judgment: do people mean anything? Can you subordinate them to a process? Or are they free human beings who can give of their ideas and energies in a way that's more valuable for everyone?

Jerome Rosow
President, Work in America Institute

From annual report of Borg-Warner Corporation

Photo opposite: Alice Denton's instruments are a propane torch and a wand of phosphorus and copper, which she wields with an artist's delicacy. A brazer at the York Madisonville plant, she seals copper coils that carry coolant through air conditioning units. "Not everyone can do this job," she says. "It takes concentration and some skill. I worked at a place once where they made bombshells. Somebody has to do it, I guess, but it bothered me making something that would kill people. Here I'm working on something to make people comfortable. I sometimes wonder who gets the air conditioners I help make . . . you hope there's nothing wrong."

Courtesy of Borg-Warner Corporation

Human relations
and direction

Human relations and direction

An understanding of human relations is essential for the effective manager in directing the activities of employees to achieve the objectives of the enterprise.

After studying this chapter, you will be able to answer the following questions related to human relations and direction:

What are the individual needs of employees?

What is the role of direction in the management process?

Which skills are required of the effective manager?

What types of leadership are found in organizations?

How can communication be improved?

Why must both formal and informal organization be considered in improving human relations?

How do status and status symbols relate to the enterprise?

How can managers develop a healthy work climate?

THE INDIVIDUAL AND THE BUSINESS ENTERPRISE

Sometimes managers, particularly those who own a business enterprise, assume that because they are completely devoted to their company's endeavors all employees will be similarly motivated. However, this is simply not true! The good manager will understand the difference between individual employees' goals and enterprise goals, what motivates individual employees, and the importance of human relations in modern management.

Individual needs versus enterprise goals

The principal goal of the business enterprise is to provide goods and services to consumers at a profit. To a certain extent persons employed by a business share this goal, since without the enterprise they would not have their present jobs. However, individuals are also concerned about their personal needs and objectives. These are distinctly separate from the principal goals of the organizations in which they are employed. It is important to provide a climate in the business enterprise that will both satisfy the employees' needs and achieve the economic objectives of the enterprise.

Individuals have physical and material needs which are met largely through wages and fringe benefits. Because of our expanding economy what will satisfy our material needs in the United States has changed greatly over the last 50 years. What was considered a luxury item only a few years ago may be considered a necessity today by a large proportion of the population. The level of wage payments is one factor affecting the morale of the work force. This topic is discussed in the next chapter on personnel management.

However, human relations involve much more. Nonmaterial needs of employees must be considered in developing a good human relations climate. These nonmaterial needs are both psychological and social. Psychological needs pertain to the individual's self-image. These include the needs for love, self-respect, and a feeling of accomplishment. Social needs arise from relations among individuals and groups. These include the needs for recognition, acceptance, and group activity.

Some of these psychological and social needs are met by the family and other groups. However, a large proportion of an individual's waking hours is spent on the job. People cannot shut off their social and psychological needs when they step into the factory or office. Employee morale can be greatly improved when management recognizes and meets these psychological and social needs insofar as possible.

Motivation of the individual

How does management motivate employees to do their work well? Workers act in order to satisfy their needs. Individuals are motivated to work satisfactorily because of their desire for more goods and services. Once material needs have been provided for, then other needs take on a greater importance. Psychologists suggest that in the United States social and psychological needs are becoming more important because we already have a high material standard of living.

The fact that material needs may be considered less important than social and psychological needs is shown by a study of nearly 1,000 managers who changed jobs. It was found that money ranked fifth among reasons they gave for quitting. The four leading factors which ranked above money were: dissatisfaction with the present job; poor chances for advancement; conflicts at work, particularly with the boss; and altered duties or status because of corporate reorganization.

DIRECTION—DEALING WITH PEOPLE AT WORK

Direction is the process of aiding an enterprise's employees in carrying out their jobs. Direction is at the heart of management. Coordinating the activities of many different workers requires the major part of most managers' time. What skills are required of a manager? What are the different types of leadership? How important is communication? As you read the following pages, look for answers to these questions about the direction function of management.

Skills required of the manager

In today's business enterprise the manager's job is complex. Different types of skills are required, depending on the manager's level in the organization. These skills may be classified as technical, human, and conceptual.[1] The mix among these three skills is illustrated in Figure 8–1.

Technical skill consists of a manager's ability in and knowledge of a particular process or technique. Technical skill requires knowledge of things rather than

FIGURE 8–1
Skills required of the effective manager

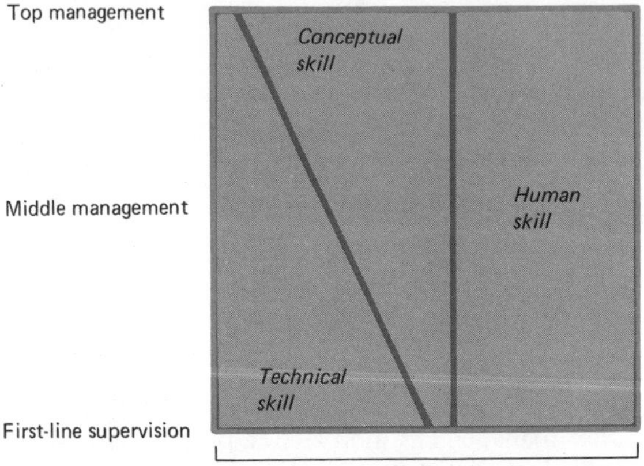

people. Examples of technical skill are to be found in the activities of typists, accountants, and engineers. Technical skill is especially important at the first level of supervision. The higher in management one moves, the less important technical skill becomes. Middle management relies more upon others for technical information than does the first level of supervision and is more involved in human and conceptual problems. A person who reaches top management devotes little or no time to the exercise of technical skills. This may be one reason why top executives with well-developed human and conceptual skills can move easily from one industry to another in positions of high responsibility.

Human skill is the ability to work with people and to build effective work teams. Training in human skills should be part of the orientation of new managers, and human skills should be developed throughout their careers.

Conceptual skill is the ability to diagnose a problem in relation to its total environment and to develop creative solutions. Conceptual skill is very important for top management in formulating long-range plans and making broad policy

---

[1] Robert L. Katz, "Skills of an Effective Administrator," *Harvard Business Review,* September–October 1974, pp. 90–102.

decisions. Conceptual skill deals primarily with ideas, human skill with persons, and technical skill with things.

Different types of leadership

Leadership is the element of direction which causes subordinates to follow. It results in accomplishment of the goals of the enterprise. Leadership can be classified as authoritarian or participative.

With *authoritarian leadership* there is centralized authority and autocratic decision making. Subordinates are given little or no discretion in carrying out work assignments. They merely follow orders! *Participative leadership* decentralizes authority among subordinates. Decisions are made by those who are situated where action is required. Suggestions from subordinates are encouraged. This type of leadership emphasizes communication from the leader to all members of the group and from the group members to the leader.

These two leadership styles, authoritarian and participative, are exercised by what one writer has called "Theory X" and "Theory Y" type managers.[2] Theory X (authoritarian) managers presumably view their employees as being basically lazy, preferring to avoid responsibility, and requiring close supervision and control to achieve enterprise objectives. Theory Y (participative) managers presumably view their employees as work-oriented, anxious to assume responsibility, and willing to exercise initiative to achieve results. These two types of direction are extremes. In practice, elements of both may be observed in most managers.

Authoritarian leadership is sometimes criticized. However, the competent manager who directs in an autocratic manner may be able to accomplish the work of the enterprise quite well, especially in the short run. Less time is required than with participative leadership. Employees do not have to exercise much independent judgment. Therefore, personnel who have fewer capabilities may be hired. Despite some advantages for authoritarian leadership, in the long run the failure to use the capabilities of all employees and the dependence on one person weaken this type of leadership for the business enterprise.

Participative leadership is widely regarded as having the most long-run advantages for the successful business enterprise. Management training programs usually emphasize direction by this method because it tends to maximize employee satisfactions and enterprise productivity. Participative leadership attempts to draw not only upon managers but upon all employees for the smooth functioning of the enterprise.

Participative leadership should not be used unless the manager is genuinely concerned about the views of subordinates. Employees will quickly perceive when it is merely a pretense, and its usefulness will then be severely limited. Under such circumstances the manager might be better advised to use authoritar-

---

[2] Douglas McGregor, *The Human Side of Enterprise* (New York: McGraw-Hill Book Company, 1960).

ian leadership openly so that employees will clearly understand what is expected of them.

Also, not all workers want to share the authority and assume the responsibility that goes with participative management. When employees have been managed autocratically by a previous manager, a new supervisor may encounter difficulties if he attempts to use participative methods. A gradual dispersion of authority throughout the enterprise or department concerned is advisable. Abrupt changes in leadership methods may result in uncertainty and lower morale for the work force. When a manager comes into a new supervisory situation, he or she is well advised to determine what the type of leadership has been before beginning to make changes.

The exercise of good leadership by the manager can result in increased efficiency among employees. With mediocre leadership subordinates will probably carry out their assigned tasks well enough to avoid reprimand or dismissal. However, good leadership can cause employees to put out extra effort above the minimum required.

The importance of good communication

Definition of communication   Good communication is essential in the process of direction. Just what is communication? *Communication* is the transmission of understanding. This requires both a sender and a receiver, each in tune with the other.

A supervisor who, preoccupied by a problem at home, comes into the shop or office one morning and fails to speak to the employees as usual may set the entire department to wondering what is wrong. This may actually reduce production for the day. Failure to greet the employees may be misinterpreted by them as displeasure with something they have done. The boss's comment to an employee, "Chuck, you're doing a hell of a job," may have either positive or negative interpretations, depending on the circumstances. Unless the intent of the boss's remark is crystal clear to the employee, a compliment may be interpreted as a criticism when it was not so intended by the boss.

Communication throughout the organizational structure   There are three dimensions of communication within the organizational structure of the business enterprise. Information can be transmitted down through the organization from superior to subordinates, frequently following the chain of command. Communication may occur as information being sent up from lower echelons to higher levels in the organization. Or there can be horizontal communication as between departments or among employees at about the same level in the organization. Figure 8–2 symbolizes these dimensions of communication.

Too often management personnel assume that the only communication going on is the orders and information they send down to subordinates. However, valuable information may be received from throughout the organization if managers are sensitive to communication feedback. The number of employee griev-

FIGURE 8–2
Diagram of vertical and horizontal communication

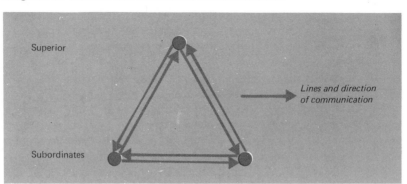

ances and their source, attitudes reflected in absences or high scrap rates, and suggestions by subordinates may be useful information when communicated upward to management. Horizontal communication in the business enterprise can improve coordination between individuals or departments.

Written and spoken communications   Both written and spoken communications have important places in the business enterprise. Written communications are used for policy statements, procedures, rules, job descriptions, advertising, press releases, office memos, letters, and legal documents. Regardless of its nature, a written communication should be stated clearly and concisely, with the reader in mind. The principal advantage of written communications is that they may be retained for future reference. Also, many persons give greater consideration to the written word since they can be more easily held accountable for it.

Written communication has two major disadvantages. First, the volume of paperwork in business and government is reaching staggering proportions. Many reports, contracts, and memorandums are saved to justify decisions should any questions ever be raised. These files frequently far outlive their necessity, and valuable space and clerical help are required for their maintenance.

Second, the fact that information is written does not guarantee that it will be carefully thought out or clearly stated. Furthermore, the written word may be costly by the time it is reproduced and sent to those for whom it is intended.

Spoken communication has the advantages of speed and possible amplification. In face-to-face communication real meaning can be conveyed through tone and facial expression as well as through discussion. The telephone industry has greatly expanded because of the advantage of instant oral communication over great distances.

As with written communication, clarity and conciseness are important in spoken communication. A meeting can involve the valuable time of many persons. Their time should not be wasted by excessive talk. A previously circulated written agenda will help make meetings worthwhile for all participants. The

"This is a recording. You're fired."

Reprinted by permission The Wall Street Journal

main weakness in spoken communication is that it may be difficult to remember exactly what was said unless some record is made of the conversation.

The importance of listening For good communication to occur there must be a communicator who clearly transmits information. It is equally important that the receiver of the information understand what is being said. Effective listening is as important to good communication as clear speaking.

The two elements to consider in effective listening are what the listener hears and what the speaker means. When the listener hears the meaning intended by the speaker, then true oral communication has occurred.

The listener needs to understand the frame of reference of the speaker. Often we do not really understand what is being said to us because instead of listening carefully we are busy evaluating the speaker's words from our own frame of reference. The question running through our minds when someone speaks to us, especially when it is the boss, frequently is, "How is this going to affect me?" A better question would be, "What is this person trying to say?" There will be time later to evaluate the remarks from our own frame of reference. First, we should attempt to understand the speaker's meaning. The next time someone comes to you with a problem or question, listen quietly to what is said without making any judgments. Listen with a view to perceiving the problem through the eyes of the speaker. By doing this, you will have made an important step in improving the communication.

When people listen more effectively they will discover that many miscommunications occur because of the failure of the speaker and the listener to have a similar perception of what the problem is. When persons attempt to discuss a situation which at least one of them views as a problem, one of the most important elements of communication is to establish the dimensions of the problem from the fame of reference of all parties. Then discussion can proceed on the merits of various solutions from the different points of view. Sometimes just a careful definition of the issue results in the conclusion that what was thought to be a problem is really not a problem after all. A lack of communication had resulted in misunderstanding, fear, or frustration.

ORGANIZATIONAL ASPECTS OF HUMAN RELATIONS

Human relations is usually thought of as interpersonal relationships. However, there are also organizational aspects to human relations. The formal and informal organization of the enterprise, the importance of status in organizations, and the labor union are three important organizational elements of human relations. The first two elements are discussed here, and the role of unions is analyzed in Chapter 10.

The formal organization

The formal organization of the business enterprise was discussed in Chapter 6. Every business enterprise of any size is organized into departments. Each department must develop workable authority-responsibility relationships, delegate decision making, and establish the width of the management span of control.

In the formal organization each person occupies a particular position or *status*. This can be diagramed on an organization chart similar to Figure 8–3. Each status position carries with it an expected behavior pattern which is referred to as the *role*. Thus, individuals perform the activities of the roles associated with the statuses they occupy. The duties and responsibilities involved in these roles continue, regardless of who performs them. This means that if the vice president for marketing retires, the status of head of the marketing department does not disappear. Someone else is selected to fill this position.

Figure 8–3 depicts part of a simple organization chart showing how the different status positions relate to one another in a typical business enterprise. There are no persons named on this organization chart. Only the statuses to be filled are given. A job description outlining the duties of each position would accompany this chart. Notice how the lines of authority and responsibility from the board of directors and the president run throughout the organization. This represents the formal and more traditional concept of the authority exercised in the enterprise.

The informal organization

The formal organization in the business enterprise makes little allowance for the natural desire of the individual to associate with other persons. In every

FIGURE 8–3

Smith Brothers Corporation (partial organization chart)

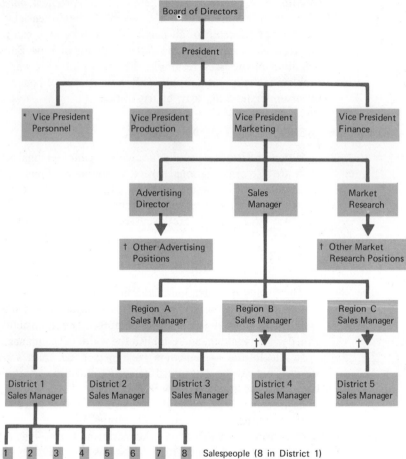

*There is an organizational structure under each vice president which is not shown here except for the marketing department.
†Not detailed here for lack of space.

enterprise informal organizations develop spontaneously to meet this social need of people. An *informal organization* is a self-grouping of employees in the work situation that is not detailed on the formal organization chart. The informal organization depends on the personalities of individuals for its being rather than on abstract statuses and roles.

Functions of the informal organization   The informal organization provides for the social needs and control of its members and for communication among employees. On an assembly line or in a large office a production worker or a clerk may not receive much recognition in the formal status hierarchy of the enterprise. However, as a member of an informal work group each is recognized, participates in exchanges of views and jokes, and has a circle of acquaintances with whom there are relationships. This can be a positive contribution to the work situation because it meets the social needs of employees.

However, sometimes informal groups become a negative factor. They may exert strong pressure on individual employees to conform. The social control exercised by informal groups frequently includes setting production standards that fit the work group's concept of a "fair day's work." These work standards will not necessarily be the same as those of management or the labor union. Various means are available to the informal work group in enforcing its standards. These means include refusing to communicate with the individual who does not accept the work group's values. More extreme sanctions include property damage and physical injury.

Informal communication—the grapevine   Another function of the informal organization—communication—is customarily known as the *grapevine*. Managements have found the grapevine to be both a help and a hindrance in operating the business enterprise.

The grapevine can be an effective means of rapidly disseminating information. Management may also get informal reactions to an idea being considered by placing information judiciously with informal group leaders. This provides management with a trial balloon to test out the idea on employees. Information gained through this means may cause changes in management's plans.

The grapevine can be a hindrance to management when rumors are passed along its channels. In the business enterprise a *rumor* is characterized as incomplete, unconfirmed information which may be incorrect or malicious in its intent. To avoid negative consequences of rumors, management should see that correct information is a part of the grapevine. This may include explaining or denying informally circulated information which is incomplete or incorrect and providing an accurate explanation of the situation. Rumors will be less of a problem in the enterprise when workers know that management seeks to inform them on matters of importance.

The nature of the informal work group   Three factors determine the nature of the informal work groups which develop in a business enterprise:

1. *The type of work performed.* People whose occupation is the same tend to group together. Thus informal work groups may be composed either of factory workers or of office workers. Only rarely will both types of workers be members of the same informal group. The difference in occupation leads to physical separation of the workplace as well as to different informal contacts based in part on the ways in which different types of workers view their status and role.

2. *The physical location of the workplace.* Generally people become members of the informal group that is located in their own work area. People naturally form associations with persons whom they meet frequently.

3. *The values held by the individuals.* The values of the members of an informal work group must be compatible if the group is to hold together. For this reason

FIGURE 8–4
Structure of an informal work group

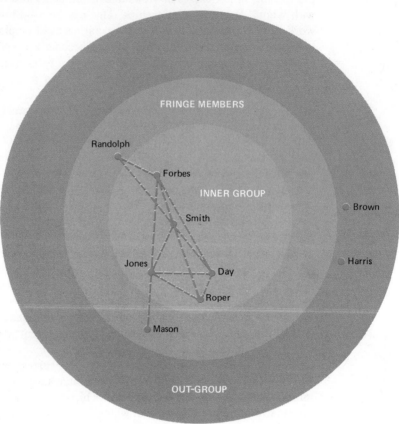

an informal work group is not likely to include union and nonunion workers
or production workers and supervisors.

    The structure of an informal work group   The structure of an informal work
group is depicted in Figure 8–4. Notice that there are three classes of individuals
who make up the group: those in the inner circle, those in the fringe area,
and those who are not members of the group (the out-group). The inner group
is the heart of the informal work group. It is composed of a closely knit group
of people who perform the same general kind of work in the same location
and hold the same values. The inner group sets the tone of the informal work
group and determines the membership. Smith, Jones, Roper, Day, and Forbes
make up the membership of the inner group. The dotted lines indicate relations
between the members in frequent contact. Notice that Randolph and Mason
are in the middle circle as fringe members of the informal group. They have
not been fully accepted by the members of the inner group, or they are not
yet willing to give full allegiance to the values of the informal social system.

Eventually they will either enter the inner circle of membership or move to the out-group status.

Brown and Harris are not members of the informal work group. They may work in the same department as the informal group members or have a formal status relationship with them. However, they do not have close informal ties with the group members or with each other. In a word, they are "loners." Usually such individuals are members of the out-group by choice. They do not want to surrender their independence to the informal work group, or their values differ in some significant way from those of the group members.

A group leader will emerge in the informal group situation. In Figure 8–4 Smith is the leader. He has frequent contact with five of the other six persons who compose the inner circle and the fringe membership in the system. Members of the inner group come to Smith with their problems and ideas. They listen to Smith's opinions and generally follow suggestions made by Smith. In short, Smith commands the voluntary respect of the members of the informal work group. In contrast, a supervisor is obeyed because of his or her status in the formal organization of the business enterprise.

THE IMPORTANCE OF STATUS

Status has been defined as a relative position in the business organization. Many persons laugh about others' concern over status and the symbols attached to it. However, these same individuals may become quite agitated when some event occurs that seems to diminish their status in an organization.

Kinds of status

When an individual works to fulfill the requirements for a particular position and attains it, this is known as *achieved status*. Being a college graduate is achieved status since a person must earn a degree. Occupational status is achieved status since a person is not born as a business manager, a banker, a physician, or a bricklayer.

However, there are some status positions which are not achieved but instead are *ascribed*—that is, persons are assigned statuses on the basis of some inherited characteristic such as sex, race, or the family into which they are born. Ascribed status can affect an individual's chances to achieve a position in a business enterprise. Although family background in business seems to be less important today than it was in earlier decades, status may accrue to a person in business because of family ties. Higher status may be afforded in industry to men than to women despite legislation which outlaws employment discrimination by business on the basis of the sex or race of individuals.

Prestige and esteem

Prestige is the recognition and regard which result from a person's status in an enterprise. A number of factors determine the prestige of a status in an organizational structure. A greater amount of formal education is generally required for higher status jobs, and therefore such jobs have more prestige than do jobs requiring less education. The type of work performed and the working conditions also determine the prestige of a status in the business enterprise. Employees who use mental skills usually have higher status and more prestige than do employees who perform manual labor.

Pay is also a determinant of the amount of prestige that is attached to a status. The level of wages is one means by which management recognizes the importance of the individual's contribution to the operation of the enterprise.

How persons perform the roles associated with their statuses determines the amount of *esteem* in which they are held. An employee such as a custodian has a position of relatively low status and prestige in the organization. However, if he or she fulfills the role well by doing a good job of keeping the office clean, the person should be held in high esteem. A person of high status and prestige, such as a vice president for sales, could be held in low esteem because of poor role behavior. This low esteem might result from lack of attention to the job, immoral conduct, or general inefficiency. Nevertheless, the vice president would still occupy a status with much prestige. If over a period of time the people who occupy certain prestigious statuses do not perform their roles well, the statuses themselves may come to have less prestige.

Status symbols

Status in business is recognized by permitting certain symbols to be part of the work environment. These status symbols are visible evidence of a person's rank in the business enterprise.

Examples of status symbols are wide ranging. They vary from desk pen sets and telephones in offices to rugs and paintings in executive suites. A cardinal rule of status symbols is that they lose their significance when they become too widespread. In one organization the vice presidents' offices had carpeted floors, and this was considered a status symbol. However, the enterprise moved into a new building where not only the offices of executives were carpeted but also those of department heads. When this occurred, the carpeted floors became a less significant status symbol. Instead, organizational status was symbolized by the floors on which offices were located. Since the building was served by automatic elevators, the offices on the highest floors were occupied by executives of higher level in the organization and connoted higher status. Also, these offices were closest to the president's office and the board of directors' meeting room, which was located on the top floor.

Although status and its symbols exist wherever people come together in organizations, management should see that these are not overemphasized if the enterprise is to function smoothly.

DEVELOPING A HEALTHY WORK CLIMATE

A healthy work climate is developed in the business enterprise as the result of conscious effort by management. Building high morale among employees requires day-to-day actions by supervisors based on sound human relations concepts. To improve the manager's awareness of human relations the following suggestions should be considered.

1. **The superior sets the tone of the enterprise** The principal responsibility for determining the work climate rests with the superior. Subordinates will tend to follow this lead. This responsibility for promoting good human relations ranges from the president of the business enterprise down to the first level of supervision. Each person who directs the activities of others should remember that subordinates will be watching to see what kind of an example is set.

Examples of ways in which a manager sets the tone for subordinates include the friendliness exhibited toward employees and how it is expressed, manner of dress, the degree of professionalism shown in associations with others, commitment to the enterprise as measured by the energy and time devoted to the job, the attitudes expressed toward the enterprise, and the prejudices which may be exhibited.

2. **Make deserved praise public; reprimand in private** "Praise publicly and reprove privately" is generally sound advice for the business manager. A private reprimand enables the individual employee to save face and may be more effective in changing behavior patterns than would publicly criticizing the employee's actions or attitudes. Most people like to have deserved public recognition despite their modest protests that "it really doesn't make any difference" whether they receive such recognition. However, there are times when the boss's most effective praise will be a quiet word of commendation for a job well done.

3. **Remember the importance of listening in good communication** Avoid making judgments until the other person has told his or her story and you believe you fully understand the situation. Try to perceive the other person's view of the situation. Listening is very difficult if you are busy thinking about what your response will be.

4. **When giving directions, make sure that others understand what you expect** Do not expect persons to respond effectively if they are not properly prepared to carry out your instructions.

5. **Preserve the dignity of the individual** A person's good self-image is important. Management should avoid placing the individual employee in a position in which he or she loses face. When this occurs, the supervisor should expect a defensive, perhaps violent, reaction that is not likely to be constructive in solving the issue at hand.

6. **How a change is made may be more important than the change itself** Although change is characteristic of today's business scene, management should recognize that change tends to disrupt the lives and work habits of people. Most of us prefer not to have our behavioral patterns interrupted. Consider your own habits. Try dressing in a different order tomorrow morning; or take a different route in coming to class. If you are typical you will resist such changes. In the work environment the same thing is true. We resent changes that require us to establish new ways of doing things. This natural resistance to change causes one of management's greatest challenges: to make necessary changes with a minimum disruption of good work habits.

In making changes, it is important that management communicate to workers the reasons for the changes. Management should recognize that changes in organizational structure, the location of offices and shops, product lines, and personnel have definite human relations implications. The more information management is able to pass along to employees regarding anticipated changes, the less disruptive the changes are likely to be.

SUMMARY

Human relations consists of providing a work climate which will both satisfy the employees' needs and achieve the broad economic objectives of the business enterprise. Employees have physical and material needs which are met largely through wages and fringe benefits. However, employees also have nonmaterial needs, both psychological and social, which management should recognize.

Direction is the process of aiding an enterprises's employees in carrying out their work activities. To be effective in exercising direction, managers need technical, human, and conceptual skills. Generally, technical skill is required to a greater degree in first-line supervision, conceptual skill is required to a greater degree at the top management level, and human skill is required at all levels of management.

Leadership is the element of direction which causes subordinates to further the accomplishment of enterprise goals. Leadership can be exercised in an authoritarian or a participative manner.

Communication, the transmission of understanding, is essential in the process of direction. Two-way communication should occur vertically and horizontally in the business enterprise. Both written and spoken communications are used in business, and each method has its advantages and disadvantages. Good communication requires both effective transmission and effective receipt of information, with the listener or reader understanding the frame of reference of the speaker or writer.

In the formal organizational structure, each person occupies a particular status and is expected to fulfill the role associated with that status. These positions can be shown in a formal organizational chart.

The informal organization is a self-grouping of employees in the workplace which depends on the personalities of the individuals for its being. Informal work groups are usually made up of workers who perform similar work in the same area and who hold similar values.

Status is a relative position in an organization. Status is achieved when a person earns it and ascribed when it is based on some inherited characteristic. Prestige refers to the recognition and regard that go with a particular status. Esteem refers to how well a person performs the role associated with a status. Status symbols are visible evidence of a person's rank in the business enterprise.

There are a number of considerations for management to remember in developing a healthy work climate:

1. The superior sets the tone of the enterprise.
2. Generally, it is good to praise in public and reprimand in private.
3. Listening is important for good communication.
4. Make sure that others know what is expected of them.
5. Preserve the dignity of the individual.
6. When a change is made, weigh *how* the change is made.

TERMS FOR REVIEW

human relations   *human skill*   *achieved status*
psychological needs *conceptual skill*   *ascribed status*
social needs   *authoritarian leadership* *prestige*
technical skill   *participative leadership* *esteem*

QUESTIONS

1. What differences are there between enterprise goals and individual needs?

2. *a.* What examples of good human relations practices have you observed in the organizations with which you have been associated?
   b. What incidents have you observed that indicated a lack of sensitivity to the importance of human relations?

3. What needs are most important to you in considering a job opportunity? What difference, if any, would it make if you were considering a summer position before returning to college instead of a permanent position?

4. Comment on the following statement by the owner of a medium-size department store: "I would like to have more participation by my supervisors and other employees, but I can't afford the time that is required for them to make a decision. Also, I feel that I know more about my business than anyone else."

5. What should you remember if you are to be an effective listener?

6. Prepare three statements that could be given opposite interpretations, depending on the frame of reference of the speaker and the listener. How could these statements be rephrased so that the transmitted message would be what was intended?

7. "Since informal organizations are bound to arise within any business enterprise, a formal organization is really of secondary importance." Comment on this statement.

8. What kinds of status symbols have you observed in the organizations of which you have been a part? Are people serious about the importance of status symbols? Why or why not?

9. Why may the way in which a change is made be as important as the change itself? Give an example to illustrate such a situation.

10. What are the implications for management in Jerome Rosow's statement in the Borg-Warner report on the first page of this chapter?

business briefs

GOING "COLD TURKEY"

A number of business enterprises are paying employees to stop smoking on the job. The managements of these enterprises believe that smoking is economically undesirable for their enterprises as well as unhealthy for employees.

An official of a California organization called GASP (Group Against Smoking Pollution) claims that cutting down on smoking boosts productivity, improves worker morale, lowers maintenance and cleanup costs, reduces fires, and cuts absenteeism. Some health insurance premiums have been reduced for companies which have provided bonus payments for workers who quit smoking.

Payments to quitters take a variety of forms. A California computer firm offered employees a $500 health bonus to quit smoking for a year. In a Texas enterprise, smokers have been awarded a 50-cent hourly raise if they go six months without smoking. In a New Mexico enterprise, employees who quit smoking for a year were paid the amount that they would have spent on cigarettes during that time. Other enterprises pay employees some of the cost of attending nonsmoking clinics.

In 1978 Johns-Manville Corporation announced that it would no longer hire smokers for its asbestos operations across the country. This enterprise also banned smoking in its asbestos plants. The company's policy has been contested by the unions involved. Arbitration cases and court battles are under way over whether the company should be required to provide smoking areas for its employees.

1. *Why should tobacco smokers be willing to quit smoking for money when they have not quit for the sake of their health?*
2. *Would a bonus program to encourage employees to quit smoking be likely to raise the level of morale in an enterprise?*
3. *How far should an enterprise go in influencing the personal habits of its employees?*

LEVI STRAUSS

Levi Strauss, the manufacturer of jeans, is a family-controlled enterprise which was founded in 1850 and still projects a family image. Its shares of common stock were sold to the public for the first time in 1971. One of its junior executives, in his 20s, states that what he really likes about the company is that it is very people-oriented. This young man was impressed that on chance meetings with the president, the top executive would speak to him by his first name. Furthermore, the junior executive feels that management is open to suggestions. People are encouraged to cross departmental lines to discuss ideas. Pride is felt that Levi Strauss has been a leader in such projects as the employment of minorities.

1. *What insights into the human relations climate at Levi Strauss can be gained from this brief?*

THE HOTLINE VERSUS THE GRAPEVINE

In Tacoma, Washington, the office employees of St. Regis Paper Company can dial a company hotline telephone for information on company developments. A recorded report provides information on local office and company-wide developments. The hotline avoids the need to have employees depend on the grapevine for rumors of change at St. Regis. After hearing the recorded telephone report, employees have an opportunity to record their comments to be heard by management.

1. *What advantages does this telephone hotline have over the company grapevine?*
2. *What limitations does such a hotline have?*
3. *What possible problems might arise from such a hotline?*

case

"LESSONS LEARNED"

Tamar Jones eyed the memos on her desk. The calendar told her that ten months had passed since she had come to Falls City to help open a new plant (see Exhibit 1) for Acme Products Company, a nationwide packaging concern. Tamar reflected on how busy the past months had been. As a group leader, she had been confronted with many problems. It had been hectic to get the plant into production on schedule. Only in the past month had things slacked up a little.

The ringing telephone summoned Tamar from her thoughts and into the office of Ms. Jackson, her department head. Handing Tamar a memo, Ms. Jackson said, "We have a request from our general manager in Chicago. He'd like to have us submit to him some of the 'Lessons Learned' by us during our new plant start-up. They'd be of benefit in planning future expansions. Can you put together some ideas?"

Tamar replied that several of the group leaders had already discussed the need for more detailed installation drawings. She then asked, "Should this be strictly technical, or should it include other problems?"

"List anything serious that has confronted you," was Jackson's reply.

During the next week, Tamar sought out the other group leaders and acquainted them with her assignment. She asked for their recommendations. Their ideas fell into three categories:

1. Facility installations and drawings.
2. Tooling tolerances and finishes.
3. Unclear personnel assignments and absence of an organization chart.

All three of these items had been subjects of discussion on numerous occasions in almost all the departments of the new plant.

EXHIBIT 1
Acme Products Company (Falls City plant organization chart)

Upon receiving the draft copies back from typing, Tamar reviewed them with the other group leaders. She then sent them for Ms. Jackson's consideration. On the following day, her draft copies were returned with Ms. Jackson's note, "Well done."

The next day Ms. Jackson left for a conference in Dallas. Tamar had not had an opportunity to discuss the final report on "Lessons Learned" with her. While Tamar was on the telephone, the executive assistant to the plant manager, Mr. Witherspoon, stormed into the department office, slammed down a handful of papers, and lashed out at the nearest secretary. "This rubbish is obviously incorrect. These conditions don't exist." The executive assistant continued, "This was written by a misguided, ignorant individual and is in poor taste, without thought of fact." As Witherspoon departed he haughtily advised that the papers should be destroyed. As the secretary returned the papers to Ms. Jackson's mailbox, Tamar saw the heading "Lessons Learned."

After completing her telephone call, Tamar turned her thoughts to the executive assistant's reaction to the "Lessons Learned" report. Some of the following thoughts ran through Tamar's mind: Should I speak to the executive assistant in an attempt to explain the report? Would it be better to go over the old-paper-shuffler's head and deliver the report direcetly to the plant manager? Had Ms. Jackson really studied the report, or had she merely rubber-stamped it? Since the general manager in Chicago had requested the report he must have considered it important.

As Tamar went to the water cooler for a drink she wondered what action, if any, she should take.

1. Discuss the central problems involved in this case.
2. a. What courses of action are open to Tamar Jones?
   b. Which of these courses do you recommend to Tamar Jones? Why?

CBS reports . . .

To a significant degree, organizational performance is the performance of people. CBS management, therefore, strives to nurture the talents and skills of all employees and to provide them with opportunities for development and fulfillment. To this end, we continually are developing and updating personnel programs, policies and procedures designed to insure our growth and success as a corporation.

The CBS School of Management, established in 1977 to help experienced executives broaden their management skills and to help them develop the skills of their subordinates, is a prime example of our management development program. The school became fully operational in 1978 and has graduated 272 executives. It will expand its activities in 1979 to include a management program for entry-level managers who are our main source of future senior executives.

In keeping with our long-standing commitment to equal job opportunity for all employees, we are dedicated to promoting from within the company whenever possible. The increased involvement of all levels of management in the promotion process, coupled with better human resources information systems, has resulted in a significant increase in the number of women and minorities in managerial and supervisory positions within the company. In addition, to insure that the company's personnel needs continue to be met, a vice president of personnel was designated for each of the four operating groups. This officer brings to each group an in-depth knowledge and understanding of the unique aspects of our corporate personnel policies as well as the requirements of the group.

From the annual report of CBS

Courtesy of CBS, Inc.

Personnel management

Personnel management

Personnel departments were a logical development as American business enterprises became larger. Personnel departments aid management in processing and maintaining the records required for a large work force. With increased awareness of the importance of the human factors in business, managements began to turn to personnel departments for assistance. Because of the broader responsibilities of the personnel function, this area is now sometimes referred to as human resources management.

After studying this chapter, you will be able to answer the following questions related to the personnel function:

What is the primary goal of personnel management?

What specific responsibilities are assigned to the personnel department?

What is the relationship between personnel management and labor relations?

How is the personnel department organized?

THE PERSONNEL MANAGEMENT FUNCTION

The primary goal of personnel management is a well-motivated and effective work force. Good personnel management emphasizes the personal development of employees. Ideally a climate is developed in which individuals may use their abilities and obtain satisfaction in their work group. A successful personnel program will integrate the individual objectives of employees with the objectives of the enterprise in order to achieve an efficient work situation.

The personnel department is in a key position to advise top management on the state of employees' morale. Personnel management can suggest methods of strengthening employee-management relations. In enterprises whose employees are unionized, the personnel department also assists in the conduct of labor relations.

Three groups carry out the personnel management function. The overall responsibility for personnel management should be assumed by top management. The president of an organization sets the tone of the work climate. The president is responsible to the board of directors for the establishment of the broad objectives and policies of personnel management. It is the president who appoints the director of the personnel department and other key executives.

The second group is made up of the supervisors throughout the enterprise. The first-line supervisors, department heads, district managers, and other managers actually put personnel policies into practice. It is important that these supervisors understand the personnel policies established by top management and actively support them.

The third group having responsibilities for personnel management is the personnel department. This department is generally established as a "staff" department. Its purpose is to provide service to other departments. The personnel department hires employees, trains them, and provides a variety of other services.

RESPONSIBILITIES OF THE PERSONNEL DEPARTMENT

The hiring and placement of employees

The responsibilities of the personnel department include the recruitment, selection, induction, and training of employees.

To provide for efficient and uniform hiring practices, employment activities should be centered in the personnel department. Here records can be kept up to date and interviews and testing can be carried out. The supervisor of the prospective employee should have the right to accept or reject any applicant recommended by the personnel department. However, centralized hiring relieves the supervisor of many details associated with the hiring and placement of personnel.

Job specifications   The first step in hiring is taken when the supervisor turns in a request for personnel to fill certain jobs. Job specifications should be drawn up to describe realistically the requirements of the positions to be filled.

Recruitment   After the request for workers has been turned in, the personnel department undertakes the recruitment phase. Sources of candidates include former employees who are qualified but have been laid off or have voluntarily left the enterprise. Also, candidates may apply as the result of advertising and of contacts with groups such as schools, unions, private employment agencies, minority organizations, and correctional authorities. The local office of the public employment service is also a helpful source of employment information.

Employee selection   The selection of individuals who will be offered employment is a six-step process. This consists of a screening interview, a written application, employment tests, a physical examination, a reference check, and a comprehensive interview. Figure 9–1 illustrates the employment process.

The *screening interview* may be conducted by an assistant in the personnel department. It provides an opportunity to make a preliminary decision about the applicants' suitability for employment. Applicants may be turned down for employment for specific jobs not only because they are deficient in some respect, but because their education or intelligence is too high for the jobs which are currently vacant. If the applicants appear to be good candidates, then the screening interview may be used to explain the rest of the employment process.

The *application form* provides information about the candidate in writing.

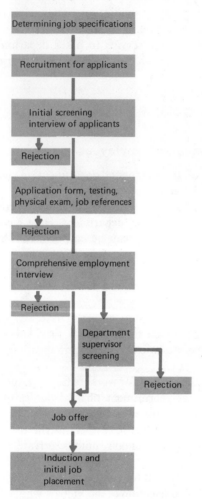

FIGURE 9–1
The employment process

It acts as a simple test of writing ability and should contain items which the enterprise has found to correlate with job success.

The development of a *testing program* is a complex undertaking. A good testing program will measure the ability of applicants to fill a particular job and will provide an objective comparison among applicants.

The *physical examination* should be given to applicants who are considered seriously for employment. Employees should not be placed in jobs which might be harmful to them or in which they might endanger other workers. The enterprise should be protected against the risk of claims from persons who have disabilities prior to employment.

The investigation into the *job references* provided by the applicant gives the

Reprinted by permission The Wall Street Journal

enterprise a check on past work records. The reference check also tests the applicant's accuracy and honesty.

The main purpose of the *comprehensive employment interview* is to complete or to correct information on the applicant which has been provided by the previous steps. Qualities of the applicant which have not been covered in previous steps may be drawn out by a skillful interviewer. This interview also provides an opportunity to explain the job's requirements fully.

If the applicants qualify in all respects they are accepted for employment, sometimes with a probationary period. Normally the supervisor for whom they would work meets the applicants before they are finally selected. The supervisor should have some authority in determining which applicants are hired into his or her department, since the supervisor is responsible for the productivity of the department. However, in large enterprises the supervisor's most important function in the hiring process is to provide a realistic list of the requirements for the positions to be filled. Then the personnel department should screen for applicants who meet those requirements.

career outlook

PERSONNEL WORKERS

Attracting the best employees available and matching them to the jobs they can do effectively are important for the success of any organization. Personnel workers interview, select, and recommend applicants who have the education and experience to fill vacancies. In addition to staffing, they counsel employees, plan training, develop wage and salary scales, and investigate methods to improve personnel operations.

Some personnel specialists handle the employer's benefits program. This often includes health insurance, life insurance, disability insurance, and pension plans. Personnel workers also coordinate a wide range of employee services, including cafeterias and snack bars, health rooms, recreational facilities, newsletters and communications, and counseling for work-related personal problems.

New personnel workers usually enter formal or on-the-job training programs to learn how to classify jobs, interview applicants, or administer employee benefits. After completing their training, they are assigned to work in specific areas.

Personnel workers should speak and write effectively and be able to work with people of all levels of education and experience. They must also be able to see both the employee's and the employer's points of view. A persuasive, congenial personality can be a great asset.

The number of personnel workers is expected to expand very rapidly through the mid-1980s, as employers recognize the need for trained personnel to maintain good employee relations. Legislation setting standards for employment practices in the areas of occupational safety and health, equal employment opportunity, and pensions has stimulated the demand for personnel workers.

A college education is becoming increasingly important for personnel work. Many employers in private industry prefer applicants who have majored in business administration or personnel administration. Other employers think that a well-rounded liberal arts education is the best preparation for personnel work.

Employee induction

A new employee should be introduced to the organization before being placed in a specific job. A good induction program provides the new employee with useful information about the enterprise, about policies affecting employees, and about the services which are provided. First impressions are important in determining future employee attitudes toward the enterprise.

A good program of employee induction has these three elements:

1. The personnel department provides introductory information to new employees either individually or in groups.
2. Additional information is provided by the new employee's supervisor about the department and the requirements of the job.

3. After the employee's first days on the job, a follow-up interview is held either by the supervisor or by the personnel department. This can check on the employee's progress, answer additional questions, or repeat information provided earlier.

An initial tour of the enterprise helps new employees to relate their jobs to the entire operation. The induction program should give the newcomer a feeling of belonging to the organization.

Employee training

Besides the induction program, the employee may need specific training for the new job. There are four types of employee training:

1. *Apprenticeship training* is used in jobs requiring long periods of training and a high degree of skill. The new employee works under the supervision of trained employees and is required to meet rigid performance standards. Employers may develop apprenticeship programs in cooperation with trade unions.

2. *Vestibule training* is off-the-job training in which workers are trained in an area of the plant physically separated from their workplace. Machinery and jobs similar to conditions in the shop are duplicated as nearly as possible. This method of training provides an opportunity for teaching the best methods of doing a particular job. Employees become accustomed to the job before actually entering the department.

3. *On-the-job training* places the workers in the shop at a machine or a workplace. There they will be trained by a supervisor, a special instructor, or an experienced employee. The effectiveness of this type of training depends on the quality of the instruction.

4. *Vocational-school training* consists of courses outside the enterprise in such areas as welding, blueprint reading, or automobile mechanics. This training may precede employment or may supplement the training provided by the enterprise in its own plant.

Training represents a continuing responsibility for management. New methods, products, and individual abilities dictate that training not be regarded as finished after the worker is placed in a shop or an office. The personnel department should stand ready to provide training programs for all employees, not merely those who were hired recently.

Job analysis

To maintain a satisfactory level of morale and employee efficiency, the wages paid employees should be adequate and fair. A good system of wage payments takes account of differences in jobs and also provides for individual differences in performance on the same job.

Job description   The first step in job analysis is to determine what jobs are performed in the enterprise. This is done by writing a *job description* that contains the essential elements of each specific job. These include such factors as physical effort, skill, responsibility, mental effort, and working conditions.

Job evaluation   Once descriptions have been written for all of the jobs in the enterprise, the process of job evaluation begins. This consists of measuring the value of each job in relation to the other jobs in the enterprise.

The simplest method of job evaluation is to identify the factors that are to be singled out for analysis and to assign weights to each factor. For example, physical effort may be assigned a maximum of 40 points, whereas the skills required may be assigned a maximum of 110 points. The determination of the maximum weights assigned to each job depends on the types of jobs which the enterprise has. Next, the personnel administrator selects several jobs in the enterprise for use as benchmarks against which all of the other jobs will be measured. These benchmark jobs are then evaluated according to the point scales established for each factor in the evaluation scheme. The benchmark jobs should each employ a number of persons and should be widely known to all employees. For example, the job of machinist first class might be assigned the following point spread: physical effort 20, skill 100, responsibility 60, and working conditions 20, for a total of 200; whereas the job of custodian might carry points as follows: physical effort 30, skill 10, responsibility 20, and working conditions 30, for a total of 90 points. Other jobs in the enterprise are then ranked in relation to the benchmark jobs. A careful handling of the point assignments and the relative rankings is necessary to maintain fairness.

Job evaluation provides management with a more desirable basis for wage determination than does a haphazard scheme of wage payments. A carefully administered program of job evaluation will result in a logical scale of jobs which can be used as a basis for setting relative wage scales. However, no job evaluation system is completely scientific. Judgments on the relative worth of different jobs are difficult to make.

Also, some jobs may be viewed by workers as of unequal attractiveness even though the point analysis makes them of equal value. Some jobs may seem to be stepping-stones to higher positions. Others may be viewed as dead-end assignments. In some cases exceptions to the job evaluation system may be necessary to attract workers to a particular job where labor is in short supply.

Remember that job evaluation rates *jobs,* not the *individuals* on the jobs. The evaluation of individuals, called performance rating, is discussed below.

Wage determination   After the job evaluation has been completed, management must fit the scale of jobs to its wage scale. The wage scale in an enterprise will depend on the local level of wages for similar jobs, on the ability of the enterprise to pay higher wages, on the bargaining strength of the labor union if employees are unionized, and on the industry of which the enterprise is a part.

In putting a new job evaluation system into effect, the best psychology is to do so at the time of a general wage increase. Then job rates which have been too high can be brought into the scale by raising other rates rather than by lowering those rates. It may require a period of time before all jobs are "in line" with a fair scale as determined by a job evaluation plan.

Performance rating

Once a system of job evaluation and wage scales has been worked out, individuals must be selected to fill the various jobs. There should be a range of pay for each job so that supervisors can pay an individual more for superior job performance. The supervisor is responsible for keeping employees informed of their progress on the job. This is done through a performance rating system, sometimes called a merit rating system (see Figure 9–2).

The performance rating system is used to make merit wage increases within job classifications and to guide management in selecting employees for promotion. Formal performance rating of employees reduces the practice of giving raises on the basis of quick judgment or favoritism.

The performance rating system provides managers with a means of rewarding effective employees and furthering the operating efficiency of the enterprise. Discussions with employees about their ratings should take a positive direction whenever possible. Morale and productivity are much easier to improve by pointing out positive elements in the employee's performance than by emphasizing weaknesses.

Performance rating is only one source of evidence for promotions or pay increases. Other information is provided by records of output, quality of work, and attendance.

Promotion

Promotion is the advancement of an employee to a better job with more responsibility, increased skill, or higher status. An important aspect of a promotion is that it results in an increased salary or rate of pay. A promotion may involve moving an employee to a more skilled job within the same basic job classification, such as from second-class machine operator to first-class machine operator. Or a promotion could be a major shift in jobs such as from a production worker to a supervisor.

Seniority and ability   Two basic factors affect promotion—seniority and ability. Labor unions usually believe that seniority should be the basis upon which promotions are decided. On the other hand, managements usually believe that ability should be the key factor in making promotions.

The supervisor in a department is responsible for the productivity of the personnel. Authority should be delegated to the supervisor to select those employees for promotion who have the abilities needed for success in new positions. Promotion should be the reward for employees who increase their skills and exhibit capability for better jobs. To promote only on the basis of seniority places an unfair restriction on management in view of the supervisor's responsibil-

FIGURE 9-2

PERFORMANCE RATING REVIEW

Name:_____ Job Title: _____ Dept .:_____ Date:_____

Instructions to Supervisor: Summarize the individual's performance by checking each of the 4 evaluation factors below. Your ratings should reflect your judgment based on your observation of the employee. Use N/E (not evaluated) if you have insufficient evidence on which to make a rating. However, normally all items should be evaluated. These ratings should indicate what the employee has actually accomplished. Remember that personnel performance rating and development represents an important responsibility of management.

Rating System: A - Exceeds Departmental Expectations
B - Meets Departmental Expectations
C - Below Departmental Expectations

Evaluation Factors   Ratings

	A	B	C
Quality of Work	Consistently does high-quality and accurate work; creative with high degree of ingenuity and practicality.	Usually can be depended upon for good work; few mistakes; practical; some creativity.	Work performed in a careless and slipshod manner; frequent mistakes; lacks creativeness.
Quantity of Work	Consistently high output; works rapidly.	Satisfactory production level; works steadily.	Below average in output; slow; wastes time.
Knowledge of Job	Expert knowledge of job and related areas; rarely requires instruction.	Good knowledge of job and related work; requires only normal instructions.	Has limited knowledge of job; requires frequent instruction and guidance.
Cooperation and Attitude	Enthusiastic and cooperative team worker; inspires confidence; loyal to company; solicits suggestions for improvement.	Responsive and cooperative; interested in job and company; accepts constructive criticism.	Lack of cooperation; little job interest; resents suggestions and constructive criticism.

Instructions: Check the appropriate block for the qualities listed below:

Capacity for Advancement: Qualifications	Is qualified for higher position with no further training or experience.	May be qualified for higher position with additional training and/or experience.	Qualified for present job, but has only limited potential for advancement.
Capacity for Advancement: Leadership Ability	Has demonstrated many of the qualifications for leadership; excellent supervisory material.	Has demonstrated some of the qualifications for leadership; possible supervisory material.	Has demonstrated few, if any, of the qualifications for leadership; not considered supervisory material.

	Yes	No
Is attendance satisfactory?	_____	_____
Is the employee punctual?	_____	_____

Remarks and/or Recommendations:

Rater's Signature_____   Supervisor's Signature_____ Date_____
Title_____   Title_____

After Supervisor's signature, forward orginal copy of Performance Rating Review to the Personnel Office. Retain copy in local files. This Review is to be discussed with the employee before it is filed.

ity for results. Seniority should be taken into account when making promotions, but only when the other qualifications of two or more candidates for a better job are substantially equal.

Senior employees should be considered for promotion on the basis of their abilities, performance ratings, production records, and personal interviews by management. The junior employee should be selected for a promotion only when he or she can be shown to be superior to the senior worker.

When seniority is used as one of the criteria for promotion, the question arises as to how it is to be computed. Seniority may be determined by length of service in the enterprise, plant, department, or job classification. An employee's seniority can start from the time of hiring into any of the above units. The basis for determining seniority is critical, because seniority will vary, depending on which unit is used.

For example, a longtime employee who has moved from one department to another has relatively little seniority on a departmental basis, but considerable seniority with the company. The question of how seniority is counted when an employee is transferred, laid off, or promoted is thus important for both the employees and management.

Whatever system of seniority is adopted, seniority lists showing each employee's standing should be publicly posted. Then all employees will have knowledge of their relative standing, and possible errors can be corrected.

Employee transfer

Promotion is an upward change in jobs. *Transfer* is the movement of an employee to another job at about the same pay and on the same level in the organization. The work done by the employee may change with a transfer. However, there is no significant change in responsibility. Employee transfers may be of various types, including shift transfers, production transfers, and remedial transfers.

Shift transfers are used when the plant operates during more than a normal eight-hour day. The evening shift usually runs from about four o'clock in the afternoon to midnight, and the night shift from midnight to eight o'clock in the morning. Most workers prefer to work the regular day shift. However, if production needs require multiple-shift operations, some workers will have to be hired for the extra shifts. One positive aspect of shift work from the employee's point of view is that the unusual shifts generally carry a pay premium.

Production transfers are necessary when there is a change in the job requirements from one department to another. Some jobs may be eliminated, and other types of work may require additional workers. In this case workers are transferred for production purposes to avoid laying off present employees and hiring new ones. Production transfers may also occur when replacements are needed because of the retirement, dismissal, or promotion of other workers.

Remedial transfers are made because of some problem with a person on a particular job. The worker may become too old to bear the physical burden of the job. Changing health conditions may make a transfer necessary. A worker may become tired of a certain job. The initial placement of the worker may have been faulty. Or the worker may simply not be getting along with the supervisor or the people in the department but may be useful in another part of the plant. Both the employee and the enterprise may benefit from a remedial transfer.

Downgrading and layoffs

Sometimes transfers, particularly production transfers, result in *downgrading*. This means that employees are moved to jobs requiring less skill than those performed previously. This may come about because the higher skills are no longer needed.

At times a company may be faced with reduced demand for its products. This means a layoff of workers, sometimes in large numbers. Although layoffs, like downgrading, may be only temporary, sometimes permanent changes in the size of the work force are required. Before making large layoffs of permanent employees, many companies lay off probationary employees and then reduce hours of work.

Discipline of employees

A good disciplinary policy provides for constructive, positive, consistent actions by supervisors under a clear set of regulations. Most employees are anxious to do what is expected of them. The enterprise's disciplinary policy should be administered so as to encourage self-discipline. At the same time, provision should be made for prompt action against the relatively small number of employees who do not conform to reasonable rules for plant conduct.

There are four essentials in every good disciplinary policy:

1. There should be a written list of clear and reasonable rules, along with the penalties which will be applied for infractions.
2. All employees should be informed of plant rules and standards of work.
3. A means should exist for informing employees of how well they are meeting standards of conduct and work.
4. A careful investigation of incidents should be carried out prior to disciplinary action. If and when guilt has been established, this should be followed by prompt corrective action.

A partial listing of conduct which will not be permitted in the plant usually includes:

Gambling on company property.

Fighting or attempting to injure others except in self-defense.

Deliberate destruction of company property.

Drinking liquor on company property or drunkenness on the job.

Violation of safety regulations.

Smoking in prohibited areas.

Unexcused absences without notifying the company.

Refusal to accept a proper job assignment.

After an employee's guilt has been clearly established, the disciplinary action may include one or a combination of the following penalties:

1. Oral warning.
2. Written warning.
3. Suspension or disciplinary layoff for a specified period of time.
4. Demotion to a less desirable job.
5. Discharge from the enterprise's employ.

The penalty to be applied depends on the nature of the offense and on whether there have been previous violations by the employee. Ordinarily either a verbal or written warning is sufficient for first offenses unless the infraction is serious enough for immediate discharge.

Safety and health

The personnel department frequently cooperates with supervisors and engineers in administering safety and health programs for employees. An important federal law went into effect in 1971 which affects every business enterprise not already covered by federal safety legislation. The *Occupational Safety and Health Act of 1970* is wide ranging. It requires employers to provide safety and health programs for the improvement of working conditions. The Occupational Safety and Health Administration (OSHA) was established to administer the legislation. OSHA has the power to set mandatory job safety and health standards. It can inspect business enterprises to determine whether they are in compliance with the law. The personnel department can assist line managers in improving safety and health conditions and can maintain the records and reports required by OSHA.

RELATIONSHIP BETWEEN PERSONNEL MANAGEMENT AND LABOR RELATIONS

When the enterprise's employees are unionized, the interaction between the union and management is called labor relations. The labor relations director is usually part of the personnel department.

When an enterprise's employees are unionized, the most significant change is in how personnel policy is formulated. When no union exists in an enterprise, personnel policy is usually determined unilaterally by management. Personnel functions such as hiring and placing employees, setting wage rates, establishing seniority rules, determining work standards, and taking disciplinary action can be carried out without consulting the labor force. The fact that personnel policies may be unilaterally determined and administered by management in the nonunion work situation does not necessarily mean that they are poor policies. An enterprise having no union can create a healthy work climate for employees. However, in the nonunion shop the employees usually have little or no chance to appeal management actions which may affect their welfare.

When a union exists in an enterprise, personnel policies are bilaterally determined. Questions relating to employees' welfare are decided by management after consultation with union representatives, or they are jointly decided by management and the union. Decisions must be within the meaning of the labor contract signed by management and the union.

The establishment of a union in the enterprise can have some benefits for management. Management is forced to analyze its position on various issues affecting employee welfare and to weigh carefully the possible implications of proposed changes. Through seniority lists and established layoff procedures, management is spared having to make individual decisions as to which workers will be released if reductions in the work force become necessary. Where labor unions negotiate contracts with a number of employers for the same wage rates, the enterprise is put on a par with other firms in the industry.

Because of the importance of unions in many industries today, the next chapter is devoted to a discussion of labor relations.

THE PERSONNEL DEPARTMENT

The personnel department acts in a staff capacity to the other departments of the business enterprise. This means that it provides certain services along with advice and assistance but is not responsible for giving orders to line supervisors in the production or marketing departments. Figure 9–3 illustrates the general organization of a typical personnel department.

The personnel manager

The head of the personnel department usually has the title of personnel manager or vice president for personnel administration. The personnel manager normally reports to the president of the enterprise. Depending on the size of the enterprise and the number of employees, there may also be labor relations personnel, recruiters, interviewers, training supervisors, and clerical assistants.

FIGURE 9–3
Partial organization chart of a personnel department

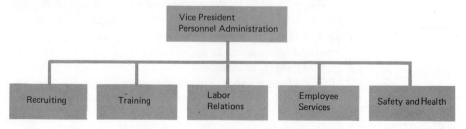

Employee services

In addition to the duties performed for line supervisors by the personnel department, most personnel departments administer a variety of employee service programs, including the insurance and retirement programs. Also, the personnel department handles the sponsoring of company recreational activities, including athletic teams, picnics, and news bulletins with information of personal interest to employees. Community activities relating to the enterprise and its employees, such as United Way drives for local charities, may be handled in part by the personnel department.

Housekeeping duties

The personnel department performs a number of housekeeping duties for the business enterprise. Records are maintained on each employee. These include data on recruitment, employment, training, health and other personal information, pay history, disciplinary actions, and promotions or transfers. These records provide information for line supervisors when historical background is needed on an employee.

Advisory role

The personnel department cooperates with other departments in the business enterprise. It works with safety engineers to see that safety regulations are enforced and to improve the safety of machinery and the production process. Personnel administrators can assist industrial engineers in motivating employees to better productivity. Personnel officials maintain contact with union officials to improve communication with management.

Finally, as adviser to top management, the personnel department can determine the level of employee morale through such data as absentee rates, labor turnover, complaints and grievances, accidents, and production efficiency. Once these data are analyzed, the department may make suggestions for improving the enterprise's work climate.

SUMMARY

The functions of the personnel department include providing staff assistance in the recruitment, selection, induction, and training of employees. The personnel department acts as adviser to management in matters of employee morale and employee-management relations. Top management and supervisors throughout the enterprise, as well as the personnel department, have important personnel roles to perform.

The personnel department performs five basic steps in the hiring and placement of employees:

1. Working with line management in determining job specifications.
2. Recruiting job applicants.

3. Carrying out the selection process.
4. Inducting new employees.
5. Coordinating a program of employee training.

The personnel department normally performs the function of job analysis to ensure that wages are fair. The first step in job analysis is to draw up a job description covering the essential elements of each specific job. Then job evaluation ranks each job in relation to other jobs in the enterprise. Following job evaluation, the wage scale is drawn up.

A performance rating system is used to evaluate each employee's performance. This is used to make individual merit increases in wages within job classifications and to guide management in selecting employees for promotion. Seniority and ability are important considerations in promotion policy.

The personnel department should formulate policy on transfers of employees from one job to another, between departments, from one work shift to another, or for remedial reasons.

Downgrading and layoffs are important areas relating to workers and should be covered by formulated personnel policies.

A disciplinary policy should provide a clear statement of what is expected of employees and should be fairly administered.

When workers are unionized, the personnel department can assist management in developing positive policies regarding organized labor and can aid supervisors in administering those policies.

The personnel department functions in a staff capacity. It includes a personnel manager and subordinates in the areas of recruiting, training, labor relations, employee services, and safety and health. The head of the personnel function should report to the president of the enterprise and be considered a member of top management.

TERMS FOR REVIEW

personnel management	job evaluation	downgrading
job specifications	performance rating	layoffs
recruitment	promotion	discipline
employee training	seniority	Occupational Safety and
job description	employee transfer	Health Act of 1970

QUESTIONS

1. Outline the steps that a personnel department might go through to add an additional shift of both skilled and nonskilled workers in a television manufacturing enterprise.

2. What types of training programs would be appropriate for the different kinds of workers hired as the result of the expansion outlined in Question 1?

3. Distinguish between job analysis and performance rating. What is the importance of each?

4. Assume the role of owner of a small manufacturing enterprise, and draw up a statement of your views on the relative importance of seniority and ability in promotions or layoffs for production workers.

5. Assume the role of labor union president in a small manufacturing enterprise, and draw up a statement of your views on the relative importance of seniority and ability in promotions and wage increases for production workers who are members of the union.

6. Why is a written disciplinary policy important for the business enterprise?

7. *a.* What changes occur in the development and administration of personnel policies when an enterprise's nonmanagerial employees become unionized?

   b. What positive and negative implications are there for management in such a development?

8. Describe the approach of CBS to personnel development as reflected on the first page of this chapter. Why do you think CBS has adopted this point of view?

---

business briefs

MARIJUANA USE IN BUSINESS

A study by Louis Harris & Associates, public opinion pollsters, indicates that over 33 million Americans over age 18 may have used marijuana. The use of marijuana by business employees and managers is increasing. Although most business managers believe that alcohol creates a more serious problem for industry than do drugs, considerable concern is expressed about marijuana.

"Grass" smoking occurs in business in a variety of circumstances. In some enterprises "pot" smoking is noticed in rest rooms, parking lots, or back offices. Marijuana may be used on the job by persons whose work lacks stimulation and variety. Night shifts can create special problems, including the use of drugs on the job.

The use of marijuana is by no means limited to blue-collar and clerical employees. Drugs are reportedly used by some business executives, attorneys, bankers, and accountants. Although most pot smoking occurs among younger persons, some middle-aged professionals and managers engage in the practice.

A wide variety of policies exist concerning the use of marijuana. Attitudes range from such statements as "We abide by all laws, federal, state, and local" to "Everybody uses it—what's the big deal?" One factory manager summarized his enterprise's policy as follows: "Our major concern is that our people not use it on the job."

Some corporations take a hard line on pot smoking, especially when hazardous work is involved. Several personnel departments have developed programs for counseling marijuana users, as is done for people with alcoholic problems.

Some enterprises take a relatively liberal policy toward drug use and tolerate pot smoking unless it interferes with an employee's work. Others have fired employees the first time they are caught using marijuana. Many company policy statements include specific penalties calling for the dismissal of anyone caught using any prohibited drug, including alcohol, on the job. However, one manager was quoted as saying, "The company feels that with a boring, high-turnover job it's all right when workers sneak off to smoke if that will make them stay on the job longer."

In presenting his view of marijuana use on the job one businessperson said, "You wouldn't go in to your boss drunk, and you wouldn't stoned either. . . . It's no fun to smoke on the job. To be stoned and go into a business meeting is a nightmare."

Just as business attitudes vary on the use of marijuana, so too do state and local laws across the country. In some states the possession of two ounces or less can bring substantial fines and jail sentences. In other areas the possession of small amounts of marijuana is treated as a minor offense similar to a parking violation.

1. *Should business managers be concerned about the use of marijuana by employees (including other managers) (a) on the job or (b) off the job? State the reasons for your answer.*
2. *Assume the role of personnel manager of a manufacturing enterprise. Frame a policy statement regarding the use of marijuana and alcohol by employees. Then outline a program for enforcement of the policy.*

PSYCHOLOGICAL TESTS FOR ALL?

An increasing number of corporations are using psychological tests and interviews in the employment and promotion processes. This testing and interviewing, which may be extensive, is being conducted by private professional psychologists as well as by company staff psychologists.

In placing prospective employees, many corporate managements are highly influenced, if not governed, by the results of such psychological testing. Psychological tests and interviews are being applied to both entry-level positions and executive applicants. Sears, Roebuck & Company, with more than 400,000 employees, makes considerable use of psychological assessment of employees and applicants for executive positions. Sears has used psychological assessment since the 1940s and reportedly believes that it improves the quality of management.

Psychological testing is designed to measure emotional strengths, mental ability, social skills, personal values, and interests. It is also used to suggest whether a person could handle additional responsibilities. One large retailer's assessment program stages phone calls from "irate customers" to see how well candidates handle complaints and behave in a situation of stress.

Corporations which have made use of psychological assessment programs include Sears, IBM, J. C. Penney, General Electric, Exxon, AT&T, Union Carbide, Delta Airlines, and Prudential Insurance.

The use of psychological testing and interviewing is not universally praised by corporations or employees. It has been criticized as an invasion of privacy when present or prospective employees are questioned about such matters as religious beliefs, sexual behavior, and family relationships. Some executives believe that reliance on psychological tests abdicates management's authority to make decisions and is not a substitute for sound business evaluations.

Defenders of psychological assessment programs respond that such tests are normally "voluntary" (though employees or applicants seldom refuse to take them). It is also claimed that if these tests improve hiring and placement decisions, they can result in more satisfied employees as well as better job performance. Testing programs may be as inexpensive as $150 per person, which supporters of such programs claim is reasonable compared with the possible costs of making a bad hiring or promotion mistake.

1. *Discuss the advantages of psychological assessment programs to business enterprises and job applicants.*
2. *What problems do you think are raised by the extensive use of such programs?*
3. *Would you be willing to submit to psychological testing as a "voluntary" condition of prospective employment? Why or why not?*

TURNOVER OF COLLEGE GRADUATES

A personnel manager for a large Midwestern manufacturing corporation recently voiced the following comment:

"We are hiring college graduates in business administration and paying them $12,000 a year and up. Top management has indicated that we are to hire more of these young people. However, we haven't been able to keep many of them more than a year. After an orientation period of two weeks they are rotated for three-month periods from one department to another in one of our factory locations. At the end of a year we put them in open spots in which they express an interest. Then the supervisor takes over their work assignments. One problem is that many of our supervisors are getting very little more in salary than these college graduates even though they have been with the company for a number of years."

1. *What personnel problems are implied in this statement?*
2. *What suggestions would you make to the personnel manager for reducing turnover in college graduates and maintaining the morale of supervisors?*

case

HEDGEPATH EARLY AMERICAN FURNITURE COMPANY

The Hedgepath Early American Furniture Company is a family-owned and family-managed enterprise. It was started 30 years ago by Ronald A. Hedgepath, Sr. who developed the business into a successful manufacturing operation employing 250 production workers.

In the summer of 1979 Hedgepath's only son, Ronald Junior, was home from college, where he was majoring in business administration. Ronald had worked in the factory in previous years. During the summer of 1979 he was employed in the main office. Because of the personnel practices he observed, and in view of what appeared to him to be a high rate of employee turnover, Ronald persuaded his father that the company needed a director of personnel administration.

The elder Hedgepath had built his business by depending heavily on his plant foremen to do the hiring, training, and firing of employees. The ten foremen had been picked by him. In the small town where the plant was located, they had considerable prestige because of their positions. Several had been with the company since its founding.

When the word got around that at young Ronald's insistence a "personnel director" was being brought in and that all hiring and firing would now be centralized, there was considerable grumbling among the foremen. In particular, the old-timers among them declared they understood company personnel needs better than an outsider ever could.

Jim Curtis, 29, was hired as the new personnel director. He had a bachelor's degree in business. He had worked five years as assistant personnel manager for a large auto manufacturer in another city.

Mr. Curtis soon found that he had his hands full in trying to work out uniform personnel policies for the Hedgepath plant. There was no union at the plant. For years each foreman had made his own "personnel policies," with considerable variation from foreman to foreman. The workers soon learned what to expect from their particular foreman. The hiring of friends and relatives was a common practice. When orders slowed down, there was no company-wide policy for laying off workers. Each foreman determined who was to be laid off. Seniority was sometimes given considera-

tion. However, the foremen generally attempted to retain the most productive employees, or relatives, or employees with whom they had special friendships. When Curtis asked one of the foremen why a particular worker with a poor attendance record was being retained, the foreman replied, "I have known Bob Jones for 18 years, and I am not about to let him go." From the tone of his remark it was obvious to Mr. Curtis that the foreman did not wish to be pressed further on the matter.

As part of his investigation of the labor turnover situation, Mr. Curtis began exit conferences with employees who were leaving the company. These conferences revealed that employees were disgruntled with such things as special friendships and nepotism in hiring and laying off workers. They also felt that there was unfair treatment in the allocation of overtime, promotions, transfers, and discipline.

When Curtis began to standardize personnel procedures, some of the foremen cooperated. However, he met resistance from others. There was also a varied reaction from the workers. Some employees welcomed the personnel director's actions because they thought they would get a "fairer shake." However, other employees resented the new personnel director.

Some employees who had complaints about their foremen began coming to Curtis to air their grievances. At the same time, several of the foremen began going to the plant superintendent whenever the new personnel director did anything that they felt threatened their power. When a decision made by Curtis failed to work out in their departments, they were quick to blame the personnel director. Curtis, in turn, claimed that these foremen were not cooperating with his attempts to work out sound personnel policies that all departments could live with.

The plant superintendent found that much of his time was occupied in settling arguments between his foremen and the new personnel director. After several weeks of this he went to the senior Mr. Hedgepath with the statement, "You're going to have to do something with that personnel man if we're going to get any work done around here!"

Exhibit 1 is a chart of the Hedgepath organization

EXHIBIT 1

Partial organization chart of the Hedgepath Early American Furniture Company

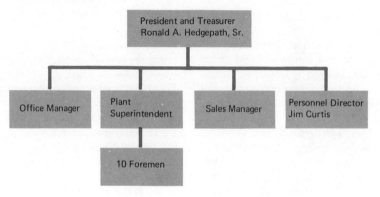

showing the major management positions in the company after the establishment of the personnel department in 1979.

1. *What are the problems involved in instituting a personnel department in the Hedgepath Company where none existed previously?*

2. *What authority should be given to the personnel director?*

3. *In what ways could the foremen participate in improving personnel policies and practices?*

4. *What should Mr. Hedgepath do in response to the statement by the plant superintendent?*

Inland Steel reports . . .

Inland's per capita employment costs increased 10 percent during 1977, primarily as a result of higher wages and benefits granted under a new three-year contract negotiated in April 1977 with the United Steelworkers of America (USW) and the extension of comparable improvements to other employees.

Average employment was 35,222, as compared with 34,476 in 1976. Employees earned a total of $650. 4 million in wages and salaries in 1977, an average of $18,465 per employee. This compared with total 1976 earnings of $586.8 million, or an average of $17,020.

Employee benefits totaled $179.7 million, or $5,101 per employee, compared with $150.8 million and $4,375, respectively, in 1976.

It is estimated that the new USW contract will increase our employment costs about 10 percent annually during the three-year period ending July 31, 1980. The contract provides for base wage increases of 80 cents per hour, increases in incentives and job class increments, and continuation of the cost of living allowance (COLA), which increased wages by $1.17 per hour, or about 13 pecent, during the term of the previous contract. Significant changes were made in employee benefits, including improvements in pensions, life insurance, medical care programs and sickness and accident benefits; a new vision care program; and the addition of one extra paid holiday. A new income security program provides additional protection for employees with 20 or more years of service.

The new contract extends to August 1, 1980, and provides that the 1980 contract will be negotiated under the Experimental Negotiating Agreement (ENA).

In August 1977 we faced a strike threat at our Indiana Harbor Works, and a walkout was narrowly averted when a settlement was reached with the local union prior to the deadline. This potential disruption prompted many of our customers to place more of their business with other steel producers to assure themselves of uninterrupted supplies.

A total of 139 production days were lost at our new Minorca iron ore mine in Minnesota as a result of an illegal industry strike on August 1, which was settled December 16. Two other iron ore sources in which we have an ownership interest also were shut down for approximately four months, and there were walkouts under a local option at two plants of our subsidiary, Joseph T. Ryerson & Son, Inc.

Prior to December 6, when the major coal strike began, there were many unauthorized stoppages at our coal mines, causing the loss of approximately 48,000 man-days of work and about 470,000 tons of coal production.

As of December 31, 1977, Inland employees represented by the United Steelworkers of America totaled 21,000. Employees represented by other unions totaled 2,800. The remainder consisted of 1,500 wage employees not represented by unions, 5,500 exempt salaried and 4,600 nonexempt salaried employees.

From annual report of Inland Steel Company

Photo by Bob McCullough

Labor relations

Labor relations

The study of human relations and personnel management leads to a third area involving the work force—labor unions. When management deals with the work force through a union, this is referred to as labor relations. The subject of labor unions produces strong emotions in many persons. There is much public interest when a major strike occurs or when some other labor dispute is widely publicized. However, most day-to-day contacts between unions and managements take place in an atmosphere quite unlike that of these relatively infrequent events.

You should approach the study of labor relations with an open mind to examine how organized labor affects the operation of business enterprises.

After studying this chapter, you will be able to answer the following questions:

How has significant legislation affected labor relations?

What has been the growth of union membership?

Why do workers join unions?

How are labor unions organized?

What provisions are normally included in the labor contract?

How does the grievance process contribute to a healthy work climate?

LEGISLATION AFFECTING LABOR RELATIONS

To understand the relationship between labor unions and business you need to see how this relationship evolved and how management's dealings with unions have been influenced by national laws. There are four pieces of legislation which are especially important: the Norris La Guardia Act, the Wagner Act, the Taft-Hartley Act, and the Landrum-Griffin Act.

The Norris-LaGuardia Act

The Norris-LaGuardia Act of 1932 was the first major labor law passed by Congress. The act limited the power of the federal courts to issue injunctions in labor disputes. Prior to its passage the courts had granted injunctions freely against unions in response to requests by employers to stifle union activity.

The Norris-LaGuardia Act protected the rights of unions to organize workers, to strike, to picket, and to inform the public of a labor dispute. In addition, the act prohibited employers from forcing workers to sign a *yellow-dog contract* agreeing not to join a union as a condition of employment.

The Wagner Act

The National Labor Relations Act of 1935, usually called the Wagner Act, represented a Magna Charta for organized labor in the United States. Before it was passed, business had used many methods to discourage employees from joining unions. It was not unusual for employees to be fired merely because they were suspected of union activity. Some employers circulated *blacklists* to other business owners with the names of former employees who had been discharged for union activities.

Employers did not limit their antiunion activities to economic pressure. They also used strikebreakers, labor spies, and armed guards in attempting to prevent unions from organizing their factories. Violence occurred, including shooting and dynamiting by both business and workers, in the battles over the employees' right to organize unions. During this period of American history the political and legal climate generally stressed property rights and favored management's attempts to avoid unionization.

Few employers were willing to recognize voluntarily the right of their employees to join a union and to bargain collectively over wages and working conditions before Congress passed the Wagner Act in 1935. The act declared that employees "shall have the right to self-organization, to form, join, or assist labor organizations, to bargain collectively through representatives of their own choosing."

The Wagner Act made illegal any interference with employees who engage in union activities. An employer cannot discharge an employee for union activity. It is unlawful to take discriminatory action against an employee for joining a union. Company unions are not permitted. Such unions had been organized by some managements to avoid bargaining with independent unions. Also, an employer cannot refuse to bargain with a union selected by employees to represent them.

The administration of the Wagner Act is the job of the National Labor Relations Board, which originally had three members. Field examiners of the board investigate complaints of unfair labor practices. Then trial examiners conduct formal hearings and pass their findings on to the board for affirmation. Decisions of the board can be appealed through the federal courts to the Supreme Court.

Another function of the National Labor Relations Board is to conduct elections to determine whether the workers in an enterprise desire a union. An election is held if a union is able to certify interest by 30 percent or more of the employees whom the union would represent in an enterprise. The union must receive a majority of votes in the election to be certified as the workers' bargaining agent.

The Wagner Act minimized the industrial disputes stemming from the issue of whether employees were to be represented by a union. The NLRB election procedure is a better means for determining whether an enterprise is to be unionized than were the strikes and violence which marked earlier representation battles.

However, the Wagner Act was not successful in reducing strikes in already organized industries. In 1946 there were almost 5,000 strikes involving more than 4.5 million workers. Excesses by unions and limitations of the Wagner Act started a movement to correct some labor abuses.

The Taft-Hartley Act

The Labor-Management Relations Act of 1947, commonly known as the Taft-Hartley Act, is actually an amendment to the Wagner Act. In an attempt to correct some abuses by organized labor, the Taft-Hartley Act adds restrictions on the activities of labor organizations. It gives employers rights not spelled out in the earlier legislation. The administration of the act remains with the National Labor Relations Board, which was increased from three to five members.

The 1947 act defines unfair labor practices by an employer in essentially the same way as the Wagner Act. However, the Taft-Hartley Act goes further by outlawing certain labor practices by unions. There is to be no restraint or coercion of employees in determining which union will represent them. The union cannot interfere in the right of an employee not to participate in union activity. The union cannot force an employer to discriminate against an employee for nonunion membership unless the union shop is authorized. In a *union shop* the employer agrees that employees must join the union after they are hired, but union membership is not a prerequisite to being hired. It is an unfair labor practice for a union which has a union-shop agreement to charge excessive initiation or membership fees.

In a *closed shop* workers must be members of the union before they may be hired by an employer. The closed shop is illegal under the Taft-Hartley Act.

Under the Taft-Hartley Act employers or self-employed persons cannot be forced to join a union. This prevents unions from forcing independent businesspersons such as plumbers to join a union even though their earnings and working conditions might affect those of unionized employees in the same occupations.

Secondary boycotts by unions are outlawed by the act. A *secondary boycott* occurs when employees of Company A with a grievance against their employer picket Company B or persuade Company B employees to strike because Company B uses Company A's products. A *primary boycott* is one in which employees refuse to use the products of the employer with whom they have a dispute. This is permitted, since it involves direct action against their own employer. Although easy to define in a simple example, in practice the secondary boycott is often difficult to distinguish from direct action against an employer.

The Taft-Hartley Act also prohibits unions from forcing employers to recognize or bargain with one union if another union has already been certified by the NLRB as the bargaining agent. The purpose of this clause is to avoid the disastrous effects on both employers and employees that may result from conflicts among different unions. *Jurisdictional strikes* which grow out of disagreements over which craft has the right to perform particular jobs are outlawed. The building-trades unions have been particularly affected by jurisdictional disputes because of overlapping of skills among their members. Another labor practice by unions that the act defines as unfair is *featherbedding,* which requires an employer to pay for services not performed. However, the interpretation of this provision allows for the payment of employees even though they do little or no productive work. An example would be the use of "standby musicians" during recorded broadcasts or when outside bands play in local theaters.

The act also requires union officers to file affidavits that they are not members of the Communist Party and that they do not support any organization which advocates overthrow of the U.S government by force.

Protection for the public   The Taft-Hartley Act protects the public from strikes which would cut off the flow of essential goods and services. When the president of the United States determines that a labor dispute threatens the national health or safety, the attorney general can obtain an injunction from a federal court. This has the effect of postponing any strike for 80 days. During this time workers cannot strike and management cannot lock workers out of the plant. Terms of work and pay are frozen, and the parties are obliged to make every effort to settle their differences. The assistance of the Federal Mediation and Conciliation Service is available to both parties. Before the 80-day injunction period is over, if no settlement has been reached, the National Labor Relations Board is required to poll employees to see whether they will accept the last offer of management. If no settlement is reached through this procedure, the president submits a report to Congress with or without recommendations for action.

The right-to-work controversy   A controversial part of the Taft-Hartley Act is Section 14b. This provides that individual states may outlaw union-shop contracts which require workers to join a union. In 1979, 20 states had these right-to-work laws.

A state right-to-work law substantially weakens unions in organizing new workers. Unless employees can be required to join a union after being hired, it is difficult to promote a solid union membership. Unions believe that all workers in a unionized factory should share the cost of the benefits secured by the union.

The Landrum-Griffin Act

Congressional investigations disclosed irregularities and questionable practices by some unions and by some managements in their relations with union officials. As a result Congress passed the Labor-Management Reporting and Disclosures Act of 1959, commonly known as the Landrum-Griffin Act. This act authorized the federal government to police the internal affairs of labor unions.

Some of the principal provisions of the Landrum-Griffin Act are:

1. Every labor union is required to have a constitution and bylaws which spell out such matters as membership eligibility, fees and dues, the handling

FIGURE 10–1
Summary of major labor relations legislation

Norris-LaGuardia Act (1932)

Limited federal courts in issuing injunctions against unions. Protected unions' rights to organize workers, to strike, and to picket. Prohibited employers from requiring yellow-dog contracts.

Wagner Act (1935)

Gave employees the right to organize unions and bargain collectively with employers.

Prohibited an employer from discriminating against an employee for union activity.

Prohibited company unions.

Required employer to bargain with the union certified as employees' bargaining agent.

Established NLRB to investigate unfair labor practices and supervise union representation elections.

Taft-Hartley Act (1947—amended Wagner Act)

Outlawed these practices by unions:

Coercion of employees in determining which union would represent them.

Union interference with the right of an employee not to participate in union activity.

Forcing an employer to discriminate against an employee for nonunion membership unless union shop was authorized.

Charging excessive initiation or membership fees when a union shop existed.

Forcing self-employed persons to join a union.

Closed shops.

Secondary boycotts.

Forcing employers to recognize or bargain with one union if another union had already been NLRB-certified.

Featherbedding.

Required union officials to file non-Communist affidavits.

Authorized president of the United States to obtain 80-day injunction to postpone a strike which threatened the national welfare.

Permitted states to have right-to-work laws outlawing union shop contracts.

Landrum-Griffin Act (1959)

Required unions to have a constitution and bylaws.

Guaranteed certain rights to individual union members.

Required unions to file financial and activity reports with secretary of labor.

Limited unions and employers to peaceful persuasion of workers in organizing campaigns.

of union funds, and the procedures for collective bargaining and strike authorizations.

2. Regardless of the union's constitution, union members have certain inalienable rights. These include safeguards against improper discipline, protection against unreasonable dues and initiation fees, and democratic controls over union

officials. Union members may enforce these rights by appealing to the federal courts if necessary.

3. Unions and union officials must file reports with the secretary of labor regarding their activities and finances. The reports are similar to those required of corporations under the federal Securities Act. (This provision put on record many of the internal workings of unions which had previously not been subject to review by any outside agency.)

4. Limitations are placed on union organizing tactics and on employer countermeasures to union organizing activities. The purpose of the limitations is to restrict these activities on both sides to the peaceful persuasion of workers.

GROWTH IN UNION MEMBERSHIP

The union movement has had variations in growth, depending on economic, political, and social factors as well as the shifting tide of public opinion and legal decisions. Figure 10–2 shows how the strength of union membership has varied from 1930 to 1976.

There was a spectacular growth in union membership between 1936 and the end of World War II. The passage of the Wagner Act in 1935 plus a keen rivalry between the AFL and the CIO stimulated the organizing efforts of the unions. The number of union members increased during World War II as the result of higher employment levels and wider union recognition.

Following the end of World War II, in 1945, numerous strikes occurred and the prestige of unions was damaged. The Taft-Hartley Act was passed in 1947. Union growth leveled off during this period.

The Korean War stimulated union growth. With the merger of the AFL and the CIO in 1955, the groundwork was laid for the achievement of a union membership of 17.5 million workers in 1956. However, the merger did not solve all of organized labor's problems. The Landrum-Griffin Act, passed in 1959, put pressure on the unions to "clean house."

By 1974 union membership had reached an all-time high of 21.6 million workers. However, the proportion of union members in the total labor force actually slipped from a 1956 high of 25 percent to about 20 percent in 1976. This can be explained in part by the changing nature of the work force. Automation has decreased the number of blue-collar workers, who have been most likely to be union members. An increasing percentage of the work force is made up of women and white-collar workers, who have traditionally been less interested in union membership.

Unions have increased their efforts to organize professional, technical, clerical, and sales employees. White-collar attitudes toward unions have been changing. As the result of inflation the wages of many white-collar workers have not kept up with increases in the cost of living. Teachers, police officers, and firefighters have become increasingly involved in union activity. These groups, along

FIGURE 10–2
Membership of national and international unions, 1930–1976

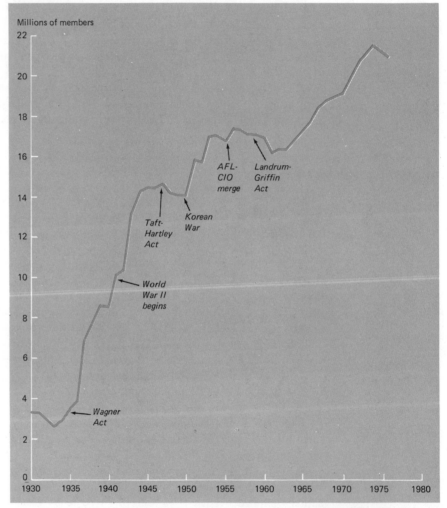

Source: U.S. Bureau of the Census, *Statistical Abstract of the U.S.: 1978* (99th ed.).

with other state and local government employees, are the most rapidly growing sector of the organized labor movement today.

WHY WORKERS JOIN UNIONS

Contrary to the belief of some managers, the desire for more pay is only one of the reasons why workers become union members. Usually a variety of economic and noneconomic considerations stimulate workers to join unions.

Economic motives for union membership

The three main economic factors which motivate workers to join labor unions voluntarily are wages, fringe benefits, and security in employment and wage income.

The prospect of higher wages does motivate workers to join unions. However, fringe benefits such as health insurance, disability compensation, life insurance, pensions, and paid vacations are becoming increasingly important. Workers also want security in employment and wage income to protect them against layoffs due to seasonal and general declines in business activity.

Noneconomic motives for union membership

The noneconomic motives influencing employees to establish or to join unions may be stronger than the economic motives. Eight noneconomic motives for union membership can be identified.

1. Employees want protection against arbitrary action by supervisors in discipline and discharge. The union provides a procedure for dealing with grievances to try to ensure fairness by management.

2. Workers desire a voice in making the decisions which affect them. Employees like to participate in decisions on such matters as how overtime will be distributed, how layoffs will be carried out, and how increased compensation will be divided between pay raises and fringe benefits.

3. Workers feel a need to establish channels of communication with top management. Such channels are provided by the union with its grievance procedure.

4. The union offers an opportunity for increased individual satisfaction associated with the work experience. This is especially true when the work environment is routine and monotonous and the employee has more than average capabilities. The employee who becomes active in the union frequently feels a sense of accomplishment from holding a union office or participating in union activities.

5. In today's complex industrial society most individuals feel a need for identification with some group. Union membership can provide an important kind of group identification.

6. Individual workers are motivated to join a union by the social pressure of the informal work group. Employees with negative or indifferent attitudes may become union members rather than face hostility and nonacceptance from fellow workers.

7. Unions, particularly in large urban areas, sometimes provide for the recreational, social, cultural, and educational needs of workers.

8. The employee may be motivated to union membership because of his or her family ties. Studies have shown that a worker with a family background of union membership is more likely to become a union member than is a worker from a nonunion family.

LABOR RELATIONS SPECIALISTS

Labor relations specialists advise management on all aspects of union-management relations. Specialists in this field work for the most part in unionized business firms and governmental agencies. In comparison with private industry, labor unions do not employ a large number of professionally trained labor relations workers. An elected union official generally handles labor relations matters at the company level. At national and international union headquarters, however, the research and education staff usually includes specialists with a degree in industrial and labor relations, economics, or law.

Labor relations specialists help company officials prepare for collective bargaining sessions. When the contract is up for negotiation, these specialists provide background information and technical support, a job that requires extensive knowledge of economics, labor law, and collective bargaining trends. The actual negotiation of the agreement is conducted at the top management level, with the director of labor relations or another top-ranking company official serving as the employer's representative. However, members of the company's labor relations staff play an important role throughout the negotiations.

Much of the everyday work of the labor relations staff concerns the interpretation and administration of the contract, the grievance procedures in particular. For example, members of the labor relations staff might work with the union on seniority rights under the layoff procedure set forth in the contract or might meet with the union steward about a worker's grievance. Doing the job well means staying abreast of current developments in labor law, including arbitration decisions, and maintaining continuing liaison with union officials.

Although the number of jobs in labor relations is projected to increase over the next decade, keen job competition is anticipated.

A growing number of people enter the labor relations field directly as trainees. They are usually graduates of master's degree programs in industrial relations, or they may have a law degree. Quite a few people, however, begin in personnel work, gain experience in that area, and subsequently move into a labor relations job.

Union membership required for employment

Where a union shop has been lawfully agreed to by an employer and a union, all members of the work force covered by the labor agreement are required to join the union within a specified time after being hired. In the union shop an employee has no option of whether or not to join a union. Membership is a condition for continued employment.

THE STRUCTURE AND ORGANIZATION OF LABOR UNIONS

Craft and industrial unions

Unions are customarily organized on a craft or an industry basis. *Craft unions* draw their members from a particular trade or occupation. An example of the craft union is the International Brotherhood of Electrical Workers, which includes electricians wherever they are employed—whether in factories, the building trades, or shipyards. The *industrial union,* typified by the United Automobile Workers, organizes the workers in a particular industry, regardless of the kind of work they do. Sometimes the line between craft and industrial unions is blurred as each reaches beyond its original scope of skills or industry to organize other workers.

Local unions

The local union is the unit which deals most directly with individual union members. The local union will usually have a business agent or a secretary-treasurer who takes care of the affairs of the union and is paid from the local union treasury.

The shop stewards are important members of the local union organization. These individuals are usually elected by the union members with whom they work. Although shop stewards are full-time employees of the enterprise, they represent union members and discuss grievances with first-line supervisors.

National union organization

The local union is generally affiliated with a national or international union. The national union has to meet the needs of its local affiliates if the national leaders are to retain their offices.

Representatives from the national organization assist local unions in negotiating either contract agreements or grievances which have not been settled at lower levels. They also act as organizers to reach nonunion employees of enterprises in their areas. The national union may provide its locals with financial aid during a strike.

THE UNION CONTRACT

When an enterprise's management bargains with its employees' union over conditions of employment, the result is a contract agreement. Union contracts customarily run for two or three years. Despite the unique nature of each union contract, there are certain issues dealt with in most contracts. These issues, discussed in the following pages, form the framework within which labor relations are conducted in the individual enterprise.

The bargaining unit

One of the first elements of a union contract is the *recognition clause,* which states that management acknowledges a certain union as representing a designated group of employees. The *bargaining unit* defines the employer and the employees covered by the union contract. On the employer side, the bargaining unit may be one business enterprise or several firms dealing with the same union, which is called *industry-wide* bargaining. On the employee side, the bargaining unit may include employees in certain job classifications or employees in a particular factory if the enterprise is a multiplant operation. When job classification is the basis for the bargaining unit, management may have to bargain with more than one union. These could represent different crafts, such as electricians, pipefitters, and carpenters.

Union security

Customarily the contract will spell out provisions for union security. In most instances this means that all employees covered by the contract must join the union within a specified time after being employed and will be required to maintain membership in the union. Frequently, a *checkoff* clause authorizes management to deduct union dues from the employee's pay and pay this sum directly to the union treasury.

Grievance procedure and arbitration

Labor contracts normally contain procedures for dealing with complaints by union members against management. A grievance usually moves through a succession of steps from lower to higher levels of management and union officials. If a dispute cannot be settled by the parties themselves, an impartial third person called an *arbitrator* is used to settle the issue. Because of the importance of the grievance process and arbitration to labor relations, this area is discussed in detail later in the chapter.

Wages and hours

Hours of work and wage rates are of major importance in collective bargaining. General wage scales are outlined in the contract, with detailed wage scales for various job classifications listed in appendices to the basic contract. Overtime premiums, bonuses, wage incentive systems, automatic wage adjustments, and wage reopening discussion clauses are usually a part of this section of the labor contract.

Pay or work guarantees

The inclusion of a guarantee of pay represents a relatively new, but important, feature of the collective bargaining agreement. As recently as 20 years ago, *supplementary unemployment benefit* plans were virtually unknown. These SUB plans consist of payments made by employers to a fund that is used to pay employees who have been laid off. This money supplements unemployment benefits paid under state plans. Unions which have negotiated unemployment benefit plans include those representing auto workers, steelworkers, and rubber workers.

In contrast to the relatively recent guaranteed pay plans, some guarantee of hours of work for employees over a given period has been in existence for years. Such work guarantees include the 36-hour-week guarantee in the meat-packing industry, a weekly hours guarantee in various transportation enterprises, and a minimum hours-per-week guarantee in sugar refineries.

Holidays and vacations

Almost all labor contracts include a statement regarding holidays. On a paid holiday employees are paid for a workday even though they do not work. Those employees who may be required to work on designated holidays are paid a premium, such as time and a half (i.e., they receive one and a half times their regular hourly rate) or double time. The number of days recognized as holidays has increased over the years, with the number now ranging from six to nine.

Paid vacations are part of the labor contract, with the length of the vacation based on the employee's years of service with the enterprise. Paid vacations usually run from one to four weeks.

Employee benefits

Employee benefits cover a broad range of insurance and pension provisions. Employee benefits have increased considerably in recent years and are an important part of the union contract. Most contracts call for some of the following types of insurance for employees: life insurance, medical and hospitalization coverage, and accidental death and disability insurance.

Most union contracts provide for pensions for employees retiring from the enterprise. The tendency in recent years has been for pension benefits to increase and for the retirement age to be liberalized. In 1974 the complex *Employee Retirement Income Security Act* was passed. It provides protection for retirement funds and generally requires that employees have *vested rights* in the pension credits they accumulate. When pension benefits are vested, employees are entitled as a matter of right to the enterprise's contribution after a specified period, whether or not they are still employed by the enterprise at retirement age. This increases the mobility of employees since they need not remain with one employer to qualify for retirement benefits in addition to federal Social Security.

Discipline and discharge

Union contracts include mention of the measures of discipline an employer may undertake for certain activities of employees. A broad reference to disciplinary measures is made in a general management rights clause. Discipline short of discharge may include oral and written warnings, suspension, transfer, demotion, and pay penalties. This section of the contract usually requires that some form of notice be given to the employee and the union. Frequently a hearing must be held before disciplinary action can be taken.

Discharge is the strongest form of disciplinary action an enterprise can take against an employee short of court action in a civil suit or supporting criminal prosecution. Almost all contracts have a section on discharge. This includes the grounds for dismissal and procedures for notification, action, and appeal. Chapter 9 discusses personnel policies dealing with discipline, plant rules, and employee conduct.

Management and union rights

It is not unusual to find a statement regarding management's rights in the labor relations contract. The general statement of managerial rights contains provisions relating to the right to direct the work force and the right to conduct the business. Frequently a statement is made that the management retains all rights except those specifically detailed in the contract as subjects for collective bargaining.

Sometimes limitations are placed on management's right to contract work, including restrictions on subcontracting. A common provision is that subcontracting is prohibited if it would result in a layoff of employees or if some employees are already in a layoff status. Other restrictions may place limits on changes in production methods and on the types of work performed by supervisors.

Union rights may include access of union representatives to the plant, control

"Quit telling me what to do, Martha! Who do you think you are—the union?"

Reprinted by permission The Wall Street Journal

of the union label (as is done in the apparel industry), and permission for union bulletin boards.

Unions may be restricted by the contract in such matters as the number of union stewards in the plant, the conduct of union activities on company time, and the solicitation of union members during company time.

Seniority provisions

Nearly all union contracts cover seniority as it affects employees in matters of job retention, promotion, and transfers. Ordinarily employees who have greater length of service with the enterprise get preference over those with lesser seniority.

There are different degrees of emphasis on the role of seniority for purposes of promotion. The most weight is given to seniority when the clause "seniority shall prevail" is the basis for determining which employee shall be promoted. However, the contract may indicate that seniority shall prevail but that the promotion will be given to the most senior candidate "if qualified." The "if qualified" clause places relatively less weight on seniority. The most senior employee could be passed over if he or she is not qualified for the promotion. Management has the most latitude in promotions when the "if equal" clause is included. The "if equal" clause means that the most senior employee will be given the position if his or her ability and qualifications are equal to those of competing candidates.

Management usually prefers to have as much latitude as possible in selecting personnel for promotion, transfer, or layoff. However, seniority systems can aid management in dealing consistently with a large work force and with the many jobs which do not require a high degree of skill.

Strikes and lockouts

Nearly all union contracts contain a no-strike clause—either unconditional or conditional. An unconditional clause bans work stoppages for the life of the contract. A conditional clause permits strikes but only if the grievance procedure is ineffective or a deadlock occurs during bargaining on a new contract or the old contract has expired.

A *strike* is action taken by workers to cease work. During a strike union members usually picket to prevent other personnel from entering the struck plant. In a similar management action, called a *lockout*, management does not permit union members to enter the enterprise's facilities because of a dispute. Customarily management will give a no-lockout pledge in the labor agreement when the union accepts a no-strike clause. Contracts with no-strike clauses may specify disciplinary penalties ranging up to discharge for individual participants in unauthorized or wildcat strikes.

Most strikes in recent years have been over wages. Other strikes have occurred because of dissatisfaction over factory administration, union security, fringe benefits, or job security. Many strikes occur while management and union officials are bargaining over the terms of a new contract after the old one has expired.

Working conditions and safety

A variety of guarantees are made that neither management nor the union will discriminate against individual employees on account of race, creed, sex, age, or some other ascribed status. Employee health and safety are referred to in the contract in clauses such as those covering union-management safety committees, safety equipment and who shall pay for it, provision for first aid, and physical examinations. Sometimes services and working conditions such as company dining rooms, parking lots, rest rooms, and locker and shower facilities are included in this section of the contract.

This lengthy discussion has only outlined the most frequently encountered provisions in the typical union contract. A great deal of time and effort by both management and the union go into its development. The union contract is an important part of the American industrial scene.

THE GRIEVANCE PROCESS AND ARBITRATION

The grievance process

The grievance process is one of the major contributions of American unionism to industrial human relations. The grievance process is customarily a three- or four-step procedure with a decision by an impartial third party if management and labor cannot settle the grievance at an earlier stage. A typical grievance procedure would include the following four steps.

First, the employee or employees with a complaint present the grievance in writing to the first-line supervisor. It is discussed by the aggrieved, the union steward or a member of the union grievance committee, and the supervisor. If the grievance is settled at this first step to the satisfaction of management and labor, the remaining steps are unnecessary. If the grievance is not settled, then the second step is taken.

Second, the grievance is discussed by the union grievance committee and the next level of management, perhaps the factory superintendent. At this stage a staff member of the industrial relations department may advise or represent management in attempting to settle the grievance. Most grievances should be settled in the first or second steps.

Third, if the grievance is not settled in the second step it is sent to a committee composed of a representative of the local's national union and the factory superintendent or some higher member of management. At this stage the local union has national assistance and the enterprise's industrial relations director is probably involved for management.

Fourth, if top management and the national union representative are unable to agree on a solution to the grievance, the issue may be dropped if the aggrieved and the union wish, or it may be submitted to a third, impartial party for arbitration. The contract will provide that issues taken to arbitration are final and binding on both parties. The arbitrator is selected with the mutual consent of both parties, with each side bearing the expenses necessary to prepare and present its own case. Customarily the cost of the arbitrator is borne equally by the business enterprise and the union.

Arbitration in industrial relations is sometimes confused with conciliation and mediation. *Arbitration* is a judicial process, with the arbitrator assuming the role of a judge. The parties submit evidence and cross-examine each other's case. After the arbitrator has heard both sides and has had a period of study, a decision is rendered.

Conciliation is the action of a third party to bring together management and labor when a dispute exists between them. The conciliator's role is merely to get the parties to talk over their dispute in the hope of reaching a settlement. On the other hand, *mediation* is the process whereby a third party brings the two sides together and *also* actively participates in the discussions. The mediator attempts to bring about a compromise which will be acceptable to both parties.

Benefits of the grievance process

A good grievance process performs several functions in the modern industrial enterprise. First, it provides an orderly procedure for resolving disputes in the administration of the labor contract. Second, by raising complaints, employees enable dissatisfactions to be examined, evaluated, and resolved. This gives employees an emotional release for dissatisfactions and frustrations. Even though a grievance may ultimately be lost, the employee feels that at least it has been called to management's attention.

Third, the grievance process enables higher management to locate poor first-line supervision. If an unusual number of grievances originate among the employees of a particular supervisor, the quality of that supervisor's management should be investigated. The grievance process is a check on arbitrary actions by supervisors.

Finally, the adjustment of grievances tends to prevent future complaints. As management seeks the underlying problems causing a grievance, it may take corrective action that will lead to a better work climate. Management should always ask the question, "What can we learn from the fact that this grievance was filed?" A properly functioning grievance process is an important tool in developing a good labor relations climate.

This discussion of the grievance process has been in the context of a unionized situation. Management may also establish a grievance procedure where no union exists, except that in the final stage arbitration will normally not be included. In a nonunionized enterprise, management should encourage employees to use the grievance process. There should be a human relations climate in which employees will not fear reprisal if they bring a grievance to management's attention.

SUMMARY

When management deals with the work force through a union, this is referred to as labor relations.

The Norris-LaGuardia Act of 1932 limited the courts in issuing antiunion injunctions and protected unions' rights in organizing workers.

The National Labor Relations Act of 1935, commonly known as the Wagner Act, represented a Magna Charta for organized labor in the United States. The Wagner Act prohibits employers from interfering with the union activities of employees. The act is administered by the National Labor Relations Board, which hears complaints of unfair labor practices and conducts union representation elections.

The Labor-Management Relations Act of 1947, commonly known as the Taft-Hartley Act, was an amendment to the Wagner Act which outlawed certain unfair labor practices by unions. The Taft-Hartley Act gave the president of the United States power to postpone any strike threatening the national health or safety.

The Labor-Management Reporting and Disclosures Act of 1959, known as the Landrum-Griffin Act, authorized the federal government to police certain internal affairs of labor unions.

Total union membership reached a high in 1974, although as a proportion of the labor force it slipped from the 1956 high.

Economic motives for joining a union include higher wages, fringe benefits, and security in employment and wage income. Noneconomic motives for union membership include the desire for protection against arbitrary actions of supervisors, and for a voice in decision making, the need to identify with a group, and prounion family ties.

Unions are usually organized on either a craft or an industry basis with local and national organizational structures.

The union contract normally includes a wide variety of provisions, such as statements on wages and hours, union security, grievance procedures, holidays and vacations, and working conditions and safety.

The grievance process provides a means whereby the complaints of employees can be resolved in an orderly manner.

TERMS FOR REVIEW

Norris-LaGuardia Act of 1932
National Labor Relations Act of 1935 (Wagner Act)
Labor-Management Relations Act of 1947 (Taft-Hartley Act)
union shop

closed shop
right-to-work laws
Labor-Management Reporting and Disclosures Act of 1959 (Landrum-Griffin Act)
union or shop steward
union contract

strike
lockout
grievance procedure
arbitration
conciliation
mediation

QUESTIONS

1. Summarize the economic, political, and social conditions that preceded the passage of the National Labor Relations Act of 1935.

2. Discuss the union shop from the point of view of:
   a. The superintendent of a factory.
   b. The local union president.

3. What are the functions of the National Labor Relations Board?

4. How do you account for the recent increase in the unionization of professional, technical, clerical, and sales employees?

5. What conditions might influence an individual to join a labor union? Consider the relative importance of economic versus noneconomic motivations.

6. Why is the labor contract an important document for both management and the union?

7. Examine current publications reporting business and economic news for labor contracts which are in the process of negotiation. What issues seem to be most important to each side in arriving at a satisfactory agreement?

8. What labor relations issues are reflected in the report of Inland Steel Company on the first page of this chapter?

---

business briefs

"WE WANT MORE!"

After many months of negotiations, in 1978 Volkswagen established its first U.S. auto assembly plant in New Stanton, Pennsylvania. Shortly thereafter its production workers voted to have the United Auto Workers represent them.

The UAW entered into negotiations with the VW management on a labor agreement. Union leaders proudly presented a proposed contract which called for a minimum wage of $7.48 hourly for unskilled workers. This rate would increase to $9.62 in 1981. The negotiated hourly rate for skilled diemakers began at $9.48 and would increase to $11.62 in 1981. The basic hourly wage rates were supplemented by fringe benefits.

The labor contract was put before the 1,800 union members at the Volkswagen plant for a vote. The workers voted down the contract by a 12-to-1 margin and went out on strike.

The workers complained that the proposed wage rates would have averaged more than a dollar an hour less than the rates paid by GM, Ford, and Chrysler.

1. a. As an outsider, what justification do you see in paying the VW workers less than the Big Three auto workers in Detroit?

   b. As an outsider, what justification do you see for the discontent of the New Stanton workers?

2. How would you react to this strike if you were:
   a. A member of the union negotiating team?
   b. The manager of the New Stanton VW plant?
   c. A Toyota executive in Japan who was considering the establishment of an auto assembly plant in the United States?
   d. A Ford Motor executive in Detroit?

3. What does this situation suggest about prospects for union-management relations in the VW New Stanton plant?

BLUE-COLLAR WOMEN

Women now make up about 40 percent of the work force in this country. In 1978 the Office of Federal Contract Compliance Programs issued goals and timetables for female participation in federally financed construction projects exceeding $10,000. These guidelines required that the proportion of women workers on such jobs be 3.1 percent in 1979, 5.1 percent by 1980, and 6.9 percent by 1981. About the same time a Labor Department regulation set 20 percent as a goal for women in registered apprenticeship and training programs.

Labor unions and business managements were already faced with a small but growing number of women in blue-collar jobs in mines, shipyards, docks, and construction projects. Women are moving into crafts and jobs which have been traditionally male dominated.

One of the big motivations for women to take these jobs is money. Women in construction, on docks, on drilling rigs, and in other similar jobs typically earn $20,000 and more annually. More traditional female clerical, custodial, and factory assembly jobs pay perhaps half as much. Some women tackle such jobs because they are attracted by the challenges of a new work environment for females.

In order to meet affirmative action standards, many enterprises actively recruit women for heavy industry and construction. The Labor Department has provided outreach programs to train women for blue-collar positions. One program in Boston puts women through a 32-week preemployment course in the painting, plumbing, carpentry, or electrical trades. The program includes physical training to teach skills of lifting heavy objects and muscle-building exercises.

The increased number of women in blue-collar jobs has accented some of the difficulties in such arrangements. In some instances lighter weight equipment has replaced traditional heavy work tools. Fiberglass ladders are available which weigh half as much as wood ladders. More mechanized equipment is being developed. However, such changes are by no means widespread. Especially on construction sites and in situations where women have not worked before, problems arise regarding the provision of toilet and washroom facilities. Some jobs involve working in an environment of heat and potentially hazardous fumes and gas. Under such conditions questions arise concerning the well-being of pregnant women and their unborn children.

The expense of equipping the workplace for women may be significant. Bethlehem Steel spent more than $10 million over five years to provide rest rooms, showers, and lockers for women.

1. *Should women be provided opportunities for blue-collar employment?*
2. *What problems do you see facing women who move into blue-collar positions in heavy industry and construction?*
3. *What problems do you see for male workers in these jobs?*
4. *What issues must managements and unions confront when women are employed in blue-collar jobs?*

case

FORTY MINUTES OF OVERTIME

The management of Amalgamated Manufacturing Company became involved in a dispute with the union over an incident which occurred on May 16, 1979. An important customer of Amalgamated had given the company short notice that it wanted certain production units revised. The customer wanted shipment on May 16 on a number of the modified units. There was a deadline of 6:00 P.M. that day for production of these units to meet the airline shipping schedule.

The changes on this model required special arrangement for tooling and measurements, along with modifications in the method of assembling the units. Amalgamated's management started to make these changes early on the morning of May 16. Certain employees were selected from other assembly lines to work on the assembly line for this job. They were instructed in the methods of assembling the units for the special rush order. Work started on this assembly line at approximately 3:00 P.M. The work was not completed at the end of the shift at 4:30 P.M.

At that time management made a decision to go ahead with the same employees. These were the assemblers who had already been instructed in the changed methods. Had management brought on other employees to complete the work, additional time would have been required to instruct the new employees. This might have prevented the order from being shipped on time. Ten employees worked overtime for 40 minutes on May 16 and completed the assembly work at 5:10 P.M. The units reached the airport in time for the 6:00 P.M. deadline.

The labor contract between Amalgamated and the union contained a provision regarding the equalization of overtime among employees. One paragraph of the contract stated:

> All overtime work shall be rotated equally among the employees on seniority in a classification. If extra employees are needed, the overtime shall then be offered on a seniority basis to employees who formerly worked in that classification.

As this provision had actually been applied, employees in a classification did not all wind up with an equal number of overtime hours. Overtime had been equalized on the basis of providing equal *opportunities* for overtime rather than on the basis of equalizing the overtime hours actually worked. Each employee who had seniority in a classification was given the opportunity for overtime work on a rotation basis, regardless of the employee's accumulated amount of overtime. If the most senior employee turned down an offer for overtime work, that employee was passed over and the next most senior employee was asked. The employees who worked 40 minutes overtime on the project were not those who would

have been entitled to work this overtime on such a rotation basis. However, to meet the emergency the management decided to go ahead and assign the overtime work to the ten experienced employees.

In the past, in similar emergency situations, the rotation of overtime opportunities had also been departed from. One case was on record in which a shop steward had agreed that overtime could be assigned on the basis of production requirements in an emergency situation.

The next day, when union officials were informed of the company's action by some of the workers, the union filed a grievance on behalf of the ten employees who would have normally been granted the opportunity for overtime. The union requested that the company pay each of these ten employees for the 40 minutes of overtime that they had been deprived of. The union referred to the contract provision and charged that management had violated the labor agreement by assigning this overtime to the ten employees who were already working on the special assembly line.

1. *What company response to this union grievance would you recommend? Why? Discuss the possible immediate and long-run consequences of the action you suggest.*
2. *Would you suggest any changes in the manner in which the company has been handling overtime? If so, what changes and why?*

The provision of goods and services

SECTION FOUR

AMP reports . . .

The "home computer" is fast emerging as a major new market made possible by rapid progress in microcircuitry. Minicomputer systems now begin as low as $600—opening the door to large volume use in consumer, business, scientific, educational and other fields. Existing AMP products meet virtually all present connection needs. For example, the logic board of this Radio Shack computer, manufactured by Tandy Corporation, uses two AMP Latch ribbon cable connectors, many board-mounted DIPLOMATE receptacles and programmable shunts, and an AMP flexible jumper cable to link the logic board to the keyboard.

From annual report of AMP Incorporated

"Home computers" offer a new avenue for AMP growth.

Photograph courtesy of Radio Shack

11

The consumer and the marketing concept

The consumer and the marketing concept

Greater attention is being paid to the consumer today. There are a variety of reasons for the increased recognition of the consumer's importance. First, consumer income has been rising. Second, consumers have become more vocal about the nature and the quality of the goods and services offered by business. Third, the protection of the consumer is being given more recognition by government. Statements from corporate executives emphasize an interest in meeting consumers' needs, dealing fairly with complaints, and acting in a socially responsible manner.

After studying this chapter, you will be able to answer the following questions regarding the consumer and the marketing concept:

What is the marketing concept of business?

What factors influence consumer behavior?

How is the consumer changing?

Why has consumerism developed?

What are government and business doing to protect consumers?

THE IMPORTANCE OF MARKETING

Marketing may be defined as the system of activities that moves goods and services from producers to consumers to satisfy needs. Recall from Chapter 1 that goods possess utility when they have the power to satisfy human wants. Marketing imparts place, time, and possession utility to goods. The production function, discussed in Chapter 13, imparts form utility to goods. However, even form utility is influenced by what can be marketed to consumers.

Marketing is as vital in today's economy as is the production of goods and services. It has been estimated that about 50 percent of the consumer's dollar is spent on marketing activities. Our market economy is directed by the spending decisions of all types of consumers. These range from the teenager spending money earned on a part-time job to the Department of Defense, which spends over $100 billion annually. Despite some poverty in the United States and despite the inflation of recent years, today the vast majority of American families are faced with decisions concerning how to spend incomes which have risen in recent years. For most American families the question is not how to put enough food on the table but what luxury goods and leisure-time activities to select.

THE MARKETING CONCEPT OF BUSINESS

Increased emphasis on the consumer in recent years has led to the development of the *marketing concept of business.* The essence of this concept is to recognize a consumer need, develop a product that will satisfy the need, and in the process earn a profit for the business enterprise. This means that management thinking throughout the enterprise must be oriented to the importance of the consumer. Marketing becomes everybody's job, not just the responsibility of a few marketing managers.

General Electric Company provides an example of an enterprise that is oriented toward the marketing concept of business. In an annual report to its stockholders General Electric stated:

> Marketing, through its studies and research, will establish for the engineer, the designer, and the manufacturing man what the customer wants in a given product, what price he is willing to pay, and where and when it will be wanted. Marketing would have authority in product planning, production scheduling, and inventory control, as well as in the sales distribution and servicing of the product.

When the marketing concept of business is applied, the act of selling a product is the last step in a sales effort which starts when the product is first conceived. Consumer appeal is built into each product from the design stage to the final marketing stage. Producing consumer satisfactions is emphasized. Goods and services have no value in themselves. Only when they are desirable to consumers do they take on value.

The enterprise must have a market for the goods and services it hopes to produce. A market consists of consumers who are willing and able to buy the goods produced by a particular business enterprise. Such markets must be created and stimulated by managers. In today's rapidly changing economy the creative management does not wait for customers to seek out its product. Management woos consumers, seeking to win them from other enterprises.

TRANSLATING CONSUMER NEEDS TO WANTS

A basic objective of marketing is to translate consumer needs into wants. To need something is to depend on it to carry out a way of life. People need all kinds of goods and services to carry on an established pattern of living. However, they are not always fully conscious of their needs. The challenge of creative marketing is to focus consumers' attention on their needs and to suggest products that will meet those needs. Through the marketing process, needs are translated into wants. To want a product is to recognize that it is available and can satisfy a need.

There is no shortage of needs in our world today, even in the United States. People need more than they have in food, clothing, shelter, health, education, and the many conveniences of life. In many instances, however, these needs are not clearly understood. Creative marketing can bring such general needs into sharper focus. It can translate a dimly perceived need into a want for a specific good or service.

Marketing is sometimes criticized on the ground that it results in the production of goods that the American people really do not need. This charge is not based on an understanding of the close relationship between needs and wants. Wants arise from needs. It is not possible to stimulate persons to want a product when they do not feel some need for it. At the same time it is clearly recognized that not all needs have the same priorities. Certain essentials of food and shelter are basic to life, whereas the need to see television shows in color is not. However, even gadgets such as electric toothbrushes meet needs. They do serve useful functions. The fact that people could survive without a particular good or service does not mean that it is not needed to achieve a certain standard of living.

Once a need has been turned into a specific want of the consuming public, the American standard of living is never the same again. Consider how much less productive American business would be without air conditioning. At one time air conditioning was virtually unknown except by primitive methods available to a few. Protection from the summer's heat and humidity was a latent need. Today it has been translated into a want of most Americans. We want air conditioning in our homes as well as at work. Out of this want has grown a new industry with new jobs and new investment opportunities.

The process of translating a need into a want is a job for marketing management. The consumer's attention must be called to the nature and the significance of the need. Many needs have an emotional rather than a rational basis. A good marketer learns when to appeal to emotion, to reason, or to a combination of both.

THE CONSUMER

Ultimate consumers

Because of the marketing concept's emphasis on the consumer, it is important that the consumer be defined and analyzed. *Ultimate consumers* are individuals or households that use goods or services for the satisfaction of personal needs. *Industrial users* purchase products for use in producing other goods or services and are discussed in the next two chapters. When the term *consumer* or *consumers* is used in this book it applies to ultimate consumers.

Individual consumer behavior

Consumers buy particular goods and services for a variety of reasons. The influence of a variety of stimuli underlies a consumer's decision to purchase some good or service. The factors affecting the consumer's behavior can be classified as economic, psychological, and social.

Economic factors Economic considerations affecting consumer behavior center on people's rational use of scarce resources to satisfy their needs. Thus, the level of consumer income, inflation, and personal savings and the availability of credit are important economic determinants of behavior. The increase in the American consumer's income is so important that it is discussed in detail later in this chapter. The price of the good, its durability, and its expense of operation are economic factors which may influence the consumer. The price of competing goods or of substitutes is also an economic consideration that may influence the consumer's decision.

Psychological factors The research and concepts of psychologists can be helpful in providing insights into buying motives. One theory of motivation is provided in Maslow's hierarchy of needs, which arrays five levels of needs in the order in which an individual tends to seek their satisfaction:[1]

1. Physiological needs—for food, drink, sex, and shelter.
2. Safety needs—for security, order, protection, and family stability.
3. Belongingness and love needs—for affection, belonging to a group, and acceptance.
4. Esteem needs—for self-respect, reputation, prestige, and status.
5. Self-actualization needs—for self-fulfillment, doing what one is best fitted for.

In addition, Maslow suggested that two other levels of needs exist for those individuals who may have satisfied the first five need levels:

1. The need to know and understand.
2. The need for aesthetic satisfaction—beauty.

In theory a person tries to fulfill all of the needs at one level before moving on to a higher level of needs. In practice most people attempt to fill needs on different levels at the same time, probably never completely satisfying the needs at any one level. However, people do have some priority of needs even if not everyone has the same priority. For example, a college student who enjoys good music may habitually skip lunch (a physiological need) while spending money to build an extensive record collection (an aesthetic need). The business manager must recognize that people have different levels of needs. For consumers to spend their income for particular goods they must be convinced that some need will be satisfied by doing so.

Social factors Marketing managers have traditionally used income as a means of predicting buying behavior. Today about half of the families in the United States have incomes of $16,000 and above. This group includes blue-collar workers as well as professional and white-collar employees. These families tend to vary in their spending patterns, depending partly on the social class with which they identify.

In addition to the social class with which consumers identify, other groups

---

[1] A. H. Maslow, *Motivation and Personality* (New York: Harper, Inc., 1954), pp. 80–97.

career outlook

MARKETING RESEARCH WORKERS

Managers of business enterprises require a great deal of information to make sound decisions on how to market their products. Marketing research workers provide much of this information by analyzing available data on products and sales, making surveys, and conducting interviews. They prepare sales forecasts and make recommendations on product design and advertising.

Most jobs for marketing research workers are found in manufacturing companies, advertising agencies, and independent research organizations. Large numbers of marketing research workers are employed by stores, radio and television firms, and newspapers.

Trainees usually start as research assistants or junior analysts. At first, they may do considerable clerical work, such as copying data from published sources, editing and coding questionnaires, and tabulating survey returns. They also learn to conduct interviews and write reports on survey findings. As they gain experience, assistants and junior analysts may assume responsibility for specific marketing research projects or may advance to supervisory positions. An exceptionally able worker may become a marketing research director or a vice president for marketing and sales.

Population growth and the increased variety of goods and services that businesses and individuals will require are expected to stimulate a high level of marketing activity. As a result, the employment of marketing research workers is expected to grow much faster than the average for other occupations through the mid-1980s.

Although a bachelor's degree is the usual entry requirement for marketing research trainees, graduate training is becoming important for some specialized positions and for advancement to higher level positions. Opportunities should be best for applicants with graduate training in marketing research or statistics. Knowledge of data processing is helpful because of the growing use of computers in sales forecasting, distribution, and cost analysis. The growing complexity of marketing research techniques may also expand opportunities for psychologists, economists, and other social scientists.

in society influence the behavior of consumers. These include the clubs to which they belong, the schools they attend, and the labor unions, athletic teams, or church groups in which they participate. The values of these formal groups as well as the values of informal groups influence the purchases of their members. Young people tend to seek approval from their peers by dressing, behaving, and buying as others do. Business managers generally act and spend in patterns which gain the approval of their associates. Even college professors are influenced by their colleagues in buying decisions.

The marketing manager should be aware of the differences which exist in the consumer market based upon social groupings. When a product has special appeal to a particular group in society, the advertising and sales promotion program should take this into account. Beverage manufacturers, magazine publishers, and fashion designers have all found that their markets may be segmented, at least partly, depending on various social classifications. Different forms of advertising may be necessary to reach these segments of the market.

THE CONSUMER OF THE 1980s

The 1980s will be a time of change for consumer markets in the United States. The proportion of high-income families has increased significantly. Changes in the age, education, and composition of the work force are also affecting spending patterns. Some of these economic, demographic, and social factors which affect business are discussed below.

Higher consumer income

The U.S. consumer market is changing. In past decades we moved from a nation of predominantly low-income families to one of middle-income mass markets. Now the move is into an era of high-income mass markets with one half of families having an income exceeding $16,000 per year. Figure 11–1 shows the changing distribution of American income since 1955. Over the past 25 years income has increased significantly for most American families.

Factors contributing to higher family income

Educational achievement Contributing to the rising income level of American families is the rising level of educational achievement. The number of college graduates has increased and is projected to become even greater in the 1980s.

FIGURE 11–1

The changing pyramid of family income (total families each year = 100 percent; based on 1977 dollars)

Income classes	1955	1965	1977
$25,000 and over	4.3%	11.8%	22.4%
$15,000 to $24,999	17.8	29.6	31.7
$12,000 to $14,999	12.5	15.0	11.3
$10,000 to $11,999	15.3	9.8	7.2
$ 7,000 to $ 9,999	20.0	12.7	10.9
$ 5,000 to $ 6,999	10.1	7.9	7.2
Under $5,000	20.0	13.2	9.3

Source: U.S. Bureau of the Census, *Current Population Reports*, series P-60, no. 116, July 1978.

Median U.S. family income in 1977, depending on educational achievement of family head

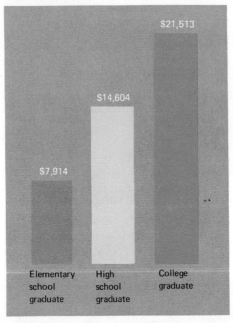

$21,513

$14,604

$7,914

| Elementary school graduate | High school graduate | College graduate |

Source: U.S. Bureau of the Census, *Current Population Reports*, series P-60, no. 116, July 1978.

Generally the greater the person's level of educational achievement, the higher the person's income. Figure 11–2 compares family income in 1977, depending on whether the head of the family had completed elementary school, high school, or college.

Working wives   The increased number of households having two wage earners has also contributed to higher family incomes. From 1950 to 1978 the overall percentage of husband-wife families with the wife in the paid labor force increased from 19 percent to over 50 percent. The median income of families in which the husband and wife were both in the paid labor force was $18,730 in 1976. This was 34 percent higher than the median income of families in which the wife was not in the work force.

More discretionary income

Discretionary income is the income left over after the family's spending for necessities has been covered. Discretionary income may be spent for luxuries or saved and invested. The rising real income of Americans provides additional discretionary income. This increases the challenge for marketing managers. They must attract the consumer's discretionary spending dollars in competition with a wide variety of goods and services. For example, more consumers are now able to make large discretionary purchases and will choose between such items as a vacation home at the lake, a trip to Europe, or a second car. Once basic transportation has been provided, the auto manufacturer competes not only with other automobile manufacturers but with the vacation home industry, travel agencies, art dealers, and producers of many other goods and services.

The job of marketing is complicated further by the fact that what one family considers necessities may be considered luxuries by another. Also, with higher standards of living the definition of what is considered a necessity will change. What were previously luxury goods will become necessities, opening up new areas for luxury spending. The consumer durable goods industries offer many examples of this concept. Thirty years ago television was considered a luxury. Today most families think of television as a necessity.

In the early 1950s the color television industry was in its infancy, but the industry grew until color television became the widespread consumer appliance of recent years. Figure 11–3 shows the degree of saturation of color television and other consumer durable goods among American households.

Figure 11–3 illustrates that there are still opportunities for further sales to expand the market for durables and to replace present models in use. However, industry is challenged to develop new products which will meet or expand consumers' needs. It remains to be seen whether mass markets will develop for such items as home trash compactors, instant home movies, or color video recorders.

FIGURE 11–3
Percentage of total U.S. households owning selected consumer durable goods, 1973

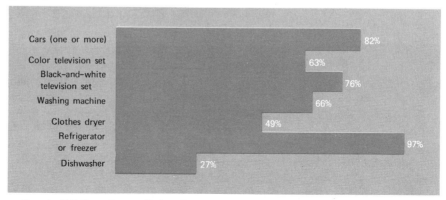

Source: U.S. Department of Labor, Bureau of Labor Statistics, *Consumer Expenditure Survey Series: Inventories of Vehicles and Selected Household Equipment, 1973* (Washington, D.C.: U.S. Government Printing Office, 1978).

Demographic changes

To predict better the kinds of goods and services that consumers will need, alert marketing executives study changes in the size and composition of the population. Although the total U.S. population continues to increase, the growth rate began a steady decline in the early 1960s until it is now less than 1 percent annually. The decreased growth rate may be attributed to a declining birthrate.

FIGURE 11-4
Estimated population growth by age groups

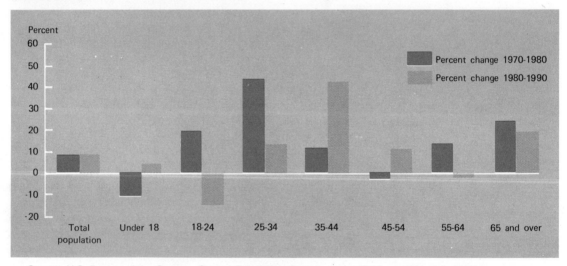

Source: U.S. Bureau of the Census, *Current Population Reports,* series P-25, no. 704, July 1977.

The lower birthrate is caused by a number of factors. These include the desire by couples for the higher standard of living which can result from having the wife work outside the home and postponing children or having fewer children. The reduction in family size from three or four children to one or two children significantly reduces the economic cost of children to the family.

In addition to changing in total size, population is changing in composition, as is illustrated by Figure 11-4. The changes in the size and composition of the population have varied meanings to different manufacturers and service enterprises. For example, the larger proportion of the population in the 25–44 age categories in the 1980s will provide increased sales opportunities for manufacturers of appliances and furniture. Also, as the family incomes of these age groups rise, additional discretionary income will be available. The substantial continued increase in persons age 65 and over will provide significant markets for retirement housing, medical services, and leisure activities for senior citizens.

CONSUMERISM AND CONSUMER PROTECTION AGENCIES

Consumerism

Most business enterprises attempt to serve consumer needs well. However, consumers express concern about poor quality of products, a lack of proper service, the use of food additives which may be harmful, unsafe products, misleading advertising, and business practices which are wasteful or contribute to pollution. The consumer protest against some products and business practices has been labeled *consumerism.*

Consumerism as a movement gained focus with the publication in 1965 of Ralph Nader's *Unsafe at Any Speed.* This book, critical of the Corvair auto, became a best-seller. Following the book's publication, sales of General Motor's Corvair dropped. In 1969 GM ceased production of this rear-engine car. Nader has continued his consumer-oriented activities. He and his followers are credited with significant influence in the passage of federal legislation intended to protect consumers in such areas as auto safety and food processing.

Governmental protective agencies

A number of federal governmental agencies have been created over the years to protect consumers' interests. These include the Federal Trade Commission, the Food and Drug Administration, and the Consumer Product Safety Commission.

The Federal Trade Commission and the Food and Drug Administration were both created before World War I. The Federal Trade Commission is responsible for policing advertising and marketing practices. It also enforces a variety of legislation, including labeling acts for wool, fur, and textile products. These responsibilities are in addition to the FTC's duties in enforcing the antitrust laws, discussed in Chapter 3. The Food and Drug Administration is charged with regulation in such areas as the maintenance of drug standards and the evaluation of new drugs, food purity, and cosmetic products.

The FTC and advertising

In the early 1970s the Federal Trade Commission responded to increasing consumer complaints about the honesty of information contained in advertising. A program was announced in 1971 requiring advertisers to be able to support advertising claims of product performance, safety, quality, or comparative price.

An industry-by-industry approach has been taken by the FTC in this truth-in-advertising campaign to see whether advertising claims can be supported. The FTC has requested supporting data from many industries. These include manufacturers of automobiles, tires, color television sets, cold remedies, pet foods, hearing aids, and air conditioners.

"There's a lot more food mixed with the additives in this one."

Evidence must be available to support objective statements such as "averages 26 miles per gallon." Subjective claims must also be documented. An example of a subjective claim is the statement by an auto manufacturer that a particular model "is the best-handling passenger car ever built in the United States."

The FTC has several ways of dealing with enterprises which do not live up to government standards in advertising. First, cease and desist orders may require a business to stop the questioned advertising. These orders may include fines. Second, the enterprise may be required to provide additional information in future ads. For example, the FTC ordered that advertising for a swimming-aid device disclose that the device was not a life preserver and that it should be used only in shallow water. Third, the FTC may require corrective advertising.

In its first such order the FTC required Continental Baking Company to spend 25 percent of its advertising budget for one year on FTC-approved corrective advertisements stating that Profile bread was not effective for weight reduction as earlier ads had claimed.

The Consumer Product Safety Commission

In the late 1960s Congress established a study commission on product safety to examine the extent to which product hazards constituted a public safety problem. The study indicated that 20 million Americans were injured annually in the home as the result of accidents associated with consumer products. Of this number 110,000 persons were permanently disabled and 30,000 were killed.

Following this study the Consumer Product Safety Act was passed in 1972. It authorized the establishment of the Consumer Product Safety Commission (CPSC), whose responsibilities include the development of safety standards for various industries, the evaluation of product safety, the collection of injury statistics, and the coordination of governmental safety enforcement. The act holds manufacturers accountable for the safety of their products sold to consumers.

The CPSC has responsibilities under several other recently passed laws. These include the *Poison Prevention Packaging Act,* which requires dangerous substances to have safety containers with caps which are difficult to remove. Also included is the *Flammable Fabrics Act,* which requires children's nightclothes to be flame retardant. The 1970 *Child Protection and Toy Safety Act* provided increased protection from toys which might have mechanical or electrical hazards.

A number of actions can be taken by the CPSC to improve product safety. It can order a manufacturer or a retailer to recall, repair, or replace any product which the commission considers unreasonably risky. The commission can seize the product or ban its sale. Managers who refuse to abide by commission rulings can be fined and jailed up to one year. However, the general approach of the CPSC has been to seek industry cooperation to improve product safety and not to emphasize penalties.

Other legislation

The following legislation passed in recent years is also important to consumers:

The *National Traffic and Motor Vehicle Safety Act of 1966* requires auto manufacturers to notify first purchasers of cars by certified mail of any safety defects discovered after manufacture and delivery. This law also provides for the issuance of safety standards for motor vehicles.

The *Wholesome Meat Act of 1967* updated and strengthened the standards for the inspection of red meat animals. Under a 1907 law, 2,000 of the 17,000 slaughterhouses and packing plants in the country, which produced 85 percent of the meat eaten in the United States, had been subject to federal meat inspection. Now, in cooperation with the states, the remaining plants are subject to standards designed to improve the quality of meat products.

In 1968 the *Wholesome Poultry Products Act* was signed into law. This act extended federal inspection standards to poultry sold intrastate.

The *Truth in Lending Act of 1968* requires creditors to furnish individuals to whom credit is about to be extended a statement of the financing charges and of the annual percentage rate of interest. Before this law was passed, practice had varied considerably on the degree of disclosure to consumers of actual annual interest rates.

The *Fair Credit Reporting Act,* passed in 1970, contained a number of provisions to protect consumers in credit matters. This act requires that all agencies reporting consumer credit rating data follow reasonable procedures to assure the accuracy of their information. Any user of credit information who rejects a consumer for credit, insurance, or employment must inform the individual of the source of the credit report. Also, consumers may use the courts to obtain identification of the sources of information behind the credit reports.

Also in 1970, the 1965 *Cigarette Labeling and Advertising Act* was amended to strengthen the warning on cigarette packages to read "Warning: The Surgeon General Has Determined That Cigarette Smoking Is Dangerous to Your Health." The act also regulated cigarette advertising, with television advertising of cigarettes ceasing after January 1, 1971.

Private groups aiding consumers

There are two nonprofit organizations which test and rate products for the benefit of consumers. They are Consumers' Research and Consumers Union. Both organizations issue monthly publications reporting the results of their studies.

Consumers can also be helped by Better Business Bureaus which are sponsored by business enterprises in metropolitan areas. The Better Business Bureaus encourage responsible business practices. They will answer consumers' questions about a particular enterprise and will advise whether they have received complaints about the business.

Some Better Business Bureaus sponsor an arbitration service to handle consumer complaints against a particular enterprise. When an unhappy customer and a business enterprise agree to arbitration, an impartial person hears both sides of the story, checks claims and counterclaims, and renders a decision on the dispute. The procedure is conducted at no charge to the consumer. It can reduce court case loads and act as a local small claims court. The early experience with the BBB arbitration program indicates that the decisions are about equally divided between complainants and businesses.

Business aid to consumers

Many business enterprises have been concerned with consumer satisfaction and product safety for years. Enterprises such as General Electric, Zenith, Sears,

3M, and RCA had product safety programs long before the passage of the Consumer Product Safety Act. However, increased consumer sensitivity and government regulations are stimulating business to do even more.

A number of enterprises, including Whirlpool Corporation, have installed toll-free telephone lines to answer customer's questions and complaints about their products. Enterprises such as Standard Oil of Indiana and Mobil Oil are giving increased attention to consumer inquiries about computer-billed charges.

A good handling of consumer complaints was the example of Calgon Corporation. The company faced charges that its Calgonite detergent caused suds to overflow in a particular type of dishwasher. The result was sometimes damaging to floors and furniture. Calgon reformulated the detergent to correct the sudsing problem and compensated consumers for known damages.

Additional business enterprises are moving toward the approach of Zenith Corporation's stated philosophy that "it isn't enough to claim that 99%—or even 99.9%—of the company's products are satisfactory." A dissatisfied consumer should be able to expect that the enterprise "sincerely wants to make an adjustment if the customer has been disappointed." The chairman of American Motors stated that an auto buyer "doesn't expect every car to be trouble-free, but he does want the troubles fixed—fixed completely, fixed without cost, and fixed carefully." American Motors adopted a "buyer protection" guaranty plan which received positive consumer reaction.

J. C. Penney is known for its emphasis on customer satisfaction. In 1974 the J. C. Penney Company's Management Conference reaffirmed the longtime commitment of that enterprise to the consumer:

The Penney Idea

1. To serve the public as nearly as we can to its complete satisfaction.
2. To expect for the service we render a fair remuneration, and not all the profit the traffic will bear.
3. To do all in our power to pack the customer's dollar full of value, quality and satisfaction.
4. To continue to train ourselves and our associates so that the service we give will be more and more intelligently performed.
5. To improve constantly the human factor in our business.
6. To reward the men and women in our organization through participation in what the business produces.
7. To test our every policy, method and art in this wise: "Does it square with what is right and just?"

Adopted: 1913.

SUMMARY

The marketing concept of business involves recognizing a consumer need, developing a product to satisfy that need, and in the process earning a profit for the business enterprise. The marketing concept means that the thinking of managers throughout the business enterprise must be oriented around the importance of the consumer. A basic objective of marketing is to translate consumer needs into wants.

Customers of business may be either ultimate consumers or industrial users. Individual consumer behavior is influenced by economic, psychological, and social factors.

The consumer of the 1980s has a rising level of real income that results in increased discretionary spending power. Since 1955 family income has increased significantly in real terms. This higher family income is attributed to higher educational achievement and to an increase in the number of families in which both the husband and the wife work. More discretionary income and changes in the size and composition of the population will present challenges for marketing managers in the future.

Consumerism is increasing in importance, with both government and private groups becoming more insistent that business avoid deceptive practices and unreliable products. Federal governmental agencies with important consumer protection responsibilities include the Federal Trade Commission, the Food and Drug Administration, and the Consumer Product Safety Commission.

Legislation passed in recent years to protect the consumer includes the Poison Prevention Packaging Act, the Flammable Fabrics Act, the Child Protection and Toy Safety Act, the National Traffic and Motor Vehicle Safety Act, the Wholesome Meat Act, the Wholesome Poultry Products Act, the Truth in Lending Act, the Fair Credit Reporting Act, and the Cigarette Labeling and Advertising Act.

TERMS FOR REVIEW

marketing
marketing concept of
  business
market
want
need

ultimate consumer
industrial user
Maslow's hierarchy of needs
family income
discretionary income
demographic changes

consumerism
Federal Trade Commission
Consumer Product Safety
  Commission

QUESTIONS

1. Is the application of the marketing concept of business more important today than it was at some other period in our economic history, such as during the depression of the 1930s or during the period immediately following World War II? State the reasons for your answer.

2. Explain why consumers do not always act in a rational manner when buying goods and services.

3. Cite ten examples of products whose advertising in the mass media makes an appeal to one or more of the five basic needs in Maslow's hierarchy.

4. Give five examples of items that you feel college students purchase more because of psychological

or social motivations than because of economic motivations.

5. What are the implications for business in the changing income distribution pyramid illustrated in Figure 11–1?

6. What do the statistics in Figure 11–3 imply for the future product development and sales promotion of durable goods manufacturers?

7. What are the implications for business in the changing composition of the population as illustrated in Figure 11–4?

8. How do you account for the interest in consumerism at a time when the incomes of American families are generally at historically high levels?

9. Outline the important consumer legislation passed by Congress in recent years.

10. From current periodicals, examine statements by consumer groups that American business and governmental bodies are not living up to consumers' expectations. Also examine statements in defense of business's actions. Write a 300-word paper summarizing your conclusions from this study.

11. From the first page of this chapter, what is the role of AMP in the production and distribution of consumer goods?

business briefs

TRYING TO MAKE IT BIG IN SMALL CARS

The flood of small imported automobiles by Toyota, Datsun, Volkswagen, and Honda in the late 1970s forced American auto manufacturers to take a hard look at how subcompact cars are sold. At the time imported cars amounted to 60 percent of subcompact sales in the United States.

American manufacturers, led by General Motors, found that their sales forces concentrated on price with prospective new-car buyers. Many salespersons were used to selling large cars. They did not really know much about the technical and performance features of their own subcompacts. In addition, they lacked knowledge of the foreign competition. By contrast, persons who sold foreign cars tended to emphasize operating and handling characteristics and technical features rather than price.

Another problem that American manufacturers and dealers had to face was the doubt by some salespersons that small cars were here to stay. Government pressure for better gas mileage is putting additional pressure on American producers to sell small cars. The federal government has mandated that by 1985 a company's auto production must average 27.5 miles per gallon.

1. *What does this brief illustrate about the importance of the marketing concept of business?*

2. *What specific steps could American auto manufacturers take to improve sales of their subcompacts?*

3. *If you own an automobile, what factors influenced you to buy that particular model? What factors might have caused you to buy some other model?*

THE COMPUTERIZED CHECKOUT REVOLUTION

A revolutionary system is under way to speed checkout at supermarkets and to eliminate hand-pricing individual items on 170 billion cans, bottles, and packages annually. The system makes use of the Universal Product Code (UPC).

The UPC marking on each container is a computer-language symbol which identifies the manufacturer and the specific product. At the checkout counter the clerk passes each UPC symbol over a laser scanner or uses a wand which reads the symbol and transmits it to a computer in the store. The computer matches the coded symbol to the product type or brand name, the size, and the correct price. The computer sends the data back to the checkout counter, where it is printed on a receipt and flashed on a display board. The entire process takes only a fraction of a second.

For stores with grocery sales of $60,000 a week, this system might effect savings of $35,000 yearly. (There would be no cost savings for stores with sales of less than $10,000 weekly.) The system would eliminate the cost of marking containers, speed checkouts, and improve inventory control. The computer can be programmed to print out such data as which items are the fastest sellers and how customers are responding to special sales.

Advocates of the system suggest that it provides these benefits for consumers:

1. Waiting time at checkout lanes will be cut by one third or more since the scanner can read the symbols faster than a clerk can operate a cash register.
2. With a properly programmed computer there is less chance of being charged the wrong price for an item.
3. The grocery receipt is more detailed, including brands and specific item designations.
4. Items can be checked out in a random manner, with price breaks calculated automatically on specials. For example, if corn is 39 cents a can or three for $1, the computer system will print out 39 cents for each of the first two cans. The third can will be priced automatically at 22 cents to complete the three for $1 deal.

Opponents of the UPC system include some consumer advocates and labor unions. The consumer advocates voice these objections:

1. Even if the shelves were marked with prices, an unethical merchant could post low prices on the shelves but program the computer with higher prices.
2. If items are not individually marked, consumers will have difficulty measuring higher prices by comparing the prices of newly purchased goods with those already on kitchen shelves.
3. The computer system costs about $20,000 per checkout lane, or over $100,000 for the average supermarket. This puts small grocery stores at a disadvantage as compared to large supermarket chains.

Grocery clerks' unions generally oppose UPC and computerized checkouts because the system reduces the need for grocery employees by about 20 percent. Although most union contracts protect the jobs of present employees, the long-run effect of the system would be savings in wage costs for merchants.

Almost 90 percent of all merchandise now bears the UPC. However, less than 2 percent of the nation's 33,000 supermarkets have the scanners and the computers that are needed to complete the system.

1. *Discuss the advantages and disadvantages of the UPC and computerized checkouts from the point of view of (a) supermarket management, (b) consumers, and (c) retail clerks.*
2. *What position would you take on legislation requiring that each item be indivdually priced if this procedure would reduce the cost savings from the computerized checkout system by 25 percent?*

BUSINESS LISTENS

In the summer of 1978 a Weslaco, Texas, couple and their daughter checked into a motel of a national chain in a nearby state. They went into the motel's restaurant 30 minutes before closing time and were served a second-rate meal which included instant mashed potatoes and a warmed-over entrée. The couple wrote a complaining letter to the chain's home office. Shortly afterward they received a letter of apology from the motel manager and an invitation to spend a night as the management's guests the next time they were in the area. Such incidents, though not necessarily commonplace, indicate that more managements are listening to customers.

Numerous large corporations have staffs to deal directly with customer complaints and inquiries. For more than 40 years General Motors has had an owner relations department. It now consists of nearly 500 employees. GM managers and quality control personnel receive copies of letters sent to this department. When a GM auto owner complains, the zone office receives the letter and contacts the dealer. If the complaint is not resolved by the dealer or the zone office to the customer's satisfaction, the Detroit office reviews the complaint to see whether everything possible was done to satisfy the customer. Because of the emphasis in the auto industry on repeat business, GM is interested in equitable handling of customer concerns.

Several hundred business enterprises now have consumer relations departments. A few consumer affairs managers hold the title of vice president and report directly to top management. However, the vast majority of consumer affairs officers have no direct contact with top management.

Not all consumer relations officers have much influence on enterprise policy or decisions concerning consumer complaints. Some consumer advocates charge that such positions are simply for public relations purposes, with little genuine concern for consumers' welfare.

1. *How important is it for an enterprise to have a consumer affairs department?*
2. *If a consumer affairs department is to be effective, what should its role be?*
3. *How would you answer this statement by a manager, "If an enterprise's manufacturing department does a good job and if products are honestly advertised, a consumer affairs department is simply a needless expense which results in higher prices for consumers"?*

J. C. Penney reports . . .

The working woman She is a powerful force in the marketplace and a prime target customer for JCPenney. Collectively, she earns more than $255 billion a year and provides a second income for approximately 40 percent of all families in the United States.

Better than half of JCPenney's contemporary customers, women who spend the most on their personal needs, are employed. These women, on the job or on the go, want to look their best.

Today, JCPenney is meeting more of the fashion needs of contemporary customers, who have regularly shopped in our stores for children's wear (42 percent of working women have children under six) and other merchandise. In many of our large regional shopping center locations, we have added higher taste level apparel and accessories, amounting to about 15 percent of our total women's offerings, including some popularly priced labels, which our customers regularly bought in other department stores.

Catalog has become a shopping habit for the time-pressed working woman. The lead pages in our recent major catalogs have been clearly aimed at her. The coordinated outfit shown here appears in our Spring & Summer 1979 catalog.

Working for the working woman . . .

This is JCPenney

From the annual report of J. C. Penney

12

The marketing mix

The marketing mix

Once consumers' needs and wants have been determined, management must create a marketing program to satisfy the needs of the firm's target customers. The marketing program is composed of four important variables which constitute the marketing mix. These variables can be abbreviated as product, promotion, price, and place and are often called the "four P's of marketing."

After studying this chapter, you will be able to answer the following questions related to the marketing program:

What factors are considered in determining the right product for the target customers of the business enterprise?

What means can be used in the promotion program to communicate effectively with the target customers?

At what price should the product be offered to target customers?

How shall the business enterprise place the goods where they can reach target customers?

THE MARKETING MIX

The four variables which make up the marketing mix are symbolized in Figure 12–1 with their focus on the consumer. The management which adopts the marketing concept of business concentrates on its target consumer group. An enterprise's management attempts to gain a competitive advantage over other firms by distinguishing its product in some way for the consumer.

A discussion follows on each of the variables of product, promotion, price, and place. Although each variable is considered separately, there is a close relationship among the four P's in the marketing mix of a business enterprise. Decisions made in one dimension of the marketing program affect the other variables. There are many trade-offs in determining a marketing mix that will meet consumers' needs profitably.

For example, a manufacturer of lawn mowers might consider selling its total production to Sears, where the mowers would be marketed under Sears' Craftsman label. Such a decision would relieve the manufacturer of promotion and place decisions and expenses. However, with only one major customer the manufacturer may lose control of the pricing decision and have to accept a lower price for its lawn mowers than it would receive if they were sold to numerous wholesalers or retailers.

FIGURE 12–1
The marketing mix

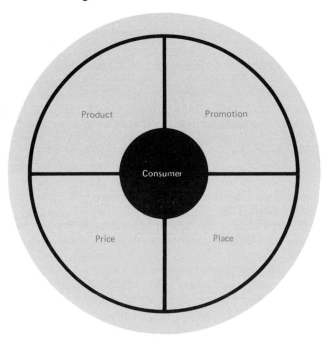

PRODUCT

Product defined

A *product* is a good or service that satisfies a consumer's need. Products may be tangible, such as houses or clothing. They may be intangible, such as the services of real estate agents or schoolteachers. Intangible products are usually called *services.* Although they do not have physical characteristics, services provide very real consumer satisfactions. Consumers are increasing their spending for services faster than their spending for tangible goods.

Tangible products may be classified as durable or nondurable goods. *Durable goods* have physical qualities and uses which generally last over a relatively long period of time. Automobiles, tape players, and golf clubs are examples of durable consumer goods. *Nondurable goods* have physical characteristics which permit them to be used only once or a few times. Hamburgers, perfumes, flowers, and newspapers are examples of nondurable consumer goods.

Features such as brand name, color, packaging, the manner of distribution, price, and service differentiate one product from another. For example, a color television set may be sold by a department store which provides credit, delivery, servicing, and a large selection. This product is not identical with the same television model purchased on a cash-and-carry basis from a discount house

BUYERS

Buyers purchase merchandise for their firms to resell (unlike purchasing agents who buy goods for direct use by the firm). Therefore, they must know what motivates customers to buy. Before ordering a particular line of merchandise, buyers study market research reports and analyze past sales records to determine what products are currently in demand. They also work closely with assistant buyers and salesclerks whose daily contact with customers furnishes information about consumer likes and dislikes.

In order to purchase the best selection of goods for their stores, buyers must be familiar with the manufacturers and distributors that handle the merchandise they need. They must also keep informed about changes in existing products and about the development of new products. To learn about merchandise, buyers attend fashion and trade shows and visit manufacturers' showrooms. They usually order goods during buying trips, but they also place orders with wholesalers' and manufacturers' sales workers who call on them.

Assisting with sales promotions and creating enthusiasm among sales personnel are part of the buyer's job.

New technology has altered the buyer's role in retail chain stores. In the past, firms employed a buyer for each store or group of stores in a local area. Now cash registers connected to a computer, known as point-of-sale terminals, allow retail chains to maintain centralized, up-to-the-minute inventory records. With these records, a single garden furniture buyer, for example, can purchase lawn chairs and picnic tables for the entire chain.

In the past, many a good buyer began in a stockroom or behind a counter and worked his or her way up the ladder without any college training. However, new buyers will find a college degree increasingly necessary. Many junior colleges and four-year colleges offer programs in marketing and purchasing.

The employment of buyers is expected to grow more slowly than the average for all occupations through the mid-1980s. Competition for jobs is expected to be keen. Prospects are likely to be best for qualified applicants who enjoy the competitive nature of retailing and work best in a demanding, fast-paced job.

with a limited selection and no service technicians. Which of these television sets you purchase will depend on the satisfactions you obtain from the extra services provided by the department store as compared to the lower price of the discount house.

Classification of consumer products

Consumer goods may be classified according to consumer buying habits as convenience goods, shopping goods, and specialty goods.

Convenience goods *Convenience goods* are purchased with a minimum of effort at the nearest available location. Convenience goods are low-priced items about which the consumer has considerable knowledge. Usually brand identification is not so strong that consumers will not accept a substitute brand if their first choice is unavailable.

Convenience goods may be classified further as staples, impulse goods, and emergency goods. *Staples* are bought and used frequently without much consideration being given to their purchase. Many food products and nonprescription drug items are staple goods. Brand identification may have some weight in the buying decision. Usually easy availability will be more important than the brand. Items such as bread, milk, and aspirin are considered staples, and easy availability to consumers is important in their distribution.

Impulse goods are items which customers buy on sight without having gone out specifically for their purchase. Their unit price is usually low. The purchase of an impulse good satisfies a need which is strongly felt at the moment. Items which customers will buy on an impulse are frequently placed near store doors or at cash registers. Candy bars, chewing gum, cigarettes, and magazines are frequently displayed in this way.

A good may be either a staple or an impulse item, depending on the purpose of the good's use and on whether the good was purchased because of an immediately felt need. Candy bars may be considered staple goods if they are purchased for lunch boxes as part of a weekly grocery shopping trip. A candy bar might be viewed as an impulse item if it were purchased and eaten on the spot because the person just happened to see it.

Emergency goods are bought only when an urgent need is felt. In this situation price is not too important. The customer needs the goods at once. Tire chains purchased at a turnpike service station during a snowstorm or ambulance service for the victim of a heart attack are examples of emergency goods.

Shopping goods   *Shopping goods* are compared with competing products for price, quality, style, or service by the customer before purchase. This presents an opportunity for personal selling by sales personnel. Shopping goods typically have a relatively high unit price and are bought less frequently than convenience goods. Examples of shopping goods include men's and women's apparel, jewelry, and furniture.

Since the customer will probably want to compare shopping goods with those sold by the competition, retail stores selling such goods find it desirable to be located close together. In some cases the name of the retail store is more important to the customer than the name of the manufacturer. Therefore, the retailer has considerable opportunity to increase sales of shopping goods through promotion.

Specialty goods   *Specialty goods* are identified by customers with strong brand preference or with features which justify a special buying effort. The customer usually has knowledge of the product before the buying trip and is willing to go out of the way to find a certain brand. Examples of specialty goods include photographic equipment, expensive clothing, and stereo sets. An automobile may be considered a specialty good by the customer who has a strong preference for a particular manufacturer's models.

Although specialty goods may have a high unit price, an inexpensive item may be considered a specialty good if the customer has a strong brand preference for it. Thus for many persons Kodak film and processing are specialty goods since they will use no other brand even though the film and processing of other manufactures may be priced lower.

Classifications change. Customers' shopping habits change over time. For example, people now buy many products in supermarkets which they formerly purchased in drugstores or variety shops. As incomes rise, families may buy as convenience goods products which were formerly shopping goods. Changes in the buying habits of consumers require managers to be alert to necessary changes in the marketing mix.

The importance of new products

Business must continually give consumers new and improved products in order to hold old customers and to win new ones. In today's markets manufacturers cannot prosper without new products. Many corporations have more than 50 percent of their sales in products which did not exist ten years ago.

Products tend to have a life cycle of sales and profit margins as shown in Figure 12–2. Both the sales and profit margin curves slope upward, reach a peak, and then decline. However, there is a significant difference in the timing of their peaks. The sales curve continues to rise after the profit margin curve has reached its peak. This can be partially explained by the competition of enterprises that produce similar goods, reduce prices, and thus force profit margins down. To ensure continued high profit margins on total sales, the business enterprise must develop new products to take up the profit slack on products

FIGURE 12–2
Product life cycle for sales and profit margin

Sales dollars and profit margin percentages

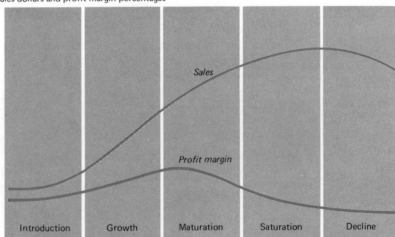

which are still increasing in sales volume. This emphasis on profits rather than sales volume is an important aspect of good marketing management.

New-product development is complicated by the actions of an enterprise's competitors. A business firm must be ahead of the competition with some of its products unless management is willing to operate with lower profit margins than those of enterprises which emphasize research and development.

Developing the product

The development of a new product should be undertaken only after a market analysis of the probable demand for the product. A market analysis enables the manufacturer to develop a product that prospective customers want, with the necessary quality to sell in a given price range. There are four stages in the typical product development program:

1. The idea stage.
2. The development stage.
3. The improvement stage.
4. The evaluation stage.

During the idea stage, creativity is encouraged. The research group should not be bound by tradition or conventional thinking. Frequently, helpful results have come from new personnel who are able to face a problem without "built-in" thinking that limits the range of imaginative new solutions.

Once the idea for a new product has been accepted, the product enters the development stage. This calls for designing the product and constructing a working model. At this stage it is important to determine what the product will look like and how it will operate, and to obtain preliminary cost estimates. Management makes frequent appraisals during the development stage. The project can be closed out if problems are encountered which cannot be solved satisfactorily.

After the development stage, the product is tested in the field to see whether there are any "bugs" in it. Generally design simplifications and other improvements are discovered during field tests. Modifications are made, and the model that will be placed on the market takes shape.

In the evaluation stage the final tests and modifications are undertaken. Final cost estimates are made up. All production details are worked out before the production lines are set up. In practice, improvement never ends. Modifications will take place even after commercial production begins. However, changes are more costly the farther along they occur in the development of the product. The use of a pilot production program and careful evaluation in the final stage of product development reduce the number of changes.

Not all new products are successful. Failure is far more common than success in new-product invention. For every five products developed to the point where they are ready for mass production, only one is ever actually produced and

career outlook

MANUFACTURERS' SALES WORKERS

Practically all manufacturers, whether they make computers or can openers, employ sales workers. Manufacturers' sales workers sell mainly to other businesses—factories, railroads, banks, wholesalers, and retailers. They also sell to hospitals, schools, libraries, and other institutions.

Most manufacturers' sales workers sell nontechnical products. They must be well informed about their firms' products and also about the special requirements of their customers.

Sales workers who deal in highly technical products, such as electronic equipment, are often called sales engineers or industrial sales workers. In addition to having a thorough knowledge of their firms' products, they must be able to help prospective buyers with technical problems.

Beginning sales workers take specialized training before they start on the job. Some companies, especially those that manufac-

ture complex technical products, have formal training programs that last two years or longer. Increasingly college graduates have been preferred as trainees.

Employment in this field is expected to grow about as fast as the average for all occupations. Growth will occur because of the rising demand for technical products and the resulting need for trained sales workers. In addition, industrial firms, chain stores, and institutions that purchase large quantities of goods at one time frequently buy directly from the manufacturer. The need for sales workers will increase as manufacturers emphasize sales activities to compete for the growing number of these valuable accounts.

Because of their frequent contact with business people in other firms, sales workers are often able to transfer to other jobs. Some go into business for themselves as independent representatives. Others find opportunities in advertising and marketing research.

distributed. Of new products placed on the market, only about half are commercially successful.

PROMOTION

Promotion of the enterprise's product to encourage the potential customer to buy is another important element of the marketing mix. Promotion is the communications dimension of marketing. Target customers are informed and persuaded regarding the product. Feedback from promotion makes management aware of the consumers' needs and reactions to a specific product. Three methods of promotion are discussed here—personal selling, advertising, and sales promotion.

Personal selling

Personal selling is almost always an important method of promotion. In some enterprises it is the only form of promotion. Selling involves some method of communication with the customer. The most direct and effective form of communication is a personal presentation. This has the advantage of tailoring the sales effort to each customer, but it has the disadvantage of a high cost for each personal communication.

Salesmanship   The heart of personal selling is salesmanship. This involves contact with prospective buyers and the preparation of appeals that will influence them to buy. Modern salesmanship provides product and service information to aid the buyer in making the best decision. Today's salespersons are equipped with knowledge regarding competitors' products as well as their own.

Personal selling is important to the entire economy as well as to the individual business enterprise. According to the U.S. Bureau of the Census, about 10 percent of the total labor force in the United States is engaged in sales work.

"Good morning, madam. We are sales representatives from the Bi-Centennial Aluminum Siding Company, Inc. . . . "

Reprinted by permission The Wall Street Journal

career outlook

ADVERTISING

Advertising requires the talents of people in many different kinds of jobs. *Advertising managers* direct the advertising programs of the businesses for which they work. They determine the size of the advertising budget, the types of ads and the media to use, and what advertising agency, if any, to employ.

Account executives are employed by advertising agencies to develop advertising programs for client firms and individuals. They first study the client's sales, public image, and advertising problems, and then create a program that suits the client's needs.

Research directors and their assistants study the market. They review possible uses for the product or service being sold, compare its advantages or disadvantages with those of competitors, and suggest ways of reaching potential buyers.

Advertising copywriters create the headlines, slogans, and text that attract buyers. *Artists* and *layout workers* plan and create visual effects in advertisements. *Media directors* (or *space buyers* and *time buyers*) negotiate contracts for advertising space or air time.

Production managers and their assistants arrange to have ads printed for publication, filmed for television, or recorded for radio. They must know which firms or free-lance workers will be able to produce the best ads for the least cost.

The employment of advertising workers is expected to increase faster than the average for all occupations through the mid-1980s. Although opportunities should be favorable for highly qualified applicants, particularly in retail advertising, others seeking entry jobs will face keen competition because the glamour of the field attracts many people.

Most employers prefer college graduates. Some employers seek persons with degrees in advertising, with a heavy emphasis on marketing, business, and journalism; others prefer graduates with a liberal arts background. Relevant work experience may be more important than educational background. Experience selling ads for school publications or radio stations, or a summer job with a marketing research service, can be a distinct advantage to the jobseeker.

Special types of sales representatives To assist the salesperson who takes orders and makes specific sales there are two types of specialists—missionary sales representatives and technical specialists. *Missionary sales representatives* work for a manufacturer to develop goodwill and generally stimulate demand on the part of potential customers. Normally they do not take orders or make specific sales. They may assist with sales promotion programs or provide training assistance for the customer's sales force. The *detail representative* who works for a drug manufacturer and calls on physicians and pharmacists is one type of missionary sales representative. The activities of the detail representative include promoting the company's reputation and the quality of its products as well as providing information on new products and distributing professional samples.

Technical specialists usually have scientific or engineering training and knowledge of an enterprise's products, so they can talk with the customer's technical personnel. They may suggest special applications of equipment or products to the customer or help solve a particular problem.

Advertising

Enterprises serving wide markets must carry on some of their promotional activities on a broad basis if they are to achieve mass distribution. Therefore, advertising becomes an important selling tool. *Advertising* is an identified sponsor's communication of a group message regarding a good, service, or idea. Through advertising it is possible to communicate ideas about a product to many persons at once.

Advertising media   The marketing manager can select from a variety of advertising media. The most widely used media include newspapers, television, direct mail, magazines, radio, and outdoor advertising.

Newspaper advertising provides a flexible and timely medium which can be used to provide coverage in a specific city or trade territory. It is adaptable to local conditions. The costs per prospect are relatively low, based on the newspaper's circulation.

Television is the newest and the fastest growing of the major advertising media. Television can be geared to a geographic market or to a particular time when a desired segment of target customers is most likely to be watching television. Television advertising is relatively expensive unless large audiences are reached by its message.

Direct mail can reach the exact market an advertiser desires and therefore may be highly selective. Its copy and form of presentation are flexible. Direct mail is costly on the basis of number of prospects reached. However, if the mailing list is current and contains the proper target customers, the message gets into the hands of interested parties.

Magazines can reach nationwide markets with a relatively low cost per prospect. Regional editions may be used for more limited geographic coverage. Specialized magazines and trade journals can reach audiences that represent clear-cut prospects for the advertiser's product.

Radio advertising offers the flexibility of saturation coverage for a limited geographic area or wider coverage on the networks. The radio ad's message and life are brief but can be repeated a number of times during an advertising campaign at a relatively low cost.

Outdoor advertising signs, if properly placed, reach a large number of people. They are generally used for products with a wide market. The outdoor ad's message must be short. The cost of a particular sign may be relatively low per person contacted, but the cost of placing outdoor signs over a wide geographic territory can be high. Outdoor signs are often used to advertise tourist facilities and to give information to travelers.

Advantages of advertising   Although advertising is less direct and less flexible than personal selling, it has the advantage of lower cost per customer contacted.

Also, advertising may provide information to the target customers which will cause them to seek out the product. It may make prospects more responsive when they are contacted personally by a sales representative. Thus, advertising can support the personal selling program of the enterprise.

Advertising reaches individuals who may be inaccessible to sales personnel. Even though a sales representative cannot get an appointment with an executive or a consumer, the advertisement can reach the desk or home to convey its sales message.

The promotion campaign for a new product usually includes advertising to inform and interest potential customers. Advertising campaigns may also be used to increase the sales of a product through more frequent replacement, such as motor oil changes; or to lengthen the selling season, for example, by encouraging consumers to buy flowers at other times than holidays or special occasions.

Product and institutional advertising   Advertising may be classified as product or institutional. *Product advertising* has the objective of providing information and selling a specific good or service. *Institutional advertising* seeks to develop goodwill for an enterprise or an industry rather than directly selling a particular product.

Product advertising may be aimed at developing consumer demand for a general product rather than a specific brand, especially in the introduction phase of a product's life cycle. Thus, in the early stages of color television the theme for advertising campaigns by RCA, the pioneer of today's color television system, was the general idea of color television instead of black and white.

In the growth and maturity stages of the product life cycle the emphasis of product advertising normally turns to promotion of a specific brand. In the growth stage of color television RCA, Zenith, Magnavox, and other manufacturers tended to stress the merits of their own brands. RCA emphasized its long experience in color television; Zenith emphasized handcrafting in its chassis; and Magnavox stressed its hand-finished cabinet quality and design.

As the product matures and reaches the saturation or sales decline phase in its life cycle, advertising may turn to reminder advertising which reinforces the product in the customer's mind. An enterprise with a dominant industry position may use this type of advertising to maintain its market position.

Institutional advertising may be used to develop a community's confidence in an enterprise. For example, banks and savings and loan associations often use institutional advertising to create an image of strength and integrity without promoting a specific service. Large worldwide corporations may use institutional advertising to emphasize the quality and research behind all their products. General Motors uses the GM "Mark of Excellence" in much of its advertising. General Electric uses the phrase "Progress Is Our Most Important Product" as part of its institutional advertising. At times an advertising campaign may contain elements of both product and institutional advertising.

Institutional advertising can also be used to counteract negative publicity or negative consumer reaction to a particular event. For example, an oil company wished to reduce criticism stemming from the pollution of beaches by oil discharges from its tanker ships. The company ran a series of television advertisements stressing the things that the company was doing to protect or enhance the environment.

Spending on advertising   Figure 12–3 shows the amount of advertising expenditures as a percentage of sales for several major industry groups. Although in total dollars the amount spent for advertising is great, advertising spending is relatively small when compared to sales. For example, automobile manufacturers spent over $600 million for advertising in 1974, but this amounted to less than 1 percent of sales dollars. For manufacturing industries in 1974, less than 1 percent of sales was spent for advertising. In contrast, many enterprises spend more than 10 percent of sales for personal selling.

Sales promotion

Sales promotion acts as a link between personal selling and advertising to make each more effective. Personal selling aims at specific customers, and advertising is directed at large numbers of potential consumers. The function of sales promotion is to fill the gap between these extremes by focusing selling efforts on selected small groups. Targets of sales promotion efforts may be the enterprise's own sales force, wholesalers, retailers, or consumers. Sales promotion includes preparing displays and other sales aids, developing materials for training sales personnel, and conducting contests and premium programs for customers.

An example of a sales promotion effort directed at the sales force is the sales contest with expense-paid trips for winners to places such as Hawaii or Mexico. Sales promotions aimed at consumers may give away free samples of toothpaste or soap or bonus trading stamps. Premiums, such as silverware redeemable by mail for boxtops or coupons, are another approach. Sales promotion to consumers may be through price incentives using coupons, refunds, or cents-off-package deals. Rexall Drug made famous the one-cent sale, in which the buyer gets two items for the price of one, plus one cent. Popular promotional devices include giving away specialty items such as calendars, pens, balloons, or paperweights with the name and address of the advertiser. Another promotional approach is to have manufacturers' representatives come into the retail store to give demonstrations of new foods, cosmetics, or fashions. The variety of these examples indicates that sales promotion activities are limited only by the imagination.

The total promotion mix

Different combinations of personal selling, advertising, and sales promotion efforts may be effective in successfully marketing a particular product. One type of promotional activity may be used as a substitute for some other type of promotion. If an enterprise uses little advertising it will probably have to rely heavily upon personal selling. The Fuller Brush Company sends very little

FIGURE 12–3
Advertising spending in selected industries, 1974–1975, expressed as percent of sales

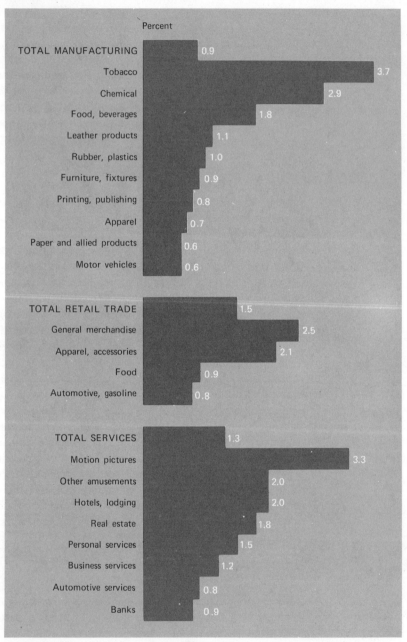

Source: U.S. Internal Revenue Service, *Statistics of Income—1974, Corporation Income Tax Returns* (Washington, D.C.: U.S. Government Printing Office, 1978).

for advertising. However, each product in its line is sold door-to-door through the use of sales promotion samples and small catalogs. On the other hand, the tobacco companies have large advertising budgets and make almost no use of personal selling in promoting their brands of cigarettes. Avon Products has introduced television advertising to support its door-to-door personal selling campaign for cosmetics. A key marketing decision is the selection of the best combination of promotional efforts.

PRICE

Pricing is one of the major elements in the marketing of an enterprise's product. Price directly affects both sales volume and profits. However, managements exercise widely varying degrees of control over the prices charged for their products. At one extreme are sellers who exercise almost no control over the prices they receive for their goods. In these cases of pure competition the seller accepts the going market price and is not able to influence price. There are few examples in industry, but there are some in agriculture, such as wheat farmers.

At the other extreme is the monopolist who is the only supplier of a particular good or service and can establish the selling price. Here too, examples in American economic life are difficult to find since our national policy is to limit the monopolist. Where natural monopolies do exist, as in the case of public utilities, the prices charged customers are regulated by public commissions. In regulated industries the objectives are to provide a fair return to the enterprise for providing the service and yet to protect consumers by keeping rates reasonable.

Between these extremes of pure competition and monopoly lies the pricing situation of most enterprises in American industry. Varying degrees of imperfect competition lead to a wide variety both of pricing practices and of emphasis upon price and nonprice competition.

Practical pricing considerations

There are several practical pricing considerations which should be taken into account by marketers. These include consumer demand, the importance of nonprice competition, costs, pricing strategy, and government controls.

Consumer demand

The marketing manager would like to know how important price is to the consumer relative to such other factors as quality, service, reliability, and sales promotion. Sometimes price is an important determinant of consumer demand. When changes in the price of a good result in substantial changes in consumer demand, the good is said to have a high degree of *elasticity of demand*. When price changes bring about little or no change in the demand for a product, the product has *inelasticity of demand*. An example of a good with a relatively high degree of demand elasticity is beefsteak. When the price of steak goes up, many people switch from steak to roasts and hamburger. As the price of steak declines, these same consumers switch back to steak. The classic example of a product which has high inelasticity of demand is table salt. Most people would not use more salt even if the price was reduced substantially. Neither would they decrease their consumption of salt if the price doubled or tripled.

Three tests may be applied to determine the elasticity of demand for a product. Generally the demand elasticity is greater when many substitutes are available, when the product is a luxury item and can be dispensed with fairly easily, or when it is a big-ticket item such as a car or a home.

The importance of nonprice competition

Where there is a tendency in an industry toward uniformity of price, market share is determined largely through nonprice competition. Nonprice competition includes promotion, quality and service competition, and fashion. Nonprice competition may reduce the importance of the pricing decision.

In the tobacco industry the chief emphasis for cigarette sales is on nonprice competition through advertising. The prices of different brands of cigarettes are essentially the same. An attempt is made by each manufacturer to distinguish its product from competing products in the mind of the consumer. This is done mainly by advertising which appeals to the emotions.

Quality and service are important nonprice considerations for a variety of products. Brand names such as Maytag, Cadillac, Texaco, Omega, and Hart Schaffner & Marx reflect an image of quality or service. This reduces the importance of price competition for these products.

Fashion is the style of a particular product which happens to be popular at a given time. Improved methods of communication and better use of advertising have contributed to an increased emphasis on fashion.

Costs

An obvious consideration in pricing is the cost associated with producing and distributing the products of the business enterprise. Over the long run the manager must cover all the costs of doing business if the enterprise is to avoid operating at a loss. An important responsibility of the marketing department is to provide top management with information regarding probable consumer reaction to different prices. In setting product prices, expected consumer reactions are considered in addition to production and marketing costs.

Pricing strategies

A range of pricing strategies may be used in the business enterprise. Skimming the cream and market penetration represent two extremes in pricing strategy.

Skimming-the-cream pricing   A policy of *skimming the cream* results in setting a price at the high end of the possible range of prices for a product. Such a policy is likely to be used with a distinctive product in the introduction stage of its life cycle or with products for which nonprice competition is emphasized. Early in the product's life, demand will probably be less elastic in response to price. Also, competition is not as intensive as it is later. High prices at the introduction stage may generate greater profits. These can be used to cover development costs. Moreover, if a mistake is made in the initial pricing of a new product, it is easier to lower the price than to raise it. Later in the product's life cycle, a series of planned price reductions can broaden the market to increase sales and meet price competition.

Market penetration pricing   In *market penetration pricing* the price is set relatively low to achieve mass market acceptance quickly. This strategy can be successful if demand for the product is highly sensitive to price and if considerable competition is expected as soon as the product is introduced. Also, lower costs per unit of production may be achieved when a large volume of goods is produced. This is especially true for products having high fixed costs that can be spread over volume production. An enterprise with a large investment in plant and equipment may profit from mass marketing early in the product life cycle. In addition, a low initial price may achieve a degree of product acceptance in the market which will help meet competition better in the future.

Government controls

In some instances prices charged by a business enterprise are directly controlled by government. This is especially true for public utilities whose service rates within a state are established by state regulatory commissions. Interstate utility services are controlled by federal governmental agencies.

The antitrust laws set the ground rules to which business pricing practices must conform. These laws include the Clayton Act and the Robinson-Patman Act, which were discussed in Chapter 3. Price-fixing in an industry is generally illegal, as are other restraints on competition. It is unlawful to practice price discrimination in interstate markets among purchasers of products of similar grade and quality where the result may tend to injure competition. Differences in price to different purchasers must be based on cost differences or on the need to meet competition. Government has generally attempted to prevent large enterprises from setting prices so low as to drive out smaller competitors. The fear is that once competition has been eliminated the larger, surviving firms will raise prices even higher than they were before the predatory price cutting.

PLACE

Place is an important dimension of the marketing mix. Place includes the factors which provide time and place utility to satisfy customers. Place decisions have to be made regarding channels of distribution and transportation and storage systems.

Channels of distribution

Channels of distribution determine the route that a product takes from the producer to the ultimate consumer or the industrial user. These channels include the producer and the final consumer, along with any intermediaries involved in the transfer of title to the goods.

In recent years there has been a tendency to reduce the number of intermediaries between the producer and the ultimate consumer. However, the marketing functions of storage, transportation, and risk-taking must be performed as goods are moved to consumers. These marketing functions can be shifted forward or backward in the channel of distribution or they can be shared, but they cannot be eliminated. In deciding which means of distribution to use, the objectives are to reduce the total distribution costs and to improve service for consumers.

Channels of distribution to ultimate consumers vary considerably in their complexity. Figure 12–4 illustrates the range of channels for consumer products. The distribution of industrial goods is discussed in Chapter 13.

The simplest channel is from the manufacturer directly to the consumer. Enterprises such as Firestone and Rexall own some of the retail outlets through which their products are sold to consumers. Goods may be sold by manufacturers to such retailers as large furniture dealers, with the retailers assuming the wholesale functions of warehousing.

More complicated channels of distribution include more than one intermediary between the producer and the consumer. These intermediaries include various wholesalers and retailers.

Wholesalers Two principal types of wholesalers are used by manufacturers to distribute their products to retailers. These are the merchant wholesaler and

FIGURE 12–4
Channels of distribution for consumer products

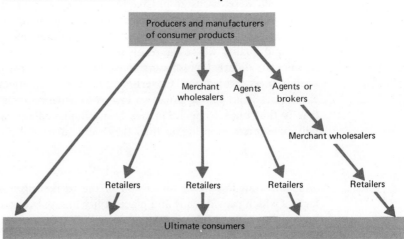

the agent or broker. In deciding which system is best for distributing their products manufacturers must analyze the alternatives in light of the characteristics of their products, the services to be provided, and the customers they wish to reach.

Merchant wholesalers perform several important functions for manufacturers. They purchase merchandise from manufacturers, take title to the goods, and assume the risks associated with selling them. The merchant wholesaler stores the product, delivers it to retail or industrial customers, handles the collection of accounts, and may provide service facilities and sales promotion.

Jobbers, drop shippers, and cash-and-carry wholesalers are other types of wholesalers that normally take title to goods as these move through the channel of distribution, but such wholesalers usually do not provide all the services that are made available by the merchant wholesaler.

The distinguishing characteristic of *agents* and *brokers* is that they customarily do not take title to goods but merely negotiate the purchase or sale of merchandise. For this service they are paid a fee or commission. They may represent specialized product lines as in the case of processed foods brokers or building supplies manufacturers' agents. Customarily the agent or broker is in close communication with potential customers and is able to provide information on the demand for goods at any time. This permits the manufacturer to avoid the expense of a sales force. A large area can be covered by a network of independent sales agents.

Retailers   *Retailers* sell goods and services to the ultimate consumer. This puts retailers in a key position to test consumer acceptance of the product, gauge whether it is priced correctly, and assist customers in making their purchases.

No longer can retailers be easily classified as department stores, drugstores, or grocery stores, depending on the merchandise sold and the services provided to customers. Retailing classifications have been blurred with the development of discount houses. Also, supermarkets and drugstores have diversified their merchandise lines so as to appear as small department stores. Today retailing ranges from highly impersonal vending machines to small specialty shops dealing in luxury merchandise with much personal service.

In the past 30 years retailing methods have changed dramatically. First came discount houses, then shopping centers, and most recently enclosed shopping malls. The retailer who can sense new ways to fulfill consumer wants will be the one who will prosper. What kind of retailing do you think will prevail in the future?

Physical distribution

Physical distribution consists of moving and handling goods through channels of distribution. For goods to have possession utility they must be at a location where they are available to the consumer at the proper time. The physical distribution system includes the transportation of goods and their storage.

INDUSTRIAL TRAFFIC MANAGERS

Industrial firms want to receive raw materials and deliver customers' goods promptly, safely, and at minimum cost. Arranging for the transportation of materials and finished products is the job of the industrial traffic manager. Industrial traffic managers analyze various transportation possibilities and choose the most efficient type for their companies' needs—rail, air, road, water, pipeline, or some combination. Then they select the route and the particular carrier.

The activities of industrial traffic managers range from checking freight bills to deciding whether the company should buy its own fleet of rail cars or trucks or contract for services. Industrial traffic managers route and trace shipments, arrange with carriers for transportation services, prepare bills of lading and other shipping documents, and handle claims for lost or damaged goods.

Some employers prefer graduates of technical and trade school programs in traffic management. Others seek college and university graduates who have either majored in traffic management or taken courses in transportation, logistics, physical distribution, management, economics, statistics, marketing, computer science, and commercial law. More than 100 colleges and universities offer programs or courses in traffic management.

Industrial traffic management is a relatively small occupation, and it is expected to grow about as fast as the average for all occupations through the mid-1980s. College graduates with a major in traffic management or transportation can expect first consideration for the available jobs.

Growth in the occupation will stem from an increasing emphasis on reducing the cost of receiving raw materials and distributing finished products. As the distance between markets becomes greater and the rate schedules and regulations governing transportation become more complex, manufacturers will increasingly require the expertise of the traffic manager.

The transportation of goods is critical to business and consumers in our interdependent society. This is highlighted during a major truck or railroad strike. Transportation systems are so important that some economists have traced the economic development of the United States by analyzing the impact of new means of transportation over the years. In selecting a form of transportation for their products, today's managers can choose among railroads, trucks, waterways, pipelines, and airlines.

Railroads   As Figure 12–5 indicates, railroads carry more intercity freight than does any other single means of transportation in the United States. Railroads are well suited for long hauls of products which are bulky and have a low value relative to their weight, such as coal, steel, and building materials.

Railroads have faced stiff competition from other forms of transportation in recent years. To counter this competition, mainly from trucks, railroads have provided a number of services to meet the needs of specific shippers. For example, when faced with the loss of the shipping of new cars from assembly plants to

FIGURE 12–5
Freight traffic by mode of transportation, 1977

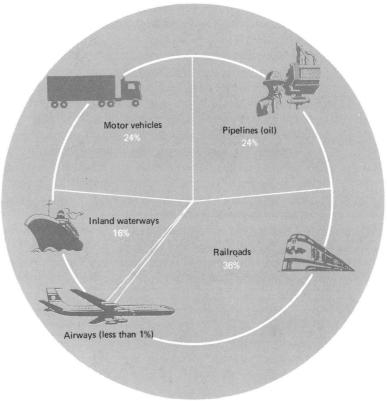

Source: Interstate Commerce Commission, *1978 Annual Report.*

dealers, the railroads designed a triple-deck car carrier. This won back a considerable amount of the business from truck operators. With the development of subcompact American automobiles the railroads devised a carrier which would stack these minicars vertically. Now more can be carried per freight car than by traditional horizontal stacking.

Another innovation by railroads is "piggyback" service, in which loaded truck trailers are carried on railroad flatcars. The transported goods can be packed at the shipper's site and not handled again until they are unloaded at the buyer's freight dock. This provides additional flexibility for the railroads, since the loaded truck trailers can be driven directly to the buyers' locations even if they are not on a rail siding. Also, with less handling the goods are not exposed to as much risk of damage or theft.

Trucks   Over the past 30 years truck transportation has more than doubled its proportionate share of freight carried. This growth has been achieved because of the flexibility of trucking operations, the improvement in the nation's highway system, and truck freight rates that are competitive with those of railroads.

Waterways   The coastal and inland waterways in the United States are used by ship and barge traffic to haul a considerable amount of bulky, nonperishable products such as mineral ore, sand, coal, cement, and petroleum products. Water transportation is the cheapest method of moving goods, but it is also the slowest, and some waterways are closed by ice in the winter.

Improvements have been made in water transport with the development of containerization. Ships are designed to take standard-size containers directly from freight cars or trucks without repackaging. "Fishyback" service using truck trailers similar to those used in rail piggyback service has been developed to increase the flexibility of water transportation.

Pipelines   Pipelines are used primarily to carry such products as crude oil and natural gas. Although water transportation is less costly for refined petroleum products, pipelines are used extensively to transport natural gas and to carry oil from the fields to refineries.

Airlines   Airlines are the newest, fastest, and most expensive means of transportation. Airfreight rates are lower now than they were just a few years ago. However, they are still higher than rail or truck rates. This has caused shippers to analyze the total cost of physical distribution in justifying this type of transportation.

The speed of air transportation has opened up new markets for fragile or perishable products. Orchids and other tropical flowers can be shipped from Hawaii to the mainland. Electronic parts can be packaged less expensively. Inventories can be reduced as the result of speedy availability through the use of air transport.

Storage

The storage function is the holding of goods from the time they are produced until their final use. For the business enterprise this involves a system of warehousing, materials handling, and order processing.

Warehousing   Warehousing, or the storage of goods, may be done by the manufacturer, the wholesaler, or the retailer. The ownership of warehouse space is an added cost of doing business. Unless there is a continuing need for warehouse space, the business enterprise may find it desirable to rent space in a public warehouse.

Public warehouses are located across the country and overseas. They provide public customers with storage space and other services associated with storage. Public warehouses may be prepared to receive goods in large quantities and to repackage them for smaller shipments to customers. A public warehouse may help finance the inventories it holds by issuing a warehouse receipt that can be used as security for a loan from a bank. The public warehouse company assumes responsibility for the damage or loss of goods placed under its custody. Storage facilities for agricultural commodities and other perishables are maintained by some public warehouses.

Materials handling   The efficient movement of goods into a warehouse and their placement, storage, and subsequent removal from the warehouse provide a challenge for materials handlers. The handling of materials is a major part of storage cost.

Moving goods vertically is generally more expensive than moving them horizontally. Therefore, older warehouses with several floors connected by slow-moving freight elevators are being replaced with new one-story warehouses.

Much mechanization is being applied to materials handling. This includes the use of forklifts, conveyor belts, and hydraulic ramps to make unloading and loading easier. Pallets, which are wooden racks that hold a number of boxes or items for easy storage or movement, are widely used in warehousing today. Containerized packaging of standard sizes is being used for easier handling, storing, and transporting. Some grocery and drug warehouses use automated order-filling equipment and radio-controlled equipment for greater efficiency.

Order processing   Once an order from a customer has been received it must be processed. Processing includes the flow of paperwork covering the transaction and the physical shipment of goods. Order processing should be done accurately and promptly to maintain customer goodwill. Mistakes in order handling or delayed shipments can undo the favorable image of the enterprise and its product which has been created by earlier steps in the marketing process.

ORGANIZATION OF THE MARKETING DEPARTMENT

When an enterprise adopts the marketing concept of business it emphasizes the profitable fulfillment of consumer wants. Perhaps the most important aspect

FIGURE 12–6

Partial organization chart of a marketing department

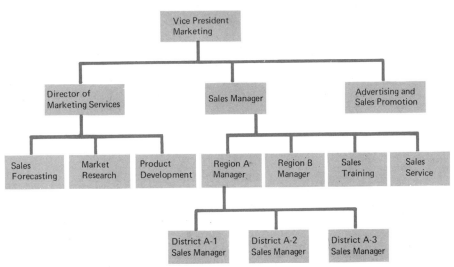

of applying the marketing concept is orienting the thinking of all personnel to improved customer service. Once top management has accepted the marketing concept of business, that concept must be communicated and implemented throughout the business enterprise.

The top marketing executive normally reports directly to the president of the enterprise. Figure 12–6 shows a partial organization chart of a marketing department. Each manager has authority and responsibility for certain functions and a number of subordinates, depending on the size and needs of the enterprise.

SUMMARY

The marketing program of a business enterprise can be thought of as being composed of four variables which constitute the marketing mix. These variables are product, promotion, price, and place. All four variables focus on the consumer, which is consistent with the marketing concept of business.

Consumer products may be classified as convenience goods, shopping goods, and specialty goods. Consumer buying habits differ for each class of products.

New products are the lifeblood of many business enterprises, since the typical product life cycle reaches a peak after which profitability and then sales begin to decline.

Promotion consists of personal selling, advertising, and sales promotion. Advertising is the communication of the enterprise's marketing message to potential consumers through a visual or oral medium. Sales promotion acts as a link between personal selling and advertising.

Pricing considerations include consumer demand, the importance of nonprice competition, costs, pricing strategy, and government controls.

Channels of distribution, transportation, and storage systems all relate to the factor of place in the marketing mix. The channels of distribution vary, depending on the customer, the product, and who is to perform the economic functions associated with moving the product from the producer to the consumer.

Transportation systems include railroads, trucks, waterways, pipelines, and airlines. The choice of a means of transportation requires careful study by marketing managers.

The storage function includes a system of warehousing, materials handling, and order processing.

The marketing department is an important part of the business system. It functions to fulfill consumer wants in a way that will result in a profit for the enterprise.

TERMS FOR REVIEW

marketing mix	*product life cycle*	*skimming-the-cream pricing*
product	*personal selling*	*market penetration pricing*
services	*advertising*	*channels of distribution*
convenience goods	*sales promotion*	*wholesaler*
shopping goods	*elasticity of demand*	*retailer*
specialty goods	*nonprice competition*	

QUESTIONS

1. Interview a retail store manager in your area to determine what products are now sold there that were not on the market five years ago. How would you classify these new products based on consumers' buying habits?

2. *a.* Based on Figure 12–2, what are the implications for the enterprise which does not market new products?

   b. How does the nature of the product line influence the need for new products?

   c. Give examples of products which have product life cycles of different lengths.

3. Evaluate the relative importance of the four P's for small specialty shops and large department stores as they compete in the same enclosed shopping mall.

4. What long-term changes in the consumer's shopping habits may result from the development of the enclosed shopping mall? What are the implications for the older, established retailers in downtown locations?

5. Select examples of product and institutional advertisements which you found appealing. What made these ads effective for you? Give an example of how your buying behavior with regard to a particular item was influenced by advertising.

6. By examining the promotion program for a product, try to determine the pricing strategy being followed by the retailer or manufacturer. To what extent is nonprice competition a factor in selling the product you selected for study?

7. Comment on the following statement by the manager of a discount store in a suburban location: "We have eliminated the wholesale distributor and buy direct from the manufacturer. Since we do our own warehousing and servicing we are able to pass these savings on to the consumer." How would you test the manager's statement?

8. After a study of library materials, write a 300-word paper either supporting or opposing the statement that advertising simply adds to the cost of goods without adding to the value received by consumers.

9. What implications for marketing managers are reflected in the report of J. C. Penney on the first page of this chapter?

business briefs

ADVERTISING PROS?

Should dentists and lawyers advertise their professional services? The legal question was answered in 1977 when the U.S. Supreme Court ruled against a regulation of the Arizona bar prohibiting advertising by lawyers. This legal decision permitted members of the professions to advertise. Previously a variety of laws and regulations had generally prohibited advertising by dentists, physicians, and lawyers.

Opponents of advertising by professionals state that quality is sacrificed for quantity when advertising is done. These opponents also believe that advertising downgrades the status of professionals. One dentist summarized this feeling when he stated that advertising is for car dealers.

Professionals who favor advertising point out that it gives consumers more knowledge about available services and results in more competitive prices.

Today more than 130,000 dentists are practicing in the United States, compared with 117,000 in 1968. Since 1968 the number of lawyers has increased from 132,000 to 432,000 in 1979.

1. *Should professionals such as lawyers and dentists advertise their services to the public?*
2. *Discuss the advantages and disadvantages of advertising by professionals from the point of view of (a) the professionals themselves and (b) consumers.*
3. *What medium and message would probably be most effective for professionals who use advertising?*

A FEW CENTS OFF!

Some 1,200 new food and health products are introduced in the United States each year. To get customers' attention for these new products, more manufacturers are turning to product sampling. In this promotional technique, free samples, often accompanied by a cents-off coupon, are given to potential consumers.

Several large firms now specialize in product sampling to target groups. One these firms employs 1,500 part-time people to pass out samples. PepsiCo used such a firm to help introduce Pepsi Light. The campaign covered 120 markets and included 4,500 stores. During a six-month period the firm's representatives passed out 5 million coupons worth 35 cents each on the purchase of Pepsi Light. The representatives who handed out the coupons were well trained and very enthusiastic. The Pepsi promotion manager observed that because of the training program "by the time the representatives reached the stores, they were so eager that they practically picked up six-packs and put them in customers' baskets."

1. *Why would a manufacturer use product sampling instead of just advertising?*
2. *Why is it important to have training programs for the part-time employees who pass out samples and coupons?*

3. *Have you ever been influenced to buy a new product by a sample in a store? Would reading about the product or hearing about it on radio or television have been equally effective in getting you to try it?*

COMPETING IN COLOR

The demand for color television sets has boomed in recent years. Normally this would be good news for television manufacturers. However, in 1978 American television producers were engaged in what may have been a life-and-death struggle for some of them.

RCA and Zenith lead in U.S. color television sales, with each of them having about 20 percent of the U.S. market. Competition from Japanese producers, which have had a price advantage over American color television sets, has proved to be significant. In 1977, however, after prodding by the U.S. government, the Japanese agreed to reduce their exports of color television sets to the United States.

Did this agreement with Japan reduce foreign competition? Although U.S. imports of Japanese color television sets dropped in 1977, there was an increasing flood of color television imports from other countries. Japanese companies are now producing color television sets in Taiwan, Korea, and Singapore at lower labor costs than they had in Japan.

Also, Japanese manufacturers are moving their production of color television sets to the United States. Sony is producing sets in a San Diego plant and plans a multimillion-dollar expansion of that plant. Toshiba has plans to build a plant in Tennessee, and Matsushita Electric Industrial is modernizing and expanding its Chicago plant, which formerly belonged to Motorola.

Some Japanese companies are working out joint ventures with American companies. Sanyo Electric now owns a majority of the shares of Warwick Electronics, with the rest of the stock owned by Sears, Roebuck & Company.

While American manufacturers are faced with this foreign competition, they are also engaged in price competition with one another. Strong marketing campaigns were waged by RCA in 1978 to take over leadership in color television sales. As a result of competition in the industry the number of U.S. television manufacturers has declined from almost 150 in 1950 to only 6 in 1978.

1. *What risks do American color television manufacturers face today in their efforts to operate profitably?*
2. *What actions can be taken by U.S. color television producers such as Zenith, Sylvania (General Telephone & Electronics), and Curtis Mathis in order to remain competitive?*
3. *What benefits can the American consumer derive from the competition that exists in the color television market?*
4. *What possible problems are there for the American consumer because of current conditions in the television industry?*

"AVON CALLING"

Since World War II American retailing has shifted its emphasis from downtown department store selling to the discount house, the suburban shopping center, and the enclosed shopping mall. Now there is an increased interest by business enterprises in direct selling in the customer's home.

Door-to-door selling has long been a part of the American retail scene. Fuller brushes and Electrolux vacuum cleaners (both now owned by Consolidated Foods) are familiar products to many housewives. Avon Products is the world's largest manufacturer of cosmetics and toiletries. These are sold worldwide by over 900,000 sales representatives. Avon has added costume jewelry and ceramics to its product line, which is sold directly in the customer's home. Avon sales more than tripled from 1969 to 1978. During that period its profits increased more than 2½ times.

Encyclopedias, other books, and magazines are widely sold on an in-home basis. Tupperware (part of Dart Industries) effectively utilizes neighborhood gatherings of housewives, called Tupperware parties, to sell its kitchenware and other products. Other retailers are also using neighborhood hostesses to organize gatherings at which company representatives display and demonstrate a variety of products.

1. *How do you account for the continued success and growth of in-home selling?*
2. *Why will consumers permit strangers to come into their homes to extol the virtues of products ranging from cosmetics to vacuum cleaners?*
3. *What types of goods are particularly suited for direct sale in the customer's home?*

AMF reports . . .

The development of MagicScore was a four-year triumph of cooperation between AMF's central technical staff, corporate test center, the company's Bowling Products Group and several outside contractors. Early in 1973, an AMF study of so-called automatic scorers, which in reality were semiautomatic models, showed that a sophisticated, fully automatic scorer could be developed for reasonable cost, using the latest advances in electronics. The microprocessor, which had emerged as a major technological breakthrough, was seen as the key to developing a self-contained scoring system that would be far more effective in reliability and performance than any device then available.

With the support of AMF's Bowling Products Group, the central technical staff contacted various companies having sophisticated microprocessor technology. Starting with AMF's own design and cost estimates, a special microprocessor was developed for the basic scoring unit. As a result, Magic-Score is the only automatic scoring system utilizing an advanced microprocessor—a silicon chip about the size of a thumbnail that actually is a complex minicomputer.

Outside contractors also were utilized to help develop the acoustical pin sensor as well as a unique counter control unit that enables the bowling proprietor to monitor, control and flash messages to up to 49 MagicScore units, each serving two lanes.

An exhaustive testing program was carried out for MagicScore. This involved not only testing of components by various contractors, AMF's bowling development center in Shelby, Ohio, and the corporate test center, but also consumer testing of numerous preproduction units at bowling establishments. The crowning achievement came in November 1976 when approval was given to the fully automatic MagicScore bowling system, equipped with the acoustic pin sensor, by the American Bowling Congress following a 2,000-game test.

MagicScore is performing well today across the country. The facts that it is easy for bowlers to operate and is simple for proprietors to maintain are major selling points. MagicScore is clearly one of AMF's most significant major new products—one that testifies to the effectiveness of the company's approach to research and development and its commitment to quality.

From annual report of AMF Incorporated

13

Production

Production

If you want a sports car you are not interested in sheets of steel, plate glass, synthetic fabrics, and unprocessed rubber. Unless these materials are combined into a completely assembled automobile they will have little value for the consumer who wants a car. Production provides goods with form utility by turning raw materials and component parts into finished goods for consumer or industrial use.

Great strides have been made in the production process in the United States during the past 50 years. The ability to mass-produce goods at prices which make them available to millions of people is one of the outstanding accomplishments of the private enterprise system. The increased productive capacity of our economy stems from the greater productivity of workers, from increased investment in capital equipment, and from the application of improved production techniques and management methods.

After studying this chapter, you will be able to answer the following questions regarding production:

How does management determine the location of new production facilities?
What factors must management consider in setting up a production system?
Why are production control and scheduling so important?
What is the role of purchasing in the production process?
How does automation relate to production?
How may the production department be organized?

THE LOCATION OF PRODUCTION FACILITIES

The importance of factory location

The selection of a factory site is a decision of major importance for any business enterprise which engages in manufacturing operations. The location of production facilities is a long-term commitment. It is not easy to dispose of buildings and large amounts of machinery if a mistake is made in the factory's location. The location of a plant involves consideration of the following factors.

Nearness to raw materials When raw materials used in the manufacturing process are bulky and expensive to transport, it is wise to locate the factory near the source of these commodities. Iron and steel plants are frequently located near sources of iron ore or coal because of the bulkiness of these raw materials. Often many different parts go into the manufacture of a product. Management must decide whether the advantage of being close to some raw materials sources outweighs other factors which influence factory location.

Nearness to markets for finished products   To achieve economies in distributing its products, a manufacturer may select a plant location close to major customers for its goods. This involves an analysis of future expected markets as well as present distribution patterns. With nationwide and international distribution of product lines this may mean having multiple-plant operations.

Quality and cost of labor available   An important question in deciding plant location is whether an adequate supply of workers is available for the new factory. Management must determine what skills are required and whether the area can supply the workers in a satisfactory cost-quality relationship. If enough skilled workers are not already available, are there persons in the community who can be trained for the new jobs? Are wage rates in the area in line with what management will encounter in other areas and with what its competitors are paying?

Access to transportation facilities   Because of the importance of time in delivering manufactured products to customers, access to good transportation facilities should be considered in factory location. The transportation facilities used depend on the nature of the product and on the importance of speed. For example, an electronics plant may locate adjacent to an airport. Then air transportation is convenient for both company products and company personnel.

Many railroads are willing to provide railroad spurs alongside new factories to encourage greater use of rail freight. Some railroads are developing industrial parks with attractive lease or purchase plans near important rail junction points.

Availability of utilities   A management interested in a new factory site wants to know whether enough electricity, gas, and water are available at economical rates for manufacturing. This is especially important if the manufacturing process consumes large quantities of utility services.

Satisfactory tax situation   Business enterprises must pay several state and local taxes. One of the most important is the property tax imposed by local and state governments on factories, equipment, and inventories. Business enterprises may also have to pay state and local sales or income taxes.

Local and state taxes are a minor portion of an enterprise's costs of doing business. Therefore, these taxes are usually not too important unless other factors are about equal in the choice among several locations. More important than the amount of taxes is whether the community is providing a satisfactory level of municipal services.

Miscellaneous factors   A variety of other factors influence factory location. These include the quality of the community as measured by its schools, colleges, cultural programs, and churches, along with the attitude of its people toward new enterprise. Land for factory sites, adequate zoning, and up-to-date building codes are necessary to encourage new industrial development.

Information regarding possible plant locations is available from local chambers of commerce, state industrial development commissions, industry trade associations, railroads, and utility companies. Management can use much of this information, but it should recognize that each locality is certain to picture itself in the most favorable light. The final decision on factory location must be made by management from its own analysis in light of the enterprise's requirements.

THE PRODUCTION SYSTEM

At its best the production system of a modern business enterprise operates as a smoothly functioning unit. Through the design of efficient production systems we have achieved mass production of goods priced within the reach of millions of consumers. An example of improved production processes which have lowered costs is the development of color television. When color television was a new product a set cost about $1,000. Technology and volume production have reduced costs. Now color television sets cost less than half as much as they did initially. The elements of the production system include research and product design, process design, production control, purchasing, and automation.

Research and product design

Research in most manufacturing enterprises is primarily *applied research*. This involves the practical application of scientific knowledge to definite problems or needs. Applied research is directed toward the development of new products or toward reducing the costs of established product lines. In contrast, *pure research* extends our frontiers of knowledge without regard to the immediate application of its findings.

In many industries up to 10 percent of annual sales is directed toward research and development. Corporations such as Du Pont, Merck, and IBM are noted for both pure and applied research in the fields of chemistry, pharmaceuticals, and computers. Governmental agencies also conduct research, sometimes in cooperation with universities and private enterprises. Both pure and applied research are important in today's economy.

Research and product design may be done by the production, engineering, or marketing departments. Sometimes a separate research department is organized. The final product developed for manufacture should be the result of close cooperation between marketing and production.

The objective in *product design* is to develop a product that will perform properly, appeal to consumers, and be sold at a price that will be profitable. Performance relates to how the product works—to its reliability, mechanical design, and ease of repair. Consumer appeal relates to the form and appearance of the product. For example, automobile designers have to consider performance and appearance as well as price in order to come up with a successful model.

Good styling alone is not enough to make a product successful. Because of mechanical or performance difficulties an auto model may be labeled a "lemon." Successful product design results in a product which rates high in both performance and appearance.

Process design

Whereas product design has to do with the characteristics of the product, *process design* is the development of the means of making it. The objective of good production management is to have the most efficient method for manufacturing a given product. Essential elements in process design include the factory layout, the type of machinery used, and the development of prototypes.

Factory layout   How machines and production lines are arranged in a factory affects the cost of production. Materials should move through the manufacturing process in the quickest and most direct manner possible. Transportation and handling should be held to a minimum. A good factory layout makes the most efficient use of the available machines and workers.

There are two basic types of factory layout. A factory may be laid out according to product or process. *Product layout* is the arrangement of machinery and assembly lines by chronological steps in the manufacture of the product. As the product moves through the plant organized on a product layout basis, there is a gradual buildup from raw materials or parts to the finished product.

Product layout is especially economical when the articles being produced are of standard specifications and are required in large volume. In product layout the use of automatic equipment, continuous production lines, and conveyors results in low costs per unit produced even though the total investment is large. The product layout moves materials through the factory rapidly, with a minimum of handling and transportation.

The advantages of product layout also provide the basis for its weaknesses. As nearly as possible all machines must be kept operating with a minimum of idle time. When something goes wrong along the product layout, it is frequently necessary to shut down the entire assembly line until the trouble is remedied. The product layout therefore requires numerous maintenance and setup personnel, materials suppliers, and engineers to back up the workers tending the machines. Attention must be given to balancing production facilities so that backlogs of materials do not pile up at any one point along the layout. Once the product layout has been set up, changing it will probably be costly.

Process layout occurs when similar types of machines or functions are located together, regardless of where the process comes in the production of a product. This means that all grinding is done in one location, all polishing in another, all drilling in another, and so on through the various steps in the manufacturing cycle. Process layout provides a great deal of flexibility. Products requiring specialized manufacturing operations can be scheduled into the different areas. Machinery can be fully occupied if scheduling is well done.

A breakdown of one machine is not as critical with process layout as with product layout. If a machine breaks down, its work can be transferred to a similar machine in the area. With no continuous production line, such as in product layout, the balancing of production time for machinery is not as important. Process layout is used when a variety of products are produced with the same machines and when job-lot orders in small quantities are being handled.

"We've decided to rehire you—the machine we bought to replace you won't work either."

Reprinted by permission The Wall Street Journal

However, process layout also presents some problems for production managers. Transportation and materials-handling costs are usually high because the conveyors and the mechanized handling used with product layouts are not present. Goods that are being processed move more slowly, resulting in higher inventories and greater financial costs. The scheduling routine of materials and the accounting for costs of production are different for every order. This is in contrast to the more standardized procedures in product layout.

Process layout and product layout each have advantages and disadvantages. In practice most manufacturing enterprises use elements of both, depending on the nature of the product, the variety of goods produced, the length of production runs, and the importance of flexibility.

Machinery selection   General-purpose or special-purpose machines are used in production. *General-purpose machines* can be used for a variety of different jobs requiring the same kind of work. A drill press is an example of a general-purpose machine. A drill press can be used to drill holes of different sizes, to different depths, and into different materials by simply changing the drill bit. General-purpose machinery is fairly well standardized and is available from a number of different manufacturers.

The general-purpose machines found in many factories include shapers, lathes, drills, presses, grinders, polishers, boring machines, and milling machines. Although each of these machines performs a different function, in general machines of this kind change the form of raw materials or semiprocessed goods by removing material, cutting holes, smoothing, bending, or shaping.

General-purpose machines are especially useful when the work in the factory is varied and the volume for any single product is small. Skilled machinists are able to operate more than one type of general-purpose machine. This provides flexibility which is necessary for the job-lot shop. However, it also results in somewhat higher unit costs than when long production runs and standardized products permit the economical use of special-purpose machines.

Special-purpose machines are designed for a particular job and have the right tools and adjustments built in. Once the special-purpose machine has been calibrated and is in operation, a semiskilled worker can be used to tend it. In some instances all a worker has to do is supply raw materials to the machine, remove the parts which have been produced, and occasionally check to see that the machine is producing to established standards. Special-purpose machines are desirable when long production runs of a part justify a large investment in a machine for that one job.

Prototypes   Frequently before production begins on a new product or before a new factory is built, a prototype is constructed. A *prototype* is a model or pattern which will be used as the basis for subsequent production. A prototype may be made of the product or the production process. A good example of a product prototype is the clay model of an automobile that is made during the design process to show its styling and appearance in three dimensions. Later hand-tooled auto models are put together, complete with mechanical work. These models are tested extensively before the final production-line car is decided upon.

A prototype of the production process, called a *pilot plant,* consists of a scale model of the complete factory or the production line. Engineers try to anticipate and eliminate as many problem areas as possible before the factory is built. The construction and testing of a pilot plant may cost thousands of dollars. However, this outlay reduces the risks involved in investing millions of dollars in the new factory and equipment.

Once the product and process designs have been settled, management must place orders for the tooling necessary to start production. *Tooling* consists of items such as cutting and grinding attachments, clamps, gauges, loading devices, and other fixtures. Tooling is designed to adapt machinery and assembly lines to the production of a particular product. It may cost from a few hundred dollars to millions of dollars, depending on the complexity of the product and on the amount of new tooling required. The automobile industry spends hundreds of millions of dollars annually for new-model tooling.

The final step before full-scale production begins is to put the new production facility through a series of test runs. Production personnel and engineers iron out difficulties which may appear despite all the precautions that have been taken. During this time the personnel department recruits and trains any additional workers necessary for the production process. Prior to this time the marketing department will have completed its analysis of the expected market for the product. Pricing and distribution decisions will have been made. Top management will be coordinating the efforts of the various departments for a smooth introduction of the new product.

PRODUCTION CONTROL AND SCHEDULING

The heart of the modern factory system is production control. *Production control* consists of a wide variety of activities, including authorization of orders, scheduling, routing, and maintaining production schedules. Production control personnel coordinate and control the production process to meet delivery schedules. Production control personnel maintain communication with the marketing department as well as with production supervisors.

A master schedule of anticipated production is normally prepared to provide a general basis for control. This master schedule is based on the factory's capacity and on the sales forecast of the demand for the enterprise's goods. The process of sales forecasting was discussed in Chapter 7.

Orders and authorization of production

Orders from customers are sent by the marketing department to production control, which has the responsibility for scheduling those orders so that delivery dates can be met. The sales department has a responsibility for coordinating its efforts with production control so that customers will not be promised unrealistic delivery dates. In some instances the sales department is not permitted to give a firm delivery date until the delivery date has been cleared with production control.

The specific orders coming from the sales department constitute the factory's authority to produce the goods. Once an order has been placed, the authorization to produce the goods is prepared by the scheduling section of production control. The specific scheduling takes into account the status of orders already in the production process, the present utilization of factory capacity, and the promised delivery date.

Production scheduling

Production scheduling covers the time span that begins when orders are received from the sales department and ends when finished goods are shipped to customers or are delivered to the warehouse for future shipment. The objectives of good production scheduling are to assure that delivery schedules are met and that the most efficient utilization of production capacity is achieved.

Before setting up production schedules, an important factor to be considered is *lead time*. This is the time necessary for all arrangements before production can begin. In the case of simple or repeat production orders the lead time may be measured in days. With model changes in automobiles, appliances, and other complex goods the lead time is measured in months. Several years of lead time are required with items such as new aircraft or aerospace products requiring new technology.

Scheduling and follow-up are valuable control devices in the modern factory. A complex system of production scheduling is required today because of the thousands of parts which go into many of the products we take for granted. For example, a portable typewriter has more than 1,750 parts. Each part must be available at the right place, in the proper quantity, at the time it is required in the assembly of the typewriter. Even more complex scheduling systems are involved in the production of aerospace products which have a multitude of parts and may require coordination among a number of manufacturing plants.

Routing An important part of production control and scheduling is routing. *Routing* includes detailed instructions as to how a particular order will move from department to department, which machines will be used, and when inspections will be made. The routing sheet provides the supervisor in each department with specific information regarding the order, how it is to be processed, and where the materials are to go after a department has completed its operations.

Maintaining production schedules There are a number of means available to see that production is on schedule. A variety of charts and control boards are used. These charts show the detailed operations that are required to fill an order, when these operations should occur, and what the actual state of production is. A master schedule is used as an overall control device to summa-

career outlook

PURCHASING AGENTS

The purchasing agent's job is to maintain an adequate supply of the items that a firm needs for its operations. Purchasing agents and their assistants obtain goods and services of the required quality at the lowest possible cost. They buy when the stocks on hand reach a predetermined reorder point or when a department in the organization requisitions items that it needs.

Because purchasing agents can often purchase from many sources, their main job is to select the seller who offers the best value. Frequently purchasing agents invite suppliers to bid on large orders. Then they select the lowest bidder among those suppliers who meet the requirements for quality of goods and delivery date.

Once an order has been placed with a supplier, the purchasing agent makes periodic checks to ensure that it will be delivered on time. This is necessary to prevent work flow interruptions due to lack of materials. After an order has been received and inspected, the purchasing agent authorizes payment to the shipper.

The purchasing agent must be able to ana-lyze numbers and technical data in order to make buying decisions and take responsibility for spending large amounts of money. The job requires the ability to work independently and a good memory for details. In addition, a purchasing agent must be tactful in dealing with salespersons and able to motivate others.

The employment of purchasing agents is expected to increase faster than the average for all occupations through the mid-1980s. Although there are no universal educational requirements for entry-level jobs, most large companies now require a college degree and prefer applicants with a master's degree in business administration. Persons with a bachelor's degree in engineering, science, or business administration whose college program included one or more courses in purchasing should also have bright prospects. Graduates of two-year programs in purchasing should continue to find ample opportunities, though they will probably be limited to small firms.

The demand for purchasing agents is expected to rise as their importance in reducing costs is increasingly recognized.

rize information on units produced, orders on the books, and the productive capacity that will be available in the future.

In many instances the electronic computer has replaced these charts and control boards. The ability of computer systems to provide instant information on the status of orders and machine use has been of great benefit to production managers in scheduling. Computer systems are used on a continuous basis to receive information from the factory machinery for constant control of the production process. Machinery or reporting stations in the factory are connected electrically to the computer. Information on jobs that are under way or have been completed is fed immediately into the computer for analysis and reporting.

PURCHASING INDUSTRIAL GOODS

In many manufacturing enterprises the value of purchased materials makes up 50 percent or more of the cost of the final product. In most manufacturing operations, purchased materials are the largest single expense in the manufacturing process.

Purchasing is the procurement of industrial materials and supplies for use or for further processing, not for immediate resale. This excludes buying merchandise for sale to the consumer without changing its form, as is done by retail and wholesale merchants.

Steps in the purchasing process

The essential steps in the purchasing process are outlined below.

1. The need arises for specific industrial goods. For maximum efficiency, purchasing schedules should be planned in advance. However, rush orders may be necessitated by emergencies, such as breakdowns or sudden changes caused by shifts in demand.

2. An accurate description of the goods is drawn up on a purchase requisition form.

3. Once the requisition has been completed and filed with the purchasing department, the negotiations with possible sources of supply are undertaken.

4. After negotiating with possible vendors, the purchasing department selects a particular vendor and places an order for the goods. The purchase order contains the precise merchandise description, quantity, price, delivery date, and the signature of the purchasing officer.

5. Prior to the delivery date, a follow-up is carried out by the purchasing department to confirm that the promised delivery date will be met.

6. Upon receipt of the vendor's invoice, an itemized statement of the merchandise shipped by the seller, the purchasing department checks to see that the goods shipped match the description on the purchase order.

7. When the industrial goods arrive they are inspected for quantity and quality and to see whether damage has occurred in transit. After the merchandise has been inspected, the invoice is approved for payment. The departments are then notified that the goods are available.

Price and quality considerations

Purchasing agents are expected to negotiate prices and to buy at the most favorable prices obtainable. However, invoice price is but one element of cost. Delivery costs must also be considered. At times a lower invoice price may be obtained through quantity purchasing. However, the expense of handling and storage may outweigh this price difference by the time the materials have been put to use. Thus, low unit prices on invoices do not always mean the lowest total cost to the purchaser.

Quality must also be taken into account in the purchase decision. Quality is a relative term. *Quality* may be defined as the possession of the characteristics which fit a product to a given use. The purchasing enterprise must define the minimum standards of quality that are required for the intended purpose.

Selecting sources of supply

In selecting the sources of supply for the enterprise, the purchasing department normally goes through four stages:

1. The information or survey stage, when possible sources for a product are considered.
2. The inquiry stage, when the relative qualifications and merits of potential suppliers are determined.
3. The analysis and selection stage, when the initial order is placed.
4. The administration or experience stage, when the vendor-customer relationship is established or when the selection process is repeated to find a more satisfactory source of supply.

THE MAKE-OR-BUY DECISION

At times the question arises as to whether it is better to manufacture a component in one's own plant or to buy the part from an outside vendor. To help management with the make-or-buy decision, comparisons should be made of costs, the quantity desired, and the necessary quality.

The *cost of purchased goods* may be determined rather easily. This should be the complete cost to the time of use. It includes the invoice price of the purchased goods plus transportation charges and costs of handling and storage. Against this purchased cost must be balanced the total estimated cost of producing the goods in the enterprise's own shop. This cost calculation should include not only the costs of materials and labor, but also investment costs, including depreciation on necessary equipment, the cost of utilities, and supervision costs. All of these costs of production must be included for a fair comparison with the cost of purchasing the product.

The *quantity of goods* required is an important consideration. Are the potential cost savings large enough to justify producing the component? Is the quantity needed great enough to realize economies by spreading the fixed manufacturing costs over many units of production?

Quality control of an item may be better if the component is produced in your own plant rather than purchased outside. This is an important consideration when strict quality control and exacting requirements are needed. Production in your own plant may make it easier to guarantee the desired quality. On the other hand, if the quality standards for the component are greater than plant employees have been accustomed to dealing with, quality may be improved by purchasing the component from a manufacturer accustomed to such high standards.

The problem of inflexibility is associated with the self-manufacture of a component part. When special equipment is necessary, the element of inflexibility is introduced. Freedom of selection is sacrificed even if cost savings later become available through outside purchase.

INVENTORY CONTROL

Inventories typically represent a substantial part of a manufacturing enterprise's assets. Inventory control is important to three different departments in the business enterprise. The production department must be assured of an adequate supply of materials on hand to manufacture goods when needed. The marketing department must be able to fill sales orders and meet customers' delivery dates. The finance department must see that funds are available to finance necessary inventories.

Manufacturing inventories are classified as raw materials, goods in process, or finished goods. *Raw materials* include unprocessed commodities and purchased components that are to be assembled into the finished product. Once inventories have been placed in the production cycle they become *work in process*. Their form is changed or other parts are added to increase their value and to move the materials nearer to product completion. When the manufacturing process has been completed and the goods await distribution to customers, they are *finished goods*. Finished goods inventories are the buffer between immediate sales needs and the ability of the factory to produce goods.

The administration of inventories includes the receipt and storage of goods, the issuance of materials to production departments, and the shipment of finished goods to customers. A system of records provides for accountability of goods, information on inventory turnover, and reorder points. The analysis of inventory turnover is discussed in Chapter 14. Today inventory control is improved by computer systems.

THE PURCHASE OF CAPITAL EQUIPMENT

The purchase of capital equipment such as machinery, transportation equipment, or office equipment requires different analysis than the purchase of materials which go into the manufacture of a product. *Capital equipment* lasts longer than a year, is used to produce other goods, and does not become part of the product being manufactured. New capital equipment may result in greater productivity, lower costs, or higher dependability.

Special attention is given to the purchase of capital equipment because:

1. Capital equipment usually involves outlays of large amounts of money which may require special financing. The purchase of capital equipment is generally a decision of major importance for the enterprise.

2. In view of the long life of most capital equipment items, the purchase of major equipment is an infrequent occurrence. The type of new capital equip-

ment purchased will probably vary from year to year. This makes the purchase of such equipment difficult to routinize.

3. The total cost of capital equipment is more difficult to determine than are raw materials costs. In addition to the initial cost, the cost of capital equipment includes obsolescence, maintenance, and idle time.

4. The characteristics of capital equipment produced by different manufacturers are seldom identical. Each machinery manufacturer normally has different features and options for a particular line of equipment. Therefore, direct comparison of machines and prices is difficult.

5. Because of the long life of capital equipment, its purchase commits management to a series of other decisions with long-run consequences. These decisions include the product to be manufactured, the method of production, and the costs of operation.

6. Consideration must be given to how the proposed capital equipment will fit into the plant layout. Extensive changes may be required in the production process when new capital equipment is introduced.

OTHER ELEMENTS OF THE PRODUCTION SYSTEM

Other important elements of the production system include motion and time analysis, quality control, and maintenance.

Motion and time analysis

Motion and time analysis is done by industrial engineers to provide a basis for production standards on factory jobs. First comes the motion analysis to determine the best way of doing a particular job by reducing waste effort to a minimum. The methods engineer studies the job and breaks it down into its essential elements, eliminating unnecessary movements and establishing a pattern for efficient production.

Once the motion analysis has been completed, the worker is trained in the new method. Then the industrial engineer conducts a time study analysis, using a stopwatch, to determine how much time is necessary to carry out the job under actual factory conditions. This time study will be the basis for setting the work standard after allowances have been made for worker fatigue, production delays, and necessary personal time.

In establishing work standards, a desirable psychological practice is to set an expected rate of production which the average worker can exceed by 10 to 15 percent by exerting a bit more than normal effort. The establishment of piece rates or hourly production standards is a tedious job. Management seeks to be fair to the workers and at the same time to hold down production costs so that the enterprise can be competitive and earn a profit.

Quality control

An important element in the production system is the maintenance of the desired quality in manufactured products. Once standards of quality have been established, a means of inspection must be devised. Many different types of inspections can be carried out on manufactured goods. These range from a skilled cook tasting a vat of soup to pronounce it fit for canning to a test driver checking out a new car off the assembly line before shipment to a dealer.

Inspection can be done as goods move along the production lines or at a central inspection facility located away from the production process. When inspection is done on the production lines, there is an opportunity to prevent the buildup of an excessive number of defective products.

The central inspection facility may act as a receiving station for products from all over a factory. This facility may be a laboratory in which detailed inspections are made under carefully controlled conditions. A central inspection facility permits more objective inspection, since the inspector is not standing by the production worker who may be responsible for the unsatisfactory work.

Sometimes every product in a factory will be inspected. However, often some form of partial inspection is used, based on a statistically selected sample.

Maintenance

The work of the *maintenance* force is to keep the factory in efficient operating order. This involves a wide variety of activities, including lubricating moving parts, repairing machinery, or fixing a plumbing breakdown. All the physical facilities in a factory start wearing out the day they are installed. Therefore, a sound maintenance program must be instituted if production is to continue, uninterrupted by breakdowns.

Hiring skilled maintenance personnel, providing them with proper tools, and keeping an inventory of spare parts are costly. However, a breakdown which stops production, causing workers and machinery to be idle, is even more costly. This means that *preventive maintenance* should be part of the maintenance program in a factory.

AUTOMATION

Automation has different meanings for different people, depending on their frame of reference. To planners it may mean the promise of factories that produce huge quantities of goods but require little human physical effort. Workers may see automation as a threat to their employment, with labor unions seeking to protect the jobs of their members against it. Business owners may view automation as a means of lowering production costs and thereby increasing profits. And idealists may see automation as a means for improving living standards through greatly increased productivity. Actually automation contains elements of all these meanings.

Automation today represents an extension of the mechanization which began in the 18th century with James Watt's invention of the steam engine. *Mechanization* is the application of power-driven tools in factory production, and it results in a saving of both human energy and time. The textile industry was the first to be mechanized. Mechanization represents the first phase in the process of automation.

The second phase in automation is the *continuous process assembly line,* in which goods are moved through the production process by automatic conveyors. The continuous production process can be seen today in such industries as steel, glass, and nonferrous metals.

The third phase in automation is the *fully automated process.* This consists of the feedback of information from a machine which inspects its own output and actuates controls to correct deviations from established standards. This phase of automation is already in use in the metalworking industries, in oil refining, and in the production of hydroelectricity. Automatic feedback and control systems are made possible through electronic data processing equipment and controls. Electronic computers and increased automation have eliminated many routine production and clerical jobs in industry. Workers with increased technical knowledge are required to program, check, and maintain these automated processes. With electronic computers, information is available to management more rapidly, in greater quantities, and in wider variety than ever before. Chapter 17 is devoted to a discussion of computers because of their importance today.

THE ORGANIZATION OF THE PRODUCTION DEPARTMENT

In a manufacturing enterprise the production department is a line department since it contributes directly to the main function of the enterprise. The complexity

FIGURE 13–1

Partial organization chart of a typical production department

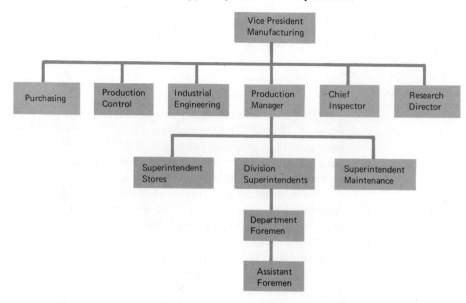

of the organization of the production department depends on the size of the enterprise and on the goods produced. The organization for the production function in a typical manufacturing enterprise is illustrated in Figure 13–1.

Manufacturing management

The executive in charge of the production function has a title such as vice president for manufacturing. The line organization directly responsible for production goes through the production manager to the division superintendents and then to the foremen and their assistants. The maintenance department headed by a master mechanic or superintendent of maintenance reports to the production manager, as does the inventory or stores superintendent.

A number of staff departments assist line managers by performing functions which support manufacturing operations. These typically include production control, industrial engineering, inspection, purchasing, and research. Other departments, particularly personnel and accounting, play an important staff role in the production function. The legal department may assist by assuring that manufacturing processes and products are properly protected by patents and that the enterprise is not infringing on patents of other firms.

The factory foreman

The role of the foreman is extremely important in manufacturing operations despite the increased use of automation and staff persons in the modern factory. Men and women who serve as foremen must be trained in the technical requirements of their departments. The foremen need to understand how the work of their departments relates to the total operation of the factory.

Important as technical skill is for the formen, they should also have an awareness of the importance of good human relations in dealing with the workers. This usually requires some training and a thorough understanding of the enterprise's policies and operating rules.

As first-line supervisors, the foremen represent the point at which management comes into direct contact with the workers. They must interpret and administer enterprise policies which affect employees. The typical factory worker views the foremen as being the management. Therefore, the impressions created by them will significantly influence workers' attitudes toward the business enterprise.

SUMMARY

Production consists of providing goods with form utility by turning raw materials and semifinished products into finished goods for either consumer or industrial use.

The location of production facilities involves consideration of such factors as closeness to raw materials and markets for finished goods, access to transportation, the availability of labor and utility services, and a satisfactory tax structure.

The first steps in the production system are research and product design and process design. These steps involve factory layout, machinery selection, and the building of prototypes. Production control and scheduling, purchasing, and inventory control are also important elements in production. Other significant elements in the production system are motion and time analysis, quality control, and maintenance. The purchase of capital equipment involves a number of special problems.

Automation progresses from mechanization to the continuous process assembly line to the fully automated process which has a control system to correct deviations from established standards.

The vice president of manufacturing is customarily in charge of the production system. In large factories an extensive organization is necessary to support the foreman, who serves as the direct contact between management and the work force.

TERMS FOR REVIEW

production	*purchasing*	*motion and time analysis*
product design	*raw materials*	*quality control*
factory layout	*work in process*	*maintenance force*
production control	*finished goods inventories*	*automation*
production scheduling	*capital equipment*	*foreman*

QUESTIONS

1. *a.* What advantages does your area have for the location of manufacturing enterprises? Talk with chamber of commerce personnel, public utilities managers, and real estate brokers to develop this information.

    b. What type of manufacturing activities would be particularly desirable for your community?

    c. What negative and positive implications are there for a community as the result of a new factory?

2. Examine current publications and find specific examples of research which has resulted in new industrial or consumer products.

3. If possible, arrange with the personnel or public relations department to tour a factory in your area. Observe the type of factory layout and the machinery which is used.

4. What are some examples of the application of "quality" to a product? Why would quality specifications be quite different for a product depending on its intended use?

5. If a manufacturer is able to produce a component for less than its purchase price, would you advise the enterprise to go ahead and produce it? Explain your answer.

6. Why is the purchase of capital equipment an important decision in most enterprises?

7. What factors make the position of factory foreman an important and difficult one? What does this imply for the top management of a manufacturing enterprise?

8. After a study of library materials, write a 300-word summary either supporting or opposing the

statement that automation results in the elimination of jobs and causes higher levels of unemployment.

9. Outline the steps involved in the development of the fully-automatic bowling scorer described by AMF on the first page of this chapter.

business briefs

METRICATION MAYHEM

Most nations except the United States, Burma, Brunei, Liberia, and Yemen are on the metric system. It is estimated that the United States loses $700 million yearly in foreign sales due to the nonmetric labeling of products. In 1975 Congress passed the Metric Conversion Act, which calls for the voluntary conversion to the metric system.

Metrication, the transition to the metric system of weights and measures, is of great interest to business managers, purchasing agents, and skilled laborers as well as the general public. For example, mechanics who provide their own tools may have to spend as much as $4,000 each for a new set of metric-measure tools. Some labor leaders have called for government subsidies to persons who are economically hurt by metrication.

Many multinational business enterprises such as General Motors, IBM, and International Harvester have shifted to metric standards without waiting for government to require or subsidize the shift. An estimated 60 percent or more of the top 1,000 manufacturing enterprises in the United States are using the metric system or are in the process of transition.

However, some U.S. enterprises are resisting the switch to the metric system. The costs of retooling, training, and product redesign place short-term pressures on the profits of many firms.

Over the long run, conversion to the metric system streamlines industrial measurements and specifications and results in lower costs. For example, the American National Standards Institute states that the new metric fastener system calls for 25 standard thread sizes instead of the present 59. Streamlined product lines, reduced inventories, and longer production runs are benefits that can result from changing to the metric system. American industry can save an estimated $500 million annually through production economies just from the new fastener system.

Consumers are resisting changing their thinking from inches, pounds, quarts, and Fahrenheit to centimeters, grams, liters, and Celsius. The Department of Agriculture found that consumers complained vigorously when asked for comments on the use of metric terms on meat and poultry labels. A strong negative reaction of the public to the conversion of highway distance signs from miles to kilometers caused federal officials to delay action in 1978.

1. *What problems will be caused by the shift to the metric system in the United States?*
2. *Why is the shift to metric inevitable?*
3. *Should government provide subsidies to business and labor for metrication? Why or why not?*

FLOAT THE GLASS

In 1975 PPG Industries announced a new "float" method for producing flat glass which yields more uniform, higher quality glass than did the previously used production process. The new process was installed in PPG's Wichita Falls, Texas, factory, where it resulted in lower operating costs. The production capacity of the new line equaled that of the plant's initial production line, which was 200 million square feet of glass yearly.

The original "float" process for manufacturing flat glass was developed more than 20 years ago by Pilkington Brothers, Ltd., in England. This method produced flat glass at lower cost than earlier methods, which involved a complicated roller system. Following Pilkington's development of the float process, PPG and other glass manufacturers paid license fees to the English enterprise for a number of years for the use of the technological process.

The new PPG float process consists of mixing and melting raw ingredients for glass in a high-temperature furnace. A "stream" of molten glass of the desired production width, normally 160 inches, is formed at the refining or exit end of the melting furnace. By a novel delivery system the stream then flows as a production-width layer of glass onto molten metal in a sealed chamber or bath. The ribbon of molten glass, supported by the perfectly flat molten metal, flows through the bath and gradually cools until its undersurface is hard enough to be conveyed by rollers without marring the finish. Then the glass is cooled, washed, and cut into the desired sizes with automatic equipment.

PPG indicates that the new process is covered by basic patents in the United States and many foreign countries. Possibilities exist for converting existing float glass production facilities to the new process. PPG may license other flat glass manufacturers to use the process for a fee.

1. *What benefits can PPG expect from this new manufacturing process?*
2. *a. What risks did PPG take in attempting to develop the new float process?*
   b. What alternative course of action could PPG have taken regarding the development of a new production process?
3. *What possible benefits for the general public may float from the new PPG process?*

---

case

THE SUNFLOWER DAIRY

The purchasing agent for the Sunflower Dairy was reviewing the sales proposals of manufacturers of metal tanks which were needed to expand Sunflower's milk-processing facilities. The purchasing agent recalled the conversation with the salesworker from the Monroe Container Company. The product of the Monroe Company cost more than the top management of Sunflower wanted to spend. However, the purchasing agent consented to visit the Monroe manufacturing plant with the chief engineer of Sunflower, who was responsible for the expansion project.

Upon arriving at Monroe's plant, the purchasing agent and the chief engineer were greeted by Monroe's sales manager, who quickly got down to business. "I want to show you firsthand what our capabilities are for producing stainless steel tanks that will meet your needs for a quality product."

The sales manager and the two visitors toured the company's manufacturing facilities. Sunflower's chief engineer was impressed by the cleanliness of the manufacturing plant and by the apparent industry of the workers as they went about their duties. When the sales manager was asked about this favorable attitude toward productivity, the executive replied, "We have had seven expansions of our plant in the past ten years. Our employees are well paid by local labor market standards. Management emphasizes high quality on all work. This attitude goes down to the first-line supervisors and to those who are doing the work. The success we have enjoyed with our products by emphasizing quality work and being willing to pay for it has justified the higher prices we have had to charge."

Using a medium-size container, the sales manager pointed out the attention that was given to finishing the outside of the tanks, with final grinding and polishing by hand. This extra work gave a pleasing appearance to the product. In designing such equipment, a special effort was made to provide more safety features than were required. "We realize," the sales manager indicated, "that many purchasers of our products have plant tours by their customers and the public. We think an attractive, well-designed piece of machinery is important from a public relations viewpoint as well as for production."

Monroe's sales manager also showed how the fillets[1] on the inside of the tanks were carefully filled in and finished to eliminate the possibility of residue buildup in the tank corners. This not only represented a health feature, but made it easier to clean the tanks and reduced maintenance costs.

---

[1] A fillet is a concave junction that is formed when two surfaces come together. In this case two metal pieces come together to form the edge of a tank, creating a concave surface inside the tank.

After the plant tour the sales manager discussed the product which the Monroe Company hoped to sell Sunflower for its expanded facility. The sales executive pointed out how some specifications of the Monroe product exceeded those called for in Sunflower's initial request for price quotations. Monroe engineers had made some design changes which they believed improved the product and made it easier to service. The sales manager frankly stated that Monroe's price was as low as possible in view of the product and its quality. In spite of this, the purchasing agent for Sunflower Dairy knew that the price was 10 percent higher than that of competing products which lacked some of Monroe's quality features but would probably provide satisfactory service.

Upon their return to the home office the two Sunflower executives discussed their trip. The chief engineer concluded, "I am very impressed with the Monroe operation. They have given me some good ideas on equipment design. However, their price is higher, and you know what the president said about costs on the new expansion."

1. What issues face the purchasing agent at this point?
2. How should the purchasing agent deal with these issues?
3. Appraise the philosophy of the Monroe Container Company in light of a competitive market for its products.

Accounting
and finance

SECTION
FIVE

Maytag reports . . .

Financial Highlights

	1978	1977
Net sales	$325,044,463	$299,402,974
Income before taxes	70,795,942	65,371,346
Taxes on income	34,100,000	30,910,000
Net income	36,695,942	34,461,346
Per cent to net sales	11.3%	11.5%
Per share of Common stock	$ 2.74	$ 2.58
Dividends paid	24,490,561	23,407,099
Per share of Common stock	1.83	1.75
Salaries, wages, pensions and other employee benefits	84,024,126	76,834,736
Working capital	83,476,615	73,120,871
Ratio current assets to current liabilities	4.25 to 1	4.21 to 1
Property, plant and equipment less depreciation allowances	$ 71,240,278	$ 67,817,798
Total assets	181,383,481	164,322,192
Shareowners' equity	148,875,233	136,295,489
Per share of Common stock	11.12	10.20
Number of shareowners	18,439	18,273
Average number of employees	3,758	3,748

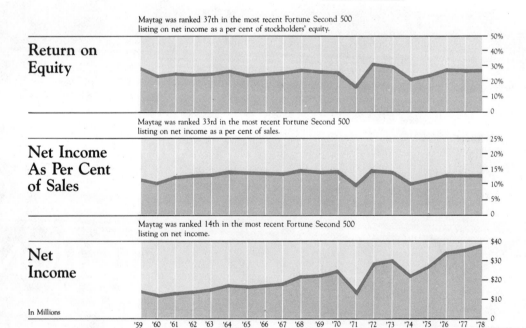

Maytag was ranked 37th in the most recent Fortune Second 500 listing on net income as a per cent of stockholders' equity.

Return on Equity

Maytag was ranked 33rd in the most recent Fortune Second 500 listing on net income as a per cent of sales.

Net Income As Per Cent of Sales

Maytag was ranked 14th in the most recent Fortune Second 500 listing on net income.

Net Income

In Millions

'59 '60 '61 '62 '63 '64 '65 '66 '67 '68 '69 '70 '71 '72 '73 '74 '75 '76 '77 '78

From the annual report of the Maytag Company

Dishwasher assembly line at Maytag

14

Understanding accounting statements

Understanding accounting statements

Accounting has been called the language of business. Accounting statements provide the basis for reporting profits or losses and for presenting the economic picture of the enterprise. You need to understand the basic accounting statements, whatever your role in the organization.

After studying this chapter, you will be able to answer the following questions regarding accounting:

How is accounting information used by management?

Why are financial statements important for groups outside the enterprise?

What are the basic accounting statements?

How are these statements analyzed?

THE USES OF ACCOUNTING INFORMATION

Accounting consists of recording, measuring, analyzing, and reporting the results of enterprise transactions in monetary terms. An enterprise's accounting system should be designed to evaluate the financial implications of decisions. Accounting statements should be prepared on a consistent basis from one time period to the next in order to make comparisons meaningful.

Management uses of accounting

To be effective, management needs regular financial progress reports. An enterprise's accounting system provides the basis for determining profits or losses over a given period of time. The measurement of income and the statement of an enterprise's financial position are important to the management process, especially for control purposes.

For control purposes, accounting provides a basis for establishing quantitative standards, measuring performance, and analyzing variations from expectations. Standards set in financial terms are easily understood and can be used to evaluate performance. Performance evaluations, in turn, may be helpful in making decisions on promotions or salary increases as well as in determining the need for corrective action, demotions, and dismissals.

Outsiders' use of accounting information

Information derived from the enterprise's accounting system is useful to individuals and organizations outside the enterprise. Outsiders that make use of accounting data include stockholders, governmental agencies, banks, and creditors of the enterprise.

Stockholders' use   In a small proprietorship or a partnership where the owners are active in the business, there is no need to publicize financial results for the benefit of the owners. The owners are already aware of the enterprise's profitability and financial condition. However, in today's large corporations there is a separation of ownership and management. The thousands of stockholders who own the corporation have no direct voice in its management. They have no knowledge of results unless published financial reports are made available to them. Managements of widely owned corporations provide this information to their shareholders through regularly published financial statements. This information is also made available to the general public. The information is needed by those who may be considering the purchase of stock in the corporation. Thus, both present and prospective shareholders are vitally interested in the financial statements of large corporations.

Governmental use   The reporting of financial information is required by numerous governmental agencies. Tax authorities require that detailed financial reports from business enterprises accompany the payment of local, state, and federal taxes. Public disclosure of the financial standing of widely held corporations is required by the Securities and Exchange Commission, a federal agency established in 1934. The SEC requires that corporations provide adequate information to investors about new security issues and reveal dealings in their own stock by enterprise executives.

Banks' and creditors' use   Accounting information is required by banks and other financial institutions before they will lend money to an enterprise. The business manager should be prepared to provide complete information about the past results of the enterprise and a financial projection of its plans for the future. Financial planning should include evidence that management has considered its needs carefully and has estimated when the loan it is seeking can be repaid.

A *trade creditor* supplies merchandise or services to an enterprise and is willing to ship merchandise without requiring cash payment upon delivery. Before a trade creditor will ship merchandise to a firm for the first time, the customer's accounting statements will be analyzed to determine that the merchandise can be paid for. The terms of trade credit vary with the industry and local circumstances. Customarily, trade credit is granted for periods of 30 to 60 days, with cash discounts of 1 or 2 percent being given for prompt payment, such as within 10 days from the date on the invoice. Whatever the credit terms, the purchasing enterprise should observe them to maintain its good credit rating.

THE BASIC ACCOUNTING STATEMENTS

The balance sheet and the income statement are the two most widely used accounting statements. They provide much information about the enterprise's financial condition and operations. An understanding of these statements is essential for financial analysis and control. A third accounting statement that is now prepared is called the statement of changes in financial position. Owners and creditors find it a useful tool in addition to the balance sheet and the income statement.

The balance sheet

The *balance sheet* is a financial picture of the enterprise at the close of business on a particular date, usually at the end of a month, a quarter, or a year. It is a statement of the assets which the enterprise owns and of the claims against those assets. The claims against the enterprise's assets are either claims by outsiders, called liabilities, or claims by the owners, called owners' equity or net worth. This balancing of the assets of the business enterprise against the claims to the assets gives the balance sheet its name. Therefore, the equation which represents the balance sheet is:

$$\text{Assets} = \text{Liabilities} + \text{Net Worth}$$

Assume that a new enterprise is started by a person who set aside $5,000 to initiate the business. The balance sheet of this new business enterprise after this initial act would be:

$$\text{Cash \$5,000 (assets)} = \text{Owner's equity \$5,000 (claims)}$$

Next assume that the owner-manager went to a bank and borrowed $3,000 to provide funds to begin operations. After this transaction the balance sheet of the enterprise would be:

Assets		Liabilities	
Cash	$8,000	Bank loan	$3,000
		Net Worth	
		Owner's equity	5,000
		Total Liabilities and	
Total Assets	$8,000	Net Worth	$8,000

The balance sheet will continue to reflect changes in the accounts of the business enterprise as additional transactions occur. The balance sheet lists only those assets which are owned by the enterprise on a specified date.

The balance sheet in Figure 14–1 illustrates the simplified year-end statement of assets, liabilities, and net worth for a typical retail corporation. A discussion of each item on the balance sheet follows.

Assets   *Current assets* are assets which are cash, realizable in cash, or expected to be sold or consumed during the year. Current assets are customarily listed on the balance sheet in order of liquidity. The liquidity of an asset is measured by how readily it can be turned into cash.

Cash is listed first, since it is easiest to transfer cash into other assets or to use cash in paying what is owed by the enterprise. Normally cash is held in

FIGURE 14–1

JEANS, INCORPORATED
Balance Sheet
As of December 31, 1979

Assets		Liabilities	
Current assets		**Current liabilities**	
Cash	$ 6,000	Accounts payable	$ 4,900
Accounts receivable	3,000	Wages payable	1,200
Inventories	9,000	Taxes payable	1,000
Prepaid insurance	600	Miscellaneous payables	300
Total Current Assets	$18,600	Total Current Liabilities	$ 7,400
		Long-term liabilities	
Fixed assets		Bank loan, due 1984 ..	7,000
Fixtures and equipment .	$15,000		
Less: Accumulated depreciation	1,500	Total Liabilities....	$14,400
Net Fixed Assets ...	$13,500		
		Net Worth	
Other assets		Common stock	$10,000
Trademarks	$ 500	Retained earnings	8,500
Miscellaneous assets	300	Total Owner's Equity	$18,500
Total Other Assets .	$ 800	**Total Liabilities**	
Total Assets ...	$32,900	and Net Worth	$32,900

bank accounts, although small amounts may be kept in the enterprise's cash drawer for making change in retail transactions or for small expenditures.

Accounts receivable are amounts owed to the enterprise by customers who have purchased goods on credit. Accounts receivable are considered to be relatively liquid since normally they will be collected within a few weeks or months.

Inventories are the cost of the stock of goods that the enterprise has available for sale to customers. The varied nature of inventories in a manufacturing enterprise was discussed in Chapter 13.

Prepaid expenses have been paid for and not yet used. A typical example is a fire insurance policy whose premium is paid for two years at a time so that the policy provides insurance protection next year as well as during the current year.

Fixed assets, sometimes called capital assets, represent long-term assets, such as land, buildings, and equipment, which will not be turned into cash but are necessary for the operation of the enterprise. The gross amount of the fixed asset account represents the acquisition cost of such assets. *Depreciation* is the accounting charge to reflect the decline in the value of fixed assets over a period of time. *Accumulated depreciation* is the total amount which has been charged as an expense of using fixed assets over the years. The accumulated depreciation is subtracted from the fixed asset accounts to show the book value of fixed assets on the balance sheet.

Other assets is a catchall category that includes assets not listed as either current or fixed. Other assets are sometimes intangible, such as patents and trademarks. *Patents* are exclusive rights to a product or process conferred on the holder by governmental authority. *Trademarks* are words or symbols which identify particular brands of merchandise. Registered trademarks are legally protected from use by unauthorized persons or enterprises.

Liabilities *Liabilities* are amounts owed by the business enterprise to its creditors. *Current liabilities* are obligations which will fall due within a short period of time, customarily within the coming year.

Accounts payable are amounts owed to suppliers for purchases of inventory goods. Sometimes *notes payable* are signed to recognize formally the enterprise's financial obligations to banks, to other financial institutions which supply money, or to vendors which supply merchandise.

Wages payable represents amounts owed to employees for their work efforts. This obligation is paid each payday. The amount which accrues will depend on the level of the wages paid and on the frequency of wage payments, such as weekly or monthly.

Taxes payable is the enterprise's current tax liability to various governmental bodies. Customarily, a large proportion of this figure covers income tax liabilities which build up with profitable operations. Taxes must be paid according to the schedules set by federal and state authorities. Sometimes the taxes payable account on the balance sheet will be divided into the types of taxes payable, such as income taxes, Social Security taxes, and property taxes.

Miscellaneous payables is a catchall account for any outsiders' recognized financial claims which have not been listed elsewhere. The *total current liabilities* is the amount of debts which management expects to have to pay within a year.

Long-term liabilities are financial obligations which do not have to be paid off during the coming year. These may arise from a variety of borrowing arrangements. In the Jeans, Inc., balance sheet there is one long-term liability, a bank loan due in 1984.

Net worth The *net worth,* or owners' equity, section of the balance sheet shows the amount of the owners' claims to the assets of the enterprise. The net worth section of a corporation balance sheet is divided into various accounts, such as preferred stock, common stock, and retained earnings. These divisions are for legal or accounting purposes and do not have much financial significance except for preferred stockholders, who constitute a different class of owners.

Preferred stock, of which there is none in Jeans, Inc., is the class of ownership shares in a corporation which has preference over common stock as to a stated amount of cash dividends each year. Preferred stockholders also have priority over common stockholders if the corporation should be liquidated. If the corporation's assets were sold, the preferred stockholders would have a claim to a stated amount of funds after all liabilities had been paid. After the preferred stockholders' interests were satisfied, the common stockholders would divide the remainder of the funds from the sale of the corporation's assets in proportion to the number of shares of common stock that each held.

"I can't pinpoint exactly when I switched from a liberal stance, but I
think it was when my net worth hit two hundred big ones."

Reprinted by permission The Wall Street Journal

When a corporation's common stock is sold, the proceeds are recorded in
the *common stock* account. This account reflects the amount of funds received
by the corporation for the common stock which has been issued. A detailed
balance sheet would normally indicate the number of shares of common stock
held by the corporation's owners. In the case of Jeans, Inc., the number of
shares of common stock outstanding is 1,000.

The *retained earnings* account, sometimes called *earned surplus,* shows the
amount of profits that the enterprise has earned over the years and has kept
in the business to strengthen and expand operations. The amount of retained
earnings varies each year, depending on annual profits or losses and on the
amount of earnings paid to the owners in dividends.

The balance sheets for corporations, partnerships, and proprietorships are
similar in the listing of assets and liabilities. The accounts will be designated
differently for the ownership interests in these different forms of business organization. However, each type of enterprise has a net worth section which shows
the owners' claims to the assets of the enterprise.

The income statement

In contrast to the balance sheet, which portrays assets, liabilities, and net
worth as of a certain date, the income statement summarizes the revenues and
expenses that have occurred in the enterprise's operations between two points
of time. Thus, the income statement covers a period such as a year over which

management wants to measure operations. The income statement is sometimes called the profit and loss statement or the operating statement. It can be expressed in the following simple equation:

$$\text{Revenue} - \text{Expenses} = \text{Net income}$$

Or using different terminology:

$$\text{Sales} - \text{Costs} = \text{Profit}$$

Example of a corporation's income statement   Figure 14–2 is an illustration of a simplified income statement, or profit and loss statement, of Jeans, Inc., for the year's operations ending December 31, 1979. Each item on the statement is discussed.

Net sales means that all cash discounts given for prompt payment of goods and credits for returned merchandise have been deducted from the gross sales.

FIGURE 14–2

JEANS, INCORPORATED
Income Statement
For the year ended December 31,1979

Net sales		$80,000
Less: Cost of goods sold		
Inventory beginning January 1, 1979	$ 6,000	
Add purchases for the year	40,000	
Cost of merchandise available for sale	$46,000	
Less ending inventory December 31, 1979	9,000	
Total cost of goods sold		37,000
Gross income on sales		$43,000
Less: Operating expenses:		
Selling expenses		
Salesclerks' wages	$11,000	
Advertising expense	3,000	
Depreciation expense—fixtures and		
equipment	800	
Supplies expense	500	
Miscellaneous expenses	100	
Total selling expenses	$15,400	
General and administrative expenses		
Manager's wages	$ 8,400	
Rent	9,000	
Insurance	700	
Miscellaneous taxes	1,800	
Miscellaneous expenses	400	
Total general and administrative		
expenses	$20,300	
Total operating expenses		35,700
Operating income		7,300
Financial expenses:		
Interest expense		500
Profit before income taxes		$ 6,800
Income taxes		1,200
Net Profit		$ 5,600

Cost of goods sold is the value of merchandise sold calculated at its cost rather than the price for which it is sold. Since a retailer or wholesaler does not change the form of goods, the calculation of cost of goods sold is relatively simple. The cost of all purchases made by the enterprise is added to the value of its inventory at the beginning of the year. This gives the cost of the goods available for sale. Then the value of the inventory at the end of the year is subtracted to give the cost of the goods sold during the accounting period.

In a manufacturing enterprise the cost of goods sold includes the costs added during the manufacturing process. Thus, a calculation of cost of goods manufactured is made by adding the costs of raw materials used during the year, direct labor, factory expenses such as utilities, insurance, and depreciation on plant and equipment. The cost of goods manufactured is added to the beginning inventory. This sum represents total manufacturing costs. From this total, subtract the value of the inventories at the end of the accounting period, and the difference is the cost of goods sold. In actual practice the determination of cost of goods is somewhat more complicated because of different types of inventories and problems of allocating various costs.

Gross income is found by subtracting the cost of goods sold from net sales and is the amount from which other expenses are deducted.

Selling, general, and *administrative* expenses are deducted from gross income to give operating income.

Operating income is the profit generated from the operation of the enterprise before interest payments and income taxes are deducted.

Interest expense is the cost of borrowed money and is deducted from operating income in Figure 14–2. Then federal income taxes are calculated based on the *profit before taxes.*

The bottom figure on the income statement is the *net profit* for the period. If this figure is negative, the enterprise has suffered a loss and the owner's equity on the balance sheet is decreased by that amount. If profits are earned, the owners' equity is increased.

Supporting records   Each of the accounts shown in the balance sheet and the income statement is a summary of detailed accounting records which reflect individual business transactions. For example, on the balance sheet of Jeans, Inc., the accounts receivable total of $3,000 is substantiated by an accounts receivable ledger showing the individual accounts of each customer who has received credit from the retailer. These individual accounts show the value of the merchandise sold, the dates of the transactions, and the amounts and dates of the payments received from the customer.

Statement of changes in financial position

A third accounting statement, that of *changes in financial position,* draws information from both the balance sheet and the income statement. This statement summarizes the funds generated from operations and other sources and reveals the use of those funds to show the changes in the enterprise's financial position occurring over the period. Sometimes this presentation is called a *source*

FIGURE 14–3

```
                    JEANS, INCORPORATED
           Statement of Changes in Financial Position—Cash Basis
                   For the year ended December 31, 1979

Cash sources (inflows):
  From operations:
    From sales ................................   $80,000
    Decrease in accounts receivable .............       500
       Total sources from operations .............   $80,500
    Less: Cash used for expenses ...............    73,600
    Cash generated from operations .............               $ 6,900
  From other sources:
    Investment by owners (new stock issued) .....   $ 3,000
    Bank loan ................................     7,000
    Cash received from other sources ...........                10,000
       Total cash sources during the year
          (inflows) ...........................                $16,900
Cash applications (outflows):
  To purchase new store fixtures ...............   $ 9,000
  To increase inventories .....................     3,000
  To reduce accounts payable .................     2,700
       Total cash applied during the year
          (outflows) ........................                 $14,700
Change—Increase in Cash Balance during the Year              $ 2,200
```

and application of funds statement. Funds may be defined in several ways. Two common ways of defining funds are as cash or as working capital (current assets minus current liabilities). In this chapter we define funds as cash.

Figure 14–3 presents a simplified statement of changes in financial position. The figures shown were taken from the income statement, the balance sheet, and other accounting data. In the interest of simplification the example will not trace through their derivation.

This statement shows the changes which occurred in the enterprise's cash position during the year. Sometimes such a statement of funds is called a "where got—where gone" statement regarding cash.

The three basic accounting statements may be summarized as follows:

1. The income statement shows the profits which were earned over a period of time.
2. The balance sheet shows the financial position of the enterprise at a specific point in time.
3. The statement of changes in financial position reflects funds flows over a period of time.

THE FINANCIAL ANALYSIS OF ACCOUNTING STATEMENTS

Once the basic accounting statements have been compiled from information provided by the enterprise's accounting system, the analyst must interpret those statements. The absolute figures contained in the accounting statements can be used to compute ratios which can be compared with the ratios for previous years or for other enterprises in the same industry. Ratios measuring an enterprise's liquidity, profitability, and solvency are useful tools of financial analysis.

Measures of liquidity

Liquidity is the ability of the enterprise to meet its current financial obligations when they become due. Measures of enterprise liquidity are widely used in analyzing short-term finances and operating efficiency.

The current ratio   The current ratio is the relationship of current assets to current liabilities. The current ratio for Jeans, Inc., is:

$$\frac{\text{Current assets}}{\text{Current liabilities}} = \frac{\$18,600}{\$7,400} = 2.5 \text{ times or 2.5 to 1}$$

This means that current assets are 2.5 times the amount of current liabilities. The larger this ratio, the stronger is the enterprise's current financial position. A widely used rule of thumb for a satisfactory current ratio is 2 to 1. The current ratio is the most commonly used balance sheet ratio.

The acid test ratio   The acid test ratio is the measure of *quick assets* to current liabilities. Quick assets consist of cash, short-term investments held instead of cash, and accounts (or notes) receivable. For Jeans, Inc., the acid test ratio is:

$$\frac{\text{Quick assets}}{\text{Current liabilities}} = \frac{\$9,000}{\$7,400} = 1.2 \text{ times or 1.2 to 1}$$

The acid test ratio is a measure of short-term liquidity as is the current ratio, except that inventories and prepaid expenses are excluded from the assets portion of the ratio. This makes the acid test ratio a more severe test of enterprise liquidity. A widely used rule of thumb for a satisfactory acid test ratio is 1 to 1.

Inventory turnover   Because much of an enterprise's current assets is typically invested in inventory, the inventory turnover ratio can be a useful calculation for management. This ratio indicates the number of times merchandise moves through the enterprise during the period under study. Inventory turnover is computed by dividing the cost of goods sold by the average inventory on hand over the period.

Average inventory is commonly determined by adding the beginning and ending inventories for the accounting period and dividing by two. The inventory for Jeans, Inc., on January 1, 1979, was $6,000, and on December 31, 1979, it was $9,000. Therefore, the average inventory for 1979 was $7,500. The average inventory turnover during the year was:

$$\frac{\text{Cost of goods sold}}{\text{Average inventory}} = \frac{\$37,000}{\$7,500} = 4.9 \text{ times}$$

Since a profit is normally earned each time inventory is sold, a relatively high inventory is desirable. However, too high an inventory turnover may mean that sales are being missed because inventories are too small in relation to potential sales. On the other hand, a lower inventory turnover may mean that sales are down or that some inventory is no longer attractive to customers.

Collection of credit sales   The *average collection period* may be calculated to analyze how promptly credit customers are paying their accounts. This is sometimes called *days' sales outstanding in receivables.* It is calculated by taking the ratio of accounts receivable to average daily credit sales.

In most manufacturing enterprises nearly all sales are made on credit. In retailing enterprises the accounting records will show which sales are for cash and which are on credit. The average daily credit sales for Jeans, Inc., during 1979 amounted to $110 a day. Thus, the calculation of the average collection period for 1979 is:

$$\frac{\text{Accounts receivable}}{\text{Average daily credit sales}} = \frac{\$3,000}{\$110} = 27.3 \text{ days' credit sales}$$
outstanding in accounts receivable

Since the clothing store's credit terms are for payment within 30 days, it would appear that on the average credit customers are paying their accounts promptly.

Measures of profitability

Overall measures of profitability may be derived from the income statement and the balance sheet. The ratios of net profit to sales and net profit to net worth are discussed with the vertical analysis of the income statement.

Vertical analysis of the income statement   The *vertical analysis* of the income statement consists of a percentage relationship of each item in the income statement to sales. Vertical analysis is useful when comparing the enterprise's current operations with past periods or with industry statistics. The percentage breakdown of the Jeans, Inc., income statement, derived from Figure 14–2, is:

Vertical analysis, income statement
For the year ended December 31, 1979

Net sales		100.0%
Less: Cost of goods sold		46.3
Gross income on sales		53.7%
Less operating expenses:		
Selling expenses	19.2%	
General and administrative expenses	25.4	
Total operating expenses		44.6
Income from operations		9.1%
Less: Interest expense		0.6
Profit before income taxes		8.5%
Income taxes		1.5
Net Profit		7.0%

The vertical analysis of the income statement highlights the relative importance of the various expenses. By comparing changes in expense percentages from one year to another, management can diagnose areas which need improvement to raise profitability.

The net profit margin   The last item in the vertical analysis shows the *net profit margin*. This important measure of profitability is the ratio of net profit to net sales. For Jeans, Inc., in 1979 the net profit margin was:

$$\frac{\text{Net profit}}{\text{Net sales}} = \frac{\$5,600}{\$80,000} = 7.0\%$$

If this ratio seems too low, an examination of the different expenses shown in percentage form in the vertical analysis can be made to determine which expenses are out of line.

The return on owners' investment   Since the profits earned by an enterprise represent the return on the owners' investment, another important measure of profitability is that of *net profit to net worth* (owners' equity). For the clothing store in 1979 this ratio was:

$$\frac{\text{Net profit}}{\text{Net worth}} = \frac{\$5,600}{\$18,500} = 30.3\%$$

This ratio shows the rate of return on the owners' investment. It is a measure of how efficiently the corporation is using the funds provided by the stockholders.

Measures of solvency

Liquidity, which was discussed earlier, refers to the ability of the enterprise to meet its cash needs for current business operations. *Solvency* refers to the enterprise's ability to pay long-term financial obligations when they fall due as well as to meet the interest payments on outstanding debt. By borrowing more money, the owners of the enterprise assume more risk, since these debts will have to be repaid in the future. Measures of solvency include the ratio of owners' equity to total debt, the ratio of long-term debt to total assets, and the number of times interest is earned.

Owners' equity to total debt   The ratio of *owners' equity to total debt* measures the owners' investment compared with the claims against the enterprise by creditors. This is an important measure of how much protection creditors have against shrinkage of the value of the enterprise's assets. For Jeans, Inc., the ratio is:

$$\frac{\text{Owners' equity}}{\text{Total debt}} = \frac{\$18,500}{\$14,400} = 1.3 \text{ times or } 1.3 \text{ to } 1$$

This means that for each $1 of liabilities outstanding on December 31, 1979, there was $1.30 of net worth. The larger this ratio, the greater is the protection for creditors and the less is the risk that the business enterprise will be faced with insolvency.

career outlook

ACCOUNTANTS

Managers must have up-to-date financial information to make important decisions. Accountants prepare and analyze financial reports that furnish this kind of information.

Accountants often concentrate on a particular phase of accounting. For example, many public accountants specialize in auditing (reviewing a client's financial records and reports to judge their reliability). Others specialize in tax matters. Still others become specialists in management consulting. Such accountants might develop or revise an accounting system to serve the needs of clients more effectively or give advice about different types of accounting equipment.

Anyone working as a "certified public accountant" must hold a certificate issued by the state board of accountancy. All states use the CPA examination, prepared by the American Institute of Certified Public Accountants, to establish certification. Most of the successful candidates have college degrees, and three fourths of the states require CPA candidates to be college graduates. Nearly all states require applicants to have at least two years of public accounting experience for a CPA certificate.

The demand for skilled accountants will rise as managers rely more on accounting information to make business decisions. The employment of accountants is expected to increase about as fast as the average for all occupations through the mid-1980s.

Although many graduates of business and correspondence schools are successful in small firms, most large public accounting and business firms require applicants for accountant and internal auditor positions to have at least a bachelor's degree in accounting or a closely related field. Many employers prefer applicants with the master's degree in accounting. A growing number of large employers prefer applicants who are familiar with computer technology.

Employers often prefer graduates who have worked part time in a business or an accounting firm while in school. Many colleges offer students an opportunity to gain experience through internship programs conducted by public accounting or business firms.

Long-term debt to total assets   The ratio of long-term debt to total assets measures the proportion of debt which falls due more than a year in the future in relation to the total assets of the enterprise. For the clothing store this ratio is:

$$\frac{\text{Long-term debt}}{\text{Total assets}} = \frac{\$7,000}{\$32,900} = 21.3\%$$

This ratio shows what proportion of the enterprise's assets are being financed by long-term debt. Both interest and principal repayments must be made according to a schedule agreed upon when long-term funds are borrowed. Since future business conditions cannot be forecast with extreme accuracy, the prudent management is unwilling to finance too great a proportion of total assets by use of long-term debt. Management should analyze its anticipated cash inflows over future years before undertaking long-term borrowing.

Times interest earned   The *number of times interest is earned* is a measure of the enterprise's ability to meet current interest charges on borrowed funds. For Jeans, Inc., this ratio is:

$$\frac{\text{Operating income}}{\text{Interest}} = \frac{\$7,300}{\$500} = 14.6 \text{ times}$$

In this instance the annual interest charge is covered 14.6 times by operating income. The more times interest charges are covered by operating income, the safer is the situation from the viewpoint of both the lender and the borrower.

SUMMARY

Accounting is the recording, measuring, analysis, and reporting of enterprise transactions in monetary terms. Management uses accounting data as a measure of operating results and for control purposes. Accounting statements are also used by present and potential owners of business enterprises, by governmental agencies, and by present and potential creditors.

The balance sheet presents a financial picture of the business enterprise's assets, liabilities, and owners' equity at a given point in time. Typical current assets include cash, accounts receivable, and inventories. Fixed assets are represented by land, buildings, and equipment. Other assets include patents and trademarks.

Current liabilities usually include accounts payable, wages payable, taxes payable, and miscellaneous payables. Long-term liabilities are items which do not fall due during the next year, such as bank loans.

Owners' equity, or net worth, shows the amount of the owners' claims to the assets of the enterprise.

In contrast to the balance sheet, which portrays assets and claims against those assets as of a certain date, the income statement summarizes what has occurred in enterprise transactions between two points of time. The income statement, or the profit and loss statement, shows the revenues during a given period and the expenses for the period. The difference between revenues and expenses is the profit for the period.

The statement of changes in financial position summarizes the funds generated from operations and other sources and reveals the way in which those funds were used between two points of time.

In financial analysis, measures of liquidity analyze the ability of the enterprise to meet its current financial obligations when they become due. The current ratio and the acid test ratio are common measures of liquidity. The average collection period for accounts receivable and the inventory turnover ratio are measures calculated to analyze current operations.

The vertical analysis of the income statement consists of a percentage relationship of each item in the income statement to sales. This shows the relative importance of various expenses.

Measures of overall profitability include the ratios of net profit to sales and net profit to net worth.

Solvency measures the enterprise's ability to pay the principal as well as to meet the required schedule of interest payments on long-term financial obligations. Measures of solvency include the ratio of owners' equity to total debt, the ratio of long-term debt to total assets, and the number of times that interest charges on borrowed funds are earned.

TERMS FOR REVIEW

accounting
balance sheet
owners' equity (net worth)
current assets
fixed assets

current liabilities
long-term liabilities
income statement (profit and
  loss statement)

statement of changes in
  financial position
liquidity
solvency

QUESTIONS

1. Why are outside groups interested in the accounting statements of corporations?

2. Explain the accounting equation.

3. Indicate how changes in the assets, liabilities, and net worth sections are reflected in the balance sheet.

4. What information does the income statement provide?

5. Examine either *Moody's Industrial Manual* or *Standard & Poor's Corporation Records* in the library for examples of balance sheets and income statements. In what ways do these vary from the examples in Figures 14–1 and 14–2?

6. Select a balance sheet and an income statement of a corporation, and suggest changes which would make it more meaningful to the average stockholder.

7. What is the purpose of ratio analysis? Explain the usefulness of the specific ratios relating to liquidity, profitability, and solvency to (a) management and (b) a potential investor.

8. If you were a stockholder of the Maytag Company would you be pleased with the financial highlights from the annual report as shown on the first page of this chapter? Why?

business brief

FIGHT OR SWITCH?

Certified public accountants act as auditors of business enterprises' accounting statements and certify to interested parties that these statements conform with generally accepted accounting principles. However, corporations and public accountants do not always agree over specific issues concerning accounting.

Sometimes these disagreements are resolved. In some cases the CPA firm will give the enterprise's accounting statements a qualified opinion.[1] Management prefers not to have a qualified opinion since this reveals to outsiders not only disagreements but sometimes potentially serious financial difficulties. On occasion a business enterprise will dismiss its CPA firm and hire a different outside auditor. Also, CPAs have withdrawn as auditors when conflicts could not be resolved satisfactorily.

An example of a disagreement between a major CPA firm and a client is the case of the enterprise which sold a large tract of Florida real estate. The enterprise wanted to realize profits on the sale immediately. However, the auditors maintained that part of the profits should be deferred until after the completion of certain improvements for which the selling enterprise had obligated itself. These improvements included the building of roads, sewers, and a golf course. The CPA finally agreed to let the land sale be reported as a completed transaction after the enterprise's management had obtained agreement from the buyers that they would assume responsibility for completion of the improvements.

---

[1] A qualified opinion briefly states the nature of the disagreement which the CPA has with the enterprise's accounting practices.

A variety of disagreements have arisen between CPAs and enterprises over such matters as how to compute tax deductions for subsidiary operations, how to determine tax liabilities in disputes with the Internal Revenue Service, and how to figure the economic life of computer equipment. In addition to changing auditors because of friction over accounting practices, enterprises change auditors because they are unhappy about the fees charged by CPA firms. Switches in accountants also occur when a CPA firm believes that the extensive use of other CPAs by a corporation's subsidiaries gives the parent corporation's CPA too little control over auditing practices.

Since 1971 the Securities and Exchange Commission has required business enterprises and CPA firms which part company because of disagreements over accounting practices to file public 8-K reports indicating the reasons for the break in relations.

1. *What is the purpose of requiring a CPA opinion of a business enterprise's accounting statements?*
2. *Should the government prohibit a business enterprise from changing its CPA firm when a disagreement between the two arises?*
3. *When a change of CPAs occurs, should the nature of the disagreement be revealed to stockholders in the corporation's annual report?*

---

cases

THE CHOCOLATE HEART CANDY STORE, INC.

The Chocolate Heart Candy Store opened in the new Parkwood Mall, an enclosed regional shopping center, in the summer of 1977 and became very popular. In addition to prepackaged assortments the store carried quality candy which was boxed to the customer's specification.

In January 1979, the owners of the shop, Mr. and Mrs. James Ford, were reviewing the first full year's operations. Up to that point the only formal accounting statements which they had used were the balance sheets and income tax returns prepared by a tax accounting service. The Fords felt that the candy store was a success, but they believed that some additional

analysis would help them make a better judgment.

In addition to the balance sheet for the year ended December 31, 1977, the records of the Chocolate Heart Candy Store included a record of all checks paid during 1978 and a file of unpaid invoices which were owed to suppliers. All candy sales were for cash.

1. *From the information given in Exhibits 1, 2, and 3 on page 330 determine:*
   a. *Sales for 1978.*
   b. *Cost of merchandise sold.*
   c. *Total expenses for 1978.*

EXHIBIT 1

CHOCOLATE HEART CANDY STORE, INC.
Balance Sheet
December 31, 1977

Assets			Liabilities		
Current assets			Current liabilities		
Cash	$	900	Wages payable	$	300
Merchandise inventory		4,100	Accounts payable		2,600
Supplies		300	Income taxes payable		250
		$ 5,300			$ 3,150
Fixed assets			Long-term liabilities		
Fixtures	$8,000		Bank loan, due 1984		3,200
Less: Accumulated			Total liabilities		$ 6,350
depreciation	400	7,600			
			Net Worth		
			Common stock	$6,000	
			Retained earnings	550	6,550
			Total Liabilities		
Total Assets		$12,900	and Net Worth		$12,900

EXHIBIT 2
Taken from the cash records of Chocolate Heart Candy Store, Inc., for 1978

Cash receipts			Cash disbursements		
Cash sales		$50,250	Wages paid................		$11,000
			Rent		5,000
			Advertising		2,500
			Utilities		1,200
			Insurance		200
			Interest		300
			Income taxes, 1977		250
			Miscellaneous cash		
			expenses...............		350
			Supplies		500
			Paid on accounts payable		
			for merchandise during		
			1978		25,600
			Total expenditures		$46,900
Cash balance,			Cash balance,		
December 31, 1977		900	December 31, 1978		4,250
		$51,150			$51,150

EXHIBIT 3
As of December 31, 1978

Inventory on hand...............	$4,700
Supplies on hand	300
Accounts payable	2,200
Wages payable	300

Annual depreciation rate on fixed assets is 10 percent of original cost.

Income tax rate is estimated to be 20 percent of taxable income.

2. *Prepare an income statement for 1978 and a balance sheet as of December 31, 1978.*

3. *How can these statements be useful to the Fords? What measures could the Fords use to determine how successful they were in their first full year of operation?*

BRADLEY CAFETERIAS, INC.

Pat Knight, a loan officer at a Dallas bank, was a stockholder in Bradley Cafeterias, Inc., an operator of cafeterias and industrial food services. In February 1979 Pat received the company's annual report for the year ended December 31, 1978, which was mailed to all stockholders. The annual stockholders' meeting would be held in approximately three weeks. Knight did not plan to attend the stockholders' meeting, but wanted to analyze the company's annual report to see what progress had been made over the year and to compare the results with those for 1977.

Exhibits 1 and 2 are summaries of information taken from the annual report.

1. *Compare the sales, profits, and total assets shown in the 1978 Bradley statements with those for 1977.*

2. *Prepare a financial analysis for 1978, using the measures of liquidity, profitability, and solvency de-*

EXHIBIT 1

BRADLEY CAFETERIAS, INC.
Balance Sheets
As of December 31
(millions of dollars)

Assets	1978	1977
Current assets		
Cash	$ 3	$ 6
Accounts receivable	6	4
Inventories	10	7
Prepaid expenses	1	1
Total Current Assets	$20	$18
Fixed assets		
Buildings, equipment, and land	48	43
Less: Accumulated depreciation	18	16
Net Fixed Assets	$30	$27
Other assets		
Investments, deposits, etc.	$ 3	$ 3
Total Assets	$53	$48
Liabilities		
Current liabilities		
Accounts payable	$ 5	$ 4
Wages payable	3	2
Taxes payable	2	2
Current loans payable	1	1
Miscellaneous payables	3	2
Total Current Liabilities	$14	$11
Long-term liabilities		
Long-term debts	9	10
Total Liabilities	$23	$21
Net Worth		
Common stock	$15	$15
Retained earnings	15	12
Total Owners' Equity	$30	$27
Total Liabilities and Net Worth	$53	$48

EXHIBIT 2

BRADLEY CAFETERIAS, INC.
Income Statement
For years ended December 31
(millions of dollars)

	1978	1977
Net sales	$120	$89
Less: Cost of goods sold*	101	73
Gross Income	$ 19	$16
Selling, general, and administrative expenses	8	7
Operating income	$ 11	$ 9
Financial expense—interest	1	1
Profit before income taxes	$ 10	$ 8
Income taxes	5	4
Net Profit	$ 5	$ 4

* Depreciation included in cost of goods sold of $3 million for each year.
Note: Cash dividends on common stock were $2 million in 1978 and $1 million in 1977.

veloped in this chapter. Compare the 1978 ratios with those for 1977.

3. What significant changes occurred in the company's financial picture during 1978?

4. As a stockholder, what additional financial information would you need to make your analysis more meaningful?

The Arizona Bank reports . . .

The Arizona Bank's branch philosophy is to identify, through extensive research, the most productive growth areas in the state and to anticipate local banking needs with the establishment of well-situated branch offices.

During the year, the bank began development of a unique computer model to improve analyses for branch site locations. These analyses will help us determine if a branch location is justified. Further, the analyses will aid us in deciding whether to build a full-service branch or whether a limited service facility, at lower cost, can effectively serve the area.

The "through-the-wall" automatic teller machines (ATMs) currently in place have been well received by customers. In addition, the usefulness of an in-lobby unit was tested during 1977. In 1978, the ATM installation program will be broadened by supporting the teller function with more automated tellers at selected branch locations.

On July 1, 1977, after a 12-month feasibility study, we began a pilot program in three branches for a new statewide "on-line" computer system. The system is one in which electronic terminals with display screens at each teller station and at administrative desks are connected by telephone lines to the central computer. Assuming continuing success, the on-line system will be extended by stages throughout the state during the next two years.

From annual report of The Arizona Bank

Photo by Abrams Photo/Graphics

Simon the Simple Teller, The Arizona Bank's 24-hour teller machine.

15
Financial institutions

Financial institutions

Financial institutions have an important influence on business. Without an effective means in the economy for regulating the money supply and for providing debt and equity funds, business would not be able to operate. Directly or indirectly, every business enterprise's success depends on the money and capital markets.

After studying this chapter, you will be able to answer the following questions regarding financial institutions:

What is the nature of our system of financial institutions?

What are the roles of the U.S. Treasury and the Federal Reserve System in influencing the financial markets?

How do the different financial institutions serve the private enterprise system?

What services are performed by investment bankers?

OUR SYSTEM OF FINANCIAL INSTITUTIONS

Financial institutions regulate the money supply and channel savers' funds to business enterprises, individuals, and governmental bodies which need them. Although business can expand by reinvesting profits, frequently additional money from outside the enterprise is required. External funds are obtained through financial institutions either as debt by borrowing or as equity by selling additional stock in the corporation.

Besides providing funds for business enterprises, financial institutions lend money to various governmental units and to individual consumers. The federal government, states, counties, cities, and school districts borrow money through the sale of bonds. In addition, other financial institutions specialize in lending to consumers.

There is a wide range of financial institutions. The U.S. Treasury and the Federal Reserve System are acitve in determining the money supply. Investment bankers act as intermediaries for channeling both debt and equity funds to business enterprises. Commercial banks, life insurance companies, savings and loan associations, mutual savings banks, pension funds, and other specialized institutions fulfill particular financial needs.

THE ROLE OF THE U.S. TREASURY

The U.S. Treasury provides part of the money supply and manages the debt of the federal government. The basic money supply in the United States, called M-1, consists of two elements—currency and demand deposits. Currency is

TABLE 15–1

Ownership of direct and fully guaranteed securities of the U.S. federal government as of March 31, 1979 (billions of dollars)

Held by:	
U.S. government agencies and trust funds	$167
Foreign and international	133
Individuals	112
Federal Reserve banks	110
Commercial banks	96
State and local governments	69
Other miscellaneous investors	66
Corporations	24
Insurance companies	15
Mutual savings banks	5
Total	$797

Source: *Federal Reserve Bulletin*, June 1979.

the token coin and paper money in circulation. Demand deposits in commercial banks (checking accounts) represent most of the public's money supply. As of April 1979, M-1 consisted of $100 billion in currency and $264 billion in demand deposits held by the public.

The U.S. Treasury is also an important borrower of money. It provides an opportunity for investors who desire a high degree of safety for their funds. The gross direct debt of the U.S. government amounted to $797 billion at the end of March 1979. The ownership of direct U.S. Treasury debt, which is fully guaranteed by the federal government, is shown in Table 15–1. Notice the wide range of lenders to the federal government.

This U.S. Treasury debt arises out of an excess of spending over receipts by the federal government over the years. A large portion of our federal debt was incurred because of deficit spending during wars which the United States fought.

THE FEDERAL RESERVE SYSTEM

The basic purpose of the Federal Reserve System is to provide for a flow of money and credit that will foster orderly economic growth and stable prices. The system was established in 1913, though its powers and functions have continued to evolve over the years. The United States is divided into 12 Federal Reserve districts, with a Federal Reserve bank in each district to meet regional needs.

The Federal Reserve System is controlled by the Board of Governors in Washington, D.C. It consists of seven members appointed by the president of the United States and confirmed by the Senate. The Board of Governors is highly influential in determining the level of bank reserves, credit conditions, and rules affecting commercial banks which are members of the Federal Reserve System.

All nationally chartered commercial banks are required to belong to the Federal Reserve System, and state chartered banks may belong. Over 70 percent of the deposits in the commercial banking system in this country are in banks which are members of the Federal Reserve System. The stock in the 12 regional Federal Reserve banks is owned by commercial banks which are members of the system. In essence the Federal Reserve System acts as a banker's bank where member commercial banks which deal with the public can maintain reserve balances, borrow when necessary, and receive advice and direction concerning the economy's movement. However, unlike commercial banks, which are profit-seeking private financial enterprises, the 12 Federal Reserve banks are not profit-oriented. Any excess income of the Federal Reserve banks is turned over to the U.S. Treasury after reserves have been provided for and a fixed percentage return has been paid on the banks' stock.

Functions of the Federal Reserve System

The Federal Reserve influence on bank reserves The availability of money and credit is a significant determinant of economic conditions. When the economy is expanding and the demand for goods and services is great, the money supply must expand to permit the economic growth. On the other hand, if too much money and credit are made available, the excessive demand will drive up prices and result in inflation. During a recession, providing sufficient money and credit with lower interest rates tends to stimulate the economy toward recovery. Through its influence on commercial banks the Federal Reserve has the important and delicate function of carrying out a constructive monetary policy for the country.

The Federal Reserve influences the supply of money and credit in our economy by regulating the reserves of commercial banks in three ways:

1. Setting the reserve requirements for commercial banks.
2. Determining the discount rate.
3. Carrying out open-market operations.

Required reserves The Federal Reserve's Board of Governors has the power to set the specific reserve requirements which commercial banks must maintain to back up their deposits. With higher reserve requirements, more funds have to be held in reserve by commercial banks against deposits and less funds are available to be loaned out. Lowering reserve requirements frees some bank reserves and permits bankers to expand their loans to business enterprises and individuals. In 1979 the required reserve ratio for demand deposits in large commercial banks was 16.25 percent.

The discount rate The Federal Reserve has the authority to change the discount rate. The *discount rate* is the interest rate that member commercial banks pay to obtain funds from the Federal Reserve bank in their district.

These funds are obtained from the Federal Reserve to strengthen a commercial bank's reserves in relation to deposits. The higher the discount rate, the less encouraging it is for commercial banks to obtain reserve funds from the Federal Reserve. When the discount rate is lowered, it becomes more attractive for commercial banks to utilize Federal Reserve funds to increase their reserve positions. This enables the banks to grant more credit to their customers.

Open-market operations   The third method used by the Federal Reserve in influencing commercial bank reserves is *open-market operations*. These involve the purchase or sale of federal government securities.

When the Federal Reserve buys government securities in the open market, the result is an increase in the commercial banks' reserves. This tends to increase the money supply and has an expansionary effect on the economy. When the Federal Reserve sells government securities, commercial banks' reserves are decreased and the money supply is reduced. This has a deflationary effect on the economy, which is desirable when inflationary pressure is present. Through open-market operations the Federal Reserve can achieve more gradual changes in bank reserves than are achieved by a change in the reserve requirements for commercial banks or a change in the discount rate.

Other functions of the Federal Reserve System   The Federal Reserve System provides a number of services for member banks. These include handling member bank reserve accounts, furnishing currency for circulation, acting as a central agency for the clearing and collection of checks, and lending to member banks. For the U.S. Treasury and other governmental agencies the Federal Reserve System acts as fiscal agent, custodian, and depository for government funds. The Federal Reserve's services to the general public include collecting and interpreting economic data, working with business and academic economists, and undertaking research on monetary and general economic problems. The Federal Reserve also examines member commercial banks for good banking practices.

SPECIFIC FINANCIAL INSTITUTIONS

Financial institutions serve different financial markets. One way of classifying financial markets is by the length of time for which debt funds are loaned. The short-term or *money market* consists of debt which matures in one year or less. Longer-term financial markets are referred to as *capital markets*. There are four types of financial institutions which are very significant in the money and capital markets. These are commercial banks, savings and loan associations, life insurance companies, and mutual savings banks. Their relative size is shown in Table 15–2. In addition, there are several types of financial institutions of a more specialized nature, which are also discussed in this chapter.

Commercial banks

The commercial banking system is the keystone of the American monetary and financial system. The 14,700 commercial banks in this country are the

TABLE 15–2

Total assets of selected financial institutions as of March 1979 (billions of dollars)

Commercial banks	$1,281
Savings and loan associations	540
Life insurance companies	400
Mutual savings banks	162

Source: *Federal Reserve Bulletin*, June 1979.

only financial institutions which accept demand deposits from the public. Commonly called a checking account, such a deposit permits the customer to request currency from the deposit at any time or to direct that it be paid to someone else.

Also, the commercial banking system, is capable of creating money through loans from its checking and savings deposit accounts. This is possible because commercial banking operates on a *fractional reserve system*. This means that each bank is required to keep only a portion of its deposits in reserve form and that it may lend out those funds which are in excess of required deposit reserves.

The multiple effect of fractional bank reserves   The following illustration shows how the fractional reserve concept may be used to expand the money supply for the commercial banking system as a whole. Suppose that a commercial bank receives $10,000 in currency from a customer to establish a checking account. We will assume that the bank is required to maintain a 20 percent reserve against such accounts. The reserves may be either in the form of deposits with the Federal Reserve or in cash in the bank's vaults. This means that a commercial bank must have 20 percent of its demand deposits in reserves but may create additional demand deposits by lending out the remaining 80 percent. Also, assume that the checks drawn on all additional demand deposits created by commercial banks are immediately deposited back into some bank in the system. As the result of all these transactions a total of $50,000 of demand deposits will be created, including the initial $10,000 deposit of currency which started the cycle.

How this expansion occurs is demonstrated by Table 15–3, which shows a total of $50,000 in demand deposits. This includes the required $10,000 in reserves plus a total of $40,000 in excess reserves which were loaned out and created the additional deposits. To achieve this maximum multiple effect permitted by fractional bank reserves, we assumed that each bank in the system would loan out all of its excess reserves. Furthermore, we assumed that all deposits were left in the banking system by the public, with none being withdrawn for currency or for transfer outside the United States.

No single bank can lend more than its excess reserves at any one time.

TABLE 15–3

The multiplying effect of new deposits in a fractional reserve banking system

Transactions	Amount deposited in checking accounts	20 percent required reserves	Excess reserves loaned out
Initial currency deposit in checking account	$10,000	$ 2,000	$ 8,000
2nd transaction (deposit of amount just loaned)	8,000	1,600	6,400
3rd transaction	6,400	1,280	5,120
4th transaction	5,120	1,024	4,096
5th transaction	4,096	819	3,277
6th transaction	3,277	655	2,622
7th transaction	2,622	524	2,098
8th transaction	2,098	420	1,678
9th transaction	1,678	336	1,342
10th transaction	1,342	268	1,074
11th transaction	1,074	215	859
12th transaction	859	172	687
13th transaction	687	137	550
14th transaction	550	110	440
15th transaction	440	88	352
Plus all additional transactions necessary to complete the cycle	1,757	352	1,405
Total for all transactions	$50,000	$10,000	$40,000

Therefore, each bank depends upon additional deposits for the funds to create additional loans. However, the fractional reserve system permits the entire banking system to achieve the multiple expansion effect of the money supply. What is loaned to a person by one bank becomes a demand deposit in that bank or other banks, thereby creating additional reserves for further loans.

Activities of commercial banks   In its ability to create money through the fractional reserve system, the commercial banking system is unique among the financial institutions which deal directly with business and consumers. All other financial institutions must use funds received from deposits, premium payments, the sale of shares in the particular institutions, borrowing, or retained profits. Equity funds from stockholders provide a relatively small proportion of the typical bank's funds. More than 80 percent of the typical bank's sources of funds are provided by demand deposits or time deposits. Since such a large proportion of bank funds must be available for payment "on demand," bankers must walk a narrow tightrope in putting money to work profitably, yet with safety.

A term often used in the news media is the *prime rate of interest.* This is the borrowing rate that commercial banks charge their most creditworthy business customers. Other interest rates are generally scaled up from the prime rate. The prime rate is raised when the demand for loans is greatest and when loan funds are in the shortest supply. Banks lower the prime rate to attract more borrowers when the demand for money lessens and they have a surplus of lendable reserves.

The total assets of commercial banks exceed those of any other class of financial institutions. Commercial banks are the main source of short-term credit for business enterprises. It has been estimated that over 90 percent of all short-term business loans in this country are made by commercial banks. Commercial banks are also important sources of funds for mortgage and consumer loans, such as loans for the purchase of a home or an automobile. Commercial banks purchase large amounts of federal, state, and local government bond issues.

Commercial banks also provide such services as time and savings deposits, safety deposit boxes and vaults, and correspondent relationships with other institutions for national and international financial transactions. Depositors in nearly all commercial banks are protected by the Federal Deposit Insurance Corporation. This governmental agency insures accounts to a maximum of $40,000 each. Commercial banks provide loan funds to other financial institutions such as finance companies and investment bankers as well as to business enterprises and individual consumers. The commercial bank has been described as the financial institution that is prepared to provide a "full range" of financial services.

Savings and loan associations

Savings and loan associations are the second largest class of financial institutions. Over 80 percent of the assets held by savings and loan associations are mortgages on real estate. Most of these funds are committed to the financing

"Federal regulations require a substantial penalty in case of early withdrawal."

Reprinted by permission The Wall Street Journal

of one-to-four family homes. Savings and loan associations hold 47 percent of the mortgage loans outstanding on homes. This demonstrates their importance in financing home construction.

Savers who place their funds with savings and loan associations technically become shareholders in the savings and loan rather than depositors. Therefore, they actually receive dividends on their savings rather than interest. Legally savings and loan shareholders could be required to wait up to 30 days before withdrawing their savings. In recent years however, savings and loan associations have customarily been willing to cash in a saver's account on demand. The vast majority of savings and loan associations are insured by the Federal Savings and Loan Insurance Corporation, a governmental agency which insures each account up to $40,000.

Life insurance companies

Life insurance companies are the third largest class of financial institutions. Many people think of the life insurance company as an institution which sells insurance protection and savings programs to individuals who pay premiums for this coverage. This underwriting of insurance risks is an important part of the operations of life insurance companies since policy premiums are their major source of funds.

However, there is another important side to the life insurance business. Life insurance companies invest the insurance premiums which they receive. The earnings from these investments are used to meet future payments to policyholders and beneficiaries, to generate income for operating expenses, to increase reserves, and to pay taxes and dividends.

Life insurance companies have a huge portfolio of investments to manage. Whereas commercial banks provide funds mostly for short-term loans, life insurance companies are able to make long-term loans because of the difference in the demands on their cash reserves. Through statistical analyses of accident and death rates, life insurance companies are able to forecast rather accurately the cash they will need for payments to policy beneficiaries. These actuarial studies enable the managements of life insurance companies to set premium rates and policy benefits in such a way as to permit the investment of funds in the long-term (capital) markets.

Life insurance companies provide funds in significant amounts to a variety of business enterprises. This includes long-term loans to industrial corporations, public utilities, and railroads, as well as mortgage money for all types of construction. In 1979 the major investments of life insurance companies fell into the following categories:

Corporate bonds	42%
Real estate mortgages	27
Corporate stocks	9
Policy loans	8
Government bonds: federal, state, and local	5
Miscellaneous investments	9
Total Investments	100%

Mutual savings banks

Mutual savings banks are financial institutions which encourage individual savers to establish deposit accounts. They are the oldest class of strictly savings institutions in the United States. All but a few are located in New England and the Middle Atlantic states.

A mutual savings bank has no shareholders. All depositors have a "mutual" interest in the enterprise's operations. Thus payments for savings accounts are dividends and not interest payments. Mutual savings banks are governed by boards of trustees which appoint their own successors. Many wealthy individuals serve as trustees for little or no compensation. They consider it an honor to be asked to serve. This view goes back to the founding of mutual savings banks when they were regarded as providing the common people with a place to save money in good times so that they could provide for themselves when times were hard.

About 60 percent of the assets of mutual savings banks are invested in mortgages. The balance of mutual savings bank investments is mostly in corporate and government bonds.

OTHER FINANCIAL INSTITUTIONS

A number of other types of financial institutions are active in particular markets. These include finance companies and credit unions, which provide funds directly to businesses and individuals. Financial institutions which purchase stocks and bonds include personal trust departments, pension funds, fire and casualty insurance companies, and investment companies. After each of these institutions has been described, the role of the investment banker is discussed.

Finance companies

A variety of enterprises fall under the general category of finance companies. Finance companies borrow large amounts of money from commercial banks and other lenders. In turn they make smaller loans to business enterprises and individuals at higher rates than the interest paid on their borrowed funds. The difference between the borrowing and lending rates of finance companies provides for operating expenses and profits. At the end of April 1979, finance companies had installment loans outstanding of $58 billion.

Finance companies which specialize in direct loans to individuals are called *consumer finance* or *personal finance companies.* A consumer finance company makes an installment loan directly to you for the purchase of an automobile, major appliances, a television or stereo set, or as a personal loan. Consumer finance companies provide a significant amount of installment credit.

Sales finance companies also specialize in installment loans. However, they do not make loans directly to individuals or business enterprises. Instead they purchase installment receivables from merchants who sell such products as autos, appliances, industrial equipment, and other durable goods. Sales finance companies also lend money to retailers and wholesalers to finance inventories. Usually installment loans and inventory loans are secured by the merchandise on which the loans are made.

Commercial finance companies provide loans to business enterprises, many of which would have difficulty in obtaining credit from commercial banks because of the small size of the enterprise or because of the risk involved. Most loans by commercial finance companies are secured by accounts receivable of the borrowers, though loans based on equipment and inventories are also made. The interest rates of commercial finance companies are generally higher than those charged by commercial banks because of the additional risks involved and because of the higher costs of handling such loans.

Another specialized type of business financing is called factoring. *Factoring* is the purchase of a business enterprise's accounts receivable by a finance company, which then collects the accounts. Factoring is widely used in the textile industry. It is a relatively expensive form of short-term financing. However, the factor (which the financial institution is called) provides a variety of services when it purchases the receivables of a business enterprise. These services include credit investigation and collection as well as assuming the loss for any bad debts which result from failure to collect the accounts.

Credit unions

Credit unions are cooperatives which promote saving on the part of their members. They also provide personal loans to members at relatively low interest rates. Credit unions are organized and sponsored by fraternal groups and labor unions, and by business enterprises for the benefit of their employees. Membership in a particular credit union is limited to individuals who are part of the sponsoring group. Because of their cooperative nature, credit unions are sometimes managed by members who serve on a part-time basis with little or no compensation. This type of financial institution is important in the consumer credit market, with $46 billion in installment credit outstanding at the end of April 1979.

Personal trust departments

The personal trust departments of commercial banks and trust companies take legal possession of personal assets and manage them for the benefit of the person creating the trust or some other designated person. The trust department of a commercial bank (called the trustee) will take possession of funds provided by a person (the trustor) and provide investment management of the money. The income from this trust fund will be paid to whomever the trustor designates; perhaps it will also be paid to the person's family upon his or her death. Personal trust departments also act as executors and administrators of estates, receivers in bankruptcy, and trustees of private pension funds.

Personal trust departments control vast amounts of wealth. Their funds are invested primarily in corporate stocks, state and local government bonds, and corporate bonds. As a class of institutions they have developed a reputation for responsible financial stewardship of the funds placed under their control.

Pension funds

Pension funds have become investors in all sectors of the capital markets since World War II. Basically pension funds are accumulated out of the contributions of employers and employees. These funds are invested in stocks, bonds, and other types of investments, such as mortgages. The purpose of the funds is to provide retirement income for the individual beneficiaries and their families.

There are two general types of pension funds—private and government. Private pension plans provide retirement benefits for employees of business enterprises, union members, and employees of nonprofit organizations such as educational and religious institutions. Private pension funds invest heavily in common stocks of corporations and corporate bonds, with smaller holdings of mortgages and U.S. government securities.

Government retirement plans also provide significant sources of funds for the capital markets. State and local government retirement monies are heavily invested in U.S. government bonds, state and local government securities, corporate bonds, and mortgages. Some states permit investment in high-grade common stocks.

The federal government sponsors a number of retirement plans. The U.S. Treasury acts as the fiscal agent for these funds which include Old-Age, Survivors, Disability, and Health Trust funds and the Federal Employees Retirement funds. These funds are obtained from Social Security payments by employees and employers, from premiums, and from contributions to specific fund accounts. After benefits are paid to recipients, the balance in these funds is invested in U.S. government securities.

Fire and casualty insurance companies

Fire and casualty companies sell insurance service to their clients to cover destruction of property by fire or other hazards. Some also provide personal liability insurance and other types of insurance protection. Whereas the life insurance company guarantees a fixed dollar return for its policyholders, the fire casualty insurance company assumes contingent liability and pays policyholders only if a loss actually occurs. The fire and/or casualty policy has a limited amount of dollar protection, depending on the terms of the policy. Also, payments to policyholders may be no higher than the amount of the loss.

The fire and casualty insurance company's funds come mainly from policyholders' premiums and from investments made by the company. These funds are invested to provide reserves to underwrite the policy risks assumed by the company. Normally most fire and casualty companies are able to meet expenses

career outlook

UNDERWRITERS

After analyzing information in insurance applications, reports from loss control consultants, medical reports, and actuarial studies (reports that describe the probability of insured loss), underwriters appraise and select the risks that their companies will insure. Some routine applications that require very little independent judgment are handled by computers. Generally, however, underwriters use considerable personal judgment in making decisions. Because these decisions are seldom reviewed at a higher level, underwriters have great responsibility. If underwriters appraise risks too conservatively, their companies may lose business to competitors. If underwriters are too liberal, their companies may have to pay many future claims.

Underwriter trainees begin by evaluating routine applicants under the close supervision of an experienced risk appraiser. They study claim files to become familiar with the factors associated with certain types of losses. As they develop the sound judgment that is re-quired, they are assigned policy applications that are more complex and have a greater face value.

For beginning underwriting jobs, most large insurance companies seek college graduates who have a degree in liberal arts or business administration, but a major in almost any field provides a good general background. Some small companies hire persons with less than a college degree for underwriter trainee positions.

The employment of underwriters is expected to rise about as fast as the average for all occupations through the mid-1980s, as insurance sales continue to expand. Over the next decade, a much larger portion of our population will enter its most productive years. As this traditional market for life insurance expands, the volume of insurance sales should also rise. The American public's growing security consciousness should also contribute to the demand for insurance protection.

and losses on policies from new premium income. This provides some flexibility for the insurance company's investment policies. However, to be able to meet calamitous losses from natural and human-caused disasters the insurance company must provide a cushion of readily marketable securities in its investment portfolio. This need is met by holding large amounts of U.S. government securities. Fire and casualty insurance companies also hold substantial quantities of corporation common stocks and state and local government securities. Unlike the life insurance companies, the fire and casualty insurance companies do not invest heavily in the mortgage and corporate bond markets.

Investment companies

An important purchaser of corporate securities, especially of common stocks, is the class of financial institutions called investment companies. *Investment companies* obtain funds by selling shares of their stock and using the proceeds to purchase securities of other corporations. The usual purchasers of shares in investment companies are individuals who have relatively small amounts of money to invest but would like the benefits of a diversified investment portfolio. Investment companies are either *closed-end* or *open-end,* depending on whether the shares in the investment fund can be increased routinely.

Closed-end investment companies have a fixed amount of capital outstanding. When an individual investor wishes to buy stock in a closed-end company, it must be purchased in the open market from someone who already owns the stock. The managers of the closed-end investment company buy and sell securities to earn income and capital gains from the funds provided when the company's shares were originally sold to the public.

Open-end investment companies, commonly known as *mutual funds,* do not have a fixed number of shares outstanding. They issue more shares whenever an investor desires to purchase shares. Shares are purchased at their net asset value. This is computed daily, based on the market value of the securities in the portfolio plus a "loading charge" to cover the sales commission and other expenses of the sale. When the individual investor desires to sell shares owned in a mutual fund, the shares are sold back to the fund at the then-current asset value, minus a small redemption charge in some funds.

Shares in some mutual funds, known as "no-load" funds, are sold to the public at net asset value without a loading charge. In these mutual funds there are no salespersons. Therefore, the individual investor saves the cost of the sales commission (loading charge). However, in order to purchase shares in such funds the investor must contact the fund's management directly. This is usually done by responding to an advertisement in a financial newspaper or magazine.

THE FUNCTIONS OF THE INVESTMENT BANKER

The investment banker performs many services as an intermediary between corporations and investors in the capital funds market. The investment banker is active in both primary and secondary securities markets.

Primary and secondary securities markets

The *primary securities markets* channel funds directly to corporations or governmental bodies in exchange for their securities. In the primary markets the proceeds from the sale of new stock or bond issues go directly to the corporation issuing the securities. When selling new stocks and bonds, an investment banker is participating in the primary securities markets.

In *secondary securities markets,* stocks and bonds which are already outstanding are bought and sold among investors. The organized trading markets for corporate stocks and bonds are examples of secondary markets. These include

career outlook

SECURITIES SALES WORKERS

When investors want to buy or sell stocks, bonds, or shares in mutual funds, they call on securities sales workers to put the market machinery into operation. In initiating "buy" or "sell" transactions, securities sales workers relay orders through their firms' offices to the floor of a securities exchange. After a transaction has been completed, the securities sales worke. notifies the customer of the details.

Securities sales workers may also provide many related services for their customers. They may explain stock market terms and trading practices to new investors; offer clients complete financial counseling; devise individual financial portfolios including securities, life insurance, and other investments; and advise on the purchase or sale of particular securities.

Because a securities sales worker must be well informed about economic conditions and trends, a college education is increasingly important, especially in the larger securities firms.

Almost all states require persons who sell securities to be licensed. A state's licensing requirements may include passing an examination and furnishing a personal bond. In addition, securities sales workers are usually required to register as representatives of their firms according to regulations of the National Association of Securities Dealers, Inc. (NASD), or of the securities exchanges where these sales workers do business. Before beginners can qualify as registered representatives, they must pass the Securities and Exchange Commission's General Securities Examination or examinations prepared by the securities exchanges or the NASD. These tests measure the prospective representative's knowledge of the securities business. Character investigations are also required.

Most employers provide training to help securities sales workers meet the requirements for registration. In member firms of all the major exchanges the training period is at least four months.

The number of securities sales workers is expected to grow about as fast as the average for all occupations through the mid-1980s, as investment in securities continues to increase.

---

the New York and American stock exchanges. In the secondary markets none of the proceeds from a securities transaction go to the corporation which issued the stocks or bonds originally. An investment banker participates in the secondary securities market by acting as a broker for the transfer of securities among investors.

Although the secondary markets do not channel any additional funds directly to business enterprises, active secondary markets for corporate securities are important because they provide liquidity to investors for purchases made in the primary markets. This liquidity makes investors more willing to participate in the primary securities markets, since they can sell their securities to other investors should they desire to do so.

Role of the investment banker

In primary securities markets	*In secondary securities markets*
1. Underwrites new issues of stocks and bonds.	1. Acts as broker in purchase and sale of securities for clients on organized exchanges and in over-the-counter markets.
2. Sells new securities issues without underwriting (best efforts).	2. Buys and sells securities for own portfolio.
3. Sells new securities issues through private placements.	3. Advises clients on investment matters.
4. Advises corporations on financial matters.	

Underwriting

The sale of a new issue of stock or bonds is relatively rare for most corporations. Therefore, when this is necessary the investment banker can provide corporate management with useful assistance. The investment banker has knowledge of current market conditions and can advise on the timing of the issue's sale, pricing, and other terms.

As underwriters, investment bankers assume responsibility for the sale of a corporation's stock or bonds. They guarantee a specified amount of money for the securities to be sold. This makes the investment banker a merchandiser of corporations' securities. The delicate job of the investment banker is to set an issue offering price that will be well received by the investing public and at the same time bring as much as possible for the issuing corporation.

Underwriting security issues involves financial risk on the part of the investment banker because of rapidly changing supply and demand conditions in the capital markets. Therefore, a grouping of investment bankers will frequently cooperate in the underwriting and sale of security issues. Such a grouping is called a *syndicate*. It is formed only to market a particular security issue. After the issue has been sold, the syndicate is dissolved.

When investment bankers underwrite an issue they are paid a fee to cover their expenses. They also sell the securities for a markup over what the issuing corporation receives for the securities. This is to compensate them for their services and for the risk they bear in the transaction. As a result of an unexpected downturn in stock or bond prices immediately after an issue comes to market, the investment bankers may be unable to dispose of the issue. This leaves the investment bankers with the choice of selling the issue at what it will bring (with a probable loss for themselves) or of holding the issue in the hope that an improvement in market conditions will enable them to sell it at a satisfactory price.

Best-efforts offering

The investment banker may also sell a securities issue for a corporation without underwriting the issue. This is known as a *best-efforts* offering. The investment banker assists with the planning and details connected with the issue and sells the stocks or bonds, but does not assume the risk for their sale. Under this arrangement the corporation accepts the risk of the sale of its securities, and the investment banker receives a fee.

Private placements

In addition to selling securities to the public, investment bankers may assist enterprises in the sale of their securities through private placements. A *private placement* is the sale of an entire issue of securities to a single investor or a small number of investors. A number of corporate debt issues in recent years have been sold through private placements to institutions such as life insurance companies and private pension funds. The investment banker's role in private placements is to advise the business enterprise during the negotiation process and to handle various details associated with the issuance of the debt securities.

The brokerage function

The brokerage function of the investment banker is the one which is best known to the public. Brokerage operations are carried on by the marketing organization of the investment banking house. As a broker, the investment banker buys and sells securities, acting as an agent for customers. For this agency service the broker receives a commission on each transaction. The commissions for most sales or purchases on the stock exchange or the over-the-counter market vary from about 6 percent on small transactions down to about 1 percent on amounts of several thousand dollars. The role of the broker is illustrated in the discussion of the stock market in the appendix to this chapter. The investment banking firm may also buy and sell securities for its own portfolio or for the portfolios of its partners or officers.

The activities of investment bankers are policed by the Securities and Exchange Commission and by industry groups. The SEC's objective is to prevent manipulation and fraud in the securities markets and in general to protect the interests of the investing public. Stock exchanges and investment advisers are also subject to federal laws and SEC regulations.

Investment banking houses are financed by equity capital provided by the individuals who own the firms. The traditional form of business organization for the investment banking house has been the partnership. However, in recent years a number of investment bankers have incorporated their operations. In 1971 the largest investment banking house, Merrill Lynch, Pierce, Fenner & Smith, Inc., sold a portion of its common stock to the public to increase its capital and to broaden its ownership.

SUMMARY

Financial institutions regulate the money supply and channel savers' funds to the business enterprises, individuals, and governmental units which want to borrow those funds.

The U.S. Treasury provides currency for the money supply and manages the federal debt.

The Federal Reserve System is made up of 12 regional Federal Reserve banks and is controlled by a seven-member Board of Governors. The Federal Reserve System is influential in determining the money supply, the level of interest rates, and the banking system's ability to provide credit to its customers.

The level of commercial bank reserves is regulated by the Federal Reserve through its purchase and sale of government securities, changes in the percentage of deposit reserves required of member banks, and changes in the discount rate for member banks in their dealings with the Federal Reserve.

Commercial banks, the largest class of financial institutions, accept demand deposits. They have the ability to create money through the use of a fractional reserve system.

Savings and loan associations, the second largest class of financial institutions, receive savings mostly from individuals. In turn they make loans for the financing of real estate, mainly one-to-four family homes.

Life insurance companies constitute the third largest class of financial institutions. The premiums they receive for underwriting insurance risks are invested primarily in the long-term capital markets.

Mutual savings banks, consumer finance companies, sales finance companies, and commercial finance companies are types of financial institutions which serve particular segments of the borrowing market.

Personal trust departments of commercial banks and trust companies take legal possession of personal assets and manage them for the benefit of the trustor or designated beneficiaries.

Pension funds are accumulated out of the contributions of employers and employees and are invested to provide retirement incomes for the beneficiaries and their families.

Fire and casualty insurance companies sell insurance coverage for fire and other hazards. They invest in U.S. government securities, corporate common stocks, and state and local government securities.

Investment companies obtain funds by selling shares and purchase securities of other corporations. Open-end investment companies, commonly known as mutual funds, are a medium of investment for the small investor who wishes to acquire a diversified portfolio of corporate securities.

The investment banker performs such services as underwriting new issues of stocks and bonds for corporations, acting as a broker in buying and selling securities for clients in the secondary securities markets, and providing advice to business enterprises in the timing and details of long-term financing.

appendix

THE STOCK MARKET AND INVESTING IN SECURITIES

THE STOCK MARKET

Organization of stock markets

A great deal of the trading of corporate securities in the secondary markets takes place on organized exchanges such as the New York Stock Exchange and the American Stock Exchange. Indeed, when people talk about "the stock market" they are normally referring to the New York Stock Exchange (NYSE), or the Big Board as it is informally called. The NYSE accounts for a majority of the trading volume on organized exchanges.

A corporation's management must apply to have its securities listed for trading on the New York Stock Exchange. In order to qualify for trading a corporation must meet certain minimum exchange requirements for demonstrated earning power, value of corporation assets, number of shares of stock outstanding, and the number of shareholders. The purpose of these requirements is to provide an active marketplace for well-established securities.

Trading on the floor of the organized exchanges is carried out by individuals and brokerage firms that hold memberships in the particular exchange. About 1,400 memberships or "seats" permit the holders to buy and sell securities on the floor of the NYSE. These memberships may be sold to other qualified individuals or firms with the approval of exchange officials.

About one fourth of the members of the NYSE are specialists who perform the function of "making a market" for one or more stocks. This means that they carry an inventory of shares in the issues in which they specialize and are willing to deal with other exchange members who are trading for themselves or their customers.

Buying and selling stock through an organized exchange

If you wished to purchase 100 shares of General Motors common stock on the New York Stock Exchange you would relay that order to your broker. The order would be sent by wire to the firm's New York office, from which it would be relayed to the trading member on the floor of the exchange. The member on the NYSE floor would take the order to the place, called a trading post, where the specialist dealing in General Motors stock is located and would carry out the transaction.

The purchase and sale of stocks on the Big Board is accomplished through the specialist, who conducts a continuous two-way auction-type operation. The specialist quotes prices for buying and selling stock of a given corporation. The "bid" price is the price at which the specialist is willing to buy stock.

The "ask" price is the price at which the specialist is willing to sell. The difference between these is called the "spread," which is the specialist's margin.

Various types of orders for securities may be placed with brokers by customers. Usually orders to buy or sell securities are placed either at a particular price or "at the market," which means that the transaction will be executed immediately for the best price your broker can obtain. Each broker who acts for a customer is charged with the responsibility of obtaining the best possible price for the customer. Stocks may be bought and sold in round lots, which normally consist of 100-share units. Smaller orders are called "odd lots," which in most stocks range from 1 to 99 shares. Recall that brokerage fees range downward from about 6 percent, depending on the amount of the transaction.

After the broker on the floor completes the transaction, both the broker and the specialist make a written notation of the deal. This information is sent to the New York brokerage office and then wired to the branch office from which the order came. At the same time, a report of the transaction is relayed to the exchange reporting service, which sends the report across the country on a wire service. The transaction is reported on the visual tape, called a broad tape, which almost every brokerage office has in continuous operation during the hours when the market is open for trading. This public report gives the symbol that represents the name of the corporation's stock, the number of shares in the transaction, and the price per share of stock. Brokerage officers may use their wire services to obtain quotations of the bid and ask prices for their customers direct from the trading floor of the exchange in a very short time. It is possible for you to receive a quotation, place an order, have it executed on the floor of the stock exchange, and receive the report back in your broker's office in less than ten minutes.

The prices of individual securities are determined by the relative supply and demand for them as received by the specialist. The specialist is charged with maintaining an orderly market for stocks. However, the willingness to buy or sell on the part of institutions and individuals interested in securities will ultimately determine the price at which transactions are completed.

Stock market averages

In addition to reports on price changes of individual stocks, illustrated in Figure 15–1, there are reports on the general movement of stock prices at a given time. The most publicized of these stock market price averages is the Dow-Jones average. Actually the *Dow-Jones average* is composed of four series of calculations of stock prices—one series for 30 industrial stocks, one for 20 transportation stocks, one for 15 utility stocks, and a composite of the total 65 stocks. The Dow-Jones Industrial average comprises some of the country's leading corporations, including American Telephone & Telegraph, Du Pont, Eastman Kodak, General Electric, General Motors, Sears Roebuck, Texaco, and U.S. Steel.

The Dow-Jones averages are made up of "blue-chip" or high-quality stocks.

FIGURE 15–1

How to read stock market reports

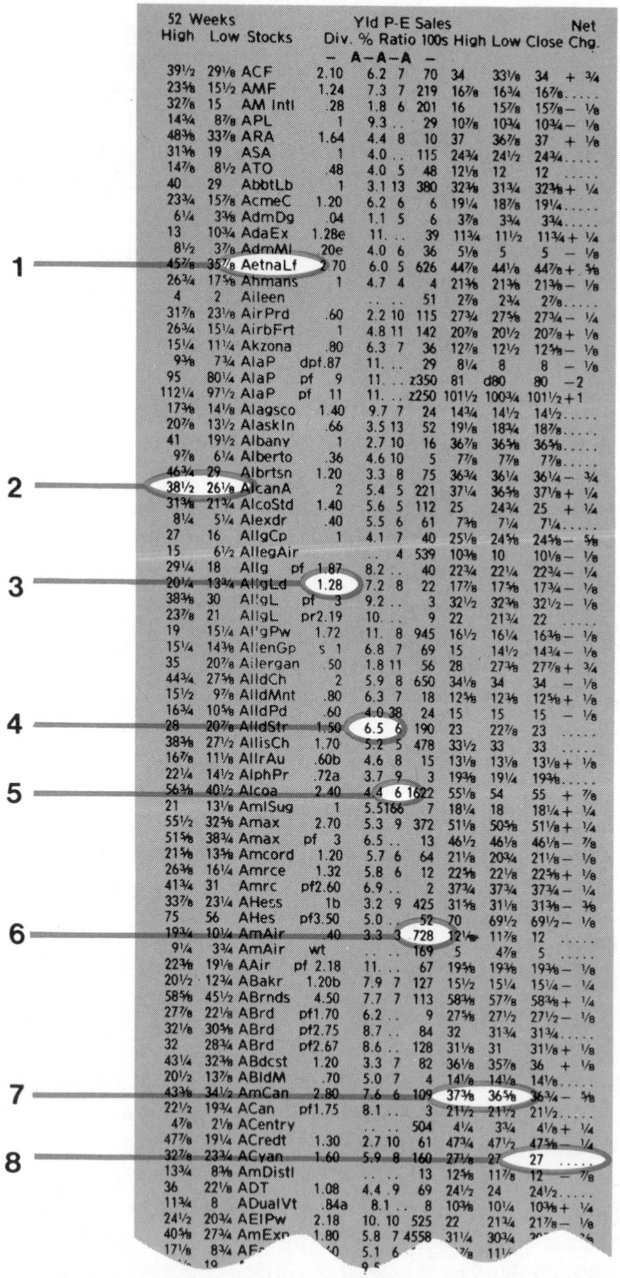

52 Weeks				Yld	P-E	Sales				Net
High	Low	Stocks	Div.	%	Ratio	100s	High	Low	Close	Chg.
			– A–A–A –							
39½	29⅛	ACF	2.10	6.2	7	70	34	33⅛	34	+ ¾
23⅜	15½	AMF	1.24	7.3	7	219	16⅞	16¾	16⅞	....
32⅞	15	AM Intl	.28	1.8	6	201	16	15⅞	15⅞	− ⅛
14¾	8⅞	APL	1	9.3	..	29	10⅞	10¾	10¾	− ⅛
48⅜	33⅞	ARA	1.64	4.4	8	10	37	36⅞	37	+ ⅛
31⅜	19	ASA	1	4.0	..	115	24¾	24½	24¾	....
14⅞	8½	ATO	.48	4.0	5	48	12⅛	12	12	.....
40	29	AbbtLb	1	3.1	13	380	32¾	31¾	32⅜	+ ¼
23¾	15⅞	AcmeC	1.20	6.2	6	6	19¼	18⅞	19¼	....
6¼	3⅜	AdmDg	.04	1.1	5	6	3⅞	3¾	3¾	....
13	10¾	AdaEx	1.28e	11.	..	39	11¾	11½	11¾	+ ¼
8½	3⅞	AdmMl	20e	4.0	6	36	5⅛	5	5	− ⅛
45⅞	35⅝	AetnaLf	2.70	6.0	5	626	44⅞	44⅛	44⅞	+ .⅜
26¾	17⅝	Ahmans	1	4.7	4	4	21⅜	21⅜	21⅜	− ⅛
4	2	Aileen		...	..	51	2⅞	2¾	2⅞	....
31⅞	23⅛	AirPrd	.60	2.2	10	115	27¾	27⅝	27¾	− ¼
26¾	15¼	AirbFrt	1	4.8	11	142	20⅞	20½	20⅞	+ ⅛
15¼	11¼	Akzona	.80	6.3	7	36	12⅞	12½	12⅜	− ⅛
9⅜	7¾	AlaP	dpf.87	11.	..	29	8¼	8	8	− ⅛
95	80¼	AlaP	pf 9	11.	..	z350	81	d80	80	−2
112¼	97½	AlaP	pf 11	11.	..	z250	101½	100¾	101½	+1
17⅜	14⅛	Alagsco	1.40	9.7	7	24	14¾	14½	14½	....
20⅞	13½	AlaskIn	.66	3.5	13	52	19⅛	18¾	18⅞	....
41	19½	Albany	1	2.7	10	16	36⅞	36⅝	36⅝	....
9⅞	6¼	Alberto	.36	4.6	10	5	7⅞	7⅞	7⅞	...
46¾	29	Albrtsn	1.20	3.3	8	75	36¾	36¼	36¼	− ¾
38½	26⅛	AlcanA	2	5.4	5	221	37¼	36⅝	37⅛	+ ¼
31¾	21¾	AlcoStd	1.40	5.6	5	112	25	24¾	25	+ ¼
8¼	5¼	Alexdr	.40	5.5	6	61	7⅜	7¼	7¼	....
27	16	AllgCp	1	4.1	7	40	25⅛	24⅝	24⅝	− ⅝
15	6½	AllegAir		...	4	539	10⅜	10	10⅛	− ⅛
29¼	18	Allg	pf 1.87	8.2	..	40	22¾	22¼	22¾	− ⅛
20¼	13¾	AllgLd	1.28	7.2	8	22	17⅞	17⅝	17¾	− ⅛
38⅜	30	Al'gL	pf 3	9.2	..	3	32½	32¾	32½	− ⅛
23⅞	21	AllgL	pr2.19	10.	..	9	22	21¾	22	....
19	15¼	Al'gPw	1.72	11.	8	945	16½	16¼	16⅜	− ⅛
15¼	14⅜	AllenGp	s 1	6.8	7	69	15	14½	14¾	− ⅛
35	20⅞	Allergan	.50	1.8	11	56	28	27¾	27⅞	+ ¾
44¾	27⅝	AlldCh	2	5.9	8	650	34⅛	34	34	− ⅛
15½	9⅞	AlldMnt	.80	6.3	7	18	12⅜	12⅛	12⅜	+ ⅛
16¾	10⅜	AlldPd	.60	4.0	38	24	15	15	15	− ⅛
28	20⅞	AlldStr	1.50	6.5	6	190	23	22⅞	23	.....
38⅜	27⅛	AllisCh	1.70	5.2	5	478	33½	33	33	....
16⅞	11⅜	AllrAu	.60b	4.6	8	15	13⅛	13⅛	13⅛	+ ⅛
22¼	14½	AlphPr	.72a	3.7	9	3	19⅜	19¼	19⅜	....
56¾	40½	Alcoa	2.40	4.4	6	1622	55⅛	54	55	+ ⅞
21	13⅛	AmlSug	1	5.5	166	5	18¼	18	18¼	+ ¼
55½	32⅝	Amax	2.70	5.3	9	372	51⅛	50⅝	51⅛	+ ¼
51⅝	38¾	Amax	pf 3	6.5	..	13	46½	46⅛	46⅛	− ⅞
21⅝	13⅝	Amcord	1.20	5.7	6	64	21⅛	20¾	21⅛	− ⅛
26⅜	16¼	Amrce	1.32	5.8	6	12	22⅝	22⅛	22⅝	+ ⅛
41¾	31	Amrc	pf2.60	6.9	..	2	37¾	37¾	37¾	− ⅛
33⅞	23¼	AHess	1b	3.2	9	425	31⅝	31⅛	31⅜	− ⅜
75	56	AHes	pf3.50	5.0	..	52	70	69½	69½	− ⅛
19¾	10¾	AmAir	.40	3.3	3	728	12⅛	11⅞	12	.....
9¼	3¾	AmAir	wt			169	5	4⅞	5	.....
22¾	19½	AAir	pf 2.18	11.	..	67	19⅝	19⅜	19⅜	− ⅛
20½	12¾	ABakr	1.20b	7.9	7	127	15½	15¼	15¼	− ¼
58⅝	45½	ABrnds	4.50	7.7	7	113	58⅜	57⅞	58⅜	+ ¼
27⅞	22⅛	ABrd	pf1.70	6.2	..	9	27⅜	27½	27½	− ⅛
32⅛	30⅜	ABrd	pf2.75	8.7	..	84	32	31¾	31¾	....
32	28¾	ABrd	pf2.67	8.6	..	128	31⅛	31	31⅛	+ ⅛
43¼	32⅜	ABdcst	1.20	3.3	7	82	36⅛	35⅞	36	+ ⅛
20½	13⅞	ABldM	.70	5.0	7	4	14⅛	14⅛	14⅛	....
43¾	34⅛	AmCan	2.80	7.6	6	109	37⅜	36⅝	36¾	− ⅜
22½	19¾	ACan	pf1.75	8.1	..	3	21½	21½	21½	....
4⅞	2⅛	ACentry		...		504	4¼	3¾	4⅛	+ ¼
47⅞	19¼	ACredt	1.30	2.7	10	61	47¾	47½	47⅝	− ¼
32⅞	23¾	ACyan	1.60	5.9	8	160	27⅛	27	27	.....
13¾	8⅜	AmDistl				12	12⅛	11⅞	12	− ⅞
36	22⅛	ADT	1.08	4.4	9	69	24½	24	24½	....
11¾	8	ADualVt	.84a	8.1	..	8	10⅜	10¼	10⅜	+ ¼
24½	20¾	AEIPw	2.18	10.	10	525	22	21¾	21⅞	− ⅛
40⅜	27¾	AmExp	1.80	5.8	7	4558	31¼	30¾		
17⅛	8¾	AF	.40	5.1	6		7⅞	11¼		

Many newspapers carry stock market reports similar to this sample taken from New York Stock Exchange transactions which occurred on April 20, 1979.

Key to Figure 15–1

1. The abbreviated name of the company issuing the stock. In this case it is Aetna Life Insurance. The stock is common stock unless the company name is followed by "pf," which indicates that the issue is a preferred stock.

2. These columns show the highest and lowest prices paid for a given stock on the exchange during the year. In this case it is $38.50 and $26.125 per share.

3. Figures following company names indicate the annual dividend rate estimated on the basis of the latest quarterly or semiannual payment. Here the annual rate is $1.28 per share. Letters following the dividend numbers indicate other data regarding dividends. For example, "b" indicates that, in addition to the cash dividend shown, a stock dividend is issued. Other symbols are explained in a footnote on the market reports page.

4. This column shows the cash dividend yield. It is determined by expressing the annual dividend rate as a percentage of the stock's closing market price for the day. For Allied Stores the dividend yield is $1.50/$23 or 6.5 percent.

5. This column shows the stock's price/earnings ratio based on the closing price of the day divided by the past 12 months' reported earnings per share. For Alcoa the P/E ratio is 6.

6. This column shows the number of shares traded for the day, expressed in hundreds. In this instance 72,800 shares of American Airlines stock changed hands during this day on the New York Stock Exchange. A "z" indicates the actual number of shares traded.

7. These two columns show the highest price and the lowest price at which the stock traded on this day. In this case the stock of American Can hit a high of $37.375 and a low of $36.625.

8. These final two columns show the closing price of the day and the change from the previous day's closing price. For American Cyanamid the closing price was $27 per share, unchanged from the previous day's close.

There are more broadly based stock market price averages, such as the 500-stock average by Standard & Poor's Corporation, a securities research organization.

The over-the-counter market

In addition to the securities trading which takes place on organized exchanges, there is the *over-the-counter* market (OTC). On the OTC, securities dealers buy and sell stock through informal dealings, usually by telephone, rather than in a central place such as an organized exchange. Many securities dealers maintain inventories of the stocks which trade over the counter. Their quotations for bid and ask prices are circulated in the investment community. When a member of the public places an order with an investment banker's brokerage office, the customer's representative will buy the stock where it can be purchased for the best price, usually after contacting two or three dealers.

Security issues which are traded in the OTC market include the stocks and bonds of typically small or medium-size business enterprises. The common stocks of most commercial banks are also traded in the OTC market, along with many insurance company stocks.

Although some U.S. government bonds are listed on the New York Stock Exchange, most federal government securities are traded in the OTC market. Municipal securities are traded exclusively over the counter. *Municipals* include the bonds of states, municipalities, school districts, and other local governmental units. Most corporate bond trading occurs over the counter, although some corporate bonds are listed on the stock exchanges.

INVESTING IN SECURITIES

Investment objectives

Investors in stocks and bonds, whether institutions or individuals, should establish their investment objectives and determine the types of securities needed to achieve these objectives. Then they are ready to select the specific securities to be included in their investment portfolios.

Although the general objective of investing is to provide a monetary return on capital, several specific factors should be considered in judging the suitability of a particular investment. Investors need to determine the relative importance of current income, growth of the investment, and the degree of risk they are willing to assume. Current income can be provided from bond interest or dividends on corporate preferred or common stocks. Capital growth results from an appreciation in the market value of securities. Safety of principal is also an important factor in establishing investment objectives, since some investments

TABLE 15–4
Securities characteristics and investment objectives

Objectives	Bonds	Preferred stocks	Common stocks
Current income	Highest	Medium	Lowest
Capital growth (appreciation)	Lowest	Medium	Highest
Safety of principal	Highest	Medium	Lowest

carry a much greater risk than others. Table 15–4 summarizes the general characteristics of bonds, preferred stocks, and common stocks in relation to these
three objectives.

There are exceptions to the generalizations outlined in Table 15–4. For example, some low-quality bonds have less safety of principal than high-quality preferred or common stocks. This emphasizes the importance of the final selection
of specific stocks and bonds. Generally the greater the risk accepted in making
investments, the higher should be the financial return to the investor.

The selection of common stocks

In attempting to evaluate the common stock of a corporation, investment
analysts use a number of measures. These include earnings and earnings growth,
cash dividends, the market price of the common stock, the price/earnings ratio,
and the quality of management.

Earnings and earnings growth   Net profit is divided by the number of shares
of common stock outstanding to determine earnings per share. If the corporation
has preferred stock in its capital structure, the cash dividends paid on preferred
stock are subtracted from net profit before the earnings per share for common
stockholders are calculated. The earnings per share and their rate of growth
in past years are important determinants of common stock prices, especially
as these may reflect the likely continued growth in earnings in the future. Most
analysts feel that earnings for at least the past five years should be studied.

Cash dividends   The amount of cash dividends per share paid to stockholders
and the trend of cash dividend payments are also factors in evaluating a common
stock. The trend of cash dividend payments over recent years should be considered along with the proportion of earnings paid out in dividends.

The market price   The present market price per share of common stock
and the price trend over the years enable the analyst to determine whether
there has been an increase in the value of corporate shares in the past. Generally
an upward trend of the market price is viewed more positively by analysts
than a downward trend unless there is some valid reason for believing that
the price trend is about to reverse itself.

The price/earnings ratio   An important measurement which takes two key
factors into account is the price/earnings ratio. The current market price per
share of stock is divided by the past 12 months' earnings per share. This measure
can be compared with the stock's P/E ratio in previous years and with the
P/E ratios of the stocks of other corporations in the same industry. Price/earnings
ratios vary widely among different common stocks as they reflect investors'
expectations of future corporate earnings.

For example, in 1979 the common stock of Ford Motor Company was selling
for a price/earnings ratio of only about four times. This very low P/E ratio
reflected investors' fears over Ford's market share of new-car sales and prospects
of lower profits. At the same time, the common stock of Merck, a quality
drug manufacturer, was selling at a P/E ratio of 18 times. This high P/E

ratio reflected investors' confidence in Merck's ability to continue its record of research and higher profits.

The quality of management   One of the most important judgments, and perhaps the most difficult for the analyst to make, is an evaluation of the quality of a corporation's management. The effectiveness of management in developing, producing, and marketing new products should be judged. Also, an evaluation should be made of the enterprise's accounting statements, with tests similar to those discussed in Chapter 14.

A number of investment advisory services provide analyses of stocks and bonds. These services include *Standard & Poor's Outlook* and the *Value Line Investment Survey*. Such analyses plus studies of corporate stocks made by brokerage firms provide a variety of reference material for the potential investor.

The fact that advisory services as well as investors differ about the desirability of a corporation's common stock at a given time makes an active market for publicly held securities. Considerable study and analysis should precede the investment decision if investors wish to manage their capital prudently. Although the long-run trend in common stock prices has been upward, significant price declines have occurred from time to time. Also, the price movement of an individual corporation's stock may not follow the general market trend.

TERMS FOR REVIEW

financial institutions
Federal Reserve System
reserve requirements
Federal Reserve discount rate
open-market operations
fractional reserve banking
 system

prime rate of interest
mutual fund (open-end
 investment company)
investment banker
money market

capital market
commercial banks
primary securities market
secondary securities market

QUESTIONS

1. What functions do financial institutions perform in the economy?
2. Outline the role of the Federal Reserve System.
3. Explain how the Federal Reserve regulates the public's supply of money and credit.
4. Outline the services performed by commercial banks which justify calling them "the keystone of the American monetary and financial system."
5. *a.* Given an initial bank demand deposit of $10,000, what is the maximum amount by

which the commercial banking system could expand demand deposits if the required reserve ratio were 16⅔ percent?
 b. What conditions would have to prevail for such a maximum expansion to occur?

6. List the major types of investments made by each of the following types of financial institutions:
 a. Savings and loan associations.
 b. Life insurance companies.
 c. Mutual savings banks.

d. Consumer finance companies.

e. Sales finance companies.

f. Commercial finance companies.

g. Credit unions.

h. Personal trust departments.

i. Pension funds.

j. Fire and casualty insurance companies.

k. Investment companies.

7. What specific functions does the investment banker perform?

8. Assume that you have $5,000 of your own money to invest in the stock market. Select a corporation's common stock from *Moody's Industrial Manual, Standard & Poor's Corporation Reports,* or some other source. Plot the stock's market fluctuations as reported in the daily newspaper over a one-month period. How do you account for the changes in the stock's market price? What seemed to be happening in the stock market as a whole over this same period of time?

9. What important elements in a person's overall financial position should be examined before that person decides to invest in the stock market?

10. What advantages for customers are provided by The Arizona Bank's computer applications described on the first page of this chapter?

business briefs

PAY-BY-PHONE

Home Federal Savings & Loan Association of Arizona announced a Pay-by-Phone service for its customers in late 1978. Under this arrangement, customers' bills will be paid by phone for 12 cents a bill by the savings and loan association. At the same time, interest of 5¼ percent compounded daily will be paid on customers' unused account balances.

Customers who sign up for this service select the enterprises that they wish to pay by telephone. Each of these enterprises bills the customer as usual. The customer then dials a special Pay-by-Phone number and gives a personal security number, the name of the company and the amount it is to be paid, and the date when the payment is to be made.

Home Federal deducts the amount from the customer's account and pays the enterprise on the next business day. Customers receive a monthly itemized statement of all transactions and are given a register in which to record transactions when they are made. At the end of the year Home Federal provides a summary by enterprise category.

Accounts are protected with personal security numbers. If unauthorized persons obtained account and personal security numbers, only customer bill payments and account transfers would be possible. Since Home Federal is a federally chartered savings and loan association, each customer's account is insured up to $40,000 by the Federal Savings and Loan Insurance Corporation.

This service was developed by a computing service corporation in Seattle, and it was reportedly being used by 60 financial institutions across the country.

1. a. What advantages does the Pay-by-Phone program afford Home Federal's customers?

   b. What possible problems might arise for Home Federal's customers?

2. What benefits may result for Home Federal from the program?

3. How would you react to such a program if you were a manager of a commercial bank or a savings and loan association in the community?

CITY FINANCING FOR HOME MORTGAGES?

In 1978, Chicago leaders faced the fact that thousands of middle-class citizens were moving out of the city. Since the mid-1950s some 50,000 families a year had moved to the suburbs. This flight tended to increase the rate of urban decay and to reduce city property tax revenues. In an experiment to encourage middle-class families to own homes in Chicago, city officials teamed up with a major investment banking firm to devise a plan for financing home mortgages through loans from the city.

The investment banker sold an issue of $100 million in tax-free municipal bonds for Chicago.[1] The $100 million in long-term bonds paid investors about 7 percent tax-free interest. The bond issue sold out in one day.

Of the $100 million issue, $14 million was put into a special fund to cover mortgage defaults and other costs. The investment banker received $3 million as its sales fee for marketing the bond issue to the public.

A savings and loan association was selected by city officials to loan out the remaining $83 million. Over 2,000 middle-class families with incomes of up to $40,000 obtained mortgages at an interest rate of just below 8 percent.

At the same time, the home mortgage interest rates of conventional savings and loan associations in the area ranged upward from 9½ percent to 10 percent.

---

[1] The interest paid investors on municipal bonds issued by cities and states is exempt from federal income taxes. Because of this, the interest rates are lower on such bonds than on the bonds issued by business corporations, the interest on which is taxable. The original intent of federal tax exemption for municipal bonds was to assist governmental units in financing public projects at reasonable interest rates.

The city's encouragement to home owning in Chicago would save more than $80 monthly in payments on a $60,000 house as compared to the cost of a conventional mortgage loan.

Whereas federal home loan subsidy programs usually go to help low-income home buyers, this program focused on middle-income families. Similar bond issues are being considered by officials in other U.S. cities.

1. How would you react to this plan if you were:
   a. A prospective borrower of these funds to finance a home?
   b. A city official faced with the population flight to the suburbs?
   c. A manager of a competing savings and loan association in the city?
   d. A taxpayer living in the city?
2. Should the lower interest costs resulting from tax-free bonds issued by a community be used for the direct benefit of a particular family or group?
3. Do you think that a program of low-interest loans can have much effect on Chicago's "flight to the suburbs" problem? What other governmental actions might be necessary to attract middle-class homeowners back to the city?

---

case

FAMILY FINANCIAL PLANNING

Tom McCormick graduated two years ago with a degree in electrical engineering. While in college he took no courses in business administration. He married during his senior year and was employed upon graduation by a large corporation which makes 30 percent of its sales to the federal government.

During a vacation to his hometown he raised the following question with his uncle who was a stockbroker. "Uncle Max," Tom began, "Jane and I have saved $6,000 over the past two years, since we've both been working. Could you give us some tips on investing in the stock market? I'm afraid we're not too sophisticated about money matters, but we seem to be living pretty well and are saving some money."

The uncle replied, "Well, Tom, each person or family should develop an overall financial program for savings. Two elements of this plan, insurance and an insured savings account, should be considered before investments in stocks are made.

"Insurance is a separate subject. However, we can make a few observations here. Especially if you and Jane plan to start a family soon, you will want to have sufficient life insurance for family financial security in case of early death of one or both parents. You probably already have a certain amount of life insurance. I would guess it would be *whole life* insurance. Whole life provides both insurance coverage and cash surrender values for the policy owner built up from the payment of premiums which are invested by the insurance company. Many young families also buy relatively low-cost *term* insurance to have added insurance protection in the child-rearing years. Term insurance provides insurance coverage for a specified period of time but has no cash surrender value. Your family should also be protected with health and disability insurance."

Tom commented, "Right now, we have whole life insurance but no term insurance. However, we haven't analyzed whether our coverage is sufficient. I have health insurance provided by my employer as a fringe benefit at a very reasonable rate. However, this group insurance is available only while I'm employed by the company."

Uncle Max went on, "Of course, you also have government Social Security insurance which would provide benefit payments to you if you became disabled or to your widow or children under specified conditions in addition to providing retirement benefits. However, Social Security payments are considered by most persons as supplementary minimum amounts and should not be considered sufficient to provide for all of a family's insurance or retirement needs.

"The second element in a person's savings program is the establishment of a savings account in a bank or a savings and loan association. This account can provide money to meet unexpected needs that arise on short notice. A recommended amount in such a savings account would cover three to six months' living expenses. Such accounts should be placed only in financial institutions which are insured up to $40,000 for each account by the FDIC or the FSLIC.

"Once these two financial keystones to a personal financial program are established, then other investment media may be considered. For many families the purchase of a house on monthly payments is an important part of their investment program as well as providing for living quarters. Before the purchase of a house is undertaken, factors to be considered include the family's preference for home ownership versus renting a house or an apartment; the location of the house under consideration; the total costs of home ownership, including taxes, insurance, and maintenance; and the length of time that the family expects to live in the area. Only after some of these factors have been considered would I recommend that you begin to invest in common stocks.

"I don't mean to make this a long lecture, Tom. But if you'll indicate how you stand on these factors, then we can talk about your investment objectives, and I'll make some suggestions for your study."

1. *Make a list of the important questions that Tom and Jane need to consider as they plan their family financial program.*
2. *Assume that Tom has adequate insurance and insured savings so that he could consider investing through the stock market. What investment objectives would you recommend to him and his wife at this time? What kinds of securities would you suggest to achieve these objectives?*

LTV reports . . .

For The LTV Corporation, its shareholders, management and employees, 1978 marked the beginning of a new era.

It was the year in which LTV merged with Lykes Corporation and became, in essence, a new LTV—more firmly based in steel than ever before and at the same time more widely diversified.

As with any change of such magnitude, there were problems to overcome and their resolution drew the focus of LTV's efforts throughout almost all of 1978. Our goal was to enhance the investment of LTV shareholders by making a merger which would strengthen the company's position in the steel business and, simultaneously, attend to the more immediate goal of restoring LTV to profitability.

By the end of the year, we had accomplished both goals. The merger was approved by shareholders of both companies on December 5, and for the year LTV achieved its highest sales record and also returned to profitability.

Simply stated, the merger was the best means available to achieve the production and other efficiencies LTV needed to improve its steel profit margins and equip it to compete more successfully within the domestic steel industry and to deal with the continuing record flow of imported steel.

Along with the creation of a new, stronger steel operation, the merger also broadened our family of companies by adding two important lines of business—shipping and energy-oriented products.

Both Lykes Bros. Steamship Co., Inc., whose ships serve ports around the world, and Continental-Emsco Company, whose drilling rigs, pumps, and other products and services are used in the drilling, production, refining, and transportation of oil and gas in many nations, are quality enterprises with established records of success and growth. Evidence of this came within a few weeks after the merger when each of them achieved an expansion in its business field.

From annual report of The LTV Corporation

Photo opposite: One of the blast furnaces at the Cleveland Works of Jones & Laughlin Steel Corporation, a subsidiary of The LTV Corporation.

Photo courtesy of The LTV Corporation

Financial management

Financial management

The finance function is vital to the profitable management of every business enterprise. Whenever a new product line is added, a new factory built, labor contracts negotiated, or dividend payments considered, quesitons relating to finance must be answered. Are the funds available to undertake the proposed course of action? Will the project make good use of resources? How should the undertaking be financed?

After studying this chapter, you will be able to answer the following questions regarding financial management of the business enterprise:

What is the finance function?

What are the responsibilities of the finance department for the profitable management of the enterprise?

What is the specific role of top management in the finance area?

How is the finance department organized?

THE FINANCE FUNCTION

The financial aspects of management should be viewed as an integrated part of the total management of the enterprise rather than as a narrow activity concerned mainly with writing checks and collecting accounts. The finance department does disburse funds for financial obligations and supervise credit management. However, this is not the heart of the finance function. The basic elements of finance are the profitable use of funds and the provision of funds to finance enterprise activities at the most economical cost.

Financial managers are responsible for analyzing the proposals for increasing profits that originate with production and marketing managers. This does not mean that the finance department makes all the critical decisions as to which investments will be undertaken by the enterprise. The proposals for production and marketing programs still originate in the production and marketing departments. Production and marketing executives should have the necessary expert knowledge to decide which equipment will do a particular job or what product is likely to sell best. However, the finance department should perform the task of review when major decisions are made to commit funds to new or continuing projects. The finance department must also be sure that funds will be available to carry out the projects that management selects.

RESPONSIBILITIES OF THE FINANCE DEPARTMENT

In its role of decision making in both the use and the acquisition of funds, the finance department should develop certain guidelines:

1. To determine the optimum size of the enterprise.
2. To select the best balance among different types of assets.
3. To provide the funds necessary to finance these assets.
4. To deal with the dilemma of profitability versus liquidity.

Size of the business enterprise

The size of a particular firm depends on the nature of the industry of which the firm is a part, the firm's legal form of organization, and the firm's operating policies.

In some industries there is not much choice as to the size of an enterprise. The management of a steel mill must provide large amounts of capital for the elaborate plant and equipment necessary to produce steel. Even the smallest steel mill requires an investment of many million dollars. On the other hand, there are industries which have a greater variation in size and financing requirements. The retail grocery industry is an example. Some grocers seek the economies of large multistore supermarket operations. This requires much capital. Other food retailers operate a single store profitably on a minimum investment.

The size of the enterprise also depends on the legal form of organization which is chosen. The corporate form of organization lends itself to raising large amounts of capital. The partnership and proprietorship normally do not have access to many of the sources of funds available to the corporation.

Specific asset management

Once the general size of the enterprise has been established, specific policies must be selected to determine the balance among the different classes of necessary assets. Policies relating to the following classes of assets involve financial management:

1. The size of cash and near-cash balances.
2. Credit policies—shall the enterprise extend credit to its customers, and, if so, what should be the terms of credit?
3. The size and composition of inventories.
4. The fixed assets that are acquired.

Size of cash and near-cash balances   An important operating responsibility of financial management is the maintenance of cash and near-cash balances sufficient to pay the bills of the enterprise as they fall due. The cash account usually consists of money on deposit in commercial banks, though some funds may be held in a *petty cash fund* for minor disbursements in cash. Retail enterprises keep working balances of currency and coin on hand to make change

career outlook

CREDIT MANAGERS

Many daily activities of businesses and individuals depend on receiving goods and services on credit. For most forms of credit, a credit manager has final authority to accept or reject a credit application.

Newly hired workers normally begin as management trainees and work under the guidance of more experienced personnel in the credit department. Here they gain a thorough understanding of the company's credit procedures and policies. They may analyze previous credit transactions to learn how to recognize which applicants should prove to be good customers. Trainees also learn to deal with credit bureaus, banks, and other businesses that can provide information on the past credit dealings of their customers.

Through the mid-1980s the employment of credit managers is expected to grow more slowly than the average for all occupations. Despite this relatively slow growth, many jobs will become available each year due to the need to replace persons who leave the occupation.

Despite increases in consumer debt, the use of computers for storing and retrieving information will enable the greater volume of credit information to be processed more efficiently. The use of telecommunications networks enables retail outlets to have immediate access to a central credit office, regardless of distance.

Another factor that is expected to slow the growth in the number of credit managers is the increased use of bank credit cards. As stores substitute bank credit cards for their own charge accounts, credit departments may be reduced or eliminated.

In the years ahead, businesses can be expected to require increasing amounts of credit to secure raw materials for production and obtain finished goods for eventual resale. It is in the area of business credit that the demand for credit managers will be strongest.

for customers. *Near-cash* is any asset which is immediately transferable into money without risk of loss of value in the process. The customary form of near-cash for many financial managers is the 91-day U.S. Treasury bill. Although the interest rate on Treasury bills is usually relatively low, short-term government securities provide some interest on funds which are in excess of immediate cash needs. At the same time the funds so invested can be turned into cash on short notice. The determination of the proper level of cash and near-cash balances may be complicated. Such factors as the fluctuation in the enterprise's scale of operations, the ability of management to predict cash receipts and disbursements, and the ability of the enterprise to depend on other sources of funds such as bank credit should be taken into account in setting the desired level of cash balances.

Credit policies   The amount that should be invested in accounts receivable depends on how important credit sales are to the sales effort and on how credit is managed. Management may decide that sales will be made on a cash-only basis. This policy would avoid the problems associated with extending credit and making collections. Funds would not be tied up in receivables from customers. The possibility of bad debt losses would be eliminated. However, a no-credit policy may result in a lower level of sales with lower profits than if the enterprise granted credit to its customers.

When credit is extended, terms are usually quoted in an abbreviated form, such as "2/10, n/30." This means that a 2 percent cash discount is allowed the customer who pays within 10 days from the date on the merchandise invoice statement or the bill is to be paid with no discount within 11 to 30 days.

Although in theory each enterprise's management is able to set its own credit terms, credit practices are strongly influenced by what is done in the industry. Terms of credit will probably be similar throughout the industry. However, management does have freedom in determining the credit worthiness of customers and in adopting collection policies to see that customers pay promptly. Whether an enterprise adopts a conservative or liberal policy regarding credit extension should be determined after considering the expected additional profits which would probably result from a proposed policy.

Size and composition of inventories   The determination of the optimum size and composition of inventories is important in both manufacturing and marketing enterprises. For the manufacturing enterprise there are three types of inventories—raw materials, work in process, and finished goods. Purchasing and production departments have primary responsibility for determining the specific levels of manufacturing inventories. However, inventory policies influence the financial needs of the business enterprise. Hence, the finance department has a responsibility for anticipating requirements for funds that result from increasing inventories. Also, the finance department should be concerned with the efficient use of inventories. For example, improvement of inventory turnover may result in lower inventories and a reduction in the amount of funds required to finance them.

Acquisition of fixed assets   The specific industry and the scale of business operations will generally determine the need for fixed assets. Fixed assets, sometimes called capital assets, include land, buildings, machinery, furniture, and fixtures. The purchase of fixed assets is important to the finance department because this usually involves a large investment. Before fixed assets are purchased, the need for the specific assets and their expected profitability should be analyzed. Funds committed to fixed assets may be tied up for many years. If borrowing is undertaken to acquire the funds, the debt must be repaid, regardless of how well the investment works out. If stockholders put up the money through the purchase of more stock they expect profitable use to be made of their funds. If the investment in fixed assets does not work out well, it may be difficult, if not impossible, to dispose of the assets at their book value. For these reasons the finance department should confer with other departments to assure that all reasonable steps have been taken to analyze the desirability of investment in a particular fixed asset.

The financing of assets

In addition to advising other departments on the acquisition of fixed assets, the finance department has the responsibility of determining the best means of providing the funds for these assets. Assets may be financed by debt, by the use of leases, or by owners.

The specific source of funds for a project will depend on how long the funds are needed, how funds have been acquired in the past, the attitude of management toward the risks of debt, and current conditions in the financial markets.

Financing by use of debt Funds provided by outsiders through short-term, intermediate-term, and long-term debt are important sources of business enterprise financing. The classification of debt on the basis of length of time until maturity varies. However, *short-term debt* falls due within a year. *Intermediate-term debt* usually represents funds obtained for periods of time running from over a year until about ten years. *Long-term debt* customarily has a maturity more than ten years in the future.

The length of time for which money is borrowed depends on the purpose of the loan. It is generally advisable to use a form of credit which has a maturity as long as the money will be needed. Thus, you should not finance a seasonal buildup in inventory for holiday needs with a long-term loan from a life insurance company. Most important, you should not finance a factory building which has an expected life of 25 years with a six-month bank loan. The bank may not renew the loan after six months.

Short-term sources of funds include bank loans and credit extended by suppliers. Short-term bank loans are an excellent way to finance inventory buildup to meet seasonal or unexpected needs for merchandise. After the merchandise has been sold, the bank loan is paid off with the proceeds from the sale. Suppliers frequently extend trade credit to their customers to finance merchandise or equipment purchases.

In this country, formal notes recognizing liability for accounts payable to a supplier have not been widely used. Normally merchandise is shipped on open-trade account. However, when an enterprise is not known to the supplier or has been slow in paying its trade accounts, the supplier may ask that a note be signed to acknowledge the indebtedness.

Intermediate credit may be obtained through banks, insurance companies, or finance companies which specialize in equipment loans for a period of years. Periodic repayments are normally made to reduce the principal amount of the loan outstanding, so that upon maturity only a small amount of the original loan remains to be paid. The conditions of the term loan are agreed upon by the borrower and the lender on an individual basis. Therefore, there is room for flexibility in the lending arrangements and the provisions for repayment.

Long-term debt funds may be obtained through direct loans from insurance companies or through the sale of bonds to groups such as corporate pension funds, other business enterprises, or the general public. A *bond* is a debt contract whereby the borrower agrees to repay a certain sum of money at some specified time in the future in exchange for a given sum of money today. A wide variety of conditions may make up the *bond indenture,* which is the legal contract giving the details of the arrangement between the borrower and the lenders. If the borrower fails to live up to the conditions set forth in the bond indenture, there will be a provision for some penalty which the bondholders may invoke. The penalty might be restricting the dividends paid to stockholders or having the bondholders take certain enterprise assets or even assume management of the enterprise.

Borrowing long-term funds is an important decision for the enterprise. Large amounts of money are involved. The projects to be undertaken are substantial in their impact on future business operations. Careful analysis of these projects and their financing is necessary. The responsibility of the finance department is to provide leadership and technical knowledge for this analysis.

Financing by leasing   The leasing of buildings and equipment has increased in importance in recent years. The *lease* is a form of long-term rental contract which an enterprise may sign to obtain the use of assets without owning them. When a lease is signed, the business obligates itself to pay money over a period of time.

One popular arrangement is the *sale-leaseback* agreement. An enterprise constructs a building to its specifications and then sells it to a financial institution such as an insurance company. Simultaneously it leases the building back for a long period of time. The result is that the enterprise has the use of the building without tying up its funds. The enterprise may then use its funds for some other purpose, such as increasing inventories, improving product lines, or opening new marketing areas. The advantages of leasing are apparent. However, there are also possible problems, such as the long-term payments required, questions as to tax liabilities, and final ownership of the property at the end of the lease.

Financing provided by owners   Besides funds provided by creditors, funds may be raised by selling additional stock in the corporation (or by acquiring additional partnership or proprietorship funds if these legal forms of organization are used).

The enterprise raises equity funds through the sale of either preferred or common stock. Compared with funds raised through debt, preferred stock has the advantage of not having to be repurchased, whereas the principal on long-term borrowing has to be repaid. However, interest payments on debt are a tax-deductible expense for the corporation, whereas dividends paid on preferred stock are not.

The sale of common stock by the corporation increases the corporation's ownership base. This not only provides funds but also increases the protection for debtors, thus making it easier for the corporation to borrow money.

Because of the relative infrequency with which a corporation sells stock, when this is done, the services of an investment banker are usually needed. Recall the discussion of investment banking in Chapter 15. An investment banker aids the enterprise's finance department by setting the price of the stock, timing its sale, achieving wide distribution of the shares if the stock is not being sold to present stockholders, and handling the legal requirements of the Securities and Exchange Commission.

In addition, funds are generated internally through profitable operations. Normally the enterprise will retain a portion of profits to finance future needs. The amount retained depends on the investment opportunities for the firm and on the amount of earnings that management decides to pay owners in the form of dividends. The determination of the enterprise's dividend policy is discussed later in this chapter.

The balance between debt and equity in an enterprise is discussed below in the section of this chapter on the capital structure of the corporation.

The dilemma of liquidity versus profitability

One way of summarizing the finance function in business is to say that the objective of financial management is to assure that funds are available to pay bills as they fall due and to promote profitability. In a very real sense these two objectives are in conflict. To avoid being short of cash to meet financial obligations, huge cash balances could be kept on hand at all times. In this case, liquidity would be extremely high for the enterprise. All bills would be paid promptly and cash balances would be available to meet any contingency, however remote. In achieving this objective of extreme liquidity, the finance department would ignore its other vital responsibility of promoting the profitability of the enterprise.

To maximize profitability the finance department might attempt to calculate the needs for cash so that cash inflow exactly matched cash outflow. No excess of cash would be on hand at any time. In this case, almost all funds would be invested in working assets such as accounts receivable, inventories, or plant and equipment. These working assets would be the basis for operations that would result in a large profit potential for the enterprise. There would be no idle cash in the bank account and no funds invested in low-interest government securities. This approach to financial management would promote profitability. However, it would subject the enterprise to the danger that liquidity might be impaired and that bills could not be paid on time.

In the dilemma posed for the finance department by liquidity and profitability, neither extreme is usually the best answer. Some funds must be invested in cash and near-cash assets to provide necessary liquidity. The credit rating of the enterprise must be maintained in good economic times. Then, when credit is needed, creditors will be willing to provide funds. At the same time, most of the enterprise's funds should be invested in assets which will be more profitable than cash and near-cash. The balance that financial managers choose between liquidity and profitability comes only after considerable analysis. Ultimately the decision will depend on whether top management as a representative of the owners prefers to "eat well" by having greater expected profitability or to "sleep well" by having greater liquidity.

THE FINANCIAL RESPONSIBILITIES OF TOP MANAGEMENT

The top management of a business enterprise includes those who head the main divisions, such as the vice presidents of marketing, manufacturing, finance, and personnel; the chief executive officer, who usually has the title of president; and the persons representing the owners of the enterprise. In the corporation the board of directors is elected by the stockholders to represent their interests and to determine the overall policies for enterprise operation. The partners in the partnership fulfill the function of the board of directors, and in the proprietorship the sole owner determines overall policies.

The members of top management have responsibilities for financial decisions in the following areas:

1. Financial planning and organizing for profits.
2. Allocating profits through dividend policy.
3. Determining the capital structure of the enterprise.
4. Deciding special issues, such as consolidation and merger proposals.

Planning for profits

In the area of financial planning for profits, top management has the overall responsibility for the effective use of enterprise funds. Investment proposals presented to top management should be analyzed for expected profitability and long-run benefits. If the financial affairs of the enterprise are not well managed, the owners stand to lose their investment. In the corporation the stockholders possess the legal right to control the management and to change it if financial results are poor.

The board of directors in a corporation is charged with specific legal responsibilities. These include observing the restrictions imposed by the corporation's charter, the state laws of incorporation, and the general prohibition against *ultra vires* acts (acts beyond the powers granted to directors). The board is required to act as a faithful steward of the enterprise's assets.

As an important part of profit planning the board of directors must select the enterprise's president and approve the selection of the financial officer. Top management must also see that the finance department is organized effectively. One of the best tools for enabling top management to evaluate and control financial operations is the budget. The use of budgets for planning, executing, and controlling the financial progress of the enterprise is discussed in Chapter 7.

Determining dividend policy

The determination of dividend policy is a second area of financial responsibility for top management. In the corporation the board of directors sets dividend policy. In the partnership the partners decide how much of the profits will be withdrawn. In the proprietorship the owner decides how much money to take from operations for private use. The basic question of profits distribution is the same for all legal forms of organization—what policy will best allocate profits to satisfy the owner's needs for income and also meet the enterprise's needs for funds for profitable growth and development. This discussion centers on the determinants of dividend policy for the corporation. However, the principles are generally applicable to the other legal forms of business organization.

The factors that top management normally takes into account in determining a corporation's dividend policy are as follows.

Amount of earnings Since dividends represent a distribution of the profits to the owners of the corporation, the amount of earnings is an important determinant of the level of dividends. Usually top management decides to distribute some proportion of earnings as cash dividends and to retain the balance for reinvestment in the enterprise. Although there is wide variation in dividend payout percentages, many corporations pay out between 40 and 60 percent of profits in dividends. Frequently, small or no cash dividends will be paid shareholders in the early stages of an enterprise's development when the need for funds is greatest. As the enterprise matures, dividend payments are usually initiated or increased.

Present level of dividends In the established enterprise in which a cash dividend policy is already in effect, the level of dividends paid by management is influenced by the level of dividends which was paid in the past. In general, managements tend to maintain the dividend rate which was paid in the previous period. Most cash dividends are paid quarterly. Directors are reluctant to increase the cash dividend rate per share from the previous quarter's payment unless they are fairly certain that the higher rate can be continued in the future. Likewise, directors are hesitant to reduce cash dividends even in the face of lower earnings if they anticipate that the drop in profits may be temporary. Directors do not like to incur the displeasure of stockholders that results from the reduction of cash dividends and from the decline in the market price of the corporation's stock which generally accompanies a lowering of cash dividends.

Profit prospects on new investments In deciding on the level of cash dividends paid to shareholders, top management also takes into account the opportunities for reinvesting profits in promising new projects. If reinvestment prospects are good, management may be reluctant to pay out as large a cash dividend as it would if good investment opportunities were not available.

Dividend practice in the industry The dividend policy which prevails throughout an enterprise's industry is another consideration for directors. The fact that a competitor has a particular dividend policy is not a sufficient reason for taking the same action. However, if the management of a corporation does deviate significantly from the dividend practice throughout the industry, there should be a reason for this variance. Otherwise, stockholders may be penalized by being offered a lower market price for the corporation's stock merely because it is "out of step" with established industry practice.

"Hello, Howard? The dividend from your feedlot investment arrived today."

Reprinted by permission The Wall Street Journal

Size of corporation's cash account   As directors consider dividend declarations, the ability of the corporation to pay the cash dividend declared is a factor which must be taken into account. This means that the finance department must manage the cash flows of the enterprise so as to be able to meet the cash dividend payments which directors authorize.

Use of stock dividends   An alternative to cash dividends is *stock dividends*. Instead of making cash dividend payments or increasing cash dividend rates, the management issues more shares of stock to shareholders. The immediate effect of these stock dividends is an increase in the number of shares in the hands of owners. However, assuming that management maintains or increases its present cash dividend rate, the long-run effect is to increase the amount of cash dividends, because cash dividends are paid on an increased number of shares. Individual stockholders have generally given a favorable reception to the distribution of stock dividends, although they have shown a preference for cash dividends when given a choice between the two.

One way in which top management can resolve the dilemma of trying to meet both the enterprise's needs for investment funds and the legitimate needs of stockholders for dividend income is to have a clearly stated dividend policy. Then stockholders will be aware of the guidelines under which management will operate in dividend matters. Stockholders may then design their individual investment portfolios to include the stock of those corporations whose dividend policy suits their needs.

Determining capital structure

An important responsibility of the board of directors is the determination of the capital structure of the corporation. The *capital structure* is defined as all the long-term funds which are committed to management's use. These long-term funds are supplied from two primary sources—owners' investment, both through the sale of stock and the reinvestment of profits, and long-term debt. The determination of the balance between long-term debt and owners' funds to finance the assets of the corporation is a tedious issue for corporate managers. At one extreme, if there is no long-term debt, there is no risk that the enterprise will ever be embarrassed by not being able to meet interest costs and principal repayments. This capital structure would provide a maximum of safety for the owners' investment. However, the sole use of ownership funds in the capital structure ignores the possibility of increasing the rate of return on the owners' investment when money is borrowed. This would occur if more is earned on the borrowed money than the cost of the interest paid. The use of debt with the expectation of increasing the rate of return on the owners' investment is called *trading on the equity.*

Does the advantage of trading on the equity mean that top management should continue to add more and more debt to the capital structure? By no means! The assumption of debt brings with it the obligation to pay interest on the borrowed money whether or not the enterprise operates profitably. Furthermore, at some time in the future the debt itself must be repaid. Thus, the advantage of an increased rate of profitability on owners' funds through borrowing is tempered by the risks associated with assuming the debt. The board of directors must determine the proper balance between long-term debt and equity. A final answer can be reached only after weighing the risks associated with debt against the possibly higher profitability returns.

Consolidation and merger proposals

The last area of financial responsibilities of top management that will be discussed here concerns special issues which arise from time to time during the operation of the business enterprise. These special issues include consolidation and merger proposals. A *consolidation* is the joining of two or more independent business enterprises into a new enterprise under a single management. A *merger* occurs when a smaller enterprise is taken over by a larger business enterprise. In either of these situations, top management must determine the value of its enterprise in relation to that of the other party to the merger or consolidation. The two basic techniques which management may use to determine the value of the enterprise are the valuation of the enterprise's assets and the valuation of the enterprise's expected stream of profits.

In using the technique of valuation of enterprise assets, the assets may be valued on the basis of *book value,* which is their worth based on original cost as shown in the accounting records; of *reproduction value,* which is what it would cost to replace the assets; or of *liquidation value,* which would be the value of the assets if they were sold. When the enterprise is valued on the basis of its *stream of profits,* management must estimate future earnings and then determine the value of the business based on the yield resulting from those earnings.

No matter what valuation techniques are used, a satisfactory merger agreement will come about only as the result of bargaining by both sides after considering all factors, financial and others. Each board of directors is responsible for protecting the interests of its own shareholders and for securing the best terms possible under the existing circumstances.

ORGANIZATION OF THE FINANCE DEPARTMENT

The broad financial policies of the board of directors set the boundaries for the finance department in the performance of its duties. Generally the finance department has considerable latitude for further decision making in matters of financial management. In a particular corporation the degree of responsibility and authority exercised by the finance officer and the finance department will vary, depending on such factors as education and experience, personality, and how much confidence the president and the board of directors have in the financial officer.

In the large corporation several executives will usually be directly concerned with financial management. Although there is a wide variation in the organization of finance departments and in the titles used from one enterprise to another, a typical finance department (see Figure 16–1) includes the following positions. The top finance officer, who may be titled *vice president for finance,* directs the overall activities of the finance department. There is a good possibility that the finance officer will be a member of the corporation's board of directors. Considerable time is spent in long-range financial planning and in the preparation of long-term budgets as well as in supervising the activities of subordinates. Besides the finance officer there will be a *treasurer* who is responsible for the custody of cash funds, securities, insurance policies, and other valuable papers. The treasurer's responsibilities include receiving incoming cash, approving cash disbursements, and preparing financial data for directors, stockholders, and the public. The treasurer's office also deals with banks and other lenders.

FIGURE 16–1

Partial organization chart of a finance department

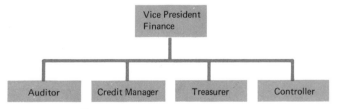

The *controller* is responsible for the accounting function in the enterprise both in keeping records and in preparing financial statements and analysis based on those records. The controller, as the chief accounting officer, checks on budget preparation and follows up to see how well the budget is adhered to by the various departments of the enterprise. The *credit manager* may report to either the treasurer or the controller. As head of the credit department the credit manager is responsible for deciding which customers shall be granted credit and the extent of that credit. The credit manager presses the collection of delinquent accounts and assists in the determination of overall credit policies. The *auditor* and the auditing staff check on the functioning of the accounting and control systems of the business enterprise. Company auditors not only verify the reported performance of the various divisions but may also act as staff advisers to make recommendations to management for the more effective operation of the enterprise.

Generally in large corporations the higher an executive is in the organizational structure of the finance department, the more time that executive spends in formulating long-range plans, with outside sources of funds such as banks, insurance companies, and investment bankers, and in working with the president and the board of directors. The finance department has a responsibility to work in a staff function with other departments to facilitate the production and sale of goods or services.

SUMMARY

The finance function is not only the disbursement of funds, the granting of credit, and the collection of receivables. In a more basic sense it includes responsibility for the profitable utilization of the funds available to management and the securing of funds at their most economical cost. The finance department in each enterprise should develop guidelines:

To determine the optimum size of the enterprise.

To select the best balance among different types of assets.

To provide the funds necessary to finance these assets.

To deal with the dilemma of profitability versus liquidity.

The dilemma of liquidity versus profitability refers to the need of the finance department to have sufficient cash on hand to pay bills as they fall due and yet to maximize profitability by investing funds in such assets as inventories or plant and equipment.

Members of top management have responsibilities for financial decisions in the following areas:

Financial planning and organizing for profits.

Allocating profits through dividend policy.

Determining the capital structure of the enterprise.

Deciding special issues, such as consolidation and merger proposals.

Dividend policy determination should take into account the present level of earnings now and the anticipated future earnings, the present level of dividend payments, the projected profits on new investments which might be made, the size of the corporation's cash account, and the prevailing dividend policy throughout the industry.

When determining the enterprise's capital structure, management must consider the desired balance between owners' investment and debt. Since creditors have a prior claim against assets, little or no long-term debt gives maximum safety for the owners but may result in a lower level of profitability for equity funds. Borrowed funds which are profitably employed can increase the rate of return on the owners' equity.

A consolidation occurs when two or more independent business enterprises are joined into a new enterprise under a single management. A merger occurs when a smaller enterprise is taken over by a larger one. In a merger or a consolidation, the two basic techniques which may be used to determine the value of the enterprises are the valuation of the assets involved and the valuation of the enterprises' expected stream of profits.

The top officer of the finance department is usually the vice president for finance, who reports to the president of the enterprise. Subordinates of the finance officer include the treasurer, the controller, the credit manager, and the auditor.

TERMS FOR REVIEW

finance function
term loan
bond indenture
lease

cash dividend
stock dividend
capital structure
trading on the equity

consolidation
merger

QUESTIONS

1. What are the major responsibilities of the finance department?

2. In what ways does an enterprise have control over the extension of credit to its potential customers? How is the enterprise limited in its control over the credit terms extended to customers?

3. List the sources of funds that are available to the large corporation. Discuss the different factors that management needs to consider in deciding on a specific source of funds for a particular project.

4. Explain the financial dilemma of liquidity versus profitability.

5. What factors should be taken into account in determining the amount of cash dividends to be paid to common stockholders?

6. a. How can the use of debt by the corporation increase the rate of return on the common stockholders' equity?

   b. How can the use of debt be detrimental to the common stockholders?

7. When a merger or a consolidation is contemplated,

what methods may be used to determine the value of the enterprises under consideration?

8. What reasons are given by management for the merger of Lykes Corporation into The LTV Corporation described on the first page of this chapter?

---

business briefs

IBM BUYS IBM

On February 22, 1977, International Business Machines Corporation announced an offer to purchase up to 4 million shares of its common stock at $280 per share. At the time, more than 150 million shares of IBM common stock were owned by investors.

Just before IBM's announcement its common stock was selling for $270 on the New York Stock Exchange. No sales commissions would be paid by shareholders who took IBM up on its offer.

The IBM offer expired on March 9, 1977. By that time over 2.5 million shares had been sold to IBM at a cost of more than $700 million. At the end of December 1976, IBM's balance sheet showed over $6 billion in cash and near-cash investments.

IBM's board chairman called the stock purchase "an attractive investment" for a portion of the corporation's funds.

The purchased shares were canceled and restored to the status of authorized but unissued shares of common stock.

1. *Why would IBM be willing to repurchase its own shares at $280?*
2. *What alternative use might IBM have made of the $700 million paid for these shares?*
3. a. *What benefits, if any, were there for the stockholders of IBM who did not sell their shares as the result of this offer?*
   b. *What has happened to the market price of IBM stock since the offer was made.*
4. *If you had owned IBM stock in early 1977, would you have tendered your shares to the corporation for $280? Why?*

THE BURDEN OF DEBT

In late 1974 Northwestern Bell Telephone, a subsidiary of AT&T, sold bonds at an interest rate of 10 percent annually. About the same time the Boston Edison and Detroit Edison electric companies had to pay over 12 percent for long-term borrowing. Some enterprises, such as Avco, Pan American, and Consolidated Edison, experienced serious difficulties in obtaining debt funds at any price either to finance operations or to pay off debt that was falling due. Commercial banks experienced an increase in demand for short-term loans, and the prime rate reached 12 percent.

At the same time that many business enterprises were having difficulty in obtaining loans, the stock market sank to a 12-year low, making it difficult for corporations to sell common stock to provide cash.

The 1974–75 recession and the simultaneous inflation put pressure on profits in many enterprises. This reduced retained earnings as a source of funds for business. In summary, enterprises which had traditionally counted on selling bonds or stocks or on retaining profits to finance expansion were in a real bind.

1. *What alternative could have been considered by top management in response to the financial problems facing business in late 1974?*
2. *What lessons from the economic and financial conditions of 1974–75 can be used by financial managers in the 1980s?*
3. *What dilemma faces the business manager who decides to limit expansion by not increasing the corporation's long-term debt?*

case

ZERO DUPLICATOR CORPORATION

Because of increasing demand for its products and good profit prospects, the Zero Duplicator Corporation's management decided to build a new factory in the Southwestern United States. The company's home office and existing manufacturing facilities were located on the outskirts of a large Eastern city and would continue to serve the company's Eastern customers.

Engineering estimates are that $5 million will be required for the new facility. Of this amount $1 million can be provided by reducing the corporation's cash and near-cash accounts, and $1 million will be generated within the coming year by retaining a large portion of expected profits in order to build this new plant. After consultation with investment bankers, management concluded that the remaining $3 million might be raised in one of the following ways:

1. Sale of 30,000 shares of 8 percent preferred stock with a par value of $100.
2. Sale of $3 million of 10 percent bonds with a sinking fund to retire the issue over ten equal annual payments, beginning the sixth year after the issue is sold.
3. Sale of 100,000 shares of common stock at $30 per share. The current market price of the corporation's stock is $35 per share. Investment bankers estimate that the new shares of stock could be sold at a price that would net $30 per share to the corporation.

For the year just ended, Zero Duplicator's balance sheet is summarized as follows:

Earnings before interest and taxes were approximately $2 million in the year just ended, or $1 per share of common stock after taxes. Management expected earnings to increase by at least 20 percent in the current year without the new plant facility. For planning purposes it is expected that income taxes will continue at about 50 percent of taxable income. Management feels that the prospects for growth are excellent. Three years ago the company successfully defended itself against a patent infringement suit by a large competitor. Although the duplicating equipment field is highly competitive, Zero's management believes that the company holds some key patents. At present, however, the company's share of the market is small.

No cash dividends have been paid to common stockholders since the corporation was organized a few years ago. The corporation's stock is rather closely held among members of management and a few wealthy investors, but some shares are held by the public. The stock is inactively traded in the over-the-counter market. No one person holds a controlling interest in the corporation's stock.

1. What key financial issues are involved in dealing with the immediate problem presented in this case?
2. Evaluate the pros and cons of each proposed method of financing.
3. What broad management policies should be considered in this case in addition to the financing of a new factory?

Current assets (including cash and near-cash)	$12,000,000	Current liabilities	$ 8,000,000
Net fixed assets	5,000,000	Common stock (2 million shares authorized, 1 million shares outstanding)	1,000,000
Other assets (including patents) ...	1,000,000	Retained earnings and other capital accounts	9,000,000
		Total Liabilities and	
Total Assets ..	$18,000,000	Net Worth ..	$18,000,000

Business in a
changing world

SECTION
SIX

IBM reports . . .

A highly automated distribution center controlled by a large IBM computer is going into operation at the IBM plant in Raleigh, N.C. The new center will reduce costs and improve operations while helping IBM meet expanded demand for terminals and other data communications products.

Products and parts are moved by the latest materials handling equipment, including more than a mile of power-driven conveyors. Up to 30,000 pallets and 300,000 small-parts locations are controlled by an IBM System/370 Model 168 computer.

The system also automatically produces up-to-date information for purchasing, finance and production control.

IBM display units are used to record data as materials enter the system. IBM printers prepare labels which are read by scanning devices in the conveyors to route parts and products throughout the system. Operator-controlled, high-lift trucks store pallets in 19,000 locations up to 45 feet high. Small-parts storage has five automatic stackers that place parts in 25-foot-high aisles.

From stockholders' quarterly report of International Business Machines Corporation

Computers

Computers

The development of electronic computers has created an industry which was unknown prior to the early 1950s. The computer has the ability to store and retrieve vast amounts of information, to make instant calculations, and to control many different operations. Major users of computers include business enterprises, governmental bodies, educational institutions, and the legal and medical professions. When the history of the mid-20th century is written, the development of computers will be considered as important as the development of nuclear energy and automation.

After studying this chapter, you will be able to answer the following questions regarding computers:

How are computers used by management?

What are the essential components of the computer?

What is involved in programming?

Which factors need to be considered in the installation of a computer?

USES OF COMPUTERS IN BUSINESS

The electronic computer has three distinctive data-handling features. These features are high speed, memory, and the ability to use programs. A *program* is a detailed set of instructions for solving problems or for performing operations on data.

High speed is achieved through the use of electronic circuitry. Electronic circuits operate at the speed of light, the speed at which electricity is transmitted. Computers can hold data and instructions in an internal memory unit which greatly speeds processing of data.

Computers can be helpful to the management of an enterprise in many ways. These include the speedup of routine record keeping, better control over purchasing and inventories, the design of more efficient production schedules and sales forecasts, and improved financial planning.

Record keeping

It is estimated that more computer time is spent in record-keeping applications than in any other single function. Records efficiently handled by computers include payrolls, inventories, purchases, customer records, and production schedules.

Payrolls When an enterprise has many employees, the preparation of payroll records is a considerable clerical task. Each employee's record usually includes gross pay; deductions such as income taxes, Social Security payments, union dues, health insurance premiums, and perhaps United Way contributions; net pay; and totals for the year to date. Payroll checks with reports for the various deductions have to be prepared frequently, in some cases weekly or twice monthly. Also, reports are usually prepared which allocate an employee's pay to a specific department or cost center. When the business enterprise has hundreds of employees, electronic data processing reduces payroll processing costs substantially.

Inventories and purchasing   To account for changes in inventories a record is kept of each item showing the number of units on hand and the cost of these units. The record must be updated each time an item goes into or out of the inventory. Even inventories in small enterprises may include thousands of different items.

Department stores and supermarkets today can tie their inventory control systems to the checkout cash register. The National Cash Register Company installs two different types of systems for this purpose. In the first system the cash register produces a magnetic-type cassette of coded data on items which have been sold. The cassette is then taken to the computer center to update inventory records. In the second system the cash register is electronically connected to the computer. Thus, when the checkout clerk enters an item on the cash register, the computer immediately updates the inventory position.

These inventory systems not only show changes in inventories but are also designed to provide calculations on optimal quantities to order and reorder points, to detect slow-moving items, and to forecast future requirements. This information is valuable to purchasing agents.

Customer records   Department stores, banks, insurance companies, manufacturers, and other business enterprises have long lists of customer records which must be accurately kept on a current basis. These records include statements of amounts owed by customers and payments received from them. Department stores use computers to keep records of charge accounts. Bank computers show current balances in individual accounts. Insurance companies use computers to bill policyholders. They also feed data regarding the personal circumstances of clients into a computer that is programmed to analyze the need for policy changes. Manufacturers use computers to keep sales accounts up to date. Computers have enabled business to handle individual customer records with increased speed and accuracy.

An account is maintained by the Internal Revenue Service for each individual and business taxpayer. A computer system reconciles individual tax returns with the wages reported by business enterprises, interest and dividend reports, and other sources of individual income. The comparison of these millions of reports is feasible only because of a nationwide computer system.

Production schedules   The complexity of coordinating personnel, raw materials, purchased parts, machine capacities, and orders for finished goods makes production scheduling a natural application for the computer. As discussed in Chapter 13, a computer program can be designed to determine the schedule which minimizes cost and most efficiently utilizes production resources. Without computers, production scheduling would be more time consuming and would probably use production resources less efficiently.

Information retrieval

Rapid advances in technical knowledge have made it more difficult to keep informed of developments even within a relatively narrow field. Business, scientific, legal, and medical data are now being stored in computer systems for use when needed. Codes enable the analyst or researcher to obtain an abstract of the information desired, along with references as to where detailed information may be obtained. Further advances in the field of information retrieval will make research more productive and less time consuming and will make greater amounts of information quickly available for decision making.

Computer information systems

Computers can do much more than process record-keeping data or retrieve information. Information systems in use today can handle all information relating to a business transaction. The computer can process a customer's order; check

"Our computer shows no record of you. We hereby declare you a non-person."

Reprinted by permission The Wall Street Journal

the customer's credit rating; fit the order into the production schedule; withdraw necessary items from inventory; calculate the cost of raw materials, labor, and overhead; provide shipping instructions; prepare the customer's statement; and notify the customer of shipment!

Real-time systems   When a computer system receives and processes data and affects the functioning of the environment *at that time,* it is called a *real-time system.*

There are different types of real-time computer systems. Continuous-process manufacturing industries, such as chemical producers and oil refiners, use real-time systems to measure and regulate the production process. Computers are programmed to control production from start to finish, with automatic feedback of the corrections needed. The response time required for the system to make changes in the production process may be less than five minutes.

An airline reservation system is another type of real-time system. A central computer maintains a record of all scheduled flights for a period of time into the future. Each reservation agent is able to communicate with the computer through a terminal to determine whether space is available on a customer-desired flight. When the customer makes a reservation, the computer records this in a memory unit and automatically reduces the number of vacant seats available on the flight. The entire process requires a response time of only a few seconds. We can expect expanded use of real-time systems with a wide variety of applications.

Time-sharing systems   An important development in computer systems is the concept of *time-sharing.* Time-sharing provides a number of users at different locations with access to a single computer for the simultaneous solution of different problems. This is possible because the computer switches from one user to another in a matter of milliseconds, which appears to the individual to be instantaneous. With time-sharing, one centralized, expensive computer can be used by many persons at a reasonable charge. Thus, the small business enterprise which cannot afford its own computer may gain the use of a computer through time-sharing.

Systems are now available for time-sharing by over 100 simultaneous users. Each user has a terminal through which electronic communication is made with the computer. These terminals have keyboards much like typewriters which give individual users access to the computer from any part of the country. The computer keeps track of each user's time on the system, makes corrections, and provides helpful hints to unskilled users.

Complex computation and business simulation

Computers can perform complex calculations which would require years of time to do by hand or by mechanical calculators. The computer's ability to store programs for repetitive use reduces the time and the cost required to solve problems. It is now possible to solve in minutes scientific and engineering problems which it was unfeasible to solve earlier because of the time or money required. At a cost of less than $50, computers can do calculations that it would take a trained operator with a desk calculator a year to do.

Computers can make calculations for mathematical models which simulate the real world. This information can be used for better management decision making. Through linear programming, mathematical models can be developed for a variety of business problems. These include achieving the optimum allocation of resources for an enterprise, developing efficient shipping schedules, and determining the most profitable combination of products for a multiple-product company. Linear programming applications may require thousands of repetitive calculations. Without the computer these calculations would be impractical.

An example of a complex problem which could be solved by a computer is the scheduling of work in a large machine shop that produces metal parts. Typically hundreds of machines are in operation and thousands of orders are in production or are waiting to be put into production. A computer could be programmed to schedule these jobs to minimize idle machine time, reduce lead time on orders, and insure punctual deliveries to customers.

An interesting application of computers is in the field of business systems simulation. A model of the enterprise and its environment is developed and programmed. Alternatives for management are fed into the computer. These include decisions on product prices, production levels, research and development spending, advertising budgets, and plant and equipment expenditures. The computer calculates the effect of these decisions on profits, market share, inventories, and financial position. Such a program is only a model of the real world. However, it can provide valuable insights to management on the possible consequences of different decisions.

COMPONENTS OF THE COMPUTER

Because of the variety of computer applications and the number of computer manufacturers, it is difficult to generalize about computers. However, all digital

FIGURE 17–1
Components of a digital computer system

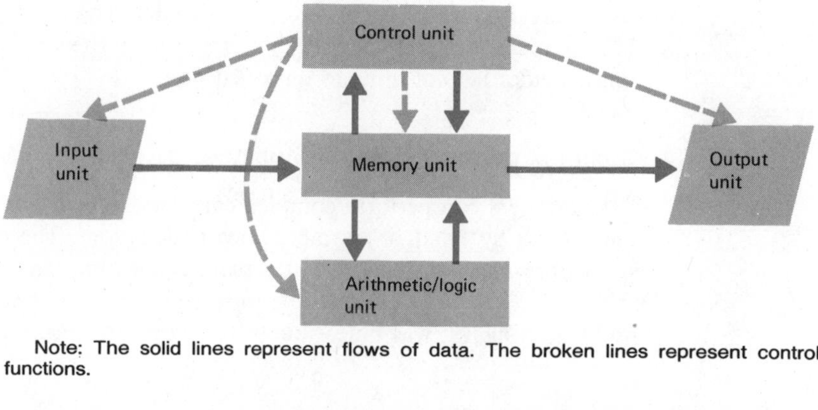

Note: The solid lines represent flows of data. The broken lines represent control functions.

computers[1] utilize the functions of data input, memory or storage, arithmetic processing, control, and output of information. The physical equipment which makes up a computer system is known as *hardware*. The program of instructions for the computer is called *software*. Figure 17–1 illustrates the components of a digital computer.

Input of data

The input unit of a computer system transmits data and instructions into the computer's memory unit. Operating instructions and the data to be processed are fed into the input unit through such means as:

1. Punched cards—such as school registration forms, utility bills, and time cards.
2. Magnetic ink characters—such as those on the bottom of bank checks.
3. Handwritten numbers—which are fed in by optical-character scanners.
4. Magnetic tapes and disks—for use with large quantities of data which require updating, such as payrolls.
5. Punched-paper tapes—such as may be prepared from cash register transactions.
6. Console typewriters—for such applications as individual use in time-sharing systems.

Whatever the means of transmitting data into the computer, the input unit translates it into a language, that the computer can electronically place in its memory unit for processing.

Memory unit

The memory unit functions as the storage and file cabinet of the computer system. This unit receives and holds not only the input data but also the program instructions for processing the data. The memory unit also receives and holds the results of the data processing from the arithmetic/logic unit before data are communicated to the user. When a very large mass of data must be stored, magnetic tapes or random-access files such as disks, drums, or punch cards can be filed outside the computer. Their data can be fed into the computer when needed.

Control and arithmetic/logic units

The control and arithmetic/logic units are the heart of the computer system. Based on the program of instructions, the control unit issues the directions

---

[1] The *digital* computer performs arithmetic operations on numbers. Because of its wide use in business data processing, the discussion in this chapter refers to the digital computer. Another kind of computer is the *analog* computer, which functions by measuring continuous conditions in physical variables such as temperature, pressure, voltages, or liquid flows. Analog computers are widely used for scientific and engineering purposes, with business use generally limited to such applications as the control of certain manufacturing operations.

career outlook

COMPUTER PERSONNEL

Computers can process masses of information rapidly and accurately, but only if they are given step-by-step instructions to follow. Because the machines cannot think for themselves, *computer programmers* must write detailed instructions called programs that list in a logical order the steps that the machines must follow to solve a problem.

Programmers usually work from problem descriptions prepared by a *systems analyst* who has examined the problem and determined the steps necessary to achieve the desired results. A systems analyst begins by determining the exact nature of a data processing problem. Then the analyst structures the problem logically, identifies all the data needed, and specifies how the data are to be processed. Analysts usually recommend which data processing equipment is to be used and prepare instructions for programmers. They also translate the final results into terms that managers or customers can understand.

Although not a universal requirement, a college degree is becoming increasingly important for systems analysts and programmers. Employers who use computers for business applications usually want college graduates with a background in accounting, business management, or economics. A background in the physical sciences, mathematics, or engineering is preferred for work in scientifically oriented organizations.

A growing number of employers are seeking applicants with a degree in computer science, information science, or data processing. Regardless of college major, most employers look for people who are familiar with programming languages. Courses in computer concepts, systems analysis, and data retrieval techniques offer good preparation for a job in the computer field.

The employment of computer programmers and systems analysts is expected to grow faster than the average for all occupations through the mid-1980s, as computer usage expands, particularly in firms that provide accounting and business management services and in organizations that are involved in research and development.

that will enable the other units of the computer to accomplish the given mission. The control unit monitors the instructions to determine that they are in the correct form and that the system is functioning properly. The control unit controls the input and output units, the transfer of data to and from the memory unit, and the arithmetic/logic unit.

The arithmetic/logic unit receives instructions from the control unit and data from the memory unit. The arithmetic portion of the unit performs computations on data, such as addition, subtraction, multiplication, and division. The logic portion of the unit makes comparisons, checks results, and may adjust instructions and computations.

The sheer volume of the calculations that can be done by computers is difficult to comprehend. The speed of computer operations may be stated in terms of MIPS (millions of instructions per second). Today large computers produced by Control Data Corporation have the capacity to calculate addition instructions at a rate of up to 15 million instructions per second (15 **MIPS**). At that speed, all the telephone numbers in the New York City telephone directory could be added up and divided by any other number in two or three seconds. Such speeds enable computer users to handle the flood of paperwork and calculations that are necessary to carry on business and scientific operations today.

Output unit

The output unit communicates the results of the computer's work in a form that can be useful to management. This is usually done through printed pages. High-speed printers are capable of printing 3,000 lines of 132 or more characters per minute. Computer output may also be in the form of punch cards or sheets for checks, invoices, or accounting statements. Output can be transmitted through visual display devices such as graph plotters, cathode-ray tubes (like television tubes), or microfilm. Voice reply systems are also available to receive information from computers.

PROGRAMMING

Programming provides the computer with a set of instructions to solve a problem or to carry out a series of operations on data. Careful steps are necessary to assure that the instructions are usable by the computer. The first step in the programming process is to analyze the data processing system. One must understand whether the computer system is capable of handling the assigned problem.

The second step in programming is to outline the necessary computer procedures in a logical fashion. At this point a program flowchart is constructed. Specific instructions in the proper sequence are necessary since the computer will process the data exactly as the program directs.

The third step in programming is to translate the program flowchart into a set of detailed coded instructions for the computer.

The final step is to test the program in order to eliminate errors. This debugging process is necessary to check the programmer's work. The output of information will be no better than the data put into the computer or the program used to process the data.

A simple flowchart for processing an office employee's payroll record is shown in Figure 17–2. As this figure indicates, computer programs must provide specific instructions to the computer under all possible conditions.

With more applications for computer problem solving and wider use of these applications, a number of packaged programs have been developed for users. These standardized programs are useful for operations that are the same from one business enterprise to another. In some instances these programs can be modified to fit individual needs.

FIGURE 17–2
Flowchart of individual payroll

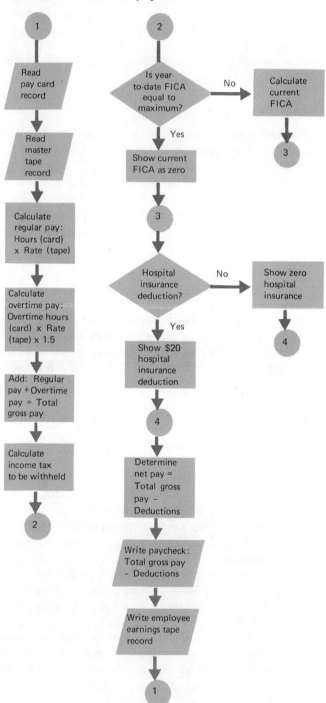

COMMUNICATING WITH COMPUTERS

The computer functions from directions given through electronic circuits which perform specific operations. Language understandable to a programmer must be translated into a language form which can be accepted by the computer. This operation is called compiling a program. Several compiler language systems have been developed to simplify the job of programming and to standardize computer operations.

There are two dominant compiler languages. FORTRAN (FORmula TRANslator) is an algebraic compiler that is particularly useful for research problems requiring the solution of mathematical or statistical formulations. COBOL (COmmon Business Oriented Language) is a commercial compiler that is useful for business problems involving file processing and record keeping. In all compiler languages certain words and symbols have specific meanings.

COBOL makes available a standard method of programming business data processing problems. Generally these applications have large files which require periodic or continous updating. Such business transactions frequently involve large volumes of input and output data but may not require elaborate processing. FORTRAN provides a means of programming scientific data and business models which require relatively limited input and output but have extensive processing.

A number of other computer languages are used, depending on the purposes to be served and the particular manufacturer's computer which is available. Two of these are BASIC and PL/1. BASIC (*Beginner's All-Purpose Symbolic Instruction Code*) is a language for solving numerical problems. It is sometimes used as a first step for students before they learn one of the more complex languages such as FORTRAN. BASIC is also useful in developing models to simulate business operations.

PL/1 *(Programming Language, Version 1)* is a language suitable for problems involving both business data processing and numerical scientific computations. It combines concepts from other computer languages, and it was developed because of weaknesses in some of the other languages. PL/1 was introduced in the mid-1960s, and it has been applied widely in fields which previously used FORTRAN or COBOL.

A person does not have to be a computer expert to make valuable use of computers. Today one can be trained in a short time to use computers for problem solving. In these instances the computer will have already been programmed for the questions which will be asked. By placing a simple code into the computer through the use of a typewriter-like terminal, the individual user can receive the answers to a variety of questions. These could include airline schedules, inventory positions, a customer's account or bank balance, and solutions to problems in mathematics, statistics, or financial analysis. Additional training and knowledge are required before one becomes thoroughly acquainted with computer operations. However, a minimum amount of training is sufficient to enable the business manager or the student to make the computer a useful tool.

CONSIDERATIONS WHEN INSTALLING A COMPUTER

Before a computer system is installed, management must come to grips with a number of problems. Two benefits may come from the installation of electronic computer systems. First, information is available faster and in better form than is possible without the computer. Not only are former data processing chores accomplished more quickly, but a variety of additional information is available for management use. Applications may come to light which were not envisioned when the computer was first installed. Volumes of data can be processed with computers which it would be impossible to process without such assistance. The second benefit that is normally expected from a computer installation is a reduction in the number of employees required for data processing. However, these employees will normally be higher paid and more skilled than the clerical employees whom the computer displaces. Different kinds of skills are required in computer centers than are typically required in many routine clerical positions.

Equipment choice

If a computer is to be acquired, several questions arise. Which computer is best for the enterprise's needs? What are the costs of computer systems from different suppliers? Will satisfactory service and software be available?

The management of the small business enterprise may consider acquiring one of the new smaller computer systems with packaged programs available. In deciding on an initial commitment to a computer, management should also analyze the advisability of acquiring an older model. Such a computer might meet the enterprise's needs effectively.

Equipment leasing or time-sharing

Management may decide to lease rather than purchase a computer. This is an important decision. Leasing may appear to be costly. However, the advantages of avoiding a large initial outlay for computer hardware and of reducing the risk that new computer technology will render present systems obsolete make leasing an alternative to consider.

Management may also consider using the time-sharing computer services discussed earlier rather than purchasing or leasing a computer. Terminals connected to a large computer center which can be miles away may provide the economy and flexibility necessary for the small or medium-size business.

Employee attitudes

A critical factor in determining the success or failure of a computer system is the attitude of employees toward the new development. Employee morale will be affected, beginning with the discussion of a computer installation. As indicated in Chapter 8 on human relations, good communication can do a great deal to reduce disruption of morale. When the computer system is installed, it is important that managerial employees as well as clerical and blue-collar workers be oriented to the system's purposes and advantages. If attitudes toward the use of a computer are not developed properly, there may be reluctance by employees to provide accurate data for input into the computer. Also, managerial employees may drag their feet in using the new information provided by the computer. Positive employee attitudes are needed for the success of a computer operation.

A variety of other problems must be faced by those managements which have new computer systems. These include the physical location of the computer, organizational relationships for computer personnel, and allocation of the cost of the computer system.

SUMMARY

The computer has made it possible to store and retrieve vast amounts of information, to make instant calculations, and to control many different operations. Computers are used in business to handle record keeping, payrolls, inventories, purchasing, customer records, production scheduling, and information retrieval.

In a real-time system the computer receives and processes data so that action is taken immediately to control the environment. Under a time-sharing system a number of users at different locations have access to a single computer for the simultaneous solution of different problems.

Computer applications are available for complex calculations and for simulation of the business enterprise's operations in order to test alternative management decisions.

The components of a digital computer system include units for input of data, memory or storage, control of operations, arithmetic/logic functions, and output of data.

Computers use programs, which are a series of machine instructions to accomplish a particular problem-solving task or to carry out a series of operations on data. Standard symbols are used in programming, and special languages have been developed to simplify the job of programming. The two dominant computer languages are FORTRAN and COBOL.

In selecting a computer system, management needs to consider not only cost but also the ability of the computer manufacturer to provide the needed service. Leasing rather than purchasing a computer has the advantage of not requiring a large cash outlay for computer hardware and minimizes the risk of being saddled with outmoded equipment in future years. Time-sharing, or leasing time on an existing computer installation, can provide the small or medium-size enterprise with a flexible and relatively economical way of obtaining the services of a computer.

When a computer is to be installed, it is important to orient employees to the computer's purposes and advantages since positive employee attitudes are needed for the success of a computer operation.

TERMS FOR REVIEW

electronic computer   *memory unit*   *program flowchart*
real-time system   *control unit*   *FORTRAN*
time-sharing system   *arithmetic/logic unit*   *COBOL*
digital computer   *output unit*
input unit   *programming*

QUESTIONS

1. Discuss the different ways in which computers can be useful to business enterprises.

2. Make an appointment with a member of management at a supermarket, a department store, a bank, an airline reservations center, or some other enterprise in your community that is using a computer.
   a. In what ways is the computer being used?
   b. What problems have been encountered?
   c. Are there plans to introduce additional uses for the computer in the future?

3. What are the advantages of a time-sharing computer system?

4. a. In what ways may data be fed into a computer?
   b. What means are available for the output of information from computers?

5. Why is attention to detail so important in computer programming?

6. If there is a computer center at your school, request a tour of the facilities. Determine what kinds of applications are handled by the computer and what compiler language is used.

7. Based on your study of this chapter and of current library materials, write a 300-word summary of the issues which management should consider in the process of installing a new computer system.

8. How could management justify the investment required for the new IBM automated distribution center described on the first page of this chapter?

business brief

MASSED MINICOMPUTERS

Even though some applications of huge computers have been made in controlling operations in continuous process industries such as oil refining and power generation, relatively little use of computers has been made in the direct control of typical manufacturing operations until recently. In the late 1960s a system was developed in which a large computer ran hundreds of different machine tools. However, this system created significant problems. When the large computer failed to function properly, all the machine tools quit working. Also, the high cost of the large computer made it difficult to justify such an operation unless many machines could be operated continuously.

Today minicomputers costing $2,000 or less are more powerful and easier to use than were large computers costing $100,000 just 15 years ago. Now a number of business enterprises have built new factories using dozens of minicomputers, each of which is programmed to control a single operation on one production machine. Production lines have been laid out to enable computers to control machine tools that measure, shape, and cut raw materials into component parts. Minicomputers test, inspect, and control automated transportation and storage systems within the factory.

Philip Morris developed a huge cigarette factory in Richmond, Virginia, designed around a minicomputer system. Two hundred million dollars was invested in this plant by its completion in 1977. Significant savings in labor and materials resulted from this investment.

General Motors uses minicomputers in its carburetor testing and materials handling system. These provide more flexibility than did an older computer system which tied more than 100 test stands together. The new system allows individual control over each test stand. It is designed to test the more complex carburetors required by today's rigorous government auto emission standards.

1. What advantages do minicomputers provide for factory managements?
2. What potential problems may be raised by the extensive use of minicomputers in the production process?
3. Contrast the application of minicomputers to new factories as compared with old plants and production lines.

Merrill Lynch reports . . .

Merrill Lynch conducts the largest international securities brokerage business of any U.S.-based firm, both in terms of revenues and in geographic coverage of world markets. The record $6 billion in international financings we managed or co-managed in 1978 made us a solid first in that area, too, among U.S.-based entities. In secondary trading in the Eurobond market, our volume almost doubled to a record $6.24 billion. The commercial lending portfolio of our London and Panama City merchant banks reached $350 million, up from $210 million at the end of 1977.

During 1978, a number of steps were taken to strengthen MLI further. We made significant additions of capital to our international underwriting and trading areas last year, and our marketing structure was reorganized geographically into Latin American, European-Mideastern, and Asian regions.

Last year marked a number of firsts for Merrill Lynch International. MLI became the first non-Japanese securities firm to receive permission for a second office in Japan, and opened its new Osaka office in late 1978.

In investment banking we were the managing underwriter of the first floating rate CD offering in the Bahrain capital market. MLI managed five offerings denominated in Kuwaiti dinars, becoming the first non-Kuwaiti manager of Kuwaiti dinar bond issues.

At the same time, Merrill Lynch International became the largest factor in the Singapore floating rate CD market. And we substantially increased our services to central banks around the globe.

From annual report of Merrill Lynch & Co. Inc.

Photo opposite, top: Traders of Asian dollar CD's in Merrill Lynch International's Singapore office keep pace with this rapidly expanding money market.

Photo opposite, bottom: In a novel and visible result of a financing, the City of Oslo installed heating pipes under certain streets to provide snowfree pedestrian malls and sidewalks. During the past year, Merrill Lynch International managed five issues in the Kuwaiti dinar market, including one for the City of Oslo.

Photos courtesy of Merrill Lynch & Co. Inc.

18

International business

International business

American business managers view foreign nations with their rising wages and increasing standard of expectations as excellent marketing opportunities. At the same time, U.S. markets are viewed aggressively by foreign manufacturers.

Business managers in Europe and the Far East are effective in international trade because of their long experience in dealing in many markets. Some foreign governments give subsidies for international trade and permit business practices which would be violations of the antitrust laws in this country. This has increased competition for American manufacturers of automobiles, motorcycles, textiles, television sets, and cameras. To meet these challenges American business is improving production and marketing practices at home and has established sales and manufacturing branches abroad.

After studying this chapter, you will be able to answer the following questions related to international business:

What is the importance of international trade to the United States?

What issues are raised by the development of the multinational corporation?

How do international monetary problems affect world trade?

What other barriers affect international business?

How does the U.S. government promote world trade?

What are the differences between management in America and management abroad?

THE ECONOMIC BASIS FOR INTERNATIONAL TRADE

The economic foundation for international trade rests on the concepts of absolute and comparative advantage.

Theory of absolute advantage

Absolute advantage means that a country should produce and sell those products for which it has lower costs than another country. Countries have lower cost advantages because of such factors as climate, natural resources, technology, capital equipment, and labor productivity. For example, because of its technology the United States has an absolute advantage over Colombia in producing computers. Because of climate and other natural factors Colombia has an absolute advantage over the United States in producing coffee. Therefore, according to the law of absolute advantage, the United States should sell computers to Columbia and buy coffee from it. The reverse is true for Columbia.

Theory of comparative advantage

In the early 1800s David Ricardo, an English economist, went farther than the concept of absolute advantage. Ricardo developed the theory of *comparative advantage* for international trade: A nation should produce those goods in which it has a comparative advantage over other countries even though it may have an absolute advantage in all goods.

This is illustrated in Table 18–1, which compares assumed amounts of time that are required to produce food and clothing in the United States and Japan.

TABLE 18–1
Assumed U.S. and Japanese production requirements for food and clothing

Product	In United States	In Japan
1 unit of food	1 hour	2 hours
1 unit of clothing	3 hours	4 hours

Stating this illustrative example in hours of labor required to produce units of food and clothing eliminates the complication of currency exchange ratios.

In this example the United States enjoys an absolute advantage over Japan in its production costs for both food and clothing. It costs Japan twice as much as the United States to produce food and $1\frac{1}{3}$ times as much to produce clothing. The law of comparative advantage states that under these conditions the United States should sell food (in which we have the greatest *relative* efficiency) to Japan and buy clothing (in which we have a *comparative* disadvantage) from Japan. Under the stated conditions, doing this would enable both countries to maximize their wealth and production. Unless the United States made purchases from Japan, Japan would be unable to buy U.S. products on a long-term basis, since eventually Japan would be drained of its currency reserves if it had no exports to sell us. The United States would have to buy goods from Japan as well as sell goods to Japan if its trade with Japan were to continue.

THE IMPORTANCE OF INTERNATIONAL TRADE TO THE UNITED STATES

Business enterprises participate in international trade by the export and import of goods and by the manufacture and sale of products in foreign countries.

The export of goods

In 1978 U.S. business exported $142 billion of goods to foreign countries. As illustrated by Table 18–2, American exports have increased over the years. Exports account for about 7 percent of our gross national product. The U.S.

TABLE 18–2

Merchandise exports and imports for the United States and U.S. gross national product, selected years, 1940–1978 (billions of dollars)

Year	U.S. exports*	U.S. imports	U.S. GNP
1940	$ 4	$ 3	$ 100
1945	10	4	212
1950	10	9	286
1955	14	11	399
1960	20	15	506
1965	27	21	688
1970	43	40	982
1975	107	98	1,529
1978	142	176	2,107

* Excludes military grants and aid beginning with 1950.
Source: U.S. Department of Commerce, *Business Statistics,* 1977; and *Economic Indicators,* February 1979.

Department of Commerce estimates that international trade provides jobs for 7 to 8 million Americans. Domestic industries which rely heavily upon export business include agriculture, automobiles, chemicals, and machinery.

The basic reason for exporting goods is that they can be sold profitably in other countries where there is a demand for them. The management of an enterprise may find it desirable to export goods in order to increase sales and to spread the fixed costs of doing business over more units of production. This lowers the unit cost of all the goods produced.

In some countries manufacturers find less competition in selling their products than in this country. Some overseas markets are less saturated than those in the United States. As standards of living increase in foreign countries, it is relatively easy for an enterprise to make large sales gains. For example, the Bureau of the Census estimates that about 90 percent of American households own refrigerators or freezers. Therefore, the growth of refrigerator sales in the United States is generally limited to replacements or to new family units. In foreign countries with rising incomes where only a small proportion of families own refrigerators, there should be a larger market for these appliances.

The import of goods

In 1978, imports of goods into the United States amounted to $176 billion. Traditionally merchandise exports have exceeded imports, as shown in Table 18–2. However, beginning in the 1970s our imports of goods from foreign countries exceeded our exports for 1971, 1972, 1976, 1977, and 1978.

The principal exports and imports of the United States for 1978 are shown in Table 18–3. There are certain commodities which the United States lacks

TABLE 18–3

**Principal commodity exports and imports of the United States, 1978
(billions of dollars)***

Exports	Amount	Imports	Amount
Agricultural products	$ 29	Coffee, cocoa, and	
Automobiles and parts	15	sugar	$ 5
Chemicals	13	Other food products	9
Civilian aircraft and		Automobiles and	
parts	7	parts	21
Computers and office		Chemicals	5
machines	5	Consumer durable	
Construction machinery	6	goods	15
Other industrial		Consumer nondurable	
machinery	13	goods	11
Consumer goods,		Industrial and com-	
except autos	5	mercial machinery	18
Electrical machinery	8	Iron and steel	8
Fuels and lubricants	5	Nonferrous metals	6
Iron and steel	2	Nonmetal industrial	
Nonferrous metals	3	supplies	4
Nonmetal industrial		Paper	4
supplies	4	Petroleum and	
Paper	3	products	40
Scientific equipment	2	All other merchandise	
Textile supplies	2	imports	30
All other merchandise			
exports	20		
Total exports	$142	Total imports	$176

 * Exports include military grant shipments and reexports.
 Source: U.S. Bureau of the Census, *Highlights of U.S. Export and Import Trade,*
FT 990, December 1978.

and must import. These include bananas, coffee, cocoa, diamonds, natural rubber, tin, and nickel. Other goods such as oil are produced in this country but not in sufficient quantity to meet demand. Some imported items have special prestige appeal, such as French fashions, perfumes, or wines.

Americans have also been heavy purchasers of foreign automobiles, steel, and other manufactured products. Some foreign manufactured goods, such as portable typewriters, shoes, textiles, and some electronic products, have been available at lower prices than comparable products manufactured in this country. The lower prices have been made possible by the lower wage rates paid foreign workers, more efficient production processes abroad, or lower costs for raw materials or parts. Figure 18–1 summarizes U.S. international trade by areas of the world.

DIRECT INVESTMENT ABROAD

In addition to buying and selling goods abroad, American business enterprises have invested substantial amounts in foreign operations. American private direct

FIGURE 18–1
U.S. exports and imports to other areas of the world, 1978 (billions of dollars)

Communist areas in Asia
$1

Japan
$13

Australia and Oceania
$3

Other Asia

Communist areas in Europe
$4

Western Europe
$40

Africa

$26

$6

$2
$37
$37
$25
$1

Canada
$34
$29

(less than ½ billion $)
$2

Latin America
$20
$2
19

U.S. exports
U.S. imports

Source: U.S. Bureau of the Census, *Highlights of U.S. Export and Import Trade*, FT 990, December 1978.

investments abroad reached a total of $168 billion at the end of 1978, compared with only $32 billion in 1960. Private direct investment in foreign countries is made from funds sent from the United States or from profits generated in American-owned foreign operations.

The incentive for investing abroad rather than expanding in the United States is the prospect for higher profits because of better market conditions, lower production costs, or lower taxes. American businesses have also invested abroad in order to avoid the external tariffs imposed by multinational groups such as the European Common Market.

To a lesser extent foreign-owned business enterprises have been investing in the United States. Foreign direct investment in the United States at the beginning of 1978 totaled $34 billion.

Multinational business corporations

In recent years the increased international investment by corporations has given rise to a new class of enterprises called the multinational corporations. A *multinational corporation* is a business enterprise which has significant operations in several countries. Not only goods but also capital, technology, and management move across national boundaries. The viewpoint of the management of the multinational corporation is worldwide rather than national.

Table 18–4 lists the ten largest U.S. industrial corporations based on 1978 sales. Notice the proportion of total profits derived by these giant enterprises from operations outside the United States.

Business managers in the United States are able to make decisions without being unduly influenced by the political boundaries of the 50 states. In the same way, decisions in multinational corporations are generally based on costs

TABLE 18–4
Ten largest U.S. industrial corporations, 1978 total sales (billions of dollars) and percentage of profits from international operations

Corporation	1978 sales	Percentage of operating profits earned abroad
Exxon	$65	52%
General Motors	63	8*
Ford Motor	43	48*
Mobil	37	46
Texaco	29	51
Standard Oil of California	24	54
International Business Machines	21	50
Gulf Oil	20	35
General Electric	20	22
International Telephone & Telegraph	19	48*

* From operations outside the United States and Canada.

and prices, regardless of national boundaries. Such independence raises questions regarding the economic power, effect on employment, and political allegiance and regulation of the multinational corporations.

Economic power   The assets, sales, and economic influence of many multinational corporations dwarf the total national product of many of the countries in which they operate. When a corporation dominates an industry or the whole economy in a country, both politicians and citizens become concerned.

Effect on employment   Some union leaders and politicians claim that multinational corporations export jobs when they build new factories in countries having relatively low-cost labor markets. However, Commerce Department surveys have shown that employment in the United States by multinational corporations has increased at a faster rate than employment by other American enterprises. There are employment problems in some industries as the nature of imports and exports changes. Even so, most economists believe that free trade and capital flows produce the greatest benefits to society.

Political allegiance and regulation   These questions regarding the multinational corporations have also been raised: What political allegiance should managements have to the countries in which they operate? What happens when the national interests of those countries come into conflict with the interests of the multinationals? How is it possible to regulate the multinational corporation, with its operations extending beyond the control of any single country? These questions and the alternative answers are being discussed now.

INTERNATIONAL MONETARY BALANCES

Balance of trade

A country's total imports of merchandise are subtracted from its total exports to determine its *balance of trade*. When exports exceed imports, the balance of trade is positive. When imports exceed exports, the balance of trade is negative or in a deficit condition.

Traditionally the United States has had a positive balance of trade. However, the picture changed as the United States experienced a $2.3 billion deficit in 1971 and a deficit of over $6 billion in 1972. The trade deficit in 1972 resulted from a strong increase in demand by Americans for foreign goods as our economy expanded. At the same time, foreign demand for our nonagricultural exports was limited by the slower improvement in business abroad.

In 1973 there was a marked improvement in our merchandise trade, with exports exceeding imports by $500 million. The devaluation of the U.S. dollar made our goods less expensive abroad. Also, agricultural exports increased. However, in 1974 the United States again had a deficit balance of $6 billion, mainly because of the increased cost of imported oil. By 1978 our merchandise trade deficit had ballooned to more than $30 billion.

Other U.S. international transactions

In addition to payments for merchandise exports and imports, there are a number of other funds flows into and out of a country over a period of time. Besides merchandise exports, transactions which result in monetary inflows for the United States include:

Receipt of income on U.S. assets abroad.

U.S. military agency sales overseas.

Other services sold, including travel.

Foreign official currency inflows.

Foreign investments made in the United States.

Besides merchandise imports, transactions which result in monetary outflows from the United States include:

Payment of income on foreign investments in the United States.

Direct U.S. defense spending overseas.

Other services purchased abroad, including travel.

Remittances, pensions, and other transfers sent abroad.

U.S. government currency transactions.

Private U.S. investment overseas.

Net funds outflows from the United States result in an increase in the number of American dollars held by foreign governments, banks, business enterprises, and individuals. The dollar deposits in European commercial banks, including foreign branches of American banks, are called *Eurodollars.*

In the past foreigners considered it desirable to hold dollars, since the U.S. dollar was considered the key currency for use in international trade. However, by 1970 the dollar had become less attractive to foreigners. The reasons included our country's balance of payments deficit; U.S. inflation, causing higher prices for American products abroad; and the U.S. government's budget deficits, which tended to cause further inflation.

Despite these problems and those discussed in the remainder of this chapter, the U.S. dollar is still an important international currency. Many nations still relate the value of their currency to the dollar and hold dollars as monetary reserves. This country's GNP is the largest in the world, and our exports and imports are greater than those of any other nation.

National currencies in international business

Business transactions in international trade are complicated by the problem of different monetary systems and by restrictions on the flow of funds among countries. Virtually every nation has its own monetary system. The U.S. currency is based on the dollar. But there is also the British pound, the Swiss franc, the West German mark, the Indian rupee, and so on for other nations. The complexity of the problem may be grasped by visualizing each of the 50 states in this country as having its own monetary system, with restrictions on the flow of funds into and out of the state.

When a U.S. business enterprise wishes to buy goods in another country, the manager must obtain sufficient foreign currency to pay the exporter. The American importer's exchange of U.S. dollars for the foreign currency is usually done through the importer's bank in the foreign exchange market. The units which one U.S. dollar will purchase in a foreign currency are expressed by the *foreign exchange rate,* which is the price of one currency in terms of the other. A bank's foreign exchange department can help the American business manager to minimize the risk of loss through fluctuating currency prices.

From time to time a country's central banking authority may find itself short of another country's currency. This may result not only in changes in foreign exchange rates but also in *exchange control.* Most governments exercise control over access to foreign currencies by their private citizens and business enterprises. Usually such exchange control is effected by holding foreign currencies in central government banks or under the control of government monetary authorities. Foreign currencies are then made available to private interests to settle international financial transactions. When a nation has a persistent outflow of its currency, the government may find it necessary to restrict private transactions during the period in which foreign exchange currencies are in short supply.

In 1946 the International Monetary Fund (IMF) was established by 39 countries, including the United States, to foster international monetary cooperation

"At least *he* still has confidence in the dollar."

Reprinted by permission The Wall Street Journal

and stability. The purposes of the IMF were to provide short-term international credit for nations, to facilitate consultation among nations on monetary policies and problems, and to achieve orderly changes in individual nations' currency exchange rates. Virtually all non-Communist countries now belong to the IMF.

The role of gold

In the past the ultimate means for settling international balance of payments deficits between nations has been the payment of gold by the deficit nation to the creditor nation. In the United States from 1933 through 1974 the government strictly controlled the possession of gold by Americans. During this period it was illegal for U.S. citizens to own gold for monetary purposes. It could be owned only for manufacturing items such as jewelry or for dental or medical uses. The U.S. government set an official price of $35 an ounce on its gold supply, which it used internationally for settling balance of payments transactions. Gold was also used domestically as a 25 percent backing of the U.S. Federal Reserve notes which formed the basis of the nation's money supply.

Following World War II the United States had a large monetary gold stock which reached a peak of $24.6 billion in 1949. However, in later years this gold supply decreased because of persistent balance of payments deficits. Gold outflows resulted from a variety of factors, including military spending overseas, government grants, American business investment in foreign countries, American tourists traveling abroad, and the lack of enough merchandise exports to overcome the total deficit. By 1968 our gold supply had dropped to $10.4 billion.

Gold tie to dollar cut   In 1968, following a $3 billion drop in the U.S. gold supply, Congress eliminated the 25 percent gold backing required for the Federal Reserve's money reserves. Thus the partial gold reserve on the country's domestic money supply was removed. However, the pressure of foreigners on our stock of gold continued. The dollar claims of foreigners built up because inflation in the United States made the prices of our goods relatively less attractive abroad and because we were importing more. In addition, America was spending huge sums overseas on military activities, especially in Southeast Asia. Finally, in August 1971, President Nixon announced that the U.S. government would no longer permit the dollars held by foreign governments, banks, and private interests to be freely exchanged into gold. Thus the international tie of the dollar to gold convertibility was cut. The United States is no longer tied to gold either domestically or internationally.

The international value of the dollar for business and individual transactions is a relationship to other nations' currencies rather than to gold. This is known as a "floating" exchange rate because it is free to move up or down rather than being fixed by the government at a particular level. An international system of currency exchange is being worked out in cooperation among government central banking authorities, the IMF, and other international bodies.

Gold markets   Two markets exist today for gold. The first market is the value placed on gold for international currency standards by the IMF. As the result of two devaluations of the U.S. dollar since 1971, the dollar is now worth

$42.22 an ounce of gold officially (although the U.S. government will not permit conversion of its gold stock into dollars at this rate). Other nations also state the value of their currencies in gold with the International Monetary Fund. The rules of the International Monetary Fund prohibit government central banks from buying gold or accepting it as an official international monetary settlement at more than the official price. Since the price of gold in the second or "free" market is substantially higher than the IMF price, virtually no international monetary settlements were being made for gold in 1979.

The second gold market operates outside the official monetary rates. Here the price of gold is determined by private buyers and sellers. In this free market for gold the metal is traded as a commodity, with its price responding to supply and demand at a given time. In December 1974, after more than 30 years, it became lawful for American citizens to own gold bullion. The price of gold on the free market was about $400 an ounce in 1979. Thus for private business enterprises and individuals a market for gold exists, just as a market exists for many other commodities, such as silver, copper, wheat, and pork bellies. Active gold markets exist in London, Switzerland, and other locations around the world. Many commercial banks and investment brokers in the United States buy and sell gold bullion and coins for their customers.

TARIFFS AND OTHER TRADE BARRIERS

Tariffs

A variety of trade barriers may be used by governments to restrict the movement of products from one country to another. *Tariffs*—taxes placed on imported goods—are frequently used to limit the flow of goods between nations. Tariffs may be a percentage of a product's value or a set amount per item. Tariffs are used to protect domestic industry from foreign competition or to produce revenues for the importing country. Protective tariffs attempt to save domestic jobs and production from lower-priced imports. They may be used to build up industry in order to enhance a nation's military self-sufficiency or to improve its international balance of payments.

Quotas

Quotas are designed to place an absolute limit on the quantity of foreign goods imported into a country. A tariff allows consumers to buy as much of an imported good as they choose but increases the price of the import. A quota restricts the quantity of foreign goods that are available at any price. Quotas are used primarily to protect domestic industries. Quotas have been used by the United States to protect American producers of such products as cotton and synthetic textiles. Sometimes quotas are the "voluntary" result of international agreements. Then an importing country does not have to resort to mandatory quotas.

Embargoes

An *embargo* is a prohibition against the movement of goods. An embargo
may be placed on products or nations. Embargoes have been used by the United
States for health and political reasons. Embargoes that are placed on goods
for health purposes include restrictions on the import of a variety of drugs.
There are also embargoes on agricultural products that may be infested with
insects harmful to domestic crops. Political embargoes have been used against
Cuba and other countries.

Aid to domestic enterprises

A government may provide assistance to domestic enterprises in order to
give them a competitive advantage over foreign producers. Direct export subsidies are sometimes used to encourage exports. Export subsidies, except for those
given to agricultural commodities, are generally contrary to international trade
agreements. However, hidden subsidies may be granted by allowing tax credits
for certain exports. In 1972 the U.S. Congress created a new corporate category
for tax purposes called the Domestic International Sales Corporation (DISC).
DISCs are entitled to defer taxes on 50 percent of their export income until
this income is distributed to stockholders.

Restrictions placed on imported goods tend to aid domestic producers. These
restrictions include health and safety standards and packaging, labeling, and
marking regulations. Usually requirements that foreign goods be prominently
labeled with the country of origin are meant to discourage consumers from
their purchase. Requiring foreign products such as automobiles to conform to
American antipollution laws places additional costs on foreign manufacturers.
On the other hand, not requiring this would place U.S. manufacturers at a
competitive disadvantage.

The U.S. Department of Commerce maintains district offices across the nation
to assist business in international and domestic trade. Government trade centers
exist abroad to encourage the sale of American goods in foreign countries.
Governments may provide financial support for research and development which
aids domestic industry. Governmental agencies may also give preference to domestic products in their purchasing policies. For example, U.S. regulations under
the *Buy American Act of 1933* require that domestic products be purchased
by governmental agencies unless their cost exceeds by a specified percentage
that of the same products when purchased from foreign sources.

Customs administration and technical regulations

Although a country's tariffs on imported goods may be low, using complicated
procedures to administer customs laws can restrict imports. Delays in the customs clearance process may arise in classifying and valuing goods to determine
tariff charges.

Most countries have antidumping regulations. *Dumping* occurs when an exporter sells a product in a foreign market at a lower price than in its home market. Most nations levy duties on dumped products to protect domestic industry.

Private barriers to trade

A variety of practices by private business enterprises can restrict competition in international trade. Licensing agreements, patents, and trademark laws can be used to divide markets. Cartels are encouraged by some foreign governments. A *cartel* is a group of business enterprises which agree to cooperate in the production and marketing of a product in order to fix prices and divide markets. A cartel reduces competition. Recall from Chapter 3 that the general policy of the U.S. government is to foster competition. Hence, cartels are illegal in this country.

INTERNATIONAL TRADE COOPERATION

The United States has generally sought to improve trade among nations through legislation and international agreements. This country's participation has come through the General Agreement on Tariffs and Trade, the Trade Expansion Act, the creation of foreign trade zones, and a variety of federal and international agencies.

The General Agreement on Tariffs and Trade (GATT)

In 1947, following World War II, the United States and 22 other nations met in Geneva, Switzerland, for the purpose of discussing international trade. Out of this conference came the General Agreement on Tariffs and Trade, which provided a means for reducing tariffs and other trade barriers among nations. Now more than 70 governments are participating in GATT, with continuing discussions on international trade problems and tariff reduction.

The Trade Expansion Act of 1962 (TEA)

In 1962 President Kennedy signed the Trade Expansion Act. This empowered the president to negotiate lower tariffs with other nations over a period of five years and to enter into international marketing agreements with foreign governments. The legislation was designed to stimulate demand for U.S. goods abroad and to reduce barriers to international trade in general. The TEA led to what was called the Kennedy Round of tariff negotiations by the member nations of GATT from 1964 to 1967. The Kennedy Round resulted in an average tariff reduction of 35 percent on a wide range of industrial products.

Foreign trade zones

As the result of 1934 legislation certain areas of the United States may be designated as *foreign trade zones.* Foreign goods or raw materials may be imported from these zones without being subject to tariffs or quotas, provided that the goods are to be exported from the United States at a later time. This means that a U.S. manufacturer operating in a foreign trade zone can import raw materials or component parts, complete the product, and reexport the goods without having to pay the usual U.S. tariffs. The purpose of the foreign trade zones is to stimulate international trade by American enterprises. The zones make American manufactured goods more competitive by taking advantage of lower-cost foreign raw materials or parts. There are 40 approved foreign trade zones in the United States, located in such cities as New York, San Francisco, Seattle, New Orleans, Kansas City, Toledo, Honolulu, Little Rock, and McAllen, Texas. The foreign trade zones have facilities for storing, inspecting, manufacturing, and repacking goods. Hundreds of business enterprises make use of these foreign trade zones.

Free ports and free trade zones exist in approximately 40 countries, usually at seaports. Many manufacturers use these areas to repack goods for shipment in smaller quantities to customers in nearby areas.

Federal and international financing agencies

A variety of federal and international agencies have been created to help finance international business projects.

The *Export-Import Bank (Eximbank),* established in 1934, is the oldest international finance agency of the U.S. government. Eximbank has financed loans totaling several billion dollars for American exports of goods such as production equipment, agricultural machinery, basic raw materials, and commodities. Eximbank provides financing for export projects where business has difficulty obtaining financing from private sources such as commercial banks. This agency also participates with commercial banks in loans and provides insurance for political and business risks.

The *Agency for International Development (AID)* is a U.S. government body which has jurisdiction over most government foreign economic aid programs. The agency encourages private American participation in foreign economic development. It provides guarantees against political and economic risks for private investments in more than 70 less developed countries. AID also has joint ventures and loan programs to foster the economic development of less developed countries by private and public organizations.

International agencies organized for the purpose of facilitating trade and international development include the global organizations of the *International Bank for Reconstruction and Development (World Bank),* the *International Development Association,* and the *International Finance Corporation.*

Regional international agencies for economic development include the *Inter-*

American Development Bank, the *Asian Development Bank,* the *European Investment Bank,* and the *African Development Bank.*

DIFFERENCES BETWEEN MANAGEMENT IN AMERICA AND ABROAD

Along with the monetary problems, tariffs, and other barriers to trade already discussed, there are additional factors to be considered in the management of foreign operatiorts. These factors can be grouped into five categories: government relations, financing commercial transactions, language and cultural barriers, relations with the home office, and the training of managers who go abroad.

Government relations

Business enterprises operating in the United States are subject, of course, to all the laws and regulations of municipal and state governments and the federal government. The business manager is usually well acquainted with these domestic regulations, including laws on taxes, labor relations, patents and trademarks, licenses, and health and safety. When an enterprise operates abroad, the manager must conform to U.S. laws and also to the regulations of foreign governments.

Areas of government regulation for international business include export and import restrictions, tariff regulations, health and sanitation laws, packaging and labeling requirements, and national security policies. As was already discussed, international monetary differences and currency exchange restrictions are important in most countries.

Besides laws on imports and exports, foreign governments affect American enterprises through regulations on manufacturing and marketing operations. When Americans move into other countries to establish factories and sales branches, it is *they* who are considered foreigners, not the local governments or people. Foreign governments are generally interested in having their economies developed without being dominated by American business. Increasingly there have been government restrictions on removing profits from the country in which they are generated. Economic nationalism is important not only in such areas as Africa, Latin America, and the Middle East but also in such long-industrialized nations as Great Britain, France, and the United States. In the United States public identification is now required of purchasers of more than 5 percent of a corporation's stock. The purpose of this law is to determine the extent to which foreign investors may have acquired U.S. enterprises.

Foreign Corrupt Practices Act of 1977   In 1974 the Securities and Exchange Commission began an inquiry into bribes of foreign officials by U.S. corporations. There was concern about attempts by business to influence the legislation of foreign countries and about the methods used by business to obtain contracts from foreign governments. As a result of the SEC study, executives from more than 400 U.S. enterprises admitted having made illegal or questionable payments abroad.

Congressional committees condemned bribes overseas by American business not only because they were unethical but also because they hurt business by eroding "public confidence in the integrity of the free market system." Congressional committees pointed out that business bribes overseas created foreign policy problems for the United States. Disclosures that U.S. corporations had bribed government officials in Italy, Japan, and the Netherlands had resulted in negative publicity for the United States.

In late 1977 Congress passed the *Foreign Corrupt Practices Act,* which was signed by President Carter. The act banned corporate payments to foreign politicians or officials for the purpose of winning contracts from other governments or of influencing legislation. The act did not mention small payments made to minor officials in order to speed up routine procedures such as license applications and customs clearances.

The act provided criminal penalties with fines of up to $1 million for corporate bribery. Corporate officials can be fined up to $100,000 and be sentenced to a maximum of five years in prison. Enterprises are required to maintain records to show cash payments abroad.

Risk of investing abroad   In addition to being exposed to the business risks described in Chapter 2, American capital invested abroad is exposed to the risk of expropriation by foreign governments. In some instances, when American business assets are taken over by a foreign government, the owners are compensated for their losses. In other cases no compensation is given. In 1960 Fidel Castro's revolutionary Cuban government expropriated without compensation all Cuban properties owned by American companies. In 1971 the government of Chile expropriated properties of some American corporations. Some of the international oil companies' production facilities in Africa and the Middle East have been taken over by the host governments.

There is some protection for private investors who lose funds in international trade and investment. The Foreign Credit Insurance Association, made up of private insurance companies, cooperates with the Export-Import Bank to provide insurance coverage for the political and commercial risks of doing business abroad. This insurance covers losses due to expropriation by a government, inability of the buyer to pay for merchandise, civil war, or cancellation of an import license prior to the arrival of goods.

Financing international commercial transactions

Most international commercial transactions are financed by bills of exchange and letters of credit. Relatively little international trade uses direct cash payment or trade credit, as is customary in the United States.

Bills of exchange, or *drafts* as they are sometimes called, are the most commonly used method of payment in international commerce. A bill of exchange is drawn by the exporter of goods. It calls upon the importer to accept the obligation to pay a specified amount of money at a stated time. The bill of exchange becomes a *trade acceptance* when an acknowledgment of the obligation is written across its face by the importer.

The three parties to a draft transaction are:

1. The *drawer,* who is the person executing the draft (the exporter or seller).
2. The *drawee,* upon whom the draft is drawn and who is required to meet the terms of the document (the importer or buyer).
3. The *payee,* who is the party to receive payment (the exporter or his bank).

Drafts can be used in various ways in business transactions. A *sight draft* calls for the drawee to pay the draft upon its presentation (on sight). A *time draft* calls for payment on a specified future date. The acceptance of a time draft obligates the drawee to pay the draft when it falls due. When drafts are drawn upon a bank and are accepted by the bank instead of by an importer, they become *bank acceptances* instead of trade acceptances. The effect of bank acceptances is to substitute the credit of the bank for the credit of the importer.

A *commercial letter of credit* is a document issued by a bank for an importer of merchandise. The terms and requirements by which payment will be made to the exporter are set forth in the letter of credit. The exporter is authorized to draw drafts on the bank. The bank agrees to honor the drafts if all the requirements are met. The business enterprise which is importing the merchandise arranges to pay the bank for the drafts that the bank accepts. For this service the bank receives a commission for the letter of credit and handling charges for the drafts. These are paid by the importer. If the drafts are time drafts, the importer must pay an interest charge.

Language and cultural barriers

Language differences   The English language is widely used throughout the world. However, it is desirable to communicate with nationals, local authorities, and customers in their own language. The resident manager must be able to think in the local language so as to be able to communicate effectively and to understand others. An unwillingness to speak any language other than English may limit a manager's effectiveness in a foreign assignment.

Cultural barriers   Cultural differences are an obvious but important consideration in the management of foreign operations. In many instances the office and plant facilities of foreign operations will be similar to those in the United States. However, the cultural values relating to business, the individual, work, and social customs may be very different.

Time will be required before an understanding is gained of social customs abroad. The formalities of Oriental politeness, the different value placed on time and on the preliminaries to business discussion in the Middle East, the different hours of work and dining, and a more reserved attitude toward strangers—these are examples of differences from American customs that may be encountered abroad. The newcomer to international business is well advised to learn the prevailing local customs in a friendly but not overly aggressive way.

The ethical concepts which prevail in this country are not necessarily followed abroad. Bribery, illegal division of markets, rigged bids, and payoffs are not totally absent from our business scene, but they are not advocated by business leaders here and they are considered scandalous when discovered. The manager who deals in foreign business operations may encounter different systems of values and different practices. This does not mean that unethical deviations from American standards must be accepted. Indeed, confidence in the word of Americans abroad is an advantage over the long run.

Relations with the home office

The problems which arise out of the relationship between the U.S. home office and foreign operations are of the same type as those which exist between the home office and decentralized operations within the United States. However, complications are caused by the greater distances between home offices and foreign operations, relations with foreign governments, and variations in the business and cultural environment abroad. The American manager of a foreign operation must be able to deal with a home office which lacks an understanding of the problems faced in the field. At the same time the manager must deal with foreign nationals and governments that have little understanding or interest in home office policies and problems.

Because of these complications, the manager abroad should have as much autonomy as possible to meet unusual circumstances. Management in the foreign office should be provided with guidelines or limits on its freedom of action. Management in the home office should try not to interfere as long as the foreign operations are being conducted under these guidelines and are fulfilling overall forecasts. At least one key person in the home office should have had sufficient foreign experience to appreciate the circumstances faced abroad.

Laws abroad and dealings with foreign governments will present problems that differ from those prevailing in this country. Managers on the scene should be permitted to cope with these problems with a minimum of interference from the home office. Often there are sound reasons for dealing differently with governments overseas than with government in this country. In overseas operations it is often virtually impossible to separate economics from politics.

Even though a substantial amount of local autonomy is desirable for foreign operations, overseas offices can benefit from the systems and procedures that have been developed in this country. Some modification may be required before these are placed in effect abroad. Usually it is desirable to issue a written policy statement outlining the decisions which can be made by managers abroad, especially regarding financial commitments. In some countries a written definition of the authority of corporate managers is required by law. An overseas manager must usually get permission from the board of directors before changing product lines, making large capital expenditures, or borrowing money in excess of a certain amount.

The foreign manager is responsible for keeping the home office informed of important developments abroad and for explaining events which may not be understood at home. The importance of good communication, stressed in Chapter 8, should be reemphasized in international business. Despite improved means of communication and jet airlines systems which make London, New York, and Tokyo only hours apart, these areas are still great distances apart in many business practices and cultural mores. Furthermore, foreign business operations are not always located in big cities, which are international centers of language and culture. Business may also be done in relatively isolated areas with inadequate communication and transportation facilities.

Communications between the home office and foreign branches are further complicated because of the difference in time zones around the world. As the manager is closing the office in London at 4:00 P.M., the members of the home office staff in San Francisco are just finishing their morning coffee and rushing off to their offices at 8:00 A.M. that day, while in Tokyo the time is 1:00 A.M. the next day.

Importance of good management

Despite the emphasis on the differences between managing in this country and managing abroad, many of the same concepts and functions of management apply both at home and abroad. The basic managerial function of directing the work efforts of employees to achieve effective results is necessary throughout the world. The same importance is placed upon good planning, organization, staffing, and control. The changed economic, political, and social environment adds a new dimension to the manager's job. The manager who is effective in this country will find that many of the skills used here apply to the foreign assignment.

TRAINING FOR OVERSEAS ASSIGNMENT

Before a domestic manager accepts a foreign assignment, the executive and the executive's spouse will want to know the duration and the compensation of the assignment, something about the local living conditions, and something about the local educational system if they have children. The manager who accepts a foreign assignment should have some special training before going abroad. For the manager this means preparation for responsibilities in a different business climate. For the manager's family it means preparation to accept new customs of living and orientation into the conditions that will be encountered at the new location.

In the area of job preparation the manager may be given special training in marketing, production, or finance to relate this knowledge to the conditions anticipated abroad. Before the executive's departure he or she should be given a thorough briefing in the relationships which will exist with home office officials and in the degree of decision-making latitude that can be exercised.

Special foreign language training should be provided in the United States if English is not the native tongue in the foreign location. A desirable policy is to include the executive's spouse in language training for good adjustment to the new location.

Representatives of American business should have an understanding of the important social, political, and economic issues that confront the United States. The ability to discuss intelligently such subjects as foreign policy, economic conditions, and the private enterprise system is vital. In many respects Americans living abroad *are* the United States to those foreign nationals with whom they come in contact.

BUILDING THE WORK TEAM ABROAD

Upon arriving at the new location, the manager will be faced with the responsibility of selecting, training, and directing the efforts of the management team. When the enterprise already has an established base of operations, this job is made easier, since an organization already exists. Even so, however, the new manager will have to review the situation carefully and may wish to make changes after understanding local circumstances. This is particularly true if the manager has been sent to correct a condition which the home office believes could be improved.

In some instances the executive will have to select personnel and organize business operations. There may be some American specialists to assist. However, the key to successful future operations is the proper selection, training, and treatment of local nationals.

In building a new organization, the manager's first step will probably be to select a national who thoroughly understands how to get things done in the country. This person can accomplish much that the new manager cannot and can act as a valuable adviser.

Other key appointments will be persons to handle buying and marketing functions in the enterprise. These assignments should go to people who have experience in these fields in the country and are fluent in the language and aware of local customs. A good legal adviser can make the local regulations understandable and can offer guidance on how to avoid legal problems.

A long-range plan should be developed to replace the enterprise's American managers with local personnel. This does not mean that no Americans will be permanently stationed abroad. However, over the long run not all key executive personnel positions should be staffed with Americans. The new manager should establish employee training programs to improve the skills of workers and to develop technical and managerial persons. The morale of employees will be higher if the nationals have an opportunity to fill management positions. In summary, the success of U.S.-based enterprises abroad depends largely on the success of American executives in putting together an effective organization of foreign nationals who understand the objectives and methods of good management.

Organization for foreign operations

The organizational structure of enterprises involved in international business is similar in many instances to that of enterprises operating only in the United States. When an enterprise has a functional departmental organization, the factory manager abroad may report directly to the vice president for production in the home office. Similarly, the sales manager for foreign products may report to the vice president for marketing or to the general sales manager. However, the organization may have a vice president for foreign operations to whom foreign managers report. When an enterprise has multinational operations, it may be desirable to decentralize those operations on a geographic basis.

Some firms which have been successful in international business have created separate organizations, with their own presidents and operational autonomy. This arrangement is especially beneficial when foreign operations have passed the initial stages of development. Then the necessary staff personnel and organization required for independent operation can be economically justified. Separate organizations have advantages of flexibility and operational mobility as well as some tax advantages. When an enterprise separate from its parent company is formed, control by the parent enterprise is maintained through stock ownership. The use of patent and trademark license agreements also provides a means of control by U.S. enterprises over their relatively independent foreign operations.

SUMMARY

The economic basis of international trade involves the concepts of absolute and comparative cost advantage.

While many American business managers view foreign countries as markets for their products, foreign manufacturers also aggressively view the United States as a great market for their products.

Although exports of merchandise make up only about 7 percent of our gross national product, these transactions provide job opportunities for 7 to 8 million Americans.

The incentives for American private direct investment abroad include:

The prospect for profits stemming from better market conditions.

Lower production costs.

Lower taxes than exist in the United States.

Avoidance of external tariffs imposed by such multinational groups as the European Common Market.

The development of multinational corporations with significant operations in several countries raises a number of key issues.

A country's balance of trade is determined by subtracting its imports of merchandise from its exports. The balance of trade is part of a broader calculation called a nation's international balance of payments. This includes all funds that flow into and out of a country over a period of time.

The U.S. dollar is no longer tied to gold convertibility either domestically or internationally. The U.S. government will not permit conversion of its gold stock at the official rate of $42.22 an ounce.

Barriers used by countries to restrict trade include tariffs, quotas, embargoes, and delays in customs clearances.

The United States has acted to improve trade among nations by participating in the General Agreement on Tariffs and Trade, the Trade Expansion Act, the creation of foreign trade zones, and a variety of federal and international agencies to help finance world trade.

Most imports are financed by bills of exchange and letters of credit. Bills of exchange may become either trade acceptances or bank acceptances.

American managers sent abroad need a knowledge of the regulations, language, and customs of the country in which they are located. Also, the American manager overseas must deal with a home office which may lack an understanding of the problems faced in the field. When building a work team abroad, it is desirable to train local nationals for management responsibilities as soon as possible.

TERMS FOR REVIEW

exports
imports
multinational corporation
balance of trade
foreign exchange rate
*International Monetary
    Fund (IMF)*

floating exchange rate
devaluation
tariff
quota
embargo
expropriation
bill of exchange

trade acceptance
bank acceptance
commercial letter of credit

QUESTIONS

1. Explain the concept of comparative advantage, using a different example than that given in the text.

2. *a.* Using the most recent *Survey of Current Business,* determine the amount of exports and imports in the following industries:
    1. Automobiles and parts.
    2. Iron and steel.
    3. Chemicals.
    4. Agricultural products.

   b. By examining current periodicals, establish what positions these domestic industries have taken toward international trade questions such as U.S. import quotas and customs duties.

3. Why do U.S. business enterprises establish manufacturing or sales branches overseas?

4. What issues are raised by the development of the multinational corporation?

5. What are some barriers to world trade?

6. What possible problems may a business enterprise encounter in foreign trade or in manufacturing operations overseas that would not normally be encountered in the United States?

7. Explain the use of the bill of exchange as a means of payment for an international transaction.

8. In 1971, U.S. imports exceeded exports. It was the first time since 1893 that this country had a trade deficit. List some of the different actions that the United States could take to correct this imbalance of trade.

9. Based on your study of library materials and this chapter, prepare a 300-word summary analyzing the following statement: "More import controls and tariffs are needed to protect such American industries as textiles, steel, and automobiles against foreign competition."

10. What are the advantages to the U.S. economy and to consumers of reducing trade restrictions throughout the world? What disadvantages may result for some industries in the United States from freer world trade?

11. What advantages are there for Merrill Lynch's stockholders and customers by having international operations as described on the first page of this chapter? What potential problems could arise because of these operations?

business briefs

PEPSI, DA!

The soft drink division of PepsiCo Inc., Pepsi-Cola, is aggressively expanding its international markets in such far-flung locations as Russia and the Middle East. In recent years this has resulted in gains of 20 to 25 percent annually in international sales. Despite this campaign, Coco-Cola still leads Pepsi in soft drink sales abroad by two to one.

In 1974 Pepsi obtained permission from the Russians to sell soft drinks in the Soviet Union. Two processing plants were in production in 1978, with three more under construction. Negotiations were under way to open five more plants in Russia. Eventually Pepsi's management hopes to operate 25 plants there.

Marketing executives see a huge market for consumer goods in the Soviet Union. Pepsi's two plants have been selling about 144 million bottles annually out of an estimated 2 billion bottles of soft drinks consumed in Russia. However, Pepsi officials believe that the potential demand for soft drinks there is 72 billion bottles annually. This leaves plenty of room for growth.

Pepsi also has about 50 plants in the Middle East. The per capita consumption of soft drinks in the Middle East is estimated at 280 eight-ounce cans per year. This compares with 480 cans annually in the United States and about 100 cans outside the United States.

A factor which spurs enterprises such as Pepsi to look overseas for expansion is the aging population of the United States. At present there are about 49 million Americans in the 13- to 24-year age group. By 1985 this age category will drop to 45 million. This teenage to young adult group consumes more than 800 cans of soft drinks per person annually.

1. *What reasons contribute to Pepsi's aggressive moves to build soft drink plants overseas?*

2. *Do you see any possible problems for PepsiCo's management from this overseas expansion?*

3. *Should the U.S. government encourage enterprises such as PepsiCo to move into underdeveloped countries where more basic economic development or food production might be desirable?*

U.S. BUSINESS IN SOUTH AFRICA

In the late 1970s many American-based multinational corporations were faced with the question of what to do about their operations in South Africa. The issue is important because of South Africa's policy of apartheid, or separation of the races.

Many critics of U.S. corporations operating in South Africa have called for a pullout by American businesses because of the South African government's racial policies. American groups with this attitude include the NAACP and a number of church and educational bodies. Some of these antiapartheid groups have elected to sell any stocks they may hold of U.S. corporations doing business in South Africa.

Another position of antiapartheid groups is to urge American corporations to work actively for change in South African policies. The Rev. Leon Sullivan, a black minister and a director of General Motors, has prepared a code subscribed to by more than 100 American corporations. This code includes a commitment to equal employment opportunities; comparable pay for all employees in the same jobs; apprenticeship and management training programs for nonwhites and their promotion to higher positions; total desegregation of company eating, work, and toilet facilities; support of nonwhite union efforts; and improvement of employees' living conditions.

Over 300 U.S. corporations have invested an estimated $1.5 billion in South Africa. These include Ford, General Motors, Exxon, Mobil, Goodyear, Firestone, and IBM. Examples of attempts by multinational corporations to reduce apartheid are numerous. Ford has established an apprenticeship program for blacks, consults with nonwhite employees on plant problems, recognizes black unions, has helped some nonwhite employees build their own homes, and has made several other moves to desegregate facilities and programs. IBM has a long-standing policy of equal pay for equal work. Mobil has training and promotion programs

for nonwhites, with most supervisory jobs in some refineries now held by nonwhites.

Other corporations have reacted differently to South African government policies and to U.S. pressures. Polaroid canceled arrangements with its South African licensee. Citibank will no longer make loans to the South African government. Some corporations have stated that they will not expand their operations in South Africa.

Some critics of American corporations in South Africa state that withdrawal would put pressure on South Africa to improve the political, economic, and social status of nonwhites. Other critics maintain nonwhites would be worse off if American corporations pulled out.

1. What dilemma faces U.S.-based multinational corporations which have operations in South Africa?
2. a. What alternatives do you see for handling this dilemma?
    b. What positive and negative consequences could come from each of the alternatives you have outlined?
3. What action on this question would you take if you were:
    a. A stockholder of a corporation operating in South Africa?
    b. A director of such a corporation?
    c. A manager of such a corporation?
    d. A person running for the U.S. Congress?

GLOSSARY
AND INDEX

Glossary

accelerated depreciation allowance A provision of federal tax law which permits a greater than proportionate depreciation charge in the early years of the life of a capital investment (such as a machine). This purpose is to reduce taxable income for the enterprise in the early years of the investment and to stimulate increased productivity.

accounting The recording, measuring, analyzing, and reporting of enterprise transactions in monetary terms.

accounts payable Amounts owed to suppliers for purchases.

accounts receivable Amounts owed the enterprise by customers who have purchased goods on credit.

accumulated depreciation The total amount of the cost of fixed assets which has been charged as an expense of using those assets over the years.

achieved status Status that comes when an individual works to fulfill the requirements for a particular position and attains it.

acid test ratio A test of an enterprise's short-term liquidity; it is the relationship of an enterprise's quick assets (cash, short-term investments, and accounts or notes receivable) to current liabilities.

actuarial studies Statistical analysis of accident and death rates for insurance purposes of calculating risks, premiums, and benefit payments.

advertising The visual or oral communication of a message to a group regarding a good, a service or an idea.

advertising media The various means by which an advertising message can be transmitted to a potential consumer, including newspapers, television, direct mail, magazines, radio, and outdoor ads.

affirmative action plan A program to provide equal opportunity for employment and promotion.

AFL-CIO The combined union organization of the American Federation of Labor and the Congress of Industrial Organizations. These two major groups were united in 1955. Today unions affiliated with the AFL-CIO represent the majority of American union members.

agents Wholesale middlemen who do not take title to goods, but negotiate the purchase or sale of merchandise for which they are paid a fee or commission.

air pollution The presence of one or more contaminants in the air in quantities great enough to be injurious to life or property.

Air Quality Act of 1967 This act extended federal authority in the field of air-quality control and provided for federal cooperation with state governments in developing air-quality control standards.

American Stock Exchange A major organized trading market for corporate stocks and bonds; located in New York City.

analog computer A computer which measures continuous conditions in physical variables such as temperatures, pressure, voltages, and liquid flows.

Antimerger Act A federal law, passed in 1950, that strengthened the Clayton Act. It provided that not only is the purchase of stock of a competing corporation a violation of the antitrust laws but that it is also illegal to acquire the assets of a competing firm.

antitrust laws Legislative acts designed to promote competition and to prevent large business enterprises from practices such as illegal price setting and division of markets.

application blank A form that a job candidate fills out, giving general personal information plus answers to questions that the business enterprise has found to correlate with job success.

applied research The practical application of scientific knowledge of definite problems or needs.

appraised value The value of an asset determined by someone with expert knowledge for taxation, insurance, or other reasons.

apprenticeship training The employee works under the supervision of trained employees and is required to meet rigid performance standards. Used in jobs that require long periods of training and a high degree of skill.

arbitration A judicial process in which an impartial third party assumes the role of a judge and makes a binding decision in a dispute.

arithmetic/logic unit The part of the computer which performs computations on data and checks results.

ascribed status Status assigned to a person on the basis of some inherited characteristic, such as sex, race, or family.

ask price The price at which a stock market specialist is willing to sell securities.

assessed value The value placed on property for purposes of taxation.

auditor The financial officer who examines the accounting and control systems, verifying assets and liabilities and making suggestions for overall management improvements.

authoritarian leadership Leadership based on centralized authority and autocratic decision making. Subordinates are given little or no discretion in carrying out work assignments.

authority The delegated power to make decisions.

automation In manufacturing, the process by which goods are produced, moved, or inspected by self-operating machinery or electronic controls.

average collection period A calculation that may be used to evaluate the quality of the enterprise's accounts receivable. It is the ratio of accounts receivable to average daily credit sales.

balance of payments The difference between the total funds that flow into and out of a country over a period of time.

balance sheet A statement of the financial position of an enterprise at a given point in time, usually the end of a fiscal period, which shows the assets that the enterprise owns and the claims against those assets.

balance of trade The difference between a country's total imports and exports of merchandise.

bank acceptance A draft drawn on a bank and accepted by the bank instead of an importer or some other private party.

bargaining unit The definition in the union contract of the employees and the employers covered by the agreement.

BASIC *B*eginner's *A*ll-Purpose *S*ymbolic *I*nstruction *C*ode, a computer language for use in solving numerical problems.

best-efforts offering An agreement whereby an investment banker will sell securities for a corporation without underwriting the issue.

bid price The price at which a stock market specialist is willing to buy securities.

bill of exchange A document drawn by the exporter of goods which calls on the importer to accept the obligation to pay a specific sum of money at a specified time. Drafts used in international business.

blacklist A list circulated by an employer of former employees who have been discharged for union activities. This has been determined by the National Labor Relations Board to be an unfair labor practice.

board of directors A body of persons elected by the stockholders of a corporation to exercise control of the corporation.

bond indenture The legal contract which details the arrangement between the issuing company (the borrower) and the bondholders (the lenders).

bonds Interest-bearing certificates of indebtedness issued by a governmental body or a private enterprise which promise to pay the holder a specified sum on a future date in exchange for a specific amount of money today.

book value The worth of enterprise assets based on original cost as shown in the accounting records of the firm.

break-even chart A projection of an enterprise's operations, assuming a pattern of variable and fixed costs to analyze the profit or loss resulting from different levels of sales volume or selling prices.

break-even point The point at which revenues equal costs. At break-even the equality of sales and costs means that there is neither a profit nor a loss.

broker An agent who receives a commission for acting as an intermediary between a buyer and a seller.

budget A financial plan that serves as an estimate of and a control over the operations of the enterprise for a specified period of time.

budgeting process The gathering of data to translate the goals of the enterprise into quantitative terms and to set a basis for control.

business cycles The recurring expansion and contraction in the level of economic activity.

business enterprise A privately owned and operated organization that brings together the factors of production to provide goods and services sold with the expectation of earning a profit.

business profit The calculation of profit by subtracting the appropriate portion of fixed and variable costs from the total receipts for a product's sale.

business systems simulation Development of a model of the enterprise and its environment, which is programmed into a computer so that business decisions can be tested to evaluate their consequences.

capital In an economic sense, capital is wealth used to produce goods and services. In accounting terminology, capital is either the amount invested by owners in an enterprise or the total long-term funds committed to management's use.

capital budget A budget that details the investment plans for assets that will last longer than a year and the means for financing those assets.

capital equipment Machinery and facilities which have a life of over one year, are used to manufacture other goods, and do not become part of the product being manufactured.

capital market The coming together of suppliers and users of long-term funds.

capital structure The composition of the long-term funds committed to management's use, including equity funds and long-term debt (if any).

capitalism An economic system in which the capital used to produce goods is privately owned and is invested with the expectation of earning a profit.

cartel A group of enterprises which agree to fix prices and divide markets. Illegal in the United States.

cash A legal medium of exchange. The most liquid of current assets.

cash budget An estimate of cash receipts and cash disbursements over a specified period of time and of cash on hand.

cash disbursement Any payment of cash by a business enterprise.

cash dividends The dollars paid to shareholders from earnings, usually stated on a per share basis.

cash flow The receipts and disbursements of an enterprise over a particular period of time.

cash receipts The cash received by a business enterprise over a specified period of time.

chain of command A detailing of authority-responsibility relationships, so that all employees know who their immediate superior is and what they are accountable for.

channels of distribution The series of enterprises through which goods flow in moving from the producer to the ultimate consumer.

charter A document issued by a government which authorizes the formation of a corporation and grants it certain powers.

check A written order that directs a bank to pay a specified amount of money on demand.

checkoff clause A clause in the union contract that authorizes management to deduct union dues from the employee's pay and to turn this sum over to the union treasury.

Child Protection and Toy Safety Act Legislation providing increased protection for children from toys which might be hazards.

Cigarette Labeling and Advertising Act Legislation which requires warnings on cigarette packages regarding the health hazards of cigarette smoking. Also regulates cigarette advertising.

Civil Rights Act of 1964 Federal legislation outlawing discrimination in voting, public accommodations, schools, federal programs, and employment.

Clayton Act A federal law, passed in 1914, directed against unfair competition. It outlawed price discrimination, exclusive and tying contracts, intercorporate stockholdings, and interlocking directorates.

Clean Air Act of 1963 Legislation with later amendments which authorized the federal government to take action in interstate air pollution matters and to establish exhaust standards for new autos.

Clean Air Amendments of 1970 and 1977 Federal legislation which set specific standards for auto emissions beginning with 1975 models, along with other pollution controls, such as on new stationary sources of pollution.

Clean Water Act of 1977 Modified the 1972 water amendments and strengthened EPA's authority to control toxic pollutants.

closed-end investment company An investment company with a fixed amount of capital stock outstanding which buys and sells securities for income and capital gains.

closed shop An employment situation in which workers must be members of the union before they may be hired by an employer. The closed shop was made illegal by the Taft-Hartley Act.

COBOL *CO*mmon *B*usiness *O*riented *L*anguage. A compiler language for computers, useful in solving business problems such as file processing and record keeping.

collateral Property pledged as security on a debt.

commercial banks Financial institutions that accept demand deposits from the public and have the power to create money through a fractional reserve system.

commercial letter of credit A document issued by a bank on application of an importer of merchandise. The bank authorizes drafts to be drawn on the bank by the beneficiary and agrees to honor the drafts if all requirements are met.

commercial paper Short-term promissory notes sold by large business corporations to raise funds.

common stock Shares of ownership of a corporation.

common stock account A balance sheet account containing a stated amount of the proceeds from the sale of the corporation's common stock.

communication The transmission of understanding.

comprehensive employment interview An interview to complete or correct the file of the applicant provided by the screening interview, application blank, testing program, and job references.

computer terminal A device with a keyboard that allows an individual to make use of a computer which may be located a great distance away.

conceptual skill The ability to diagnose a problem in relation to its total environment and to develop creative solutions.

conciliation Action of a third party to bring together management and labor when a dispute exists between them.

conglomerate merger The joining together of enterprises that produce or distribute unrelated product lines.

consolidation The joining of two or more independent business enterprises into a new enterprise under a single management.

constant dollars Dollar amounts which have been adjusted for changes in the purchasing power of the currency to permit dollar comparisons between one time period and another in real terms.

consumer durable goods Products used by individuals and households that typically last over a period of years, including automobiles, television sets, refrigerators, and other appliances.

consumer goods Goods that satisfy individual needs directly rather than being used in the production process or for resale.

consumer price index The measure of relative prices for food, durable and nondurable goods, services, and housing over a period of time.

Consumer Product Safety Commission Federal agency to improve the level of safety in product design and to protect the public from unsafe products.

consumerism The movement by consumers to exert pressure on business and government to improve the quality of products sold and to protect the interests of ultimate consumers.

continuous process assembly line The movement of goods from one stage of the production process to another by use of automatic conveyors.

contract An agreement between two or more parties which can be enforced by law.

control A systematic measuring of the progress the business enterprise is making toward its objectives, including the process of correcting deviations in performance.

control unit The part of the computer which issues directions based on the program to other units of the computer.

controller The financial officer who is responsible for the accounting system and for developing the necessary financial controls to assure the security and efficient use of funds.

convenience goods Products which are usually low-priced and are purchased by consumers with a minimum of effort at the nearest available location.

copyright An exclusive right granted by law to the control of an artistic, literary, or musical work or a merchandising label for a period of 28 years with the option of one renewal for another 28 years.

corporation A legal entity, separate and distinct from its owners, who are called stockholders. A business corporation receives a charter from the state, which outlines its powers to engage in business activity. The corporation may have perpetual life, and the stockholders have limited liability.

cost accounting The branch of accounting that classifies, records, allocates, summarizes, and reports current and prospective costs.

cost of goods sold The value of merchandise sold, determined by adding together the costs of materials, labor, overhead, and other expenses involved in the production of the goods, but not including selling costs or the general costs of management.

Council of Economic Advisers Three professional economists appointed by the president to analyze and interpret economic developments and recommend national economic policy. The council was created by the Employment Act of 1946.

Council on Environmental Quality The federal governmental agency which reports to the president and is responsible for studies and policy recommendations on the quality of the national environment.

craft union A union that organizes workers who perform a particular skilled type of work. En-trance into full status in the craft is usually preceded by an extensive training and apprenticeship program.

credit manager The financial officer who administers trade credit, including the determination of which customers will receive credit.

credit rating The estimate of an individual's or an enterprise's ability and willingness to meet payments when they are due.

credit unions Cooperatives that promote saving by their members and also make loans to members at relatively low interest rates.

currency Token coin and paper money in circulation.

current assets Assets that are cash, realizable in cash, or expected to be sold or consumed during the year.

current liabilities Obligations that will fall due within a short period of time, customarily within one year.

current ratio A test of an enterprise's short-term liquidity; it is the relationship of current assets to current liabilities. The current ratio is one of the most widely used balance sheet ratios.

customs duty A tax or tariff on goods imported from a foreign country.

debt Money owed to another by an agreement that creates a legal obligation to pay.

decentralization The dispersion of decision making throughout an organization. Also, the location of facilities over a wider geographic area.

deficit spending The condition in which expenditures exceed revenues; applied to government finances when spending exceeds tax collections.

delegation of authority The authorization of a subordinate to make certain decisions, thereby creating a new responsibility relationship from the subordinate to the superior.

demand deposit A deposit in a commercial bank that may be withdrawn on demand (without advance notice); commonly called a checking account.

demographic changes Changes in the size and composition of the population.

departmentalization The division of the business enterprise into units or subsystems to accomplish the objectives of the firm.

depletion allowance A charge made to account for the reduction of a natural resource such as oil or minerals over a period of time. This reduces the amount of income taxes paid by enterprises in these industries.

depreciation The decline in value of an asset over a period of years.

depression A pronounced and prolonged recession in the business cycle.

devaluation Reduction in the value of one currency in terms of gold or another currency.

digital computer A computer which performs arithmetic operations on numbers, utilizing the functions of data input, memory or storage, arithmetic processing, control, and output.

dilemma A situation in which one must choose between two or more alternative courses of action, each of which will have undesirable consequences.

direction The process of aiding an enterprise's employees in carrying out their work activities.

discipline Rules affecting conduct or actions in the business enterprise.

discretionary income The income left after deducting the amount of income required for necessities.

dividend The amount of profits distributed to shareholders in proportion to their ownership of stock in a corporation.

dividend payout percentage The proportion of earnings that an enterprise distributes to shareholders as cash dividends.

Dow-Jones average An average price for a composite of 65 common stocks of some of America's largest industrial, transportation, and utility corporations.

downgrading Transfer of an employee to a job that requires less skill than the job previously performed.

draft An order directing the payment of money from one party to another.

dumping Selling a product in a foreign market at a lower price than in its domestic market.

earnings Profits generated by an enterprise. When applied to individual workers, usually stated in terms of dollars per hour or per week.

earnings per share The amount of a corporation's net income (profit) divided by the number of shares of common stock outstanding.

economic indicator A measurement of one part of the economy that can help in evaluating the entire economy and in forecasting its future course. Economic indicators are classified as leading, lagging, or coincident with the general level of economic activity.

economic profit The calculation of profit by subtracting opportunity costs from business profit; the difference is called economic profit.

economic resources All the scarce natural, synthetic, and human factors that go into the production of goods and services.

economics The study of how scarce resources are allocated in a society of unlimited wants.

effluent charges Payments that would be made to the government by an industry based on the amount of pollutants it discharged. Such charges would presumably stimulate industry to install antipollution systems or would provide funds to combat pollution.

elasticity of demand The responsiveness of demand to changes in price. Elastic demand is the condition in which a change in the price of a good results in a greater than proportionate change in demand for the good.

electronic computer A data processing device which is capable of the storage, processing, and retrieval of data through the use of electronic circuitry, memory elements, and programmed instructions.

embargo A prohibition against the movement of goods.

employee hiring The hiring of nonmanagerial personnel.

employee induction A program of providing new employees with useful and accurate information about the enterprise, the policies that will affect them, and the services that may be provided for their benefit.

Employee Retirement Income Security Act (ERISA) Enacted in 1974, this complex law provides protections for retirement funds and generally requires that employees have vested rights in the pension credits they accumulate.

employee training Instruction for a new job such as apprenticeship training, vestibule training, on-the-job training, or vocational-school training.

employee transfer The movement of an employee from one job to another at about the same wages and on the same level in the organization.

Employment Act of 1946 Federal legislation that stated as a matter of national policy the responsibility of the federal government for assisting the private sector of the American economy to promote maximum employment, production, and purchasing power.

Energy Research and Development Administration (ERDA) Governmental agency which replaced the Atomic Energy Commission in 1974 and broadened its activities to include other energy sources.

entrepreneur Originally a French word meaning enterpriser. The entrepreneur is a person who provides the managerial ability to bring together land, capital, and labor to produce goods and services; one who assumes the risk of doing business.

Environmental Protection Agency The federal agency established to carry out the policies of the Council on Environmental Quality.

Equal Employment Opportunity Commission This commission, established as a result of the Civil Rights Act of 1964, is charged with combating employment discrimination based on such factors as race and sex.

Equal Pay Act of 1963 Federal legislation which requires employers to pay men and women equally for the same work.

equity funds Ownership financing provided through the sale of stock in a corporation or through the retention of earnings. Also applies to owners' funds in partnerships or proprietorships.

esteem The recognition and regard resulting from how well a person performs the role associated with his or her status.

ethics A code of conduct and values that is accepted by society as being right and proper.

eurodollars U.S. dollar deposits in European commercial banks, including foreign branches of American banks.

exchange control Government control over access to foreign currencies by private citizens and business enterprises.

excise tax A tax levied on goods or services in-side a country at the time of their manufacture, sale, or use.

Executive Order 11246 A presidential directive prohibiting federal government contractors from engaging in discriminatory employment practices.

Export-Import Bank (Eximbank) Federal agency to assist in financing international trade. Established in 1934.

exports Goods sent out of a country to be sold in a foreign nation.

expropriation Action by a government of transferring ownership of private property to the state.

facilitating enterprise A business enterprise that performs auxiliary functions in fields such as finance, insurance, transportation, construction, or services.

factoring The purchase of a business enterprise's accounts receivable by a finance company, which assumes the responsibility for collecting them.

factors of production The four ingredients necessary for the production of goods and services—natural resources, labor, capital, and management.

factory layout The arrangement of machines and production lines in a factory in order to move materials through the manufacturing process.

Fair Credit Reporting Act Legislation designed to protect consumers in credit matters, including individual credit ratings and their use by merchants, insurance companies, or employers.

fair employment practices (FEP) A type of legislation passed in most of the states which outlaws discrimination in the hiring, promotion, and discharge of individuals.

family income The total money income received by family units over a specified period of time before deductions for personal taxes.

featherbedding A union practice that requires an employer to pay for services not performed. Declared an unfair labor practice by the Taft-Hartley Act.

federal Department of Energy A governmental agency that assists the executive branch in carrying out national energy policy.

Federal Deposit Insurance Corporation (FDIC)

A governmental agency that insures depositors' accounts up to $40,000 each in commercial banks that are FDIC members.

federal income taxes Taxes on annual profits or earnings which enterprises and individuals must pay to the federal government.

Federal Insurance Contributions Act (FICA) taxes Employment taxes which provide for old-age, survivors', disability, and health insurance payments from the federal government.

Federal Reserve discount rate The interest rate that member banks must pay to obtain funds from the Federal Reserve bank in their district.

Federal Reserve System A system of 12 Federal Reserve banks, presided over by a seven-member Board of Governors in Washington, D.C. It is charged with the responsibility of providing for a flow of money and credit that will foster orderly economic growth and stable prices.

Federal Savings and Loan Insurance Corporation (FSLIC) The governmental agency that insures each saver's account up to $40,000 in savings and loan associations that are members of FSLIC.

Federal Trade Commission (FTC) A quasi-judicial administrative agency of the federal government established to strengthen the observance and enforcement of the antitrust laws. The FTC also has responsibility for policing advertising and marketing practices for consumer protection.

Federal Trade Commission Act A federal act passed in 1914 to deal with the prevention and punishment of monopolistic business practices. The act also established the Federal Trade Commission to police the antitrust laws and to protect consumer interests.

feedback of information The inspection by a machine of its own output and the activation of controls to correct deviations from established standards.

finance companies Financial institutions that make loans to enterprises and individuals. Those that specialize in direct loans to individuals are called consumer finance or personal finance companies. Those that provide loans to business enterprises are called commercial finance companies.

finance function The activity involving the provision of funds from various sources for an enterprise's operations and the profitable use of those funds.

financial institutions Establishments that regulate the money supply and channel savers' funds to business enterprises, individuals, and governmental bodies which need them.

finished goods Goods that have completed the manufacturing process and have been placed in storage to await distribution to consumers.

fire and casualty insurance companies Companies that sell insurance service to their clients to cover destruction of property by fire or other hazards. Some of these companies also provide other types of insurance protection, such as personal liability insurance.

first-line supervisor The management person who is directly responsible for the work efforts of employees in producing goods or providing services.

fiscal period A span of time over which financial transactions are reported.

fixed assets Sometimes called capital assets. These are long-term tangible assets, such as buildings, land, and equipment, which will not normally be turned into cash but are necessary for the operation of the enterprise.

fixed costs Costs not directly affected by the number of units produced, such as rent, property taxes, and interest on borrowed money.

Flammable Fabrics Act Legislation which required children's nightclothes to be flame retardant.

floating exchange rate The international value of a nation's currency stated in relation to other currencies. The floating exchange rate fluctuates, depending on supply and demand, in contrast to a one-price government-imposed and guaranteed rate for international transactions.

Food and Drug Administration The federal agency which has responsibility in such areas as the safety and effectiveness of drugs, cosmetics, and food products marketed in the United States.

foreign exchange rate The price of the currency of one country in terms of the currency of another.

foreign exchange transaction The purchase or sale of the currency of one nation with the currency of another.

foreign trade zones Areas where goods may be imported, reprocessed, and exported without being subject to tariffs or quotas.

foreman A supervisor who is the first level of management and is in direct contact with workers engaged in the production process.

form utility Utility that stems from a good's possession of the physical characteristics necessary for its purpose.

formal organization A detailing of the status positions and lines of authority and responsibility from the board of directors and the president throughout the enterprise.

formal training programs Structured training such as lectures, courses, discussions, or provision for employees to attend an institution of higher learning for professional management training.

FORTRAN *FOR*mula *TRAN*slator. An algebraic compiler language for a computer that is particularly useful for research problems requiring the solution of mathematical or statistical formulations.

fractional reserve banking system The system of financial reserves used by commercial banks, whereby each bank is required to keep only a portion of its deposits in reserve form and may lend out those funds in excess of the required deposit reserves.

frame of reference the perspective from which a person views his or her environment. It is influenced by the person's past experiences and value system.

franchise The right to market a good or a service in a particular area, sometimes on an exclusive basis.

fringe benefits Items provided to employees that, in effect, increase real income but are not included in the basic wage. Fringe benefits include health insurance, disability benefits, sick leave, life insurance, pensions, and paid vacations.

fully automated process Manufacture of a good by a process that includes automatic inspection of production which actuates controls to correct deviations from established standards.

functional departmentalization Organization of an enterprise by grouping together the activities of a similar nature, such as production, marketing, or finance.

GATT (General Agreement on Tariffs and Trade) International agreement for continuing discussions on trade and tariff reductions.

general partnership A partnership form of business organization in which all partners have unlimited liability.

general-purpose machine A machine that can perform a variety of jobs for the same type of work, such as drill press that can drill different numbers of holes, in different sizes or depths, and for different materials.

General Services Administration The federal governmental agency responsible for the maintenance and upkeep of federal buildings. Also negotiates purchasing contracts for supplies and services.

geographic departmentalization Organization of a business enterprise on a territorial basis.

geothermal power Utilization of steam deep in the earth to produce electricity.

gold convertibility The ability to exchange a nation's money into gold. The U.S. dollar is no longer tied to gold convertibility either domestically or internationally.

good In economic terms, anything useful in satisfying a human want.

grapevine Informal communications that stem from informal work groups.

grievance procedure A specified succession of steps through which workers' complaints are to be processed from lower to higher levels of management and union officials.

grievances Complaints expressed to management by employees about the work situation.

gross income Net sales less the cost of goods sold.

gross national product The total retail market value of all the goods and services produced in a nation, usually stated in annual terms.

gross profit Another term for gross income.

guaranteed loan A loan which will be paid back by the government or some other institution or individual in the event that it is not repaid by the borrowing enterprise.

guide A recommendation for action.

hardware   When used regarding a computer system, the physical equipment which makes up the computer.

horizontal merger   A joining together of two or more companies that manufacture or distribute the same product.

housekeeping staff   Staff personnel who perform custodial and maintenance duties, record keeping, health services, and routine personnel functions.

human relations   The interactions arising out of the association of two or more persons. Management's actions to provide a climate in the business enterprise that will satisfy the employee's needs and achieve the broad economic objectives of the enterprise.

human skill   The ability to work with people and to build effective work teams.

human subsystem   That element of the work system which consists of the values, motivations, and interactions of persons in an enterprise.

imports   Goods brought into a country that have been purchased in a foreign nation.

income statement   A summary of the revenues and expenses of an enterprise's operations over a specified period, such as a year. The income statement is also called the profit and loss statement.

income tax   An annual tax on the income of persons or corporations.

industrial union   A union which draws members on an industry-wide basis, regardless of the jobs performed.

industrial user   An enterprise which buys products for use in producing other goods or services.

industry   Business enterprises engaged in the same type of economic activity.

industry-wide bargaining   A situation in which a single series of collective bargaining negotiations results in an agreement or agreements covering substantially all the firms in an industry.

inelasticity of demand   The condition in which changes in the price of a product bring about little or no change in the demand for it.

inflation   An increase in the price of goods or services which takes place when the supply of money or credit in the economy expands faster

than the ability of the economy to produce more goods and services.

informal organization   A self-grouping of employees in the work situation based on the personalities of individuals rather than on formal organizational relationships.

injunction   A court order that directs an individual or an organization to do or not to do some act. A violator of an injunction is subject to a contempt of court proceeding.

input unit   The system of feeding information into computers by such means as punch cards, punched-paper tapes, magnetic ink tapes, optical-character scanners, or console typewriters.

installment credit   A credit system in which a purchased article is paid for by a series of payments over a specified period of time.

institutional advertising   An advertising message which seeks to develop goodwill for a business enterprise or an industry rather than to sell a specific product.

insurance premium   The amount paid periodically to an insurance company or its agent for coverage that will provide reimbursement in case of damage or loss.

interest   The amount paid for the use of borrowed funds. In an economic sense, the return on capital resources.

intermediate-term credit   Debt instruments that have a maturity of from over one year to approximately ten years.

International Monetary Fund (IMF)   An international agency formed to foster monetary cooperation and stability among nations. Established in 1946.

Interstate Commerce Commission (ICC)   A federal agency that regulates carriers engaged in interstate commerce, created in 1887.

inventory   The stock of goods available for sale to customers. As a balance sheet item, inventory includes the cost of finished goods, work in process, and raw materials.

inventory turnover   A ratio indicating the number of times that merchandise moves through the enterprise during a period of time. Computed by dividing the cost of goods sold by the average inventory on hand over the period.

investment banker   An institution or a person that functions as a middleman between corporations and investors in the capital funds market by selling new securities in the primary securities market and acting as a broker for the purchase and sale of securities in the secondary securities market.

investment company A financial institution that sells its shares and uses the proceeds to purchase securities of other corporations.

investment portfolio The list of stocks, bonds, and other investments owned by a financial institution or an individual.

investment tax credit A direct reduction of an enterprise's federal income taxes because the enterprise purchases a specified type of capital equipment. Designed to stimulate investment and increase business activity.

invoice An itemized statement of merchandise shipped by the vendor.

job description A description of the essential elements of a specific job, including such factors as physical effort, skill, responsibility, mental effort, and working conditions.

job evaluation A measurement of the value of each job in the enterprise in relation to the other jobs in the enterprise.

job references A list of previous positions held by a job applicant, used to check the applicant's past work record.

job rotation A planned approach to management training which involves transfer of the trainee through a series of different positions.

job specifications A list of the requirements for a specific position.

jurisdictional strike A work stoppage that grows out of disagreements over which craft union has the right to perform particular jobs or over which union should organize the workers in a particular industry. Jurisdictional strikes were outlawed by the Taft-Hartley Act.

labor All physical and mental talents that individuals expend in producing goods and services, with the exception of entrepreneurial talent, which is classified separately.

labor contract See Union contract.

Labor-Management Relations Act of 1947 (Taft-Hartley Act) A series of amendments to the National Labor Relations Act of 1935 which added certain unfair labor practices for unions, permitted the president of the United States to obtain an 80-day injunction to postpone a strike threatening the national welfare, and allowed the states to have right-to-work laws outlawing the union shop.

Labor-Management Reporting and Disclosure Act of 1959 (Landrum-Griffin Act) Federal legislation that imposed certain limitations on unions in organizing workers and in the internal management of union affairs.

labor relations A situation in which management bargains over wages, hours, and working conditions with employees as a group through union representatives.

laissez-faire capitalism In its most extreme form laissez-faire capitalism, whose name stemmed from a French term meaning "let people do as they choose," limited government's participation in economic activity to providing essential services such as police and fire protection.

land In economics, all natural resources used in the production process, including timber, oil and mineral deposits, and water, as well as land itself.

layoff A reduction in the size of the work force frequently stemming from a drop in demand for the enterprise's products.

lead time The time required in development of the production process before goods can be produced.

leadership The element of direction that causes subordinates to follow a superior and results in accomplishment of the goals of the enterprise.

lease A form of long-term renting contract through which an enterprise obtains the use of assets without owning them.

liabilities Claims against the enterprise's assets by outsiders.

life insurance companies Business enterprises which provide insurance coverage on the lives of policyholders and acquire capital through investment of the insurance premiums they receive.

limited liability When applied to a corporation, a legal concept which means that if the enterprise fails, the stockholders' losses are limited to the amount of their investment in the enterprise.

limited partnership A partnership form of business organization in which some partners have limited liability. There must be at least one general partner with unlimited liability.

line functions Those activities that specifically and directly result in achievement of the goals of the business enterprise.

linear programming Determining the best allocation of limited resources through the use of linear equations and relationships by analyzing a number of variables given certain constraints.

liquidation value The value of the enterprise's assets if they were sold.

liquidity The degree of ease with which an asset can be converted into cash. Liquidity measures the ability of an enterprise to meet its current financial obligations when they become due.

lockout Management's refusal to permit union members to enter the enterprise's facilities because of a dispute.

long-term debt Loans that mature in more than ten years.

long-term liabilities A balance sheet category made up of financial obligations that fall due more than one year in the future.

McGuire Act A federal law, passed in 1952, that permitted states to include the nonsigner clause in their resale price maintenance laws. It provides that all retailers in a state are bound by resale price agreements as long as one retailer in the state signs such an agreement.

macroeconomic analysis The study of the functioning of the economy as a whole.

maintenance force Employees whose work is to keep production facilities in efficient operating order.

management The achievement of results by directing the activities of other people. Also, the group of individuals in an enterprise who are responsible for the achievement of results.

management succession The process of providing for a source of qualified management personnel either by training and promoting employees or by hiring executives from outside the enterprise.

manufacturer's sale branch An office operated by a manufacturer separate from the factories for use by sales and service personnel. It may or may not carry inventories from which orders are shipped directly.

manufacturing enterprise A business enterprise that fabricates consumer and producer goods out of raw materials and/or components.

market A group of consumers who are willing and able to buy the goods produced by a business enterprise.

market penetration pricing A policy of setting a relatively low initial price for a product in order to achieve quick mass market acceptance.

market system The coming together of buyers and sellers with money as a medium of exchange for goods and services.

marketing The business activities that move goods and services from producers to consumers to satisfy needs. Marketing imparts place, time, and possession utility to goods.

marketing concept of business An approach to business that centers management thinking on the importance of the consumer by recognizing a need, developing a product to satisfy the need, and in the process earning a profit for the enterprise.

marketing enterprise A business enterprise that distributes finished goods to consumers.

marketing mix The market program of a business enterprise consisting of the variables of product, promotion, price, and place.

Maslow's hierarchy of needs A priority of human needs discussed by the psychologist A. H. Maslow, including physiological, safety, love, esteem, and self-actualization needs.

mass media advertising The promotion of a product to many people at the same time through newspapers, television, radio, magazines, or outdoor signs.

maturity The date on which a financial obligation comes due.

mechanization The application of power-driven tools in factory production, which results in a saving of both human energy and time.

median In a series of data, the midway point that divides the number of units in half.

median family income The midway point in the distribution of family income, with half the families having incomes above this amount and half having incomes below it.

mediation The process whereby a third party brings together the two sides involved in a dispute and actively participates in the discussions in order to bring about a compromise acceptable to both parties.

memory unit The part of the computer which receives and holds the input data and the program instructions for processing data.

merchant wholesaler A distributor who purchases merchandise from manufacturers and thereby takes title to the goods and assumes the risks associated with their sale.

merger The taking over of a smaller business enterprise by a larger business enterprise.

MESBIC A *Minority Enterprise Small Business Investment Company* which is formed to provide capital and management assistance to minority-owned business enterprises.

microeconomic analysis The study of the functioning of a specific unit of the economy, such as a given business enterprise.

middlemen Enterprises or individuals, such as wholesalers and retailers, who handle goods as they move from the producer to the ultimate consumer.

Miller-Tydings Act A federal law passed in 1937 as an amendment to the Sherman Act in order to aid small business by exempting resale price maintenance contracts from antitrust laws if they were permitted by state law.

minority group A part of the population that is distinguished from the dominant society by some characteristic such as race, nationality, language, or religion.

miscellaneous payables A catchall account for any outsiders' recognized financial claims against the enterprise not listed elsewhere in the balance sheet.

money market The coming together of lenders and borrowers of short-term debt which matures in one year or less.

monopoly Control over the supply of a good or service in a given market by a single producer.

monopoly profit The additional profit of an enterprise resulting from higher prices because of the enterprise's sole control over the production or distribution of a product.

mortgage The pledging of property by a borrower to a lender as security for payment of a debt.

motion analysis A determination by industrial engineers of the method for accomplishing a particular job that reduces waste effort to a minimum.

motion and time analysis Work done by industrial engineers to provide a basis for production standards on factory jobs.

multinational corporation A business enterprise which has significant operations in several countries.

mutual fund An open-end investment company that does not have a fixed number of shares outstanding. It issues more shares whenever an investor wants to purchase shares in the fund, and it stands willing to repurchase its shares from investors.

mutual savings banks The oldest class of savings institutions in the United States. A mutual savings bank has no shareholders, but all depositors have a mutual interest and receive dividends for their savings.

National Alliance of Businessmen A voluntary organization of business leaders formed in 1967 to expand employment opportunities, especially for persons who were considered unemployable because of a lack of job skills.

National Energy Act of 1978 Legislation providing for the deregulation of natural gas prices and for a variety of energy conservation measures.

National Environmental Policy Act of 1969 Legislation which commits the federal government to a continuing policy of improving the environment for present and future generations. The act established the Council on Environmental Quality.

national income The total earnings of labor and property that result from the production of goods and services by the nation's economy. National income is the sum of employees' compensation, proprietors' income, rental income, net interest, and corporate profits.

National Labor Relations Act Federal legislation passed in 1935 which guarantees the right of workers to form and join labor unions and to bargain collectively with employers. It defined certain unfair labor practices and established the National Labor Relations Board to enforce the act.

National Labor Relations Board (NLRB) The five-member body that administers and enforces the National Labor Relations Act.

National Traffic and Motor Vehicle Safety Act of 1966 Legislation which provides for the setting of standards for auto and highway safety and requires auto manufacturers to notify first purchasers of cars of safety defects discovered after delivery.

near-cash Any asset immediately transferable into money form without risk of loss of value in the process, such as 91-day U.S. Treasury bills.

need A lack of something that is useful, required, or desirable to carry out a way of life.

net profit The amount that remains after all relevant costs, including income taxes, have been deducted from revenue; the final figure shown on the income or profit and loss statement.

net sales Gross sales less cash discounts given for prompt payment for goods and credits for returned merchandise.

net worth The amount of the owners' claims to the enterprise's assets; also called owners' equity.

New York Stock Exchange The largest organized trading market for corporate stocks and bonds; located in New York City.

nonprice competition Factors other than the cost of a product that influence consumer demand, such as sales promotion efforts, quality and service competition, and fashion.

Norris-LaGuardia Act of 1932 The first major labor legislation which limited the power of federal courts to issue injunctions in labor disputes. Protected unions' rights.

no-strike clause A clause in the union contract that prohibits work stoppages by employees.

notes payable A balance sheet item showing debts for which written acknowledgments have been made.

objectives Statements that embody the broad goals toward which the group activity of the business enterprise is directed.

occupational distribution The proportion of persons in various job categories.

Occupational Safety and Health Act of 1970 A federal law requiring employers to provide safe and healthful working conditions.

odd lot Generally defined as the purchase or sale of stock in units of less than 100 shares.

Office of Federal Contract Compliance A Department of Labor agency which coordinates the administration of executive orders to prevent discriminatory employment practices by government contractors.

Office of Minority Business Enterprise (OMBE) A Department of Commerce agency which is designed to assist minority persons in establishing and operating business enterprises.

oligopoly Control over the supply of a good or service in a given market by a few producers.

on-the-job training The worker is placed in the shop at a machine or a workplace to be trained by a supervisor, a special instructor, or an experienced employee.

OPEC (Organization of Petroleum Exporting Countries) The cartel dominated by Arab governments which controls the export of oil from most of the oil-exporting countries.

open account Extension of credit to a customer without requiring either specific collateral or a written acknowledgment of the financial obligation by the purchaser.

open-market operations The purchase or sale of federal government securities by the Federal Reserve System to affect the level of commercial bank reserves.

operating income The profit generated from the operation of an enterprise before interest payments and income taxes have been deducted.

operations budget A budget that covers operating revenue and expenses. Consists of a forecast of expected sales, along with an estimate of the costs necessary to achieve the sales goal. Operations budgets can be subdivided into budgets for sales, sales promotion and advertising, production, purchases, maintenance, and overhead.

opportunity cost An economic concept that represents the cost assumed when a person or a business enterprise forgoes the alternative of making some other use of economic resources.

organizational subsystem That element of the work system which consists of the way in which the technical and human subsystems are organized, directed, coordinated, and controlled by management to achieve the enterprise's objectives.

other assets A catchall category on the balance sheet that includes all assets not listed as either current or fixed, such as patents and trademarks.

output unit Any of the numerous means of showing the results of a computer's data processing, such as a printer system or a visual display.

over-the-counter market The purchase and sale of securities through informal dealings, usually by telephone, rather than on an organized exchange.

owners' equity (net worth) The value of the assets claimed by owners of the business enterprise.

participative leadership The decentralization of authority among subordinates. Suggestions are encouraged, and an emphasis is placed on communication between the leader and all members of the group.

partnership A form of legal organization of a business enterprise in which two or more individuals share in the ownership according to a contractual agreement. At least one partner must have unlimited liability.

patent Exclusive rights to a product or process for 17 years, conferred on the holder by government authority.

peak The high point in economic activity during a business cycle.

pension funds Funds accumulated from the contributions of employers and employees and invested to provide retirement income for the individual beneficiaries and their families.

performance rating A formal rating of an employee, used to make merit wage increases within job classifications and to guide management in making promotions.

personal assistants Staff persons who provide executives with information or who handle details that the manager may not have time for but does not want to delegate to a lower level in the organization.

personal income The total money income received by individuals before personal taxes are deducted.

personal selling A method of promotion that involves an individual presentation of a product to a customer.

personnel management The function in the enterprise of recruitment, selection, induction, and training of employees to build a well-motivated and effective work force.

philanthropy Services and gifts to help humanity.

physical distribution The process of moving and handling goods as they flow through the channels of distribution.

pilot plant A prototype of the production process, which usually consists of a scale model of the complete factory or the production line.

PL/1 *Programming Language, Version 1,* is a computer language suitable for problems involving business data processing and numerical scientific computations.

place The dimension of the marketing mix which provides products with time and place utility to satisfy customers. Includes determination of the channels of distribution and the transportation and storage of goods.

place utility Utility that stems from goods being where the consumer has access to them.

planning The process of rational decision making done sufficiently in advance to promote the more effective operation of the enterprise.

Poison Prevention Packaging Act Legislation requiring manufacturers to distribute dangerous substances in containers with safety caps which are difficult for children to remove.

policy A statement of principles or purposes that provides a framework for decision making consistent with the objectives of the enterprise.

pollution An undesirable change in the environment which can impair the quality of life.

portfolio A list of securities owned.

possession utility Utility that stems from a person being able to own or control a good.

preferred stock The class of ownership shares in a corporation that has preference over common stock to a stated amount of cash dividends each year. Preferred stockholders have priority over common stockholders in claims to assets if the corporation is liquidated.

prepaid expenses A balance sheet item that represents a portion of an outlay for a benefit that will extend over more than one accounting period, such as for insurance or royalties.

prestige The recognition and regard that result from a person's status.

price/earnings ratio A measure for analyzing common stock prices which is calculated by dividing the stock's current market price by the past 12 months' earnings per share.

primary boycott Employees' refusal to use the products of an employer with whom they have a dispute.

primary securities market The market that channels funds directly to corporations or governmental bodies in exchange for their securities.

prime rate of interest The borrowing rate that commercial banks charge their most creditworthy business customers.

private enterprise system The form that capitalism has taken in America. It is characterized by private property, the profit motive, competition in the marketplace, a particular relationship between business and government, and consumer freedom of choice.

private placement The sale of an entire issue of securities to a single investor or a small number of investors.

private property Property owned by an individual who therefore has the right to exercise substantial control over it.

procedure A specific method or a series of steps carried out in a particular sequence to implement a given policy.

process design The development of the means by which a good will be produced.

process layout The location in one place of similar types of machines or functions, regardless of the order in which they enter the production process—i.e., all grinding would be done in one location, all drilling in another, and so on.

processing enterprise A business enterprise that transforms natural resources from mines, forests, farms, or oceans into the raw materials used to manufacture goods.

producer goods Machines and equipment used to make consumer goods or other producer goods; thus satisfy individual needs indirectly.

producer price index The measure of relative prices for finished goods, consumer and capital equipment, and materials used in the production of food and nonfood products over a period of time.

product A good or a service that satisfies consumer needs.

product advertising An advertising message that provides information and attempts to sell a specific good or service.

product design The development of a product that will perform properly, have consumer appeal, and be sold at a price that will be profitable.

product layout The arrangement of machinery and assembly lines by chronological steps so that as the product moves through the factory there is a buildup from parts or raw materials to the finished product.

product life cycle The pattern of a product's sales and profit margins. The profit margin reaches a peak first and begins to decline while the sales continue to rise for a period of time before reaching their peak and then declining.

product line departmentalization Organization of a business enterprise according to the various types of products that it manufactures and sells.

production The provision of goods with form utility by turning raw materials and semifinished products into finished goods for either consumer or industrial use.

production control The coordination and control of the production process to meet delivery schedules.

production scheduling A detailing of the sequence and timing of orders from the time orders are received from the sales department until finished goods are shipped.

production transfer Changing an employee's work assignments from one department to another because of a change in a department's job requirements.

profit The residual after all appropriate costs have been deducted from business revenues; the return to enterprises or individuals for risk bearing, innovation, or some degree of market control.

profit and loss statement See Income statement.

profit center A responsibility center in which revenues are generated, enabling management to measure profitability as well as costs.

profit motive The desire to engage in economic activity in order to earn profit; a central controlling mechanism in a capitalistic economy.

program A mixture of policies and procedures that have been developed to achieve the outlined objectives of management.

program flowchart Properly sequenced instructions that enable the computer to process the input data. The flowchart is translated into a set of detailed coded instructions for the computer.

programming Providing a computer with a set of instructions for solving a problem or carrying out a series of operations on data.

promotion In personnel management, the advancement of an employee to a job with more responsibility, increased skill, or higher status and an increased salary. In marketing, the communication of information that will persuade potential customers to buy a product.

property tax A tax levied on the assessed value of tangible property such as land; business buildings, equipment, and inventories; and individuals' houses, automobiles, and home furnishings. Sometimes a tax is assesed on intangible property such as stocks and bonds.

proprietorship The legal form of business organization in which ownership is by a single individual. The most common form of business enterprise, it is generally small in size and its owner has unlimited liability.

prototype A model or pattern used as the basis for subsequent production, such as a clay model of an automobile made up during the design process to give a three-dimensional view of styling and appearance.

proxy The written authority given to a person or an organization to act for the signer in some matter, such as in voting at a corporation's meeting of stockholders.

psychological needs Needs that pertain to the individual's self-image, including the need for love, self-respect, and a feeling of accomplishment.

public relations Those functions concerned with creating a favorable image of the business enterprise and with communicating its purposes and programs to the different groups who constitute the public.

purchase contract A purchase order that has been accepted by a vendor.

purchase order A document that authorizes a vendor to deliver described goods at a specified price.

purchase requisition A formal request for the purchase of a particular item.

purchasing The procurement of industrial materials and supplies for use or for further processing, not for immediate resale.

pure research Research carried on to extend our frontiers of knowledge without regard to the immediate application of its findings.

quality Possession of the necessary characteristics that fit a product to a given use.

quality control A system of inspection to determine which goods should be accepted or rejected, and a means for preventing the continued production of unsatisfactory goods.

quota A limit on the quantity of foreign goods which may be imported.

ratio of profits to owners' equity The profitability of a business enterprise or an industry measured by profits as a percentage of owners' equity.

ratio of profits to sales The profitability of a business enterprise or an industry measured by profits as a percentage of sales.

raw materials Unprocessed commodities and components purchased by a manufacturer to be assembled into a finished product.

real income The actual purchasing power of a person's or a family's income after adjustment for changes in the prices of goods and services.

real-time system A computer system which receives and processes data so as to affect an environment *at that time.*

recession (or contraction) A decline in economic activity in the business cycle.

recognition clause A union contract provision that defines the bargaining unit and recognizes a particular union as the bargaining agency for the employees.

recovery (or expansion) The upturn in the business cycle characterized by greater demand for goods and services, higher production, and improved profits.

recruitment The process of seeking and hiring new employees.

remedial transfer A transfer made because of some problem that has arisen with a particular employee on a job.

rent In an economic sense, the return that accrues to land.

repatriation of funds The returning of monies from business operations in another country to the home country of the business enterprise.

reproduction value The amount it would cost to replace the assets of an enterprise with others of like characteristics.

reserve requirements The amount of reserve funds held by commercial banks to back up deposits, usually stated as a percentage of deposits.

Resource Recovery Act of 1970 Federal legislation which provided for research programs to encourage the development of innovative solid waste disposal systems.

responsibility Accountability to others by those who have authority.

responsibility centers A designated unit of a subsystem in which the manager can be held responsible for the control of costs.

retailer A merchant who sells goods or services directly to individual consumers.

retained earnings The amount of profits earned by an enterprise over the years and kept in the business to strengthen and expand operations; less frequently called earned surplus.

right-to-work laws State laws that make illegal the provisions in labor contracts under which workers are required to join the union after a specified period of time.

Robinson-Patman Act A federal law passed in 1936 as a revision of Section 2 of the Clayton Act. It sought to give increased protection to smaller retailers against unfair competition from large retailers.

role The expected behavior pattern associated with a status.

round lot Generally defined as a stock transaction unit of 100 shares.

routing The detailed instructions on how a particular order will move from department to department, which machines will be used at each point along the line, and when inspections will be made.

rule Regulation that must be obeyed.

rumor Incomplete, unconfirmed information, which may be incorrect or malicious in its intent.

sale-leaseback agreement An arrangement in which an enterprise constructs a building to its specifications, then sells it to a financial institution such as an insurance company and simultaneously leases it back for a long period of time.

sales budget A subdivision of an operating budget that translates the goals of the enterprise into anticipated sales revenues and the expenditures necessary to generate those revenues.

sales finance companies Financial institutions that specialize in installment loans by purchasing installment receivables from retailers who sell durable goods, such as autos and appliances. Sales finance companies also lend retailers and wholesalers money to finance their inventories.

sales promotion An attempt to bridge the gap between personal selling and mass media advertising through the use of displays and other sales aids, material for training salespersons, and contests and premium programs for customers.

sales tax A tax levied on goods or services at the time they are sold to consumers.

savings and loan association A financial institution to promote thrift and home ownership. The savers who place their funds in the association become shareholders and receive dividends on their savings.

savings deposit An account which draws interest in a commercial bank or some other savings institution.

scarce economic resources All the natural, synthetic, and human factors that go into the production of goods and services.

screening interview An interview to make a preliminary decision about an applicant's suitability for employment.

seasonal changes Fluctuations in economic activity due to the changing seasons of the year, holidays, or the calendar.

secondary boycott Action by workers against a company with which they have a dispute by bringing pressure against a third party that is not directly involved in the dispute. The secondary boycott was declared illegal by the Taft-Hartley Act.

secondary securities markets Security markets in which stocks or bonds already outstanding are bought and sold among investors.

Securities and Exchange Commission (SEC) A federal governmental agency that regulates interstate corporation stock transactions. The SEC requires corporations to provide investors with information about new stock and bond issues, and to reveal dealings in their own stock by enterprise executives, and in general protects the interests of the public. Created in 1934.

security A general term that encompasses transferable certificates of stock or debt. The term is sometimes used to mean collateral for a loan.

seniority Priority or status attained by an employee, based on length of service in the enterprise.

services Intangible products which provide consumer satisfactions.

share One of the equal parts into which a corporation's ownership interest is divided.

Sherman Act A federal law, passed in 1890, which made restraint of trade and monopolization federal offenses.

shift transfer The transfer of an employee from one time shift to another.

shop steward A worker elected or appointed by a union to represent employees in a factory department or area, particularly with regard to grievances.

shopping goods Products which are compared with competing products for price, quality, style, or service by the customer before purchase.

short-term debt Debt which matures in one year or less.

sight draft A document that calls for the drawee to pay the draft on its presentation (on sight).

single-project-type departmentalization The organization of an enterprise to carry out by department one-time projects that will extend over a period of months or years, such as highway construction.

skimming-the-cream pricing A policy of setting a relatively high price for a product, usually in the introduction stage of the product's life cycle or when nonprice competition is important.

small business An enterprise which is not dominant in its field and is independently owned and operated. The SBA has specific criteria which apply to the maximum size of an enterprise for it to receive loan assistance from the SBA.

Small Business Administration (SBA) A federal agency concerned with the problems of small business management, created in 1953.

Small Business Investment Company (SBIC) A privately owned investment company which provides equity and long-term debt capital to new or small enterprises.

social needs All the needs that grow out of a person's relation to other individuals and groups, including the need for recognition, acceptance, and group activity.

socialism An economic system in which the concept of private profit is lacking and the means of producing and distributing goods are owned by the state rather than by individuals.

software The program of instructions for a computer.

solar energy Utilization of the sun's rays to produce electricity or for heating or cooling.

solid waste pollution Pollution caused by the disposal of agricultural, mineral, industrial, and residential products or wastes.

solvency The enterprise's ability to pay long-term financial obligations when they fall due and to meet the interest payments on outstanding debt.

span of control The number of subordinates a manager can supervise.

special-purpose machine A machine specifically designed to produce a particular product or to do a given job.

specialist A member of a stock exchange who makes a market in a particular stock by offering to buy or sell the security through a continuous two-way auction.

specialty goods Products for which customers show brand preference or which have features that encourage a special buying effort by customers.

spread The gross margin or profit between the price that investment bankers or specialists pay for the securities they buy and the price they hope to sell them for.

staff function All activities that assist the line management in fulfilling the enterprise's objectives.

staff personnel Personnel necessary to support the line activities. These personnel include technical advisers, personal assistants, housekeeping staff, and other specialists. They can advise but normally do not issue orders to line organizational units.

staffing The provision of qualified managerial personnel for the enterprise.

Standard Metropolitan Statistical Areas Areas of the United States that have at least one city with a population of 50,000 or more and have been designated by the Bureau of the Census as urban areas.

standards Predetermined performance levels. These include monetary standards, physical standards, and intangible standards.

statement of changes in financial position The accounting statement which summarizes the funds generated from operations and other sources and shows how these funds are used over a period of time.

status A particular position in the formal organization of the enterprise.

status symbol Visible evidence of a person's rank in the business enterprise or some other organization.

stock dividend Additional shares of its own stock that the distributing corporation issues to shareholders.

storage function The holding of goods from the time they are produced until their final use, including warehousing, handling, and order processing.

stream of profits An approach to determining the value of an enterprise based on the yield of its estimated future earnings.

strike Action taken by workers to cease work. Picketing usually follows to prevent other personnel from entering the struck plant.

Subchapter S corporation A corporate form of business organization with a small number of stockholders which may be taxed similarly to a partnership.

subsidiary A business enterprise which is owned or controlled by another company.

subsidy Government assistance to a private enterprise.

subsystem The elements within a system.

supplementary unemployment benefit plan A plan whereby employers make payments to a fund that is used to pay employees who have been laid off. This money supplements unemployment benefits paid under government programs.

surtax An extra tax in addition to the tax already levied. Sometimes used to increase the tax rate that must be paid if income exceeds a specified level.

syndicate A group of investment bankers that is organized for the purpose of marketing a particular security issue.

system A set of elements which have a relationship to one another.

tariff A tax on imported goods.

taxes payable The amount of tax liability owed to various governmental units.

technical advisers Staff personnel, such as lawyers, public relations experts, and engineers, who provide information of a highly specialized nature.

technical skill A manager's ability in and knowledge of a particular process or technique.

technical subsystem That element of the work system which consists of the equipment, layout, and technology required to produce and distribute a particular product.

technology The accumulated fund of knowledge which promotes efficient organization for the production of goods and services.

Tennessee Valley Authority (TVA) The federal governmental agency which produces and distributes electricity and provides flood control, recreation areas, and other services in connection with the Tennessee River system.

term loan The customary name for intermediate credit; a loan running for more than one year and less than ten years.

thermal pollution The presence of excessive heat in a body of water as the result of some industrial process, such as the generation of electric power.

time deposit A type of bank deposit that bears

interest. Formal notice must be given before withdrawal of funds.

time draft A draft that calls for payment on a specified future date.

time-sharing system A computer system that provides a number of users at different locations with access to a single computer for the simultaneous solutions of different problems.

time study analysis A determination by an industrial engineer of how much time is necessary to carry out a job under actual factory conditions.

time utility Utility that stems from goods being available when they are wanted.

tooling The attachments for machine tools, gauges, loading devices, and other fixtures to adapt machinery and assembly lines to the production of a particular product.

trade acceptance A bill of exchange with an acknowledgment of the obligation written across its face by the importer that obligates the importer to pay the amount specified at the designated time.

trade credit The credit extended by suppliers to business enterprises for merchandise or equipment purchases, usually for stated periods of from 30 to 60 days.

trade creditor An individual or enterprise supplying merchandise or services to a business customer and willing to ship merchandise without requiring cash payment on delivery.

Trade Expansion Act (TEA) Law passed in 1962 which permitted negotiations to reduce tariffs and to stimulate world trade.

trade journal A periodical that specializes in a specific field, such as a particular industry or business function.

trademarks Words or symbols that identify a particular brand of merchandise. Trademarks may be registered for 28 years and the registration renewed for another 28 years, which prevents their use by unauthorized persons or enterprises.

trading on the equity An increase in the return on the owners' investment by using borrowed funds profitably in the business enterprise.

transfer payment Income paid to a person from whom no service is currently received, such as a Social Security payment or a veteran's benefit.

treasurer The financial executive who is responsible for the company's valuable papers, management of cash receipts and disbursements, and the development of banking relationships.

trend The underlying long-run tendency that persists despite short-term cyclical or seasonal fluctuations in economic activity.

trough The low in cyclical economic activity during a recession before recovery takes place.

trust A business combination that is created when the owners of the shares of stock in corporations transfer control of their shares to trustees in exchange for trust certificates that entitle them to a share in the profits of the combined corporations.

trust company A financial institution that takes legal possession of personal assets and manages them for the benefit of the person who created the trust or for some other designated person. A trust department of a commercial bank also performs this service.

Truth in Lending Act of 1968 Legislation requiring creditors to furnish individual borrowers with a statement of the amount of the financing charges and the annual percentage rate of interest on the loan.

type-of-customer-served departmentalization Organization of an enterprise so that each particular department will be geared to meet the requirements of a particular class of consumer.

ultimate consumers Individuals or households that use goods or services for the satisfaction of personal needs.

***ultra vires* acts** Actions beyond the powers granted to a board of directors.

underwriting As applied to investment banking, the assumption of responsibility for the sale of a corporation's stock or bonds, guaranteeing the corporation a specified amount of money for these securities.

undistributed profits The amount of earnings retained by a business corporation rather than being paid out to owners as dividends. Also called retained earnings.

unemployment insurance tax Taxes paid by business enterprises to finance payments to workers who are out of work.

union contract The agreement negotiated by management and union representatives which spells out the terms agreed on with regard to wages, hours, and working conditions.

union shop A labor agreement provision that requires a worker to join the union after a specified period of employment, often within 30 days.

utility In economics, the power to satisfy human wants.

value A belief held by persons in a society as to the rightness or wrongness of an action, a custom, or an institution. In economic terms, the monetary worth of a good or service.

variable costs Costs directly influenced by the number of units produced, such as materials used in production and the wages of production workers.

vendor One who sells goods or services.

vertical analysis of the income statement A percentage breakdown of the income statement to show what proportion of sales the various expenses are, and the profit margin.

vertical merger The joining together of enterprises involved in the successive stages of production or distribution of a product.

vested interest in pension plans A pension plan whereby after a specified period the employees are entitled as a matter of right to the amount contributed by the employer for the employees' pension, whether or not they are still employed by the enterprise at retirement age.

vestibule training Off-the-job training in which workers are trained in an area of the plant physically separated from their workplace, but with machinery and under conditions similar to those of the shop in which they will work.

vocational school training Special practical training taken by employees outside the enterprise—such as courses in welding or blueprint reading.

wages The amount paid to labor.

wages payable An account that reflects what is owed to employees for services they have performed.

Wagner Act The name sometimes used to refer to the original National Labor Relations Act passed in 1935.

want A recognized need.

water pollution The presence of one or more contaminants in bodies of water in quantities great enough to be injurious to life or property.

Water Pollution Control Act Amendments of 1972 Legislation setting the goal of eliminating all pollution discharge into U.S. waters by 1985, with the interim goal of making waters safe for fish, wildlife, and people by 1983.

Water Quality Act of 1965 Federal legislation providing for the establishment of water-quality standards and plans for their implementation.

Water Quality Improvement Act of 1970 Federal legislation which provided that the cleanup costs of oil spills or other water pollution would be the liability of the persons or enterprises causing the pollution.

wholesalers Middlemen who perform the economic functions of storing, financing, and distributing a manufacturer's output to retailers.

Wholesome Meat Act of 1967 Legislation which updated and strengthened the inspection standards for red meat animals at slaughterhouses and packing plants.

Wholesome Poultry Products Act of 1968 Legislation which extended federal interstate inspection standards to poultry sold within a state.

work in process Materials that have been placed into the production cycle and increase in value as they move through production.

work system A model of the business enterprise which includes technical, organizational, and human subsystems. The inputs to the work system are material and human resources. The outputs are goods and services and other satisfactions of human needs.

workers' compensation tax Insurance payments required of business to finance payments to workers who may lose income because of job-related accidents or injury.

working capital The amount of current assets after the deduction of current liabilities. Also, funds used for current operations.

yellow-dog contract An agreement signed by workers stating that as a condition of employment they will not join a union. Such an agreement is unenforceable under federal and state anti-injunction acts, and is an unfair labor practice under the National Labor Relations Act.

zero-base budgeting A method of budgeting which requires a justification for every spending request for proposed operations or programs.

Index

This book has been set VideoComp in 10 point and 9 point Times Roman, leaded 2 points. Section numbers are 36 point Vanguard Medium and section titles are 30 point Vanguard Medium. Chapter titles are 30 point Vanguard Light and 24 point Vanguard Medium. The size of the maximum type page is 35½ picas x 47 picas.